Methods in BIOSTATISTICS

Methods in
BIOSTATISTICS

Dr. K.S. NEGI, Ph.D.,
Professor (Biostatistics)
Deptt. of Community Medicine
Himalayan Institute of Medical Sciences
HIHT University
Swami Ram Nagar (Jolly Grant), Dehradun
Uttarakhand, India

AITBS PUBLISHERS, INDIA
MEDICAL PUBLISHERS
J-5/6, Krishan Nagar, Delhi-110051 (INDIA)
Tel: 22054798, 22549313; Fax: 011-22543416
Email : aitbs@bol.net.in & aitbsindia@gmail.com

First Edition : 2012

ISBN: 978-93-7473-505-3

Published by :
Virender Kumar Arya for
AITBS Publishers, India
MEDICAL PUBLISHERS
J-5/6, Krishan Nagar, Delhi 110051, INDIA
Phone : 22054798, 22549313; Fax : 011-22543416
E-mail : aitbs@bol.net.in & aitbsindia@gmail.com

Printed by AITBS, Delhi.

Preface

It gives me an immense pleasure and satisfaction in presenting ***Methods in Biostatistics*** for undergraduate and postgraduate students. It is also useful for para medical students, nursing students and other health professionals.

The present edition is written lucidly on the unknown to known format with more emphasis given on the logical presentation of the subject matter by illustrating many more examples and exercises, ***i.e.***, problem based learning methodology. For quick summarization of important and conceptualized words, glossary is often preferred. Thus, glossary is an extension and additive support to the learning material (book).

There are several features that distinguish this book from other textbooks in the field of Biostatistics.

I hope that this book **"Methods in Biostatistics"** will very useful for para medical students, nursing students and other health professionals.

I also thankful to Virender Kumar Arya and his team at AITBS Publishers, India, for their meticulous efforts in the direction of bringing out this book on time.

–Dr. K.S. Negi

Contents

CHAPTER

1

Introduction

• ***Statistics***	• ***Data***	• ***Precision***
• ***Descriptive***	• ***Inference***	• ***Sample***
• ***Census***	• ***Surveys***	• ***Population***

MEANING OF STATISTICS

The word statistics has been derived from Latin word status and it has several meanings. It is generally used to refer recorded data such as number of patients attending a hospital, number of road accidents, number of offsprings in different cities. Statistics is also used to denote characteristics calculated for a set of data, *e.g.,* mean, standard deviation, coefficients of correlation and regression. In advanced context, statistics refer to statistical methodology and theory.

Precisely, statistics is the study of techniques and procedures for collecting, classifying, summarizing, analysing and interpretating the numerical data.

IMPORTANCE OF STATISTICS

A knowledge of statistics is essential for people into research management or graduate study in a specialized area. Persons active in research will find that a basic statistics is useful in conducting clinical studies and field surveys, in the effective presentation of their findings in report, in journals, and at professional meetings.

An understanding of statistics is helpful to those who are preparing, or may be called upon to evaluate research proposals.

A person with appropriate knowledge of statistics is better able to decide whether his or her professional colleagues use their statistics to highlight or merely to support their personal biases, *i.e.,* it helps one to decide whether the claims are valid or invalid.

With the aid of statistics, it is usually possible to achieve greater precision at minimum cost by effectively using the resources available.

Uncertainties (or variability) in medicine are enormous which can be better understood by applying statistical methods (statistics). When statistics is applied in biology including human biology, medicine and public health, it is known as biostatistics. Francis Galton (1822–1911) has been called the father of Biostatistics. Biostatistics is also called Biometry.

DESCRIPTIVE AND INFERENTIAL STATISTICS

It is helpful to distinguish between the two major categories of statistics. Descriptive statistics deals with the enumeration, organization, and graphical representation of data. Inferential statistics provides the procedures to draw an inference about the conditions that exist in a larger set of observations, *i.e.,* an entire population from study of a part of that set, *i.e.,* sample. This branch of statistics is also known as sampling statistics.

An example of descriptive statistics is the decennial census of India, in which all the residents are requested to provide such information as age, sex, religion, marital status, education and occupation. The data obtained in such a census can then be compiled and arranged into tables and graphs that describe characterstics of the population at a given time.

An example of inferential statistics is to test the efficacy of a new hypotensive drug, in which the physician will have only a limited number of hypertensive patients with whom to work. It is unlikely that a second physician will be interested in the particular group of patients studied in the experiment rather than those patients who are in a large group, *i.e.,* population on the basis of studying a small sub set, *i.e.,* sample.

In summary, the distinction is that the methods of descriptive statistics are those of describing a population given all the relevant data. The methods of inferential statistics are those of making inferences from a sample about a larger population that remains unseen but that yields the sample.

DATA AND ITS COLLECTION

In observing various phenomena, we are usually interested in obtaining information on specific characteristics, *e.g.*, age, sex, weight, height, marital status, occupation, blood pressure, body temperature. These characteristics are referred to as variables; the values of the observations recorded for them are referred to as data. Data are the raw materials of statistics. There are two types of statistical data: Primary data and Secondary data.

Primary Data: It is the data collected by a particular person or organisation for his or her own use from the primary sources.

Secondary Data: It is the data collected by some other person or organisation for his or her own use but the investigator can also use it. It means that a data can be primary for one person and secondary for the other.

QUANTITATIVE AND QUALITATIVE DATA

The specific characteristics (*e.g.*, age, sex, height, weight, occupation) that we may want to assess for a certain population are referred to as variables. Variables may be categorized further as qualitative or quantitative. Variables that yield observations on which indivisuals can be categorized according to some characteristics or quality are referred to as qualitative variables. Examples of qualitative variables are sex, occupation, marital status and education level.

One the other hand, variables that yield obervations that can be measured are considered to be quantitative variables (*e.g.*, height, weight, blood pressure, serum cholesterol level, body temperature). Quantitative variables can be classified further as discrete or continuous. The number of children in a family, pulse rate, ESR, blood sugar, blood pressure are termed as discrete variables, *i.e.,* they must always be whole numbers. Variables such as temperature, height, weight, chest circumference may be measureable on fractional values (*i.e.,* 17°C, 165.2 cms, 57.3 kg., 35.2 km) are referred to as continuous varibles.

Population and Sample

Population (or universe) in statistics means the totality of the individual observations about which inferences are to be made. A population may refer to variables of a concrete collection of objects (or creatures) such as heights of all students studied in a class, haemoglobin levels of all adult women, weights of all the albino rats, etc. Population under study can be finite and infinite in numbers.

Sample is a part of the population. It can be a representive (if drawn carefully) of the population from which it is drawn large number of samples may be drawn from the same population. The composition of samples may vary in size, quality and in the technique of drawing the sample, thereby their statistics also vary. Inferences drawn from a sample refer to the defined population from which sample or samples or drawn. A representative sample will have its characteristics almost equal to the parameters of the entire population.

PROCEDURES FOR COLLECTING DATA

There are two acknowledged procedures for collecting of data. These are given below:

(i) By Complete Enumeration or Census

(ii) By Sample Survey

When information is collected in respect of every individual person or object of a given population, the object of a given population, the investigation is said to have been carried out by means of complete enumeration or census. This process is known as Census Survey.

But in most of statistical enquiry because of limitations of time and money a portion of the population, *i.e.,* sample is examined. This procedure of partial enumeration is known as Sample survey. The results and findings are however made applicable to the whole field of enquiry, *i.e.,* population. This process is known as sampling. The primary reason for selecting a sample from a population is to draw inferences about that population. Note that the population may consist of person, object, or the observations of a characteristic.

The set of observations may be summarised by a descriptive characteristic, called a parameter. When the same characteristic pertains to sample, it is called a statistic. Sample statistics help us draw inferences about population-parameters. The value of the population parameter is constant but usually unknown. The value of statistics is known because it is computed from the sample. Observations differ from one sample to the next; consequently, the value of statistic varies from sample to sample.

SURVEYS AND EXPERIMENTS

The two fundamental kinds of investigations are surveys and experiments. Data from a survey may represent observations of events or phenomena over which few, if any, controls are imposed. The study of the effects of poisonous gas leakage in Union Carbide Ltd., *i.e.*, Bhopal gas disaster on the inhabitants of the Bhopal city in and around is an example of survey. In this case, the ill effect of gas to which the survivors were exposed (referred to as "treatment" in statistics) was a no way controlled or assigned. By contrast, in an experiment we design a research plan purposely to impose controls over the amount of exposure (treatment) to a phenomenon.

The distinction between them is that an experiment imposes controls on the methods, treatment, or conditions under which it is performed, whereas in a survey such controls are seldom possible.

An experiment in Clinical Pharmacology, a new medication is administered to one group of patients suffering from a disease and a placebo (inactive or inert substance) to another group in order to assess the comparative response.

In this example the state of nature is altered by the investigator to gain comparative information.

RETROSPECTIVE AND PROSPECTIVE STUDIES

Health reseachers conduct surveys on human populations all the time. These surveys may be categorised as retrospective or prospective. Retrospective studies gather past date from selected cases and controls to determine differences, if any, in the exposure to a suspected factor. They are commonly referred to as case-control studies. The purpose of the comparison is to determine if the two groups differ as to their exposure to some specific factor.

In retrospective studies, the unit is the individual rather than the group. The investigator identifies individuals with a specific disease or some other health problem (cases) and also identifies a comparable sample without that disease or health problem (controls). An example is a study that compares the smoking habits of women who delivered premature babies to those of women who carried their pregnancies to full term. Given the comparative data, the investigator, then seeks to determine whether there is a statistical relation between the possible stimulus variable, or causative factor (smoking), and the outcome variable (prematurity).

Prospective studies are usually cohort studies, in which one enrolls a group of healthy persons and follows them over a certain period to determine the frequency with which a disease develops. The group is divided statistically according to the presence or absence of a stimulus variable, *e.g.*, smoking history.

This is done because the group can not be divided according to a disease that has not yet occurred, *e.g.,* the presence or absence of lung cancer. The prospective study then compares the proportions of smokers (exposed cohort) who developed lung cancer to the proportion of non-smokers (non exposed cohort) who developed the same disease.

CLINICAL TRIALS

A clinical trial is an experiment that seeks to detemine the effectiveness of a new drug or treatment under controlled conditions. Clinical trials have been used by healthy investigators to evaluate the effectiveness of streptomycin in the treatmentn of tuberculosis, polio vaccine, Tolbutamide for the control of diabetes and many of the new cancer chemotherpeutic agents. A clinical trial involves a comparison of two or more comparable groups of patients. The treatment group, which receives a potentially therapeutic agents, is compared with a similar control group, which receives a placebo. In such type of study, the investigator is interested not only in establishing comparable groups, but also in liniting the amount of bias entering a trial. One way to do this is to design the experiment as a single-blind study. In this type of experiment, the patient does not know whether he or she is in the treatment or the control group. The other better way is to design it as a double-blind study, in which neither the patient nor the experimenter knows to which group the patient is assigned. A neutral person keeps the code as to whose who and discloses it only at the end of data collection.

MEASURMENTS OF STATISTICAL DATA

Generally, there are four types of measurements of data (NOIR):

1. Data on Nominal Scale,
2. Data on Ordinal Scale,
3. Data on an Interval Scale,
4. Data on Ratio Scale.

1. **Data on Nominal Scale:** Sometimes the variables under study is classified by some quality it possesses rather than by an amount or quantity. In such cases, the variables is called an attribute. For this we use a nominal scale of measurement. On a nominal scale (nominal being from Latin word the 'name') persons might be classified as male or female; healthy or ill; rich or poor.
2. **Data on Ordinal Scale:** When variables are dealt with their relative differences rather than with quantitative differences, such data consist of an order of measurements and are said to be on an ordinal scale of measurement ('Ordinal'

is from Latin word for 'order'). For example, in examination grades might be recorded as A, B, C or D; educational level and physical activity status are examples of ordinal variables.

3. **Data on an Interval Scale:** An interval scale has equal unit but an arbitrary zero point. Temperature is an example of an interval scale datum. Interval scale units may be added or subtracted but they may not be multiplied or divided. For example, the two common temperature scales; Celsius (C) and Fahrenheit (F). We can see that the same difference exists between 10°C (50°F) and 20°C (68°F as between 25°C (77°F) and 35°C (95°F), *i.e.,* the measurement scale is composed of equal-sized intervals. But we can not say that a temperature of 20°C (68°F) is twice as hot as a temperature of 10°C (50°F), because the zero point is arbitrary.
4. **Data on Ratio Scale:** Measurement scales having a constant interval size and a true zero point are said to be ratio scales of measurement. Variables such as height, weight, volume, rate, and time which we can compare meaningfully with one another (*e.g.,* 30 kg is thrice of 10 kg; 20 cm is twice of 10 cm; 8 hours is four times of 2 hours) are said to be measured on a ratio scale.

PROPORTIONS, RATES AND RATIOS

A proportion is the number (a) observations with a given characteristic divided by the total number of observations (a + b) in a given group, *i.e.,*

$$\text{Proportion} = \frac{a}{a+b}$$

- A proportion is always defined as a part divided by the whole.
- A percentage is the proportion multiplied by 100.
- A percentile is a number that indicates the percentage of a distribution that is equal to/or below that number.

Note: The proportion is really a special case of the average in which the observations with the given characteristic (such as persons with having disease are assigned the value 1), observations without the characteristic (such as persons without having disease are assigned the value zero). Then the ΣX in the numerator of the formula for the average is simply the sum of the zeros and 1s (and is equal to a) ; the denominator is still n.

A ratio is the number (a) of observations in a given group with a given characteristic divided by the number (b) of observations without the given characteristic, *i.e.,*

$$\text{Ratio} = \frac{a}{b}$$

A ratio is always defined as a part divided by an other part, *i.e.,* when the numerator and the denominator are two distinct quantities. For example, among physicians taking aspirin, the ratio of those who had an MI to those who did not is 62/5200 = 0.012. In the placebo group, the ratio of MI to no MI is 110/5100 = 0.02.

An index is a summary measure intended to reflect relationship among variables. It is often expressed as a ratio. Examples are as follows: weight/height, weight/height^2 and weight/(height – 100).

Rates are similar to proportions except that a multiplier (*e.g.,* 1000, 10,000 or 100,000) is used and they are computed over a specified period of time. The multiplier is called the base. Hence the formula is

$$\text{Rate} = \frac{a}{a+b} \times \text{Base}$$

The rates, in general, are of two types: Crude and Specific.

Crude rates are general rates calculated without specification of sections of the population whereas **Specific rates** are for the specific group of the population such as for a particular age, gender, marital status, education and occupation.

➤ EXERCISES ≺

1.1. Define: Statistics, Clinical trial, Experiment and Survey.

1.2. Explain clearly what do you understannd by Descriptive and Inferential Statistics.

1.3. Explain with illustration the distinction between

(i) Qualitative and Quantitative data

(ii) Population and Sample

1.4. Distinguish between census and sample survey.

1.5. Describe retrospective and prospective studies.

1.6. Explain the various level of measurements of statistical data.

1.7. Defferentiate between proportion, rate and ratio.

1.8. Define discrete and continuous variables. Give two examples for each variable.

1.9. What is Index? How does it differ from Ratio?

1.10. Differentiate between interval and ratio scales.

⌖⌖⌖⌖⌖

CHAPTER

2

Presentation of Data

- *Frequency Distribution*
- *Tally Sign*
- *Graphs*
- *Pie*
- *Class Interval*
- *Tabulation*
- *Ogive*
- *Histogram*

Once data is collected, it must be arranged purposively, in order to bring out the important points clearly. Therefore, the method in which the data is presented is the matter of concern. There are several methods of presenting data:

1. Frequency distribution;
2. Graphic presentation;
3. Line diagram;
4. Pictures and Special curves.

FREQUENCY DISTRIBUTION

Data recorded in an arbitrary manner after their collection from the field of enquiry are called 'Raw data'. These data will not serve any purpose until we classify and arrange them in tabular form.

A classification showing the different values of a variable and their respective frequencies (*i.e.,* the number of times each value occurs) side by side is called a frequency distribution of the values.

Suppose there are 50 students in a class and their respective heights (in cms) are listed in Table 2.1.

TABLE 2.1

Student Roll No.	Height (cms)	Student Roll No.	Height (cms)	Student Roll No.	Height (cms)
1.	105	20.	109	39.	120
2.	100	21.	103	40.	100
3.	109	22.	108	41.	117
4.	106	23.	106	42.	120
5.	122	24.	107	43.	107
6.	103	25.	104	44.	116
7.	122	26.	103	45.	119
8.	107	27.	105	46.	122
9.	102	28.	102	47.	122
10.	105	29.	106	48.	107
11.	103	30.	103	49.	106
12.	100	31.	109	50.	117
13.	119	32.	114		
14.	116	33.	122		
15.	120	34.	114		
16.	122	35.	100		
17.	115	36.	116		
18.	119	37.	115		
19.	118	38.	110		

Data presented in the above table are raw data. This type of presentation will not furnish any useful information to a investigator.

If somebody wants to know that how many students are of similar height. It would be difficult to tell from the Table 2.1.

To make this easier, the data should be arranged either in ascending order or descending order of magnitude and accordingly it could be easily known that how many students belong to a particular height. This technique is called a frequency distribution, and is illustrated in Table 2.2.

TABLE 2.2

Height (cm)	Number of students	Height (cm)	Number of students
100	4	110	1
102	2	114	2
103	5	115	2
104	1	116	3
105	3	117	2
106	4	118	1
107	4	119	3
108	1	120	3
109	3	122	6

Here, heights are called variates and the number of students who belong to a particular height is called frequency of the variate. Thus frequency is the number of times a variate has been repeated.

GROUPED FREQUENCY DISTRIBUTION

The representation of data as a simple frequency distribution (Table 2.2) is better than an arranged data (Table 2.1) but it does not concise the data to the desired extent, and the frequency table appears lengthy. The next step is, therefore to condense the data by classifying them into groups or classes. These groups are called class-intervals. The number of items or values belonging to each class-interval is called the class frequency. Such an arrangement of data is known as grouped frequency distribution (Table 2.3).

The two end values of a class-interval are called class limits. The smalkler of these two values is called the lower class limit and the larger one is the upper class limit . The mid value or class mark of a class-interval is an average of its both limits, (*e.g.*, the mid value of a class interval, 100-104 cm, is 100 + 104/2 = 204/2 = 102) and is used as a representative value of the class-interval.

TABLE 2.3

Class-interval (Height in cm)	Tally	Frequency (Number of students)
100-104	~~IIII~~ ~~IIII~~ II	12
105-109	~~IIII~~ ~~IIII~~ ~~IIII~~	15
110-114	III	3
115-119	~~IIII~~ ~~IIII~~ I	11
120-124	~~IIII~~ IIII	9
Total		50

Class boundaries are points that demarcate the true upper limit of one class and the true lower limit of the next, for example, the class boundary between classes (100-104) and (105-109) is 104.5; it is the upper boundary for the former and the lower bounday for latter. Class boundaries may be used in place of class limits.

There are two types or grouped frequency tables.

(i) Inclusive type and

(ii) Exclusive type.

Under the inclusive type of tabulation, the upper limit of a class is included in that class whereas, in a group frequency distribution of exclusive type, the upper limit of one class is the lower limit of the next class and in the case class limits of a class coincide with the class boundaries of that class.

Relative frequency is the class frequency expressed as a rate of total frequency, *i.e.*,

$$\text{Relative frequency} = \frac{\text{Class frequency}}{\text{Total frequency}}$$

If the classes of a frequency distribution are not of equal width (upper class boudnay-lower class boundary), we can not compare the frequencies of the different classes. In that case, frequency densities of the classes are used for comparing the concentration of frequencies in the classes. Thus, the frequency density of a class is the frequency per unit width of the class, *i.e.*,

$$\text{Frequency density of a class} = \frac{\text{Frequency of the class}}{\text{Width of the class}}$$

A relative frequency distribution is illustrated in Table 2.4.

TABLE 2.4

Class-interval (Heights in cm.)	Frequency (No. of students)	Relative Frequency or percentage
100-104	12	12/50 = 0.24 or 24%
105-109	15	15/50 = 0.30 or 30%
110-114	3	3/50 = 0.06 or 6%
115-119	11	11/50 = 0.22 or 22%
120-124	9	9/50 = 0.18 or 18%
Total	50	1.00 or 100%

CUMULATIVE FREQUENCY DISTRIBUTION

In classification of statistical data, it is sometimes necessary to find the number of observations (or values) less than or more than a desired value. In such cases, it is done by accumulating, *i.e.,* adding the frequencies upto or above the desired value. This accumulated frequency is called cumulative frequency for that value. Thus cumulative frequency are of two types:

(i) Less than cumulative frequencies and

(ii) More than cumulative frequencies.

For a grouped frequency distribution (Table 2.5), the cumulative frequencies should be shown against the class boundary points.

Cumulative frequency distribution is also used to determine median, quartiles, and percentile scores.

GRAPHIC PRESENTATION

Sometimes significance of figures (*i.e.,* numbers) in tabular presentation is not easily understood. In such cases, health researchers and other executive prefer diagrammatic presentation which is readily understood with the help of graphs, charts, or diagrams. Graphs of statistical data bring out clear and relative importance of different figures and are helpful in finding out the relation between two or more sets of data.

TABLE 2.5

Class-interval (Height in cm)	Frequency No. of Students	Cumulative Frequency distribution		
		Class boundary points	Cumulative Frequency	
			Less than	More than
100-104	12	99.5	0	50
105-109	15	104.5	12	38
110-114	3	109.5	27	23
115-119	11	114.5	30	20
120-124	9	119.5	41	9
Total	50	124.5	50	0

TYPES OF GRAPHS

There are various type of graphs in the form of charts and diagrams. Some of them are:

- Line graph
- Bar chart
- Pie diagram
- Histogram
- Frequency polygon
- Cumulative frequency polygon

Although there are many types of graphs but an understanding of few general types will be sufficient for the presentation of data. The choice of particular type of graph to be used is often a matter of personal preference.

As we know that the data in the form of raw scores is known as ungrouped data and when it is organised into a frequency distribution, then, it is referred to as grouped data. Therefore, seperate methods are used to represent each of them.

For the ungrouped data, we usually make use of the following methods of representation:

(i) Line chart

(ii) Bar chart

(iii) Pie diagram

Line Chart: It is the most widely used in medical science or any other sphere where data are collected over a long period of time. To draw line chart, we take the values of the independent variable along the horizontal X-axis and those of the dependent variable along the vertical Y-axis.

If one of the variable is time, its values are always taken along the horizontal X-axis. With reference to X-axis and Y-axis, the given data may be plotted as points on a graph paper. These consecutive points or dots are then joined by straight lines. Line graph is illustrated though the following example:

EXAMPLE 2.1: Population of India (1901-2001)

Year	1901	1911	1921	1931	1941	1951	1961	1971	1981	1991	2001
Popn. (in Mil.)	238	252	251	279	391	361	439	548	683	844	1027

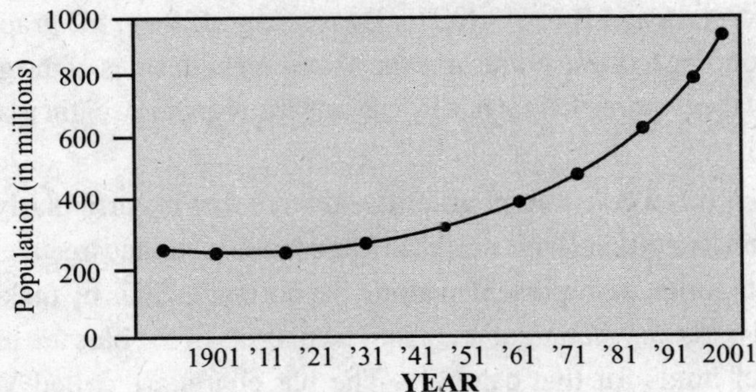

Fig. 2.1: Showing the population trend in India

The shape of line chart may alter with the chage of scale on the vertical or horizontal axis but the trend indicated will remain the same.

Graphical Interpolation: When the graphs of continously varying variable are drawn, we may find the values of the variable at any intermediate stage from the graph itself. This process is known as interpolation by graphical method.

EXAMPLE 2.2: The data given below are of the height and weight of a man at different ages:

Age (yrs)	5	7	9	11	13	15	17	19
Heights (cms)	75	90	105	125	140	150	175	185
Weight (kg)	20	25	35	40	45	55	60	65

Draw two line charts on the same graph to represent the above data. Find graphically the height and the weight of the man when he was 12 years old.

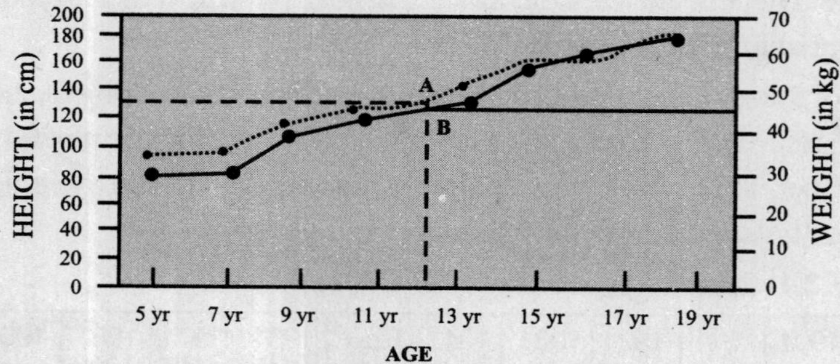

Fig. 2.2: Gives the two lines chart

The height and the weight of the man when he was 12 year old are shown in the graph by the points A and B respectively. By reading off from the graph paper the values corresponding to these points one the Y-axis on both sides of the graph. Here, we observe that the required height is 138 cms and the required weight is around to be 42 kg (Fig. 2.2).

Bar Chart: It is a convenient graphical device that is particularly useful for displaying nominal or ordinal data, *e.g.*, data like ethnicity, sex and treatment category. The various categories are represented along the horizontal axis by making equally spaced vertical baris *i.e.*, rectangular areas. The heights of the bars are proportional to the values of items for that category. The bar charts are called Vertical Bar Charts (or coloumn charts) if the bars are placed vertically. When the bars are placed horizontally, we get Horizontal Bar Charts.

Column Bar Charts are used in time-series (*i.e.*, when two or more set of data over a certain period of time are to be compared), and Horizontal Bar Charts are used for the data classified by attributes.

Bar Charts are of three types:

(i) Simple Bar Chart,

(ii) Multiple Bar Chart (or Compound Bar Chart),

(iii) Component Bar Chart.

The following figures are sufficient to understand about various bar charts:

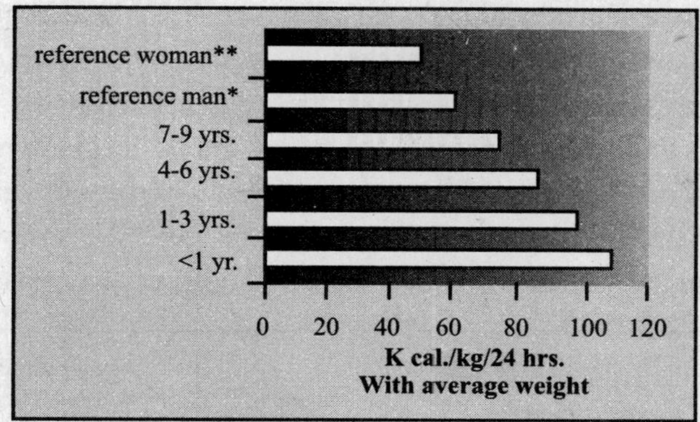

Fig. 2.3: Showing bar chart

*An Indian reference man is between 20 and 39 years of age and weight 60 kg (healthy and fit for active work).

**An Indian reference woman is between 20 and 39 years of age healthy and weight 50 kg.

The above simple bar diagram (chart) shows the recommended daily intake of energy by I.C.M.R., New Delhi. (Fig. 2.3)

Multiple or Compound Bar Chart: It is used when a number of items are to be compared in respect of two or more values at a time. For convenience, the bars are differently shaded. (Fig. 2.4)

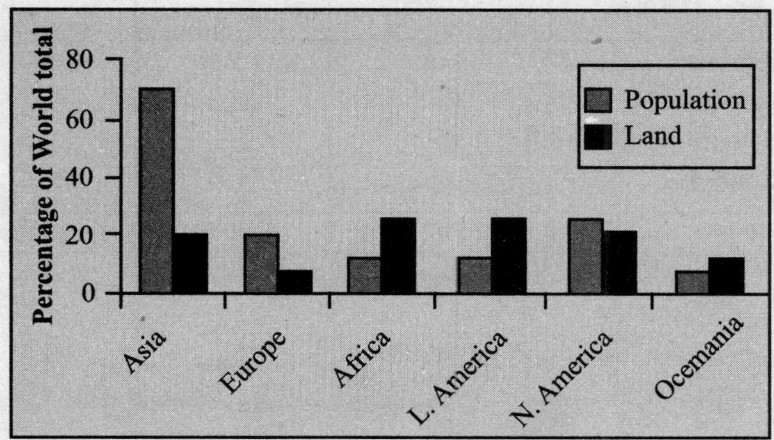

Fig. 2.4: Population and Land area by region

Component or Proportional Bar Chart: In the component bar chart, the bars are divided into two or more parts. Each part of the bar represents a certain item and proportional to the magnitude of that particular item. The under given figure represents such a chart (Fig. 2.5).

Pie Chart or Sector Diagram: It is another useful pictorial device for representing discrete data of qualitative characters such as blood groups and social groups in a population. A pie chart consists of a circle subdivided into sectors by a radii in such a way that the areas of the sectors proportional to the values of the component items under investigation. The whole are of the circle represents the entire data under consideration. The name pie diagram is given to a circle diagram because in determining the circumference of a circle we have to take into consideration a quantity known as pie which is symbolically written as π.

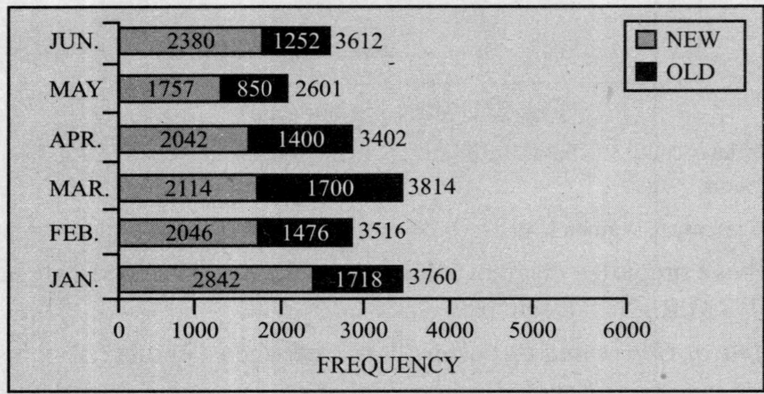

Fig. 2.5: Showing new and old out-door patients' attendance in six months

Types of Leprosy	No. of patients	Percentages	Degrees
Tuberculoid	148	61.7	222°
Lepromatous	64	26.7	96°
Indeterminate	18	7.5	27°
Borderline	10	4.1	15°
Total	240	100.0	360°

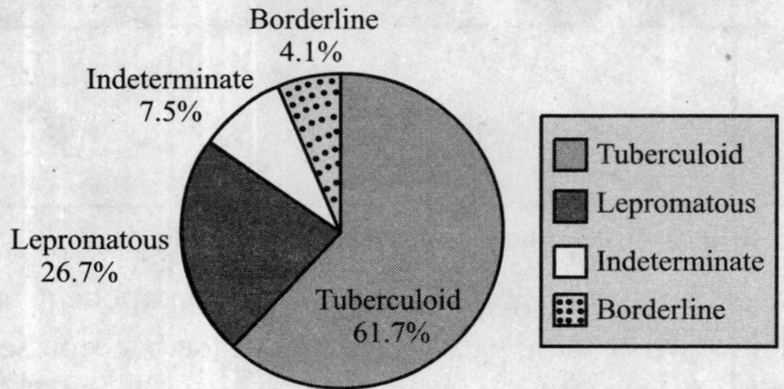

Fig. 2.6: Pie diagram showing the types of Leprosy

In order to draw a Pie chart, we first express the different components of the given data as percentages of the whole. Now the total angle at the centre being 360°, it will represent the whole, *i.e.,* 100%. Therefore 3.6° will represent 1% of the whole. Consequently if X be the percentage of a certain component (or sector) with X × 3.6°. In this way, the central angles of the sectors corresponding to the different components are determined. The different sectors thus obtained may be shaded differently. This is shown in Fig. 2.6.

SCATTER DIAGRAM OR CORRELATION CHART

When two variables are observed on the same individual, sometimes it may become necessary to study the possible relationship between the two variables. In such cases scatter diagram is used to interpret any relationship that may exist between the two variables. For every paired observation (X, Y) a point is plotted on the graph and when large number of paired observations (bivariate variable) are plotted on the graph, the graph resembles a band of region which gives an approximate idea of the type of correlation that may exist between the two variables. The scatter diagram is shown in Fig. 2.7.

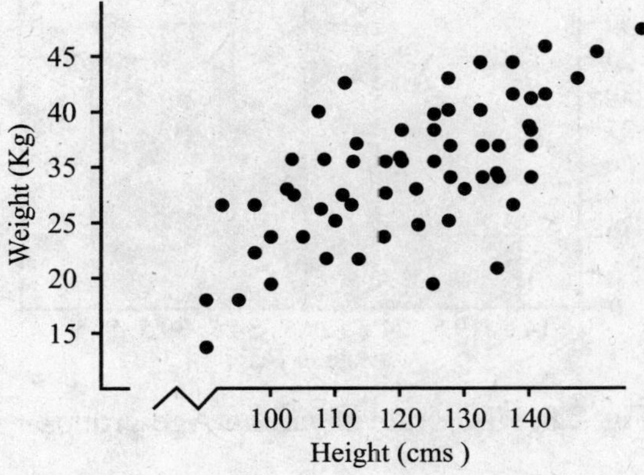

Fig. 2.7: Scatter diagram showing height and weight of individuals

Histogram: It is the most commonly used diagram to depict grouped frequency distribution graphically. A histogram consists of a series of continuous vertical rectangles (*i.e.*, a set of compact vertical bars drawn side by side), each being drawn to represent the size of the class interval by its width and the frequency in each class-interval by its height. The area of a rectangle is proportional to the frequency of the corresponding class-interval and the total area of the histogram being proportional to the total frequency of all the class-intervals. In constructing a histogram, the class boundaries are considered to be very important and they are taken on the horizontal axis. When the class-intervals are not of equal widths, the heights of rectangles are make proportional to the frequency-densities.

The following frequency distribution is represented graphically in the form of histogram:

Age groups in years	15-19	20-24	25-29	30-34	35-39	40-44
No. of Female	10	25	38	45	40	32

Here the given data is in inclusive series so that it needs to be transformed into exclusive series by having class-boundaries of the corresponding class-intervals, *i.e.*, the class-boundaries are (14.5-19.5), (19.5-24.5), (24.5-29.5), (29.5-34.5), (34.5-39.5), (39.5-44.5).

Now we take class-boundaries along the horizontal axis and frequencies along the vertical axis. The histogram for the above data has been drawn in the Fig. 2.8.

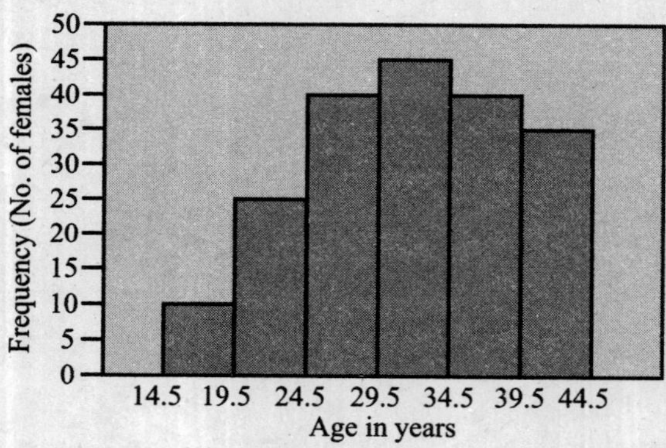

Fig. 2.8: Histogram of various Age-groups

AGE AND SEX PYRAMID

This graph is useful for representing the age and sex pattern of a community. In this graph two histograms are draw on both sides of the vertical axis with their bases adjoining to each other with a common scale. One histogram corresponds to the age distribution of males and the other to that of the females. Unlike in other histograms here the frequencies, *i.e.,* the number of persons (males and females) in any age group in taken on the X-axis and the variable, *i.e.*, age groups, is taken on the Y-axis Fig. 2.9.

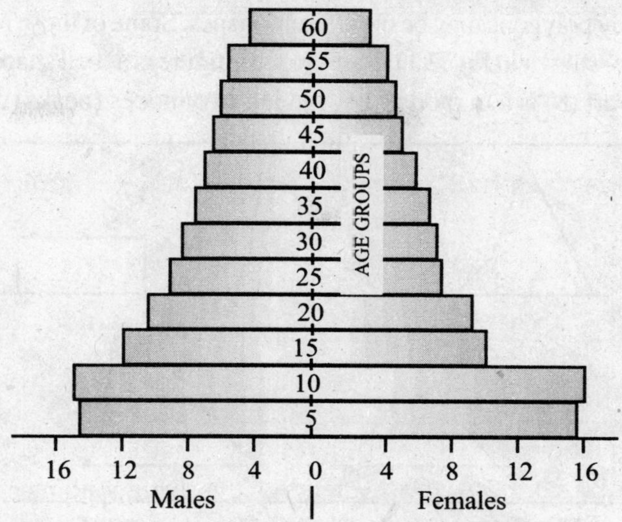

Fig. 2.9: Age and Sex pyramid of a sample population

Frequency Polygon

It is the curve obtained by joining the mid points of the tops of the rectangles in a histogram by straight lines. In order to complete the drawing of a frequency polygon the two endpoints of it are joined to the horizontal axis at the mid-points of the empty class-interval at both ends of the frequency distribution Fig. 2.10.

The construction of frequency polygon is illustrated by the following examples:

Marks obtained	0-10	10-20	20-30	30-40	40-50
Number of students	8	12	22	28	20

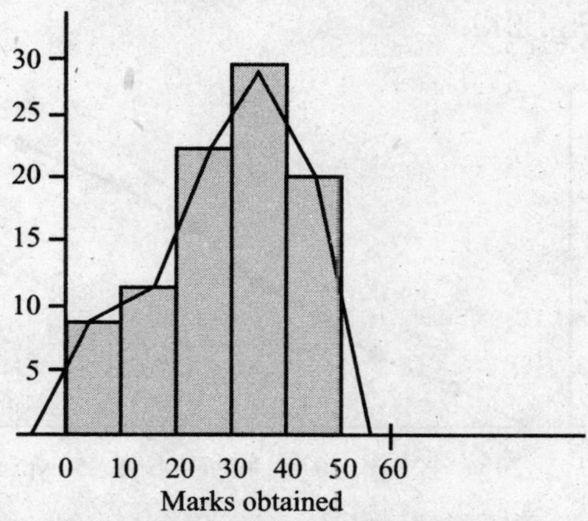

Fig. 2.10: Frequency polygon for the data given above

Frequency polygons may be of different shapes. Some of those mose commonly encountered are shown in Fig. 2.11. Part (a) of the figure is a 'bell shaped' symmetrical distribution. Part (b) is a bi modal, *i.e.,* having two modes (peaks) distribution that

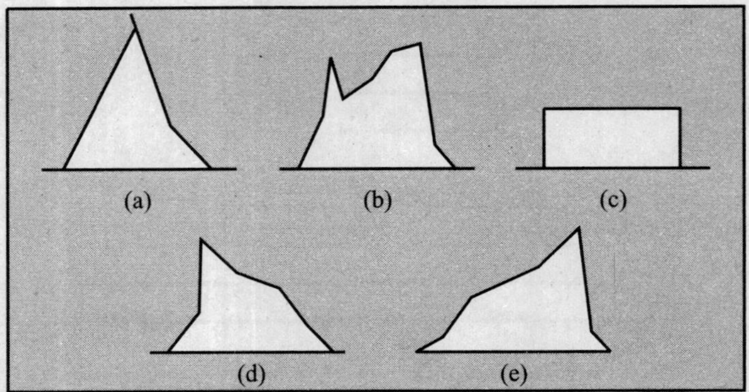

Fig. 2.11: Various shapes of frequency polygon

could represent an overlapping group of males and females. Part (c) is a rectangular distribution. Part (a) and (c) are symmetrical, whereas parts (d) and (e) are skewed or asymmetrical. The frequency polygon of part (d) is positiviely skewed since it tapers off in the positive direction, and part (e) is negatively skewed.

Cumulative frequency Curve or Ogive: It is a graph which represents the data of a cumulative frequency distribution. To draw the ogive, an ordinary frequency distribution table of a quantitative data has to be converted into cumulative frequency table. The cumulative frequencies are then plotted corresponding to the upper limits of the classes. The points corresponding to cumulative frequency at each upper limit of the classes are joined by a free hand curve. Ogive or cumulative frequency curve has been shown in Fig. 2.12.

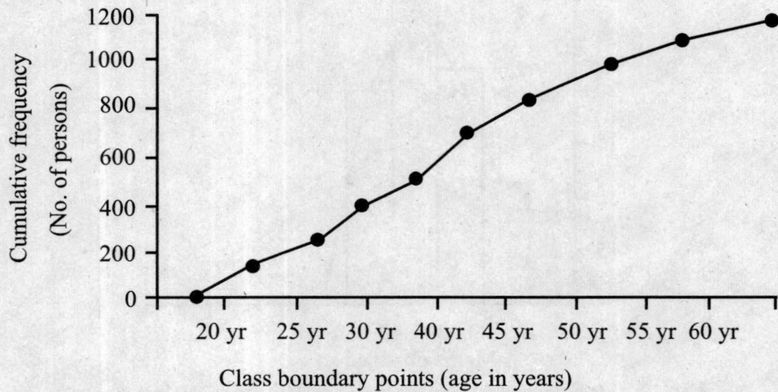

Fig. 2.12: Showing cumulative frequency curve (ogive)

Class interval (Age in Yrs.)	Class Boundary (Age in Yrs.)	Frequency (No. of persons)	Cumulative Frequency (Less than Ogive)
------	20	0	0
20-25	25	110	110
25-30	30	130	240
30-35	35	155	395
35-40	40	185	580
40-45	45	170	750
45-50	50	140	890
50-55	55	90	980
55-60	60	70	1050
Total	—	1050	—

Ogive is used to find median, quartiles and percentiles. It is also used to find the number of observations which are expected to lie between the two given values. Ogives are useful in comparing two sets of data, for example, data on healthy and diseased individuals.

➤ EXERCISES ≺

2.1. Write short notes on the following:

(a) Bar chart (b) Histogram

(c) Ogive (d) Pie diagram.

2.2. Following are the marks obtained by 50 students in the examination:

30, 41, 45, 45, 40, 35, 28, 25, 35, 49, 62, 60, 56, 55, 44, 65, 52, 50, 47, 42, 54, 43, 28, 35, 42, 45, 57, 68, 62, 65, 35, 30, 35, 42, 47, 25, 28, 48, 50, 72, 60, 56, 68, 75, 49, 55, 78, 57, 65, 55.

Construct a Histogram with class-interval of 10.

2.3. In a study of diabetic patients, the following data were obtained:

Age (in Years)	No. of Patients
10-20	2
20-30	10
30-40	25
40-50	15
50-60	5
60-70	3

Draw a frequency polygon for the above data.

2.4. Diastolic blood pressure reading in persons aged 20-45 are presented in the following table:

Diastolic B.P. (mm Hg)	No. of Males	No. of Females
70-75	10	12
75-80	22	18
80-85	55	30
85-90	20	10
90-95	13	5
95-100	5	—

Draw cumulative frequency curve for above data.

2.5. Following are the education levels found in a community survey:

Level	*No. of persons*
Illiterate	225
Primary	472
Middle	293
Higher Secondary	201
Graduation	104
Post-graduation	55

Prepare a pie chart for the above data.

2.6. Following are the fasting blood glucose level of 100 persons:

BGL (mg/dl):	80-84	85-89	90-94	95-99	100-104	105-109
Number of persons	2	15	33	35	13	2

Draw a suitable diagram.

2.7. Construct a group frequency table, histogram and frequency polygon for the following data (*i.e.,* daily protein intake (gm) of 50 adult males):

21, 28, 43, 12, 69, 23, 51, 45, 44, 47, 42, 48, 43, 69, 65, 57, 49, 55, 41, 31, 27, 28, 32, 42, 38, 16, 24, 51, 30, 70, 65, 27, 58, 38, 49, 28, 57, 48, 40, 38, 30, 46, 35, 16, 50, 74, 66, 45, 33, 39.

2.8. Age specific death rates by sex are presented below:

Age (yrs.)	0-4	5-14	15-34	35-49	≥50
Male	34.5	2.2	2.6	6.6	38.0
Female	36.5	2.6	3.4	5.2	32.0

Construct a suitable diagram for the above data.

2.9. Differentiate between Component bar chart and Age-Sex pyramid.

2.10. Distinguish between class-limits and class-boundaries.

⌖ ⌖ ⌖ ⌖ ⌖

CHAPTER

3

Central Tendency

• ***Average***	• ***Median***
• ***Percentiles***	• ***Percentiles***
• ***Quartiles***	• ***Harmonic***
• ***Cumulative Frequency***	• ***Weighted Mean***
• ***Unimodal***	

It is observed that in many frequency distributions, the tabulated values show small frequencies at the beginning and at the end very high frequency at the middle of the distrubution. This indicates that the typical values of the variable lie near the central part of the distribution and other value cluster around these central values. This tendency of the data about the concentration of the values in the central part of the distribution is called the central tendency of the data. This central tendency is measured with the help of mathematical quantities (or typical values). A central value which is representative of entire distribution is known as "average" and, therefore, gives a measure of central tendency.

There are five common measures of central tendency:

(i) Arithmetic Mean (ii) Median (iii) Mode

(iv) Geometric Mean (v) Harmonic Mean

(i) ARITHMETIC MEAN

It is the most common and useful measure of central tendency. The Arithmetic mean (or simply mean) is computed by adding all the values in a series and dividing the sum by the number of values.

Symbolically, $\overline{X} = \dfrac{x_1 + x_2 + \dots\dots\dots + x_n}{n}$

or $\overline{X} = \dfrac{\sum_{i=1}^{n} X_i}{n}$

In these expressions the symbol $\overline{X}$, representing the sample mean; X_i, the ith in a series of values (*i.e.*, = 1, 2, 3, ..., n). The symbol Σ is the Greek letter sigma and denotes "the sum of", n is the total number of values in the series.

EXAMPLE 3.1: Find the mean incubation period of 10 polio cases given below:

17, 20, 18, 24, 16, 19, 21, 22, 23, 20

$$\overline{X} = \frac{\sum_{i=1}^{10} X_i}{10} = \frac{17 + 20 + 18 + 24 + 16 + 19 + 21 + 22 + 23 + 20}{10}$$

or $\overline{X} = \dfrac{200}{10} = 20$

i.e., mean incubation period is 20.

Mean of grouped data: Let $x_1, x_2, \dots\dots\dots, x_n$ be n values of a variable X and let $f_1, f_2, \dots\dots\dots, f_n$ be their respective weights (or frequencies), then the weighted mean $\overline{X}$ is given by

$$\overline{X} = \frac{f_1 x_1 + f_2 x_2 + \dots\dots\dots + f_n x_n}{f_1 + f_2 + \dots\dots\dots + f_n}$$

or $\overline{X} = \dfrac{\sum_{i=1}^{n} f_i x_i}{\sum_{i=1}^{n} f_i} = \dfrac{\sum_{i=1}^{n} f_i x_i}{N}$, where $N = \sum_{i=1}^{n} f_i$ = total frequency

EXAMPLE 3.2: Find the mean weight of 100 persons from the following frequency distribution:

Weight (in kg)	45	50	55	60	65	70	75
No. of persons	5	12	18	20	33	10	2

SOLUTION:

Weight in kg (x)	No. of persons (f)	fx
45	5	225
50	12	600
55	18	990
60	20	1200

65	33	2145
70	10	700
75	2	150
Total	100	6010

Here, $\Sigma f = 100$ and $\Sigma fx = 6010$

$$\therefore \quad \text{Mean} = \overline{X} = \frac{\Sigma fx}{\Sigma f} = \frac{6010}{100} = 60.1$$

i.e., the mean weight is 60.1 kg.

EXAMPLE 3.3: Compute the average marks (mean) of the following data:

Marks	0-10	10-20	20-30	30-40	40-50
No. of students	3	22	35	30	10

SOLUTION: Here, the individual values of the variable (*i.e.,* marks) and their frequencies are not known. So the mid-value of a class-interval is taken to represent all the values of the variable falling within that class-interval with a frequency equal to that of the class-interval (*i.e.,* the class-intervals are replaced by their respective mid-values). After this the mean is calculated by the following method as under:

Marks (Class-intervals)	**Mid-values (x)**	**No. of students (f)**	**fx**
0-10	5	3	15
10-20	15	22	330
20-30	25	35	875
30-40	35	30	1050
40-50	45	10	450
Total	—	100	2720

$$\therefore \quad \text{Average marks (mean)} = \overline{X} = \frac{\Sigma fx}{\Sigma f} = \frac{2720}{100} = 27.2$$

Short cut method of calculating mean for discrete series:

This method is applied when the frequencies and the values of the variable are quite large and it becomes very difficult to compute the mean. In such a distribution, the assumed mean is taken as the values of x (mid value of the class-interval) which corresponds to the highest frequency lying near the middle of the distribution and the deviations of the variates from this assumed mean are found. Then the mean is calculated by the formula:

$$\text{Mean } (\overline{X}) = A + \frac{\Sigma fd}{N}$$

where A = Assumed mean

d = X–A = deviation of any variate from assumed mean

and N = Σ f = total frequency

EXAMPLE 3.4: The heights of 9 boys aged 14 years are given below. Find the mean.

Heights (in cms): 145.8, 146, 147.2, 148, 150.6, 151.5, 152.2, 155, 157.5.

SOLUTION:

	Heights in cms (x)	Deviation from 150.6 d = (x–A)	
	145.8	– 4.8	
	146.0	– 4.6	– 15.4
	147.2	– 3.4	
	148.0	– 2.6	
A = Assumed mean	150.6	0	
	151.5	+ 0.9	
	152.2	+ 1.6	
	155.0	+ 4.4	+ 13.8
	157.5	+ 6.9	
–	Total	Σd = – 1.6	

Here, N = 9 (number of boys), Σd = –1.6, A = 150.6

$$\therefore \quad \overline{X} = A + \frac{\Sigma d}{N}$$

$$= 150.6 + \left(-\frac{1.6}{9}\right)$$

$$= 150.6 - 0.18$$

or $\overline{X} = 150.4$

EXAMPLE 3.5: Find average number of days of confinement of 75 pregnant women after delivery from the following data:

Days of confinement (x)	5	6	7	8	9	10	11	12
No. of pregnant women (f)	10	15	17	12	9	3	4	5

SOLUTION: Here, x = Days of confinement

f = No. of pregnant women

	x	*f*	*d = (x − A)*	*fd*	
	5	10	−2	−20	−35
	6	15	−1	−15	
A=Assumed Mean	7	17	0	0	
	8	12	+1	+12	80
	9	9	+2	+18	
	10	3	+3	+9	
	11	4	+4	+16	
	12	5	+5	+25	
Total		N = 75	–	Σ fd = 45	

$$\therefore \quad \overline{X} = A + \frac{\Sigma fd}{N}$$

$$= 7 + \frac{45}{75}$$

or $\overline{X} = 7 + 0.6 = 7.6$

Step deviation method of calculating mean for continuous series:

When the class intervals in a grouped data are of equal widths, then the calculation can be simplified by taking out the common factor from the deviations. This common factor is the equal width among the class-intervals. The deviations from assumed mean are divided by the common width, i. Thus mean is calculated by the formula:

$$\overline{X} = A + \frac{\Sigma fd}{N} \times i$$

where $d = \dfrac{X - A}{i}$ and i = the common width of the class intervals.

EXAMPLE 3.6: In a medicine OPD the following patients of different ages were examined. Find the mean age of the patients.

Age in yrs.	10-20	20-30	30-40	40-50	50-60	60-70
No. of Patients	5	19	26	35	15	3

SOLUTION:

Age in years (class intervals)	Mid values (x)	$d = \frac{(x - A)}{i}$	No. of patients (f)	f d
10-20	15	−3	5	−15
20-30	25	−2	19	−38
30-40	35	−1	26	−26
40-50	45=A	0	35	0
50-60	55	+1	15	+15
60-70	65	+2	3	+6
Total	–	–	N = 103	Σfd = −58

$$\therefore \quad \overline{X} = A + \frac{\Sigma fd}{N} \times i \quad \text{(Here, } i = 10)$$

$$= 45 + \frac{(-58)}{103} \times 10$$

or $$\overline{X} = 45 - 5.6 = 39.4$$

Note: If in a grouped frequency distribution, the lower limit of the first class-interval and the upper limit of the last class-interval are not known. In that case, the widths for the open end class-intervals are to be taken equal to the common width of the closed class-intervals and then mean is calculated by the method mentioned above.

Mean of Composite Group

If a series of n_1 values has mean $\overline{X}_1$ and another series of n_2 values has mean $\overline{X}_2$ then the mean of the composite series of $(n_1 + n_2)$ values is obtained by the formula

$$\overline{X} = \frac{n_1\overline{X}_1 + n_2\overline{X}_2}{n_1 + n_2}$$

Merits of Mean:

- Mean is easy to calculated, based on all the observations.
- It is least affected by sampling fluctuations but it is affected very much by extreme values.
- Mean is unique in any set of observations.

EXAMPLE 3.7: The means of two samples of sizes 30 and 50 are 32.5 and 54 respectively. Find the mean of sample of size 80.

SOLUTION: Here $n_1 = 30, n_2 = 50$

$\overline{X}_1 = 32.5, \overline{X}_2 = 54$

$$\therefore \quad \text{Required Mean } \overline{X} = \frac{n_1\overline{X}_1 + n_2\overline{X}_2}{n_1 + n_2} \quad \text{or} \quad \overline{X} = \frac{30 \times 32.5 + 50 \times 54}{30 + 50}$$

$$\overline{X} = \frac{975 + 2700}{80} = \frac{3675}{80} = 45.94$$

(ii) MEDIAN

It is another measure of central tendency. If a series of values of a variable are arranged in ascending or descending order of magnitudes, then the value of the middle term or the average of the values of middle two terms according to the number of values either odd or even respectively, is called median. Median is a positional average. It divides the arranged series in two equal parts.

EXAMPLE 3.8: The weights (in kgs.) of 15 students are given below. Find the median.

30, 37, 34, 28, 35, 43, 27, 31, 42, 44, 29, 32, 41, 45, 36.

SOLUTION: Arranging the given values in ascending order of magnitudes.

27, 28, 29, 30, 31, 32, 34, 35, 36, 37, 41, 42, 43, 44, 45.

There are 15 terms (*i.e.,* odd number of values), therefore, there is only one middle term whose value is 35.

Hence, the median weight is 35 kg.

EXAMPLE 3.9: Systolic blood pressure (in mm of Hg) of 8 male patients are recorded below. Find the median.

110, 100, 90, 120, 130, 140, 150, 160.

SOLUTION: First we arrange the values in ascending order of magnitudes, *i.e.,*

90, 100, 110, 120, 130, 140, 150, 160.

Now we see that there are 8 values (*i.e.,* even number of values therefore, there are two middle terms 4th and 5th whose values are 120 and 130 respectively.

$$\text{Hence, the median} = \frac{120 + 130}{2} = \frac{250}{2} = 125$$

i.e., the median B.P. is 125 mm of Hg.

When the series is continuous, *i.e.,* the data is given in the form of grouped frequency distribution. Then the median is obtained with the help of mathematical formula under given.

Median, $$Md = L_m + \frac{N/2 - cf_m}{f_m} \times i_m$$

where L_m = Lower limit of median class interval,

N = Total frequency,

cf_m = Cumulative frequency of the class preceding the median class-interval,

f_m = Frequency of median class-interval,

i_m = Width of median class-interval.

EXAMPLE 3.10: In a community survey of 100 families, the following distribution of number of children was obtained:

No. of children	1-3	3-5	5-7	7-9
No. of families	20	42	30	8

Find the median of the above distribution:

SOLUTION: We prepare the following table which includes cumulative frequency column, *i.e.*,

No. of children (Class-interval)	No. of families (Frequency)	Cumulative frequency
1-3	20	20
3-5	42	62
5-7	30	92
7-9	8	100

Here, N/2 = 100/2 = 50, this 50th value lies in the class-interval (3-5) because cumulative of this class-interval is 62 which includes 50th value. Therefore, the median class is (3-5).

Again $L_m = 3$, $f_m = 42$, $cf_m = 20$ and $i_m = 2$

Now putting these values in the following formula:

$$\text{Median, } Md = L_m = \frac{N/2 - cf_m}{f_m} \times i_m$$

$$= 3 + \frac{50 - 20}{42} \times 2 = 3 + \frac{30}{42} \times 2$$

$\therefore$ Median = 3 + 1.5 = 4.5

Merits of Median:

- Median is easy to calculate and is not affected by extreme values.

- It is not based on all the observations.
- Median is one and only one in the set of observations.
- It can be located graphically.

QUARTILES, DECILES AND PERCENTILES

If a series of values of a variable is arranged either in ascending or descending order of magnitudes, the middle most value which divides the series into two equal parts is the median. Similarly, we can find three values Q_1, Q_2 and Q_3 which would devide the series into four equal parts. These Q_1, Q_2 and Q_3 are called the first (or lower) quartile, second quartile (or median) and third (or upper) quartile respectively.

The nine values which divide the series into ten equal parts are called deciles denoted by D_1, D_2, ..., D_9 and the 99 values dividing the data into 100 equal parts are called the Percentiles denoted by P_1, P_2, ..., P_{99} respectively.

Quartiles, Deciles and Percentiles are calculated by the following formulae after arranging the data in ascending order of magnitude:

$$Q_1 = \text{the value of the } \frac{N+1}{4} \text{ th term,}$$

$$Q_3 = \text{the value of the } \frac{3(N+1)}{4} \text{ th term,}$$

$$D_1 = \text{the value of the } \frac{(N+1)}{10} \text{ th term,}$$

$$D_9 = \text{the value of the } \frac{9(N+1)}{10} \text{ th term,}$$

$$P_1 = \text{the value of the } \frac{(N+1)}{100} \text{ th term,}$$

$$P_{99} = \text{the value of the } \frac{99(N+1)}{100} \text{ th term,}$$

Note: Here N = Number of values (or total frequency).

EXAMPLE 3.11: Find the quartiles of the following raw scores:

27, 19, 25, 33, 29, 35, 20.

SOLUTION: First arranging the given raw scores in ascending order of magnitude, *i.e.*, 19, 20, 25, 27, 29, 33, 35.

$$\text{Here} \quad N = 7; \quad \frac{N+1}{4} = \frac{7+1}{4} = 2; \quad \frac{3(N+1)}{4} = \frac{3 \times 8}{4} = 6$$

$$Q_1 = \text{Value of } \left(\frac{N+1}{4}\right) \text{th term}$$

$$= \text{Value of 2nd term} = 20$$

and
$$Q_2 = \text{Value of } \left(\frac{N+1}{2}\right) \text{th term}$$

$$= \text{Value of 4th term} = 27$$

and
$$Q_3 = \text{Value of } \frac{3(N+1)}{4} \text{ th term}$$

$$= \text{Value of 6th term} = 33$$

EXAMPLE 3.12: Find the quartiles from the following distribution:

Age in Yrs.	Number of employees
< 20	10
20-25	40
25-30	52
30-35	68
35-40	95
40-45	75
45-50	45
50-55	20
55-60	5

SOLUTION: First we have to construct cumulative frequency distribution table.

Age in yrs. (Class-interval)	No. of employees (frequency)	Cumulative frequency
< 20	10	10
20-25	40	50
25-30	52	102
30-35	68	170
35-40	95	265
40-45	75	340
45-50	45	385
50-55	20	405
55-60	5	410

Here $N = 410$, $\frac{N}{4} = \frac{410}{4} = 102.5$, $\frac{N}{2} = \frac{410}{2} = 205$

and $\frac{3N}{4} = \frac{3 \times 410}{4} = 307.5$

For Q_1: class interval is (30-35),

Q_2: class interval is (35-40),

and Q_3: class interval is (40-45).

First Quartile, Q_1 is calculated by the formula

$$Q_1 = L + \frac{\frac{N}{4} - c.f.}{f} \times i$$

$$= 30 + \frac{102.5 - 102}{68} \times 5 = 30 + \frac{0.5}{68} \times 5$$

$$\therefore \quad Q_1 = 30 + 0.04 = 30.04$$

Second Quartile,

$$Q_2 = L + \frac{\frac{N}{4} - c.f.}{f} \times i$$

$$= 35 + \frac{205 - 170}{95} \times 5 = 35 + \frac{35}{95} \times 5$$

$$\therefore \quad Q_2 = 35 + 1.8 = 36.8$$

and Third Quartile,

$$Q_3 = L + \frac{\frac{3N}{4} - c.f.}{f} \times i$$

$$= 40 + \frac{307.5 - 265}{75} \times 5 = 40 + \frac{42.5}{75} \times 5$$

$$\therefore \quad Q_3 = 40 + 2.8 = 42.8$$

Quartiles are used for measuring central tendency, dispersion and skewness. Percentiles are widely used by the Paediatricians in constructing growth charts for the monitoring of children growth by age and sex wise.

(iii) MODE

It is also a measure of central tendency of a variable. Mode of a series of values of a variable is that value which occurs with the maximum frequency, *i.e.*, it is the most frequent value. For example, in the series of values 2, 4, 7, 5, 2, 7, 5, 8, 9, 5 we see that 5 occurs most frequently, *i.e.*, 3 times and other values do not occur so often, therefore, 5 is the mode which represents the true characteristic of the series.

For grouped frequency distribution, mode is usually calculated by using the following formula:

$$\text{Mode} = L_{mo} + \frac{f_{mo} - f_1}{2f_{mo} - f_1 - f_2} \times i_{mo}$$

where, L_{mo} = lower limit of the modal class

f_{mo} = frequency of modal class

f_1 = frequency of the class preceding the modal class

f_2 = frequency of the class succeeding the modal class

i_{mo} = width of the modal class (or modal interval).

Note: The modal class is the class in a frequency distribution (*i.e.,* grouped data) which has maximum frequency.

EXAMPLE 3.13: Following is the frequency distribution of weights of 60 students:

Weight in kg.	30-35	35-40	40-45	45-50	50-55	55-60
No. of students	3	8	12	20	15	2

Find the modal value.

SOLUTION: Here the class-interval (45-50) has the maximum frequency, *i.e.*, 20. Therefore, modal class is (45-50).

Now we can calculate the modal value of using the formula

$$\text{Mode} = L_{mo} + \frac{f_{mo} - f_1}{2f_{mo} - f_1 - f_2} \times i_{mo}$$

Again we have $L_{mo} = 45$, $f_{mo} = 20$, $f_1 = 12$, $f_2 = 15$ and $i_{mo} = 5$;

$$\therefore \quad \text{Mode} = 45 + \frac{20 - 12}{2 \times 20 - 12 - 15} \times 5$$

or Modal value $= 45 + 3.07 = 48.1$ kg

Generally, mode values are used for nominal scores, medians for ordinal scores, and means for interval scores. The empirical relation between Mean, Median and Mode is given by

$$\text{Mode} = 3 \text{ Median} - 2 \text{ Mean}.$$

Merits of Mode:

- Mode is used when the values are widely varying.
- It is capable of being ascertained graphically.
- There can be more than one mode for a series of values.

(iv) GEOMETRIC MEAN

If the observations instead of being added are multiplied, the geometric mean would be the nth root of the product (*i.e.*, entire multiplication). Geometric mean is denoted by GM or $\bar{x}_g$. Therefore, the geometric mean of n observations $x_1, x_2, x_3, ..., x_n$ is calculated by the following formula:

$$\text{Geometric Mean (GM)} = \sqrt[n]{(x_1)(x_2)(x_3)...(x_n)}$$

or

$$GM = (x_1\ x_2\ x_3\ ...\ x_n)^{1/n}$$

Taking logarithm on both sides, we have

$$\log(GM) = \log(x_1\ x_2\ x_3\ ...\ x_n)^{1/n}$$

$$= \frac{1}{n}(\log x_1 + \log x_2 + \log x_3 + ... + \log x_n)$$

$$\log(GM) = \frac{\Sigma \log x_i}{n}$$

Anti-logarithmic value of this log mean is the geometric mean, *i.e.*,

$$GM = \text{Antilog}\left(\frac{\Sigma \log x_i}{n}\right)$$

EXAMPLE 3.14: The geometric mean of the radiologic counts 4 and 9 is $\sqrt{(4)(9)} = \sqrt{36} = 6$.

EXAMPLE 3.15: Compute the geometric mean of the following data (Food intakes in gms): 185, 227, 122, 101, 198, 114, 184, 109, 135, 196, 217, 148, 233.

SOLUTION:

$$GM = \sqrt[n]{(x_1)(x_2)(x_3)...(x_n)}$$

or

$$\bar{x}_g = \sqrt[13]{(185)(227)(122)...(233)}$$

Since it is difficult to find 13th root, we use the formula

$$\log GM = \log[(185)(227)(122)...(233)]^{1/13}$$

$$= \frac{1}{13}[\log 185 + \log 227 + ... + \log 233]$$

$$\log GM = \frac{28.6665}{13} = 2.2051$$

The anti-logarithm value of 2.2051 is 160.3.

Therefore, the Geometric Mean, GM $(\bar{x}_g) = 160.3$.

Merits of Geometric Mean:

- When the variation between lowest and highest values is very high, use of geometric mean is preferred.

- GM can not be determined if one of the values is either zero or negative.
- Geometric mean is used in microbiology for computing average dilution titers.

(v) HARMONIC MEAN

The harmonic mean of a set of observations is the reciprocal of the arithmetic mean of the reciprocals of the observations, *i.e.*, if the observations are $x_1, x_2, x_3, ..., x_n$ then the harmonic mean (HM) is

$$HM = \frac{1}{\frac{1}{n}\sum\frac{1}{x_i}} = \frac{n}{\sum\frac{1}{x_i}} = \frac{n}{\left(\frac{1}{x_1}\right)+\left(\frac{1}{x_2}\right)+\left(\frac{1}{x_3}\right)+...+\left(\frac{1}{x_n}\right)}$$

Harmonic mean is often denoted by $\overline{x}_h$.

EXAMPLE 3.16: Determine the average velocity of a car that has travelled the first 10 km of a trip at 30 km/hour and the second 10 km at 60 km/hour.

SOLUTION: Average velocity can be calculated as the harmonic mean of the velocities 30 km/hour and 60 km/hour, *i.e.*,

$$HM = \frac{n}{\sum\frac{1}{x_i}} = \frac{2}{\frac{1}{30}+\frac{1}{60}} = 40 \text{ km/hour}$$

Example 3.17: For the numerical values 1, 2, 3, 4, 5, 6, 7, calculate the harmonic mean (HM).

Solution: $HM = \dfrac{1}{\frac{1}{n}\sum\frac{1}{x_i}} = \dfrac{1}{\frac{1}{7}\,\frac{1}{1}+\frac{1}{2}+\frac{1}{3}+\frac{1}{4}+\frac{1}{5}+\frac{1}{6}+\frac{1}{7}}$

or $\qquad \overline{x}_h = \dfrac{7}{1+0.5+0.33+0.25+0.2+0.17+0.14} = \dfrac{7}{2.59}$

∴ $\qquad$ HM = 2.7.

(vi) WEIGHTED MEAN

If we have observations $x_1, x_2, x_3, ..., x_n$ with weights $w_1, w_2, w_3, ..., w_n$ the weighted average (mean) of the x's is calculated by the formula

$$\overline{x}_w = \frac{\Sigma w_i\, x_i}{\Sigma w_i}$$

EXAMPLE 3.18: Three well-standardised laboratories in the same area are investigating throat cultures for presence of type A beta-haemolytic streptococci.

Laboratory A investigates 40 cultures of which 20 are positive, so the positively rate is found to be 50% Laboratory B examines 100 cultures, finding 75 positive for a positively rate of 75% Laboratory C examines 120 cultures, finding 30 positive for a rate of 25%. Compute a weighted average of the individual laboratories percentage.

SOLUTION: Here $n = 3$, $x_1 = 50\%$, $x_2 = 75\%$, and $x_3 = 25\%$;
$w_1 = 40$, $w_2 = 100$, and $w_3 = 120$.

Since weighted mean, $\bar{x}_w = \dfrac{\Sigma w_i x_i}{\Sigma w_i}$

$$= \frac{40(50\%) + 100(75\%) + 120(25\%)}{40 + 100 + 120}$$

$$\therefore \quad \bar{x}_w = \frac{12500\%}{260} = 48\%$$

➤ EXERCISES ≺

3.1. Write short notes on:
(i) Median, (ii) Quartiles (iii) Percentiles.

3.2. Find the mean, median and the mode of the following: Erythrocyte Sedimentation Rate of 20 patients are 3, 7, 5, 7, 4, 5, 7, 3, 4, 5, 6, 4, 7, 5, 4, 3, 7, 5, 4, 3.

3.3. The following data give the amount of creatinine in mg per 100 ml. in a 24 hour urine specimen for normal male persons:

1.55, 1.61, 1.08, 1.58, 1.83, 1.57, 1.47, 1.86, 2.02, 1.52, 1.44, 1.15, 1.66, 2.00, 1.60, 1.46, 1.65, 1.56, 1.31, 1.42, 1.23, 1.38, 1.59, 1.51, 1.40.

Find mean and median.

3.4. Following still birth rates per 1000 total births were reported by 20 cities:

25, 36, 40, 28, 27, 30, 29, 26, 35, 37, 36, 27, 29, 40, 34, 25, 30, 40, 30, 35.

Prepare a frequency table with class-interval of 5 and then calculate the mean.

3.5. The following are the marks obtained by 96 students in an examination:

Marks obtained:	1-9	10-19	20-29	30-39	40-49
No. of Students:	7	23	46	15	5

Find median, first and third quartiles.

3.6. Calculate mode and 10th percentile (P_{10}) from the following distribution:

Age in Yrs.	No. of persons
20-30	42
30-40	65
40-50	35
50-60	13
60-70	5

3.7. Following is the distribution of heights of a group of 60 students.

Height in cm.	No. of students
145.0-149.9	2
150.0-154.9	5
155.0-159.9	9
160.0-164.9	15
165.0-169.9	16
170.0-174.9	7
175.0-179.9	5
180.0-184.9	1

Find the modal height and 20th percentile.

3.8. Calculate the mean, median and the mode of the following frequency distribution:

Marks obtained		No. of students
Below	10	3
"	20	8
"	30	17
"	40	20
"	50	22

3.9. Blood serum chloestrol levels of 20 patients are as under:

250, 245, 280, 260, 240, 255, 285, 270, 263, 277, 258, 288, 290, 275, 247, 253, 265, 245, 270, 240.

Find the quartiles (*i.e.*, Q_1, Q_2 and Q_3).

3.10. The mode of a series is 26.1 and its average is 24.6. Find the median of the series.

3.11. Find the geometric mean of 2, 4, 8.

3.12. The price of certain article becomes 1½ times in first year, 13/8 times in the second year and 7/3 times in the third year. What is the average change per year?

3.13. Find the harmonic mean of 2, 4, 8, 10, 12.

3.14. Calculate the average speed of a car running at 30 km/hr during the first 60 kms; at 40 km/hr during the second 60 kms and at 50 km/hr during the third 60 kms.

3.15. In a cirtain workshop, a unit of work is completed by A in 10 minutes, by B in 15 minutes, by C in 20 minutes and by D in 30 minutes. What is their average rate of working?

3.16. Complete the simple and weighted mean of the monthly salaries from the following data:

Designation	Monthly salary	Strength of the Cadre
Officers	₹ 20,000	5
UDC	₹ 10,000	10
LDC	₹ 7,500	25
Peons	₹ 3,500	10

CHAPTER

4

Dispersion or Variability

• *Variation*	• *Standard Deviation*	• *Range*
• *Skewness*	• *Kurtosis*	• *Absolute*

In the previous chapter, we saw that measures of central tendency provide useful summary information about the data in a single typical value, known as average, *i.e.*, mean, median or mode. However, this is not sufficient enough to describe the data completely and one can not come to know in what manner the values or measurements of variable are dispersed or scattered about the average. Considering two groups of male and female patients whose erythrocyte sedimentation rates (ESR) are 3, 2, 3, 3, 3, 3, 2, 6, 2, 3 and 2, 3, 3, 3, 4, 3, 3, 3, 3, 3 respectively. These series have much in common. They have the same mean, median and mode (*i.e.*, 3) but the values in the first series are more dispersed than the values in the second series. Thus it is necessary to know the scatter (or dispersion) of the values from their mean (*i.e.*, average).

There are seven measures of dispersion of which four are absolute measures and three are relative measures.

ABSOLUTE MEASURES OF DISPERSION

Include range, quartile deviation, mean deviation and standard deviation.

RELATIVE MEASURES OF DISPERSION

Include coefficient of variation, coefficient of quartile deviation and coefficient of mean deviation.

Range: It is the simplest absolute measure of dispersion. Range is obtained by subtracting of lowest value in a series of values from the hightest value. Although it is easy to calculate, but it is not generally used for practical purposes, as it is based only on two extreme values (*i.e.*, the lowest and the highest values).

QUARTILE DEVIATION OR SEMI-INTERQUARTILE RANGE

The range of a variable such as height between first quartile, Q_1 and third quartile, Q_3 is called interquartile range. Half of this range is considered as semi-interquartile range or sometimes quartile deviation which is a measure of dispersion slightly better than the range because it gives a little more knowledge about the distribution by including the middle half of the values in the series.

Pecentile Range = 90th percentile – 10th Percentile, *i.e.*, P.R. = $P_{90} - P_{10}$.

Note: In case of open end data and also when class intervals are unequal, quartile deviation as an appropriate measure of variation.

EXAMPLE 4.1: Find the quartile deviation of the weights (in kg) of 7 persons given below:

$$55, 50, 62, 58, 65, 48, 52.$$

SOLUTION: Arranging the given values in ascending order of magnitudes, *i.e.*,

$$48, 50, 52, 55, 58, 62, 65.$$

Here, $N = 7$

$$\therefore \quad Q_1 = \frac{N+1}{4} = \frac{7+1}{4} = \text{2nd value} = 50$$

and
$$Q_3 = \frac{3(N+1)}{4} = \frac{3 \times 8}{4} = \text{6th value} = 62$$

$$\text{Hence quartile deviation} = \frac{Q_3 - Q_1}{2} = \frac{62 - 50}{2} = 6$$

i.e., 6 kg. of weight.

EXAMPLE 4.2: Following is the age-distribution of 220 students in a school.

Age (years)	5-7	7-9	9-11	11-13	13-15	15-17
No. of students	22	63	55	38	30	12

Find the quartile deviation.

SOLUTION:

Age (years)	No. of students (frequency)	Cumulative frequency
5-7	22	22
7-9	63	85
9-11	55	140
11-13	38	178
13-15	30	208
15-17	12	220
	N = 220	

Here $\frac{N}{4} = \frac{220}{4}$ 55,

and $\frac{3N}{4} = 3 \times 55 = 165$

$$Q_1 = 7 + \frac{55-22}{63} \times 2 = 7 + \frac{33}{63} \times 2$$

or $Q_1 = 7 + 1.04 = 8.04,$

and $Q_3 = 11 + \frac{165-140}{38} \times = 11 + \frac{25}{38} \times 2$

or $Q_3 = 11 + 1.3 = 12.3$

Hence quartile deviation,

$$Q = \frac{Q_3 - Q_1}{2} = \frac{12.3 - 8.04}{2} = 2.13$$

COEFFICIENT OF QUARTILE DEVIATION

$$\text{Coefft. of Q.D.} = \frac{(Q_3 - Q_1) \div 2}{(Q_3 + Q_1) \div 2} = \frac{Q_3 - Q_1}{Q_3 + Q_1}$$

EXAMPLE 4.3: From the following data calculate coefficient of quartile deviation. Also find out the range of wages of (i) middle 50% of labourers and (ii) middle 80% of labourers.

Wages (₹) Less than:	10	20	30	40	50	60	70	80	90
No. of labourers:	5	12	15	25	30	38	40	45	50

SOLUTION:

Wages (₹)	No. of labourers (f)	Cumulative frequency
0–10	5	5
10–20	7	12
20–30	3	15
30–40	10	25
40–50	5	30
50–60	8	38
60–70	2	40
70–80	5	45
80–90	5	50
Total	N = 50	—

Calculations of coefficient of quartile deviation, interquartile range and percentile range

Here $\frac{N}{4} = \frac{50}{4} = 12.5 = q_1$

Since 12.5 belongs to the class (20 – 30) which is Q_1 (first quartile) class.

Now, $Q_1 = l + \frac{i}{f}(q_1 - cf)$

(here $l = 20$, $i = 10$, $f = 3$, $q_1 = 12.5$ and $cf = 12$)

$$= 20 + \frac{10}{3}(12.5 - 12)$$

$$= 20 + 3.33(0.5)$$

$\therefore$ $Q_1 = 20 + 1.67 = 21.67$

for $Q_3 = \frac{3}{4}N = \frac{3 \times 50}{4} = \frac{150}{4} = 37.5 = q_3$

$q_3 = 37.5$ belongs to the class (50 – 60) which is Q_3 (third quartile) class.

Since $Q_3 = l + \frac{i}{f}(q_3 - cf)$

where l = lower limit of Q_3 class (*i.e.*, 50)
i = class interval of Q_3 class (*i.e.*, 10)
f = frequency of Q_3 class (*i.e.*, 8)
cf = cumulative frequency of the class preceding the Q_3 class (*i.e.*, 30)

$$\text{then } Q_3 = 50 + \frac{10}{8}(37.5 - 30)$$

$$= 50 + \left(\frac{10 \times 7.5}{8}\right)$$

$$Q_3 = 50 + 9.37 = 59.37$$

Since, coefficient of Quartile deviation

$$= \frac{Q_3 - Q_1}{Q_3 + Q_1} = \frac{59.37 - 21.67}{59.37 + 21.67} = \frac{37.70}{81.04} = 0.47$$

Now range of wages of (i) middle 50% of labourers = Inter Quartile Range

i.e., $Q_3 - Q_1 = 59.37 - 21.67 = 37.7$

and (ii) middle 80% of labourers = Percentile Range = $P_{90} - P_{10}$

We have P_{10} = Size of $\frac{N}{10}$ th item = Size of $\frac{50}{10}$ th item

or $P_{10} = 5$

∴ (0 – 10) is the P_{10} class

Since $P_{10} = 1 + \frac{i}{f}(p_{10} - cf)$

∴ $P_{10} = 0 + \frac{10}{5}(5 - 0) = 0 + 10 = 10$

[Here, cf = Cumulative freq. of the class preceding the class (0 – 10) *i.e.,* zero]

∴ P_{90} = Size of $\frac{90}{100}$ Nth item

= Size of $\left(\frac{9 \times 50}{10}\right)$ th item

or $P_{90} = 45$

∴ (70 – 80) is the P_{90} class

Since $P_{90} = 1 + \frac{i}{f}(P_{90} - cf)$

$$P_{90} = 70 + \frac{10}{5}(45 - 50)$$

$$P_{90} = 70 + 10 = 80$$

The Percentile Range = $P_{90} - P_{10}$

i.e., P.R. = 80 – 10 = 70

MEAN DEVIATION

It is the average variation or dispersion of all the absolute values (ignoring the sign) from either the mean or median.

Mean deviation for ungrouped data is given by

$$M.D. = \frac{\Sigma |X - A|}{N} = \frac{|d|}{N}$$

Where 'd' stands for the deviation from the mean or median and | d | is always positive whether d itself positive or negative and this is called absolute d, denoted by | d |.

N is the total number of values.

For grouped data, Mean deviation is calculated by

$$M.D. = \frac{\Sigma f\,|(X - A)|}{\Sigma f} = \frac{\Sigma f\,|d|}{N}$$

STANDARD DEVIATION

It is the most important measure of dispersion. Standard deviation is defined as the square root of the average (mean) of the squared deviations of all the values from their mean. It is also called as Root Mean Square Deviation and usually denoted by the Greek letter σ, pronounced as sigma.

i.e., $$\sigma = \sqrt{\frac{\sum_{i=1}^{n}(Xi - \bar{X})^2}{n}}$$

when X < 30 (*i.e.*, small sample) then

$$\sigma = \sqrt{\frac{\Sigma(X - \bar{X})^2}{n - 1}}$$

where $\bar{X}$ = mean,

n = total number of values.

The square of standard deviation, σ^2 is known as variance.

EXAMPLE 4.4: Find the standard deviation of the respiration rate per minute found to be 16, 18, 19, 17, 21, 24, 22, 23, in eight individuals.

SOLUTION: $$\bar{X} = \frac{16 + 18 + 19 + 17 + 21 + 24 + 22 + 23}{8} = \frac{160}{8} = 20$$

The deviations of all values from the mean (*i.e.*, 20) are respectively – 4, – 2, – 1, –3, 1, 4, 2, 3.

The squares of the above deviations are 16, 4, 1, 9, 1, 16, 4, 9

$$\therefore \quad \sigma = \sqrt{\frac{\Sigma(X - \bar{X})^2}{n - 1}} = \sqrt{\frac{60}{8 - 1}} = \sqrt{\frac{60}{7}} = 2.93$$

Where (n – 1) is called degrees of freedom of the data.

Standard deviation for a frequency distribution

$$\sigma = \sqrt{\frac{\Sigma fd^2}{\Sigma f}}, \text{ where } d = (X - \overline{X})$$

and this can be expressed as $\sigma = \sqrt{\frac{\Sigma fd^2}{\Sigma f} - \left(\frac{\Sigma fd}{\Sigma f}\right)^2}$

where n = total frequency.

EXAMPLE 4.5: Find the standard deviation for the following distribution:

Age in yrs.	25	30	35	40	45	50	55	60
No. of persons	15	28	42	50	30	20	10	5

SOLUTION:

Age in years X	Deviation d = X – AM	f	d^2	fd	fd^2
25	–15	15	225	–225	3375
30	–10	28	100	–280	2800
35	–5	42	25	–210	1050
40 = A.M.	0	50	0	0	0
45	5	30	25	150	750
50	10	20	100	200	2000
55	15	10	225	150	1500
60	20	5	400	100	500
Total		Σf = 200		Σfd = – 115	Σfd^2 = 11975

∴ Standard Deviation

$$\sigma = \sqrt{\frac{\Sigma fd^2}{n} - \left(\frac{\Sigma fd}{n}\right)^2}$$

$$\sigma = \sqrt{\frac{11975}{200} - \frac{-115}{200}^2} = \sqrt{59.9 - 0.3} = 7.7$$

EXAMPLE 4.6: Find the standard deviation of the following data:

Heights (cm)	95-105	105-115	115-125	125-135	135-145
No. of children	20	55	95	70	60

SOLUTION: First we prepare the following table to calculate standard deviation:

Heights (cm)	Mid value (X)	No. of Children (f)	$d=\frac{X-AM}{i}$	fd	fd^2
95-105	100	20	−2	−40	80
105-115	110	55	−1	−55	55
115-125	120 = AM	95	0	0	0
125-135	130	70	1	70	70
135-145	140	60	2	120	240
Total		$\Sigma f = 300$		$\Sigma fd = 95$	$\Sigma fd^2 = 445$

Here $i = 10$

∴ Standard Deviation,

$$\sigma = i\sqrt{\frac{\Sigma fd^2}{n} - \left(\frac{\Sigma fd}{n}\right)^2} = 10\sqrt{\frac{445}{300} - \left(\frac{95}{300}\right)^2}$$

$$= 10\sqrt{1.48 - 0.10}$$

$$= 10\sqrt{1.38} = 11.75$$

Note: The calculation of standard deviation can be made easier by changing the origin and the scale conveniently.

RELATIVE MEASURES OF DISPERSION

Absolute measures expressed as percentage of a measure of a central tendency (mean or median) gives relative measures of dispersion.

To compare the deviations of two or more variables which are in different units as well as with marked difference in the size of the means, comparison with standard deviation is not suitable. In order to compare the deviations (or variations) of such variables of data, the standard deviation is expressed as a percentage to the mean value and this quantity is known as coefficient of variation.

The three relative measures of dispersion are given below:

(i) *Coefficient of variation.* It is the ratio of the standard-deviation to the mean, expressed as a percentage,

i.e., Coefficient of variation $= \frac{\sigma}{\overline{X}} \times 100$

(ii) *Coefficient of quartile deviation*

$$= \frac{\text{Quartile deviation}}{\text{Median}} \times 100 = \frac{Q}{Q_2} \times 100$$

where $Q = \frac{Q_3 - Q_1}{2}$

(iii) *Coefficient of mean deviation* $= \frac{\text{Mean deviation}}{\text{Mean or Median}} \times 100$

EXAMPLE 4.7: In a series of 100 individuals, the mean blood glucose in mg/dl was found to be 155 with standard deviation 52. In the same individuals the mean serum cholesterol levels in mg/dl was found to be 210 with standard deviation 36. Find which character shows greater variation.

SOLUTION: Coefficient of variation for blood glucose (bg)

$$= \frac{\sigma bg}{\bar{X}bg} \times 100 = \frac{52}{155} \times 100 = 33.5\%$$

Whereas Coefficient of variation for serum cholesterol (sc)

$$= \frac{\sigma\, sc}{\bar{X}\, sc} \times 100 = \frac{36}{210} \times 100 = 17.1\%.$$

Thus, Blood glucose is found to be more variable character as compared to serum cholesterol.

SKEWNESS AND KURTOSIS

SKEWNESS

A frequency distribution is said to be symmetrical when the values of the variable equidistant from their mean value, *i.e.*, Mean = Median = Mode. If a frequency distribution is not symmetrical, it is said to be asymmetrical or skewed. Any deviation from symmetry is called skewness, *i.e.*, skewness is the lack of symmetry.

Skewness may be positive or negative. A distribution is said to be positively skewed if the frequency curve has a longer tail (or steepness) towards the higher values of the variable. For a positively skewed distribution, Mean > Median > Mode.

A distribution is said to be negatively skewed if the frequency curve has a longer tail towards the lower values of the variable. For a negatively skewed distribution, Mean < Median < Mode.

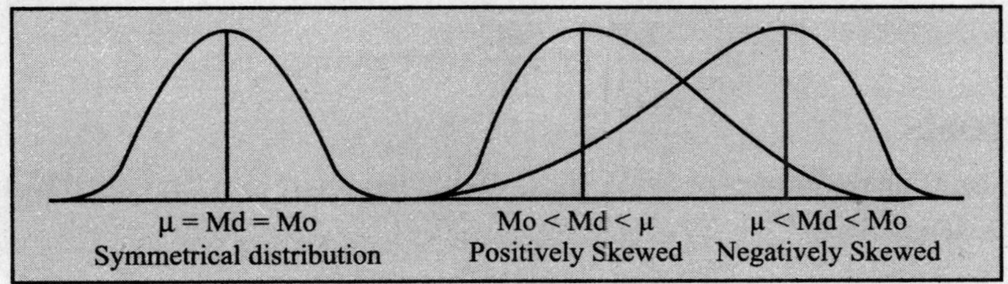

Fig. 4.1

The coefficient of skewness is a pure number and is zero for a symmetrical distribution. If coefficient of skewness is positive, the distribution is positively skewed. If the value of coefficient of skewness is negative, the distribution is a negatively skewed. This relationship can also be illustrated in the following manner:

If $Q_3 - Q_2 = Q_2 - Q_1 \Rightarrow$ No skewness (*i.e.*, symmetrical)

If $Q_3 - Q_2 > Q_2 - Q_1 \Rightarrow$ Positively skewed

If $Q_3 - Q_2 < Q_2 - Q_1 \Rightarrow$ Negatively skewed

Measures of Skewness

The degree of skewness is measured by its coefficient. The common measures of skewness are as follows:

(i) Pearson's First measure, *i.e.*, skewness

$$= \frac{\text{Mean} - \text{Mode}}{\text{Std.}} = \frac{\mu - \text{Mo}}{\sigma}$$

(ii) Pearson's Second measure, *i.e.*, skewness

$$= \frac{3\ \text{Mean} - \text{Median}}{\text{Std. dev.}}$$

(iii) Bowley's measure, *i.e.*, skewness

$$= \frac{(Q_3 - Q_2) - (Q_2 - Q_1)}{(Q_3 - Q_2) + (Q_2 - Q_1)}$$

or Coefficient of skewness $= \dfrac{Q_3 + Q_1 - 2Q_2}{Q_3 - Q_1}$

where Q_1, Q_2 and Q_3 are first, second and third quartiles respectively.

Measure of Skewness (based on moments)

The coefficient of skewness is

$$\beta_1 = \frac{\mu_3}{\mu_2{}^3} \text{ where } \mu_3 = \frac{\Sigma d^3}{N} \text{ or } \frac{\Sigma fd^3}{\Sigma f} \text{ (for grouped data)}$$

and $$\mu_2 = \frac{\Sigma d^2}{N} \text{ or } \frac{\Sigma df^2}{\Sigma f} \text{ (for grouped data)}$$

KURTOSIS

The relative flatness or peakedness of the frequency curve is called Kurtosis and it is denoted by

$$\beta_2 = \frac{\mu_4}{(\mu_2)}, \text{ where } \mu_4 = \frac{\Sigma d^4}{N} \text{ (in case of individual values)}$$

and $\mu_4 = \frac{\Sigma fd^4}{\Sigma f}$ (in case of frequency distribution)

and $\mu_2 = \frac{\Sigma fd^2}{N}$ (in case of individual values) and $\mu_2 = \frac{\Sigma fd^2}{N}$ (in case of frequency distribution).

β_2, coefficient of Kurtosis can also (based on Percentiles) be calculated as

$$\beta_2 = \frac{P_{75} - P_{25}}{P_{90} - P_{10}}$$

Conditions and types of Kurtosis:

(i) if $\beta_2 = 3$, then the frequency curve is called **Meso-kurtic**

(ii) if $\beta_2 > 3$, then the frequency curve is called **Lepto-kurtic**

(iii) if $\beta_2 < 3$, then the frequency curve is called **Platy-kurtic**

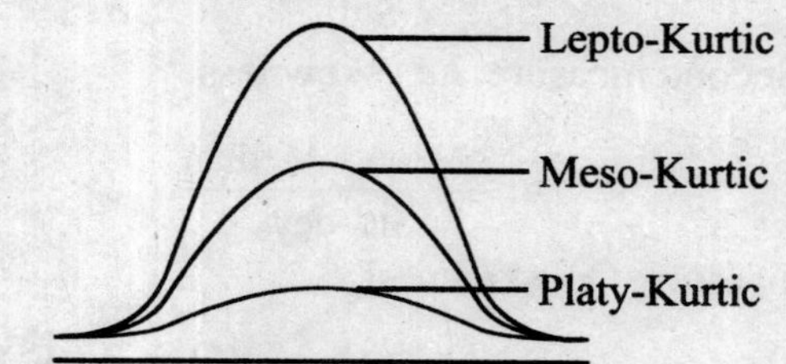

Fig. 4.2: L.M.P. – Kurtic Curves (Kurtosis)

EXAMPLE 4.8: Find the appropriate measure of skewness from the following data:

Age (yrs.):	< 20	20-30	30-40	40-50	50-60	60 and above
No. of employees:	15	35	105	200	98	27

SOLUTION: Since the frequency distribution has open end classes, therefore, the appropriate measure of skewness is Bowley's measure, *i.e.*, skewness based on quartiles.

Age (yrs.)	No. of employees (f)	Cumulative frequency (less than)
20	15	15
30	35	50
$Q_1 \rightarrow$		$\leftarrow 120 = \frac{N}{4}$
40	105	155
$Q_2 \rightarrow$		$\leftarrow 240 = \frac{N}{2}$
50	200	355
$Q_3 \rightarrow$		$\leftarrow 360 = \frac{3N}{4}$
60	98	453
and above	27	480
—	N = 480	—

$$\frac{N}{4} + \frac{480}{4} = 120, \frac{N}{2} = \frac{480}{2} = 240, \text{ and } \frac{3N}{4} = \frac{3 \times 480}{4} = 360;$$

Now we have $Q_1 = 1 + \frac{\frac{N}{4} - cf}{f} \times i = 30 + \frac{120 - 50}{105} \times 10$

$$\therefore \quad Q_1 = 30 = \frac{700}{105} = 30 + 6.67 = 36.67$$

$$Q_2 = 1 + \frac{\frac{N}{2} - cf}{f} \times i$$

$$= 40 + \frac{240 - 155}{210} \times 10$$

$$\therefore \quad Q_2 = 40 + \frac{850}{210} = 40 + 4.05 = 44.05$$

and $\quad Q_3 = 1 + \frac{\frac{3N}{4} - cf}{f} \times i$

$$= 50 + \frac{360 - 355}{98} \times 10$$

$$\therefore \quad Q_3 = 50 + \frac{50}{98} = 50 + 0.51 = 50.51$$

Now $\quad \text{skewness} = \frac{(Q_3 - Q_2) - (Q_2 - Q_1)}{(Q_3 - Q_2) + (Q_2 - Q_1)}$

$$= \frac{(50.51 - 44.05) - (44.05 - 36.67)}{(50.51 - 44.05) + (44.05 - 36.67)}$$

$$= \frac{6.46 - 7.38}{6.46 + 7.38} = \frac{-0.92}{13.48} = -0.07$$

EXAMPLE 4.9: Find out Kurtosis to the following frequency distribution:

Class-intervals:	0-2	2-4	4-6	6-8	8-10
Frequency:	5	14	17	10	4

Comment on the nature of the distribution.

SOLUTION: Kurtosis is measured by the coefficient β_2 which is given by $\beta_2 = \frac{\mu_4}{(\mu_2)^2}$, where μ_2 and μ_4 are the second and fourth central moments.

Calculations for the first four central moments:

Class Intervals	Mid value (x)	No. of Children (f)	$\frac{X-5}{2} = dx$	fdx	fd_x^2	fd_x^3	fd_x^4
0-2	1	5	−2	−10	20	−40	80
2-4	3	14	−1	−14	14	−14	14
4-6	5	17	0	0	0	0	0
6-8	7	10	+1	+10	10	+10	10
8-10	9	4	+2	+8	16	+32	64
Total	—	50	—	−6	60	−12	168

Moments from assumed mean (*i.e.*, A=5)

$$\upsilon_1 = \frac{\Sigma fd_x}{N} = \frac{-6}{50} = -0.12$$

$$\upsilon_2 = \frac{\Sigma fd_x^2}{N} = \frac{60}{50} = 1.2$$

$$\upsilon_3 = \frac{\Sigma f d_x^3}{N} = \frac{-12}{50} = -0.24$$

$$\upsilon_4 = \frac{\Sigma f d_x^4}{N} = \frac{168}{50} = 3.36$$

Central moments from Arithmatic Mean

$$\mu_1 = (\upsilon_1 - \upsilon_1) \times i = (-0.12 + 0.12) \times 2 = 0$$

$$\mu_2 = (\upsilon_2 - \upsilon_1^2) \times i^2 = \{1.2 - (-0.12)^2\} \times 2^2 = 4.74$$

$$\mu_3 = (\upsilon_3 - 3\upsilon_2\,\upsilon_1 + 2\upsilon_1^3) \times i^3$$

$$= [-0.24 - \{3 \times 1.2 \times (-0.12) + 2 \times (-0.12)^3] \times 2^3$$

$$= [-0.24 - \{3.6 \times (-0.12) + 2\,(-0.002)\}] \times 8$$

$$= [-0.24 - \{-0.43 - 0.004\}] \times 8$$

$$= [-0.24 - \{-0.434\}] \times 8$$

$$= (-0.24 + 0.43) \times 8 = 1.52$$

and
$$\mu_4 = (\upsilon_4 - 4\upsilon_3\upsilon_1 + 6\upsilon_2\upsilon_1^2 - 3\upsilon_1^4) \times i^4$$

$$= [3.36 - 4(-0.24)(-0.12) + 6 \times 1.2\,(-0.12)^2 - 3(-0.12)^4\,] \times 2^4$$

$$= [3.36 - 0.115 + 0.104 - 0.001] \times 16 = 53.57$$

Now we have $\beta_2 = \frac{\mu_4}{(\mu_2)^2} = \frac{53.57}{(4.74)^2} = \frac{53.57}{22.47} = 2.38$

Since $\beta_2 < 3$, the frequency curve of the given distribution is Platy-kurtic.

➤ EXERCISES ≺

4.1. Following are data for 12 individuals daily sodium intake:
6.5, 7.0, 6.8, 7.3, 6.9, 6.9, 7.2, 7.0, 6.4, 7.1, 7.5, 7.3, 7.0.
Find the standard deviation.

4.2. The following table gives the marks obtained by 50 students in a subject.

Marks	No. of students
10-20	2
20-30	3
30-40	12
40-50	23
50-60	7
60-70	2
70-80	1
Total	50

Find the variance.

4.3. From the data given below, state which series is more consistent (variable).

Variable	Series A	Series B
10-20	10	18
20-30	18	22
30-40	32	40
40-50	40	32
50-60	22	18
60-70	18	10

4.4. The mean and standard deviation of the haemoglobin level of a group is 12.5 gm % and 1.5 gm % respectively while the mean and standard deviation of the body weight of the same group is 60 kg and 2.4 kg respectively. Which variable has greater variation?

4.5. Find the quartile deviation from the following data:

Height (in cm)	No. of persons (frequency)
160-164	20
164-168	30
168-172	35
172-176	40
176-180	25

4.6. Find mean incubation period in days of Tuberculosis and its standard deviation, when in 12 patients was found to be 22, 26, 28, 30, 32, 24, 22, 28, 24, 30, 28, 22.

4.7. Distinguish between 'Dispersion' and 'Skewness'.

4.8. Compare the variability of systolic B.P. in children of age-group 5-10 years with that of adults of age group 30-40 years. When the means and standard deviations are 100 and 10 in children and 120 and 12 in adults respectively.

4.9. Total serum proteins (gm%) of 20 patients are given below:

5.8, 7.2, 7.8, 6.6, 6.9, 7.5, 6.8, 7.4, 6.8, 7.5, 7.0, 7.3, 7.4, 7.5, 7.2, 7.8, 7.2, 7.8, 7.2, 7.3.

Determine the standard deviation and coefficient of variation (C.V).

4.10. The CV of two series of observations are 17% and 20% with standard deviation 3.4 and 5 respectively. What are their mean values?

4.11. Find out the skewness and kurtosis of the following distribution:

Class Interval:	0-10	10-20	20-30	30-40
Frequency:	1	3	4	2

Comment on the nature of the distribution.

4.12. Calculate the coefficient of skewness (based on the quartiles) of the following distribution:

Age (yrs.):	<10	10-20	20-30	30-40	40-50	50-60	60 and above
No. of patients:	15	30	55	120	100	70	10

CHAPTER

5

Probability

- *Probability*
- *Event*
- *Experiment*
- *Likelihood*
- *Trial*
- *Permutation*
- *Combination*
- *Random*
- *Variable*
- *Binomial*

To understand probability, we must know about some important terms which will be used in defining Probability.

EVENTS

The outcomes of experiments or observations are called events. Events may be either elementary (or simple) or composite, *i.e.*, compound. Elementary events can not be decomposed further, while composite events can be decomposed into elementary events. For example, "Falling Head on tossing a coin" is an elementary event while "appearance 7 points by throwing two dice at a time in a single cast" is a composite event, *i.e.*, (1, 6) or (2, 5) or (3, 4) or (4, 3) or (5, 2) or (6, 1) each of which is a simple event.

Equally likely events: A number of events are said to be equally likely if, there is no reason to expect any one of the events in preference to the others. For example:

(i) As a result of drawing a card from a well-shuffled pack of 52 cards, any card may appear in the draw so that the 52 different cases are equally likely.

(ii) In tossing a perfect coin, the two possible outcomes Head and Tail are equally likely.

(iii) If a fair die, *i.e.*, unbiased die is cast, all the six possible outcomes 1, 2, 3, 4, 5, 6, are equally likely.

Mutually exclusive events: Events are said to be mutually exclusive when only one of the events can occur and two (or more) events can not appear simultaneously. In the case of tossing of a coin Head and Tail are mutually exclusive events, because if head turns up, Tail can not happen and vice versa, *i.e.*, Head and Tail can not occur simultaneously.

Probability: May be defined as the relative frequency or probable chances of occurence with which an event is expected to occur on an average such as giving birth to a boy in the first delivery, chances of one drug being better than the other.

Probability is usually expressed by symbol 'P'.

It ranges from 0 to 1. When the occurrence of an event is an absolute certainty then the probability of its occurrence, *i.e.*, $p = 1$, *e.g.*, death for any living being. If there is no chance of an event happening or its occurrence is an absolute impossibility, *e.g.*, chances of survival after rabies, in this case the probability of its occurrence, *i.e.*, $p = 0$.

In other words, probability measures the likelihood that a particular event will or will not occur. If the probability of an event happening is p and that of not happening is represented by the symbol q, then $q = 1 - p$ or $(p + q) = 1$, for example, the probability (chances) of getting Head or Tail in one toss are fifty-fifty or half and half, *i.e.*, $p = 1/2$.

Similarly, chances of getting male child (boy) or female child (girl) in one pregnancy are also fifty-fifty, (*i.e.*, $p = 1/2$ and $q = 1/2$), where p denotes the probability of getting a male child and q of not getting a male child or getting a female child. Thus, the probability of an event, p, is defined as the proportion of times a favourable events will occur in a long series of repeated trials:

$$p = \frac{\text{Number of favourable outcomes}}{\text{Number of possible outcomes}}$$

If n = Number of favourable outcomes

N = Number of possible outcomes or number of trials then symbolically,

$$p(\text{event}) = \frac{n}{N}$$

For example, if a surgeon performs renal transplants in 150 cases and succeeds in 63 cases then probability of survival after operation is calculated as:

$$p = \frac{\text{Number of survival after operation}}{\text{Total number of cases operated}}$$

$$= \frac{63}{150} = 0.42$$

and chances of not surviving, *i.e.*, probability of dying cases, q or (1 – p) is 1– 0.42 = 0.58 which can be shown as:

$$q = \frac{\text{No. of cases died after the operation}}{\text{Total number of cases operated}}$$

$$= \frac{87}{150}$$

$$= 0.58 = 0.6 \text{ approximately}$$

In a fair (unbiased) dice, the probability of getting each of 1, 2, 3, 4, 5 or 6 in one throw of dice will be 1/6.

Counting rules: In computing the probabilities of various events it is necessary to know that in how many possible ways such events can occur. For example, if one wants to know the probability of having two boys and girl in a three-child family, in this case it is essential to know the order of their birth.

There are eight different possibilities of having three children:

(i)	boy	boy	girl;	(ii)	boy	girl	boy;
(iii)	girl	boy	boy;	(iv)	boy	boy	boy,
(v)	girl	girl	boy;	(vi)	girl	girl	girl;
(vii)	girl	boy	girl;	(viii)	girl	boy	boy;

There are only three favourable outcomes, *i.e.*, (boy boy girl); (boy girl boy); (girl boy boy) out of eight possible outcomes. To know the number of different possibilities of a certain events, the following general rules are helpful in obtaining counts:

RULE-1:

Number of ways: If an event A can occur in n_1 distinct ways, and event B can occur in n_2 ways then the events consisting of A and B can occur in $n_1 \times n_2$ ways. For example, if three-different diet choices by amount of protein (low, medium, high) and three different choices by amount of fat (low, medium, high), then there will be:

$$n_1 \times n_2 = 3 \times 3 = 9 \text{ different possible diets.}$$

RULE-2:

Permutations: A permutation is a selection of 6 objects from a group of n objects, taking order of selection into account. The number of different ways in which n objects may be arranged is given by n! pronounced 'factorial n' means n (n–1) (n–2) .... 3.2.1. Thus 5! = 5.4.3.2.1. = 120, and 0! (*i.e.*, factorial zero) = 1 (one). For example, if a nurse wants to identify vials of a vaccine by using three different symbols, x, y and z, then there will be 3! (*i.e.*, 3.2.1 = 6) different ways of identifications like xyz; xzy; yxz; yzx; zyx; and zxy.

To know the number of ways of selecting objects from a set of n object and order is taken into consideration. We use the formula:

$$P(n, r) = \frac{n!}{(n-r)!}$$

where P (n, r) denotes permutation (selection) of r objects from a group of n objects.

EXAMPLE 5.1: If there are three effective ways of treating a cancer patient– Chemotherapy (C), Radiation (R) and Surgery (S). In how many different ways can a patient by treated with two different treatments, if order of treatment is important?

$$\text{Here } P(3, 2) = \frac{3!}{(3-2)!} = \frac{3.2.1}{1} = 6$$

i.e., CR, RC, SC, CS, RS and SR.

RULE-3:

Combinations: Sometimes we are interested to know the number of arrangements of a group of objects when the order is immaterial. A combination of selection of a sub-group of distinct objects without considering any order. Thus, the number of ways of selecting r objects from n objects without any order of selection, is:

$$C(n, r) = \frac{n!}{r!(n-r)!}$$

where C denotes the total number of combinations of objects.

EXAMPLE 5.2: In how many ways can a committee of five persons be chosen out of nine persons?

$$\text{Here} \qquad C(9, 5) = \frac{9!}{5!(9-5)!}$$

$$= \frac{9.8.7.6.5.4.3.2.1}{5.4.3.2.1.(4.3.2.1.)}$$

$$= \frac{9.8.7.6.}{4.3.2.1.} = \frac{3024}{24} = 126$$

Hence there are 126 ways of selecting a five persons committee from nine persons under consideration.

The probability of occurrence of an event is expressed as a fraction or a decimal number, *e.g.*, the probability of getting head or tail in one toss of a coin is 1/2 or 0.5. Sometimes probability is expressed as "chances in a hundred." For example, someone might say the probability that event, A will occur in 5 chances in 100, *i.e.*, $p(A) = 5/100 = 0.05$. Occassionally, probability is also expressed as the odds in favour or against an event occurring, *e.g.*, a bag contains 3 white and 5 black balls, what is the chance that a ball drawn at random will be black? Find the odds in favour of the event and against the event.

Here the total number of balls is 8; hence the number of possible outcomes for the event is 8. Again, one black ball can be drawn out of 5 black balls in $C(5, 1) = 5$ ways, hence the total number of favourable outcomes to an event is 5. Therefore, the chance that the ball drawn is black is 5/8 or 0.625.

Now, total number of outcomes unfavourable to the event $8 - 5 = 3$.

∴ The odds in favour of the event are as 5:3, *i.e.*, the odds in favour of an event

$$= \frac{\text{No. of favourable outcomes}}{\text{No. of unfavourable outcomes}}$$

and the odd against the event are as 3:5, *i.e.*, the odds against the event

$$= \frac{\text{No. of unfavourable outcomes}}{\text{No. of favourable outcomes}}$$

PROBABILITY RULES

There are two indispensable rules for determining the probability of two or more individual events. These are the addition rule and the multiplication rule.

ADDITION RULE OF PROBABILITY

The addition rule is concerned with determining the probability of occurrence of any one of several possible events.

(i) When there are only two possible events, A and B. The addition rule states that the probability of occurrence of A or B is equal to the probability of occurrence of A plus the probability of occurrence of B minus the probability of occurrence of both A and B.

Symbolically, p (A or B) = p (A) + p (B) – p (A and B), *e.g.*, In tossing two coins, one person may be, interested to know the probability of having a head on the first coin, *i.e.*, H_1 or on the second coin, *i.e.*, H_1 or on both coins, *i.e.*, H_1 H_2. To determine this, the addition rule is applied as

$$p(H_1 \text{ or } H_2) = p(H_1) + p(H_2) - p(H_1 \text{ and } H_2)$$

$$= \frac{1}{2} + \frac{1}{2} - \frac{1}{4} = \frac{3}{4}$$

EXAMPLE 5.3: In rolling a fair dice once, what is the probability of appearing 2 or 3?

The addition rule gives as:

$$p(2 \text{ or } 3) = p(2) + p(3) - p(2 \text{ and } 3)$$

Here, p(2 and 3) is zero because both events can not occur together in one roll of a fair dice.

$$= \frac{1}{6} + \frac{1}{6} - 0 = \frac{1}{6}$$

(ii) When two events are mutually exclusive, the probability of both events occurring together is zero. Then the addition rule becomes

$$p(A \text{ or } B) = p(A) + p(B)$$

The addition rule may also be applied in situations where there are more than two events, and the events are mutually exclusive, then the probability of occurrence of any one of the events is equal to the sum of the probability of each event, *i.e.*, p (A or B or C or....... or Z) = p(A) + p(B) + p(C) +......... + p(Z).

Conditional Probability: Among n equally likely cases of a random experiment if m cases are favourable for the occurrence of an event A, and among such 'm' cases, r events are favourable for the event B as well, then the conditional probability of B given that A has already materialized is $p(B|A) = r \div m, m > 0$.

THE MULTIPLICATION RULE OF PROBABILITY

In discussing the multiplication rule, it is necessary to distinguish among two conditions:

(i) When the events are mutually exclusive and

(ii) When the events are independent.

Two events are said to be mutually exclusive if they both can not occur together (or simultaneously), *i.e*., the occurrence of one of the events prevents the occurrence of others.

Whereas two events are independet if the occurrence of one has no effect on the chance of occurrence of the other, *e.g*., the outcomes of repeated tosses of a coin illustrate independent events, for the outcome of one toss does not affect the outcome of any future toss.

The multiplication rule states that the probability of occurrence of two independent events, A and B, is equal to the product of the probabilities of the individual events.

Symbolically, p (A and B) = p (A) p (B).

EXAMPLE 5.4: In tossing two coins, what is the probability that a head will occur both on the first coin and on the second coin?

SOLUTION: Since the outcome with the first coin has no effect on the outcome of the second coin, there is independence between events. Thus, p (a head with first coin and a head with the second coin) = p (a head with first coin) p (a head with second coin)

$$= \frac{1}{2} \times \frac{1}{2} = \frac{1}{4}$$

EXAMPLE 5.5: A dice is thrown twice in succession, what will be the probability of appearing 2 and 5?

SOLUTION: Here the probability of appearing 2 in the first throw of a dice and 5 in the second throw of the same dice, *i.e*.,

$$p(2 \text{ and } 5) = p(2)\, p(5)$$

$$= \frac{1}{6} \times \frac{1}{6} = \frac{1}{36}$$

EXAMPLE 5.6: What is the chance that a leap year selected at random will contain 53 Sundays ?

SOLUTION: A leap year consists of 366 days in which there are 52 complete weeks and 2 more consecutive days (*i.e*., 366 ÷ 7 = 52 weeks and 2 days). 52 days contain 52 Sundays. Therefore, leap year will contain 53 Sundays if these two consecutive days contain one Sunday. 2 consecutive days can be selected from the 7 days in a week in the following possible ways:

(Sunday, Monday), (Monday, Tuesday), (Tuesday, Wednesday), (Wednesday, Thursday), (Thursday, Friday), (Friday, Saturday), (Saturday, Sunday). Here we see that out of 7 possibilities only 2 (the first and the last) contain Sunday, *i.e.*, Number of favourable cases = 2. Hence the required chance = $\frac{2}{7}$.

Application of the multiplication rule, when the two children are born one after the other, the possible outcomes will be any of the following:

First birth	Second birth		Outcomes	Probability
Male	Male	→	Male and Male	$\frac{1}{2} \times \frac{1}{2} = \frac{1}{4}$
	Female	→	Male and Female	$\frac{1}{2} \times \frac{1}{2} = \frac{1}{4}$
Female	Male	→	Female and Male	$\frac{1}{2} \times \frac{1}{2} = \frac{1}{4}$
	Female	→	Female and Female	$\frac{1}{2} \times \frac{1}{2} = \frac{1}{4}$

Therefore, the chances of getting two males = 1/4 = 25% and the chances of getting two females are also 1/4, *i.e.*, 25% whereas chances of getting one of either sex will be 1/4 + 1/4 = 1/2, *i.e.*, 50%.

So, if a female child is born first and a second child is desired, the probability of the second delivered child being male will be (1 – 1/4) = 3/4, *i.e.*, 75% and of its being femail 25%.

PROBABILITY DISTRIBUTIONS

If we know the various probabilities associated with different outcomes of a given phenomenon, we can determine which outcomes are common and which are not. This help us to reach to a decision as to whether certain events are significant. A complete list of all possible outcomes, together with the probability of each, constitutes a probability distribution. The outcomes of events may be described numerically (*e.g.*, the number of three-boy families). The symbol X usually denotes the variable of interest. This variable, which can assume any number of values, is called a random variable because it represents a chance or random outcome of an experiment. Thus, a probability distribution is a list of the probabilities associated with the values of the random variable obtained in an experiment.

Examples of probability distribution are given below:

Toss of two coins		Roll of a Dice		Sex of three-child family	
Events	**p(E)**	**Events**	**p(E)**	**Events**	**p(E)**
Head & Head	1/4	1	1/6	3 boys	1/8 = 0.125
Tail & Tail	1/4	2	1/6	3 girls	1/8 = 0.125
Head & Tail	1/4	3	1/6	2 boys & 1 girl	3/8 = 0.375
Tail & Head	1/4	4	1/6	2 girls & 1 boy	3/8 = 0.375
	1.0	5	1/6		1.000
		6	1/6		
			1.0		

BINOMIAL DISTRIBUTION

It serves as a model for outcomes limited to two choices like ill or healthy, dead or alive, at risk or not at risk. For such a dichotomous population, we may wish to know the probability of having a number of 'r' successes on 'n' different trials, where the probability of success on any one trial is p. The probability distribution is algebraically obtained from the expansion of the binominal term $(p + q)^n$, where p is the probability of a successful outcome, $q = (1 - p)$ is the probability of a unsuccessful outcome and n is the number of trials. The binominal expansion is applicable, providing that

(i) Each trial has only two possible outcomes – success or failure.

(ii) The outcome of each trial is independent of the outcomes of any other trial.

(iii) The probability of success, p, is constant from trial to trial under these conditions. The probability of an event consisting of r successes out of n trials is

$$p(r) = \frac{n!}{r!(n-r)!} p^r q^{n-r}$$

where n = the number of trials in an experiment

r = the number of successes

(n – r) = the number of failures

p = the probability of success

q = (1 – p), the probability of failure

This is a term from the binominal expansion, *i.e.*,

$(p + q)^n = p^n + {}^nc_1\, p^{n-1}\, q + {}^nc_2\, p^{n-2}\, q^2 + \ldots\ldots\ldots\ldots\ldots\ldots + q^n$

The two independent constants 'n' and 'p' are called parameters of the Binomial Distribution and the complete distribution can be known when the values of 'p' and 'n' are given.

PROPERTIES OF BINOMIAL DISTRIBUTION

(i) Binomial Distribution is a discrete probability distribution in which the random variable r (the number of successes) assumes the values 0, 1, 2, 3, ..., n.

(ii) Mean = n p and variance = n p q and therefore, the standard deviation $= \sqrt{n\,p\,q}$.

(iii) If p = q = 0.5, the curve will be symmetrical.

(iv) For any fixed value of p and q, if n is sufficiently large, then binomial distribution tends to be a normal distribution.

EXAMPLE 5.7: A fair dice is thrown three times. Getting a '3' or '6' is considered a successes. Find the probability of at least two successes.

SOLUTION: Let p (x) be the probability of getting the number x in a toss of a dice. Then

$$p\,(3) = \frac{1}{6} \text{ and } p\,(6) = \frac{1}{6}$$

$$\therefore \quad p\,(3 \text{ or } 6) = \frac{1}{6} + \frac{1}{6} = \frac{2}{6} = \frac{1}{3}$$

$$\therefore \quad q = 1 - \frac{1}{3} = \frac{2}{3}$$

Now $\quad p\,(r) = {}^nc_r\, p^r\, q^{n-r}$

Here $\quad n = 3$ (because dice is thrown three times)

$$p(2) = {}^3c_2\, p^2\, q^{(3-2)}$$

$$= {}^3c_2 \left(\frac{1}{3}\right)^2 \left(\frac{2}{3}\right)^{3-2} = \frac{3}{1} \times \frac{1}{3} \times \frac{1}{3} \times \frac{2}{3}$$

or $$p(2) = \frac{2}{9}$$

and $p(3) = {}^3c_3\, p^3\, q^0$

$$= 1.\left(\frac{1}{3}\right)^3 .1 = \frac{1\times1\times1}{3\times3\times3} = \frac{1}{27}$$

$$\text{p (at least 2 sucesses) } p(2) + p(3) = \frac{2}{9} + \frac{1}{27} = \frac{7}{27} = 0.3 \text{ approximately.}$$

EXAMPLE 5.8: Five coins are tossed simultaneously. What is the probability of (i) 3 heads, (ii) at least three heads (iii) more than 3 heads?

SOLUTION: Let 'falling head by tossing a coin' be a 'success' then

$$p = \frac{1}{2}, q = (1-p) = \frac{1}{2}$$

Now $p(r) = {}^nc_r\, p^r\, q^{n-r}$ here n = 5

$$= 5c_r \left(\frac{1}{2}\right)^r \left(\frac{1}{2}\right)^{5-r}$$

Taking (i) case, *i.e.*, probability of getting three heads is given by

$$p(3) = {}^5C_3 \left(\frac{1}{2}\right)^3 \left(\frac{1}{2}\right)^{5-3} = \frac{5.4.3.2.1.}{3.2.2.1.} = \left(\frac{1}{2}\times\frac{1}{2}\times\frac{1}{2}\right)\left(\frac{1}{2}\times\frac{1}{2}\right)$$

or

$$p(3) = 10\times\frac{1}{8}\times\frac{1}{4} = \frac{5}{16}.$$

(ii) p (at least three heads) = 1 – [p(0) + p(1) + p(2)]

$$= 1 - \left[{}^5C_0 \left(\frac{1}{2}\right)^0 \left(\frac{1}{2}\right)^{5-0} + {}^5C_1 \left(\frac{1}{2}\right)^1 \left(\frac{1}{2}\right)^{5-1} + {}^5C_2 \left(\frac{1}{2}\right)^2 \left(\frac{1}{2}\right)^{5-2}\right]$$

$$= 1 - \left[1.1\left(\frac{1}{2}\right)^5 + \frac{5.1}{2}\left(\frac{1}{2}\right)^4 + \frac{5.4}{2.1}\left(\frac{1}{2}\right)^2\left(\frac{1}{2}\right)^3\right]$$

$$= 1 - \frac{1}{32} + \frac{5}{32} + \frac{10}{32} = 1 - \left(\frac{16}{32}\right) = \frac{1}{2}$$

(iii) Probability of getting more than 3 heads

1 – (Probability of getting not more than three heads)

1 – [p(0) + p(1) + p(2) + p(3)]

$$= 1 - \left[\frac{1}{32} + \frac{5}{32} + \frac{10}{32} + \frac{5}{16}\right] = 1 - \left(\frac{13}{16}\right) = \frac{3}{16}$$

EXAMPLE 5.9: What is the probability of having two boys and one girl in a three-child family if the probability of having a girl is 1/2?

SOLUTION: Here n = 3, p = 1/2 and r = 2

$\therefore \quad p(2B, 1G) = {}^3c_2 (p)^2 (q)^{3-2}$

$$= \frac{3.2}{2.1}\left(\frac{1}{2}\right)^2\left(\frac{1}{2}\right)^1$$

or $\quad p(2B, 1G) = \frac{3}{1} \times \frac{1}{2} \times \frac{1}{2} \times \frac{1}{2} = \frac{3}{8} = 0.37$ approx.

EXAMPLE 5.10: The probability of a patient recovering from a certain disease is 0.9. The distribution of the number of recoveries among 6 patients is as follows:

Let x denotes the number of recoveries among 7 patients (i.e., x = 0,1, 2, 3, 4, 5, 6, 7) and p = 0.7 the probability of recovery of a patient from a certain disease. Therefore, q = 1 – p = probability of no recovery of a patients = 1 – 0.7 = 0.3. The discrete random variable x is said to follow the binomial distribution with parameters n and p or briefly, x ~ B (n, p).

SOLUTION: Probability of x recoveries, $P(x) = {}^7C_X p^x q^{7-x}$, where x = 0, 1, 2, 3, 4, 5, 6, 7. The following table gives the probability distribution of x recoveries.

(x = Number of recoveries)	P(x)
0	${}^7C_0 (0.7)^0 (0.3)^7 = 0.00022$
1	${}^7C_1 (0.7) (0.3)^6 = 0.00357$
2	${}^7C_2 (0.7)^2 (0.3) = 0\ 02500$
3	${}^7C_3 (0.7)^3 (0.3)^4 = 0.09724$
4	${}^7C_4 (0.7)^4 (0.3)^3 = 0.22689$
5	${}^7C_5 (0.7)^5 (0.3)^2 = 0.31765$
6	${}^7C_6 (0.7)^6 (0.3) = 0.24706$
7	${}^7C_7 (0.7)^7 (0.3)^0 = 0.08235$

Average number of recoveries = np = 7 × 0.7 = 4.9 ≃ 5.

POISSON DISTRIBUTION

Poisson distribution is a discrete probability distribution in which the random variable x assumes the infinite set of values 0, 1, 2, 3, ..., ∞

Symbolically, $p(x) = \frac{e^{-\lambda} \lambda^x_5}{x!}$, x = 0, 1, 2, ...

where λ is a positive constant called the parameter of the distribution and e = 2.72. Poisson distribution is the limiting form of the Binomial distribution when the number of trials n becomes very large and the probability of success, p in a trial very small (*i.e.*, n p = λ).

SOME EXAMPLES OF POISSON DISTRIBUTION

(i) The number of Maruti cars passing a certain point in one minute.

(ii) The number of telephone calls per minute at a switch board.

(iii) The number of defective electric bulbs manufactured by reputed factory.

(iv) The number of deaths in a district in one year by a rare disease.

(v) The number of air accidents in India in one year.

(vi) The number of organisms visible in a square under a microscope lens.

EXAMPLE 5.11: The mortality rate for a certain disease is 5 persons per 1000 population. What is the probability for just 3 deaths due to this disease in a group of 600 persons? (Given $e^{-3} = 0.05$)

SOLUTION: Here p = probability of mortality due to certain disease

$$= \frac{5}{1000}$$

$$n = 600$$

$$\therefore \quad \lambda = np = 600 \times \frac{5}{1000} = 3$$

where λ is the parameter of poisson distribution.

$$\text{Now} \qquad p(x) = \frac{e^{-\lambda}\lambda^x}{x!}, \; x = 0, 1, 2, \ldots\ldots\ldots\ldots \infty$$

$$\therefore \quad p(3 \text{ deaths}) = \frac{e^{-3}\lambda^3}{3!} = \frac{0.05 \times 3^3}{3!} = \frac{0.05 \times 27}{3.2.1} = \frac{1.35}{6} = 0.225$$

Note: In the poisson distribution, its mean equals to its variance, *i.e.*, λ = mean = variance.

EXAMPLE 5.12: A district hospital usually admits 50 patients per day. On an average, 6 patients in 100 require special facilities found in special ward. On the evening of a certain day, it is found that there are six such rooms available. Assuming that 50 patients will be admitted, find the probability that more than 6 patients will require such special rooms. (Given $e^{-3} = 0.0498$)

Solution: Here $n = 50, \quad p = \frac{6}{100} = 0.06$

$$\because \quad \lambda = np$$

$$\therefore \quad \lambda = 50\,(0.06) = 3$$

$$\text{Now} \qquad p(x) = \frac{e^{-\lambda}\lambda^x}{x!}, \; x = 0, 1, 2, 3, \ldots$$

Hence $\quad p(0) = e^{-3}\dfrac{3^0}{0!} = 0.0498 \times 1 = 0.0498$

$$p(1) = e^{-3}\frac{3}{1!} = 0.0498 \times 3 = 0.1494$$

$$p(2) = e^{-3}\frac{3^2}{2!} = 0.0498 \times \frac{9}{2} = 0.2241$$

$$p(3) = e^{-3}\frac{3^3}{3!} = 0.0498 \times \frac{27}{6} = 0.2241$$

$$p(4) = e^{-3}\frac{3^4}{4!} = 0.0498 \times \frac{81}{24} = 0.1681$$

$$p(5) = e^{-3}\frac{3^5}{5!} = 0.0498 \times \frac{243}{120} = 0.1008$$

$$p(6) = e^{-3}\frac{3^6}{6!} = 0.0498 \times \frac{729}{720} = 0.0504$$

$$p\,(x \le 6) = 0.9667$$

$$\because \quad p\,(x > 6) = 1 - p\,(x \le 6)$$

$$\therefore \quad p\,(x > 6) = 1 - 0.9667 = 0.0333 \; (i.e.,\ 333 \div 10{,}000)$$

CONTINUOUS PROBABILITY DISTRIBUTION

In discrete probability distributions (*e.g.*, Binominal and Poisson distributions) the random variable can assume either a finite set of values or at most a countable infinite set of values. But a continuous distribution is one in which the random variable can assume any value between certain limits. The number of all possible values is then uncountable infinite and it is impossible to know the probability of each value. In this case, we consider the probability that the value of variable will fall within a specified interval in the range of the continuous random variable.

Both Binomial and Poisson distribution are discrete (discontinuous) distribution which are concerned to only whole numbers, *e.g.*, number of persons in a family, number of deaths in a hospital, number of birth in a community. But we encounter a number of biological measurements where the variables are continuous in nature, *e.g.*, height, weight, blood pressure, incubation period, serum cholesterol level, pulse rate. They can be adequately described only by a continuous probability distribution, *i.e.*, normal distribution.

➤ EXERCISES ⮜

5.1. If probability of getting Rh +ve is 0.9 and the probability of newborn being mole is 0.5, then find out the probability of newborn being a male with Rh +ve.

5.2. In a random selection of children for a specific investigation, what is the probability of getting children either with Vit. A deficiency or Vit. B-complex deficiency? Also find out the probability that the children are likely to be normal.

5.3. Anand speaks truth in 75% and Vinod in 80% of the cases. In what percentages of cases are they likely to contradict each other in stating the same fact ?

5.4. Mr. X and Mr. Y appeared for an interview for two vaccanics. The probability of Mr. X's selection is $\frac{1}{3}$ and that of Mr. Y's selection is $\frac{4}{5}$. Find the probability that only one of them will be selected.

5.5. In a pathology laboratory, the results of blood test for carcinoma of abdomen yielded 20 false positive results in 200 healthy persons. What is the probability that for any single positive result of this type of blood test ?

5.6. What is the probability of having two boys followed by a girl (*i.e.*, a sequence of BBG) in a three-child family ?

5.7. Cardiologist has observed that 140 patients, out of 210 heart attacks have survived from heart attack. Remaining 70 patients lived for 15 years. What proportion of all heart attack patients survived for 15 years?

5.8. In District TB Centre, Tuberculin test is done everyday. Usually two in 100 give positive test, Average skin test per day has been five during the present month. What is the probability that two will give negative test?

5.9. Cobalt Therapy on cancer patients showed five year survival rate of 60%. Now 12 patients are subjected for chemotherapy. In chemotherapy it is also showed 40% of survival rate. What is the probability that all 10 patients will be living at the end of the five years?

5.10. The mean number of organisms per sample tested is 2. Assuming that the number of organisms follows Poisson distribution. Find the probability that a sample will contain 2 or more organisms. [Given e^{-2} = 0.1353]

5.11. If the probability that an individual suffers a bad reaction from a particular injection is 0.001. Find the probability that out of 3000 individuals (i) exactly four (ii) more than three individuals will suffer a bad reaction. [Given $e^{-3} = 0.0498$]

5.12. Emergency hospital admissions are found to follow Poisson distribution. An investigation showed that there are three admissions per day. Find the probability that exactly two emergency admissions will occur on a given day.

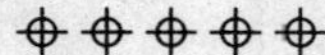

CHAPTER

6

Normal Distribution

- *Normal Curve*
- *Probability Function*
- *Confidence Limits*
- *Z-Scale*
- *Asymptotic*

It is the most important continuous probability distribution. This distribution is concerned to all continuous changing variables. In normal distribution generally maximum cases fall in the middle of scale. For example, if we study the age at menarche in Indian women, the age of the menarche of most of the women will fall between 13-15 years, very few women will fall between 9-11 years (*i.e.*, lower end of scale) and between 16-18 years (higher end of scale). This frequency distribution is also known as Gaussian distribution, *i.e.*, Normal curve.

Mathematically, the probability function of the normal distribution with mean, μ and standard deviation, σ is given by

$$p(x) = \frac{1}{\sigma\sqrt{2\pi}} e^{-1/2\left(\frac{x-\mu}{\sigma}\right)^2}, -\infty \le x \le \infty$$

where $\pi = 3.14$, and $e = 2.72$ approximately.

STANDARD NORMAL DISTRIBUTION

If we convert the basic scale of X values in order that we measure on a standard scale with zero value corresponding to μ and with a measurement unit of 1 (one) standard deviation, *i.e.*, Z (Standard Normal Variate) = $\frac{x-\mu}{\sigma}$

When $X = \mu$, then $Z = 0$

When $X = \mu + \sigma$, then $Z = 1$

When $X = \mu + 2\sigma$, then $Z = 2$

When $X = \mu + 3\sigma$, then $Z = 3$

Similarly if we take $X = \mu - \sigma$, then $Z = -1$

$X = \mu - 2\sigma$, then $Z = -2$

and $X = \mu - 3\sigma$, then $Z = -3$

Geometrically

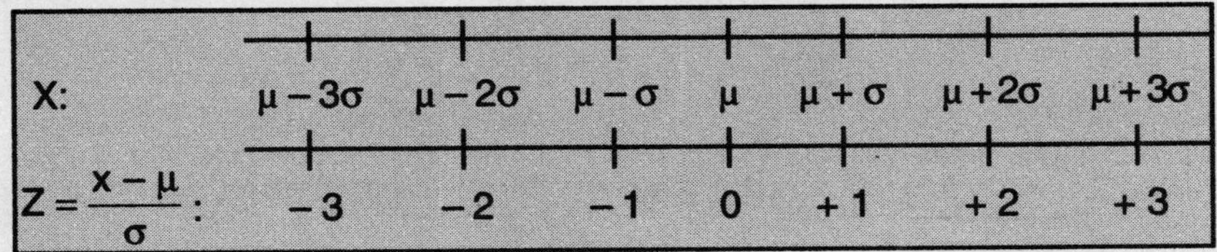

Fig. 6.1: Conversion of scale of measurement to standardize Z-scale

The above figure shows that Z is positive, when X is greater than μ and negative, when X is less than μ.

Mathematically,

$$P(Z) = \frac{1}{\sqrt{2\pi}} e^{-z^2/2}; (-\infty < Z < \infty)$$

i.e., the probability of Z variate with mean zero and standard deviation 1 (one).

Properties of Normal Distribution Curve

1. It is bell shaped curve.
2. The curve is symmetrical and asymptotic (*i.e.*, touches at infinity).
3. All measures of central tendency are equal and stable on the highest peak axis, *i.e.*,

   Mean = Median = Mode
4. The total area under the curve is equal to unity. The quartiles Q_1 and Q_3 are equidistant from the mean μ and $Q_1 = \mu - 0.67\sigma$, $Q_3 = \mu + 0.67\sigma$ approximately.
5. On the basis of mean, μ and standard deviation, σ the area of normal curve is distributed as:

   (i) $\mu \pm 1\sigma = 68.27\%$

   (ii) $\mu \pm 2\sigma = 95.45\%$

   (iii) $\mu \pm 3\sigma = 99.73\%$

Besides this, $\mu \pm 0.67\sigma$ covers 50% area

$\mu \pm 1.96\sigma$ covers 95% area

$\mu \pm 2.58\sigma$ covers 99% area

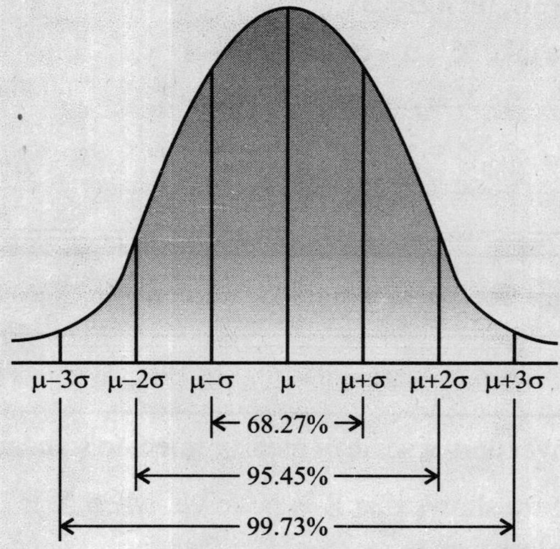

Fig. 6.2: Showing areas under the normal curve.

IMPORTANCE OF THE NORMAL DISTRIBUTION

Normal distribution plays an important role in the sampling theory. It has been found that:

(i) Data obtained from Biological measurements approximately follow normal distribution.

(ii) Binomial and Poisson distribution can be approximated to normal distribution.

(iii) For large samples, any statistic (*i.e.*, sample mean, sample standard deviation) approximately follows normal distribution and as such it can be studied with the help of normal curve.

(iv) Normal curve is used to find confidence limits of the population parameters.

(v) Normal distribution also forms the basis for the tests of significance.

EXAMPLE 6.1: The mean height of 500 students is 165 cm and the standard deviation is 5 cm. Assuming that the heights are normally distributed. Find how many students will have height between 153 cm and 180 cm.

SOLUTION:

Here, μ = mean = 165 cm, σ = std. dev. = 5 cm.

We have $Z = \frac{X-\mu}{\sigma} = \frac{153-165}{5} = \frac{-12}{5} = -2.4$

and $Z = \frac{180-165}{5} = \frac{15}{5} = 3.0$

Therefore, proportion of students whose heights are in between 153 cm and 180 cm.

= Area under the standard normal curve between Z = – 2.4 and Z = 3.0

= (Area between Z = –2.4 and Z = 0) + (Area between Z = 0 and Z = 3.0)

= (Area between Z = 0 and Z = 2.4) + (Area between Z = 0 and Z = 3.0)

= 0.4918 + 4987 [see Appendix Table I]

= 0.9905

Hence the required number of students whose heights are in between 153 cm and 180 cm = 0.9905 × 500 = 495 (approximately).

EXAMPLE 6.2: A Hospital records the weights of every new born child at the hospital. The distribution of weights is normally shaped, has a mean, $\mu = 2.9$ kg., and has a standard deviation, $\sigma = 0.45$.

Determine the following:

(i) The percentage of new borns who weighed under 2.1 kg.

(ii) The percentage of new borns who weighted between 1.8 kg. and 4 kg.

(iii) If 1500 babies have been born at the hospital, how many weighed less than 2.5 kg.?

SOLUTION: Here $\mu = 2.9$ kg., $\sigma = 0.54$ kg.

(i) To find the percentage of new borns who weighted under 2.1 kg we must first convert x score, *i.e.*, 2.1 kg to its corresponding Z score, thus,

$$Z = \frac{X-\mu}{\sigma} = \frac{2.1-2.9}{0.45} = -1.78$$

From Appendix Table I, we find the area beyond a Z-score of 1.78 is (0.5000 – 0.4625) = 0.0375.

Hence, the percentage of new borns who weighted under 2.1 kg.

$$= 0.0375 \times 100 = 3.75\%$$

(ii) Here Z transformation of 1.8 kg., *i.e.*,

$$Z = \frac{1.8 - 2.9}{0.45} = -2.4$$

and transformation of 4 kg., *i.e.*,

$$Z = \frac{1.8 - 2.9}{0.45} = 2.4$$

To locate the areas corresponding to Z = – 2.4 and Z = 2.4 (by using Appendix Table I).

We have, area under the standard normal curve between Z = – 2.4 and Z = 2.4

= (Area between Z = –2.4 and Z = 0) + (Area between Z = 0 and Z = 2.4)

= 0.4918 + 0.4918 = 0.9836

Hence the required percentage of new borns who weighted between 1.8 kg. and 4.0 kg.

$$= 0.9836 \times 100 = 98.4\%$$

(iii) Z transformation of 2.5 kg. is

$$Z = \frac{2.5 - 2.9}{0.45} = -0.89$$

Now area (Z = 0.89) = 0.3133 [See Appendix Table I]

and the total area equals to 0.5000 + 0.3133 = 0.8133.

Thus the required number of babies who weighed less than 2.5 kg = 0.8133 × 1500 = 1220.

EXAMPLE 6.3: Assume that the age at onset of disease X is distributed normally with a mean of 50 years and a standard deviation of 12 years. What is the probability that an individual afflicted with X had developed it before age 35 years ?

SOLUTION: Here μ = 50 yrs., σ = 12 yrs.

Now the Z corresponding to X = 35 yrs. is

$$Z = \frac{X - \mu}{\sigma} = \frac{35 - 20}{12} = \frac{-15}{12} = -1.25$$

By using Appendix Table I, area under standard normal curve, *i.e.*, Z = – 1.25 is 0.3994.

Hence the area under standard normal curve below Z = – 1.25, *i.e.*, 0.5000 – (area between Z = – 1.25 and Z = 0)

= 0.5000 – (area between Z = 0 and Z = 1.25)

= 0.5000 – 0.3944 (by symmetry) = 0.1056

$\therefore$ The required probability $p(x < 35) = Z(-1.25)$.

or $p(x < 35) = \text{Area} = 0.5000 - 0.3944 = 0.1056$.

EXAMPLE 6.4: The mean of a normal distribution is 60 and 6% of the values are greater than 70. Find the Standard deviation of this distribution. (Given: the area under standard normal curve between Z = 0 and Z = 1.56 is 0.44).

SOLUTION: Here $\mu = 60$, $\sigma = ?$

Since $Z = \dfrac{X - \mu}{\sigma}$ = Standardized value of X.

Therefore, standardized value of 70 is $\dfrac{70 - 60}{\sigma} = \dfrac{10}{\sigma}$

Probability that the random variable assumes a value greater than 70 is 6% (or 0.06).

By the condition of the problem, 0.06 must be the area under the standard normal curve to the right of $Z = \dfrac{10}{\sigma}$. It is also given that the area between Z = 0 and Z = 1.56 is 0.44.

$\therefore$ Area to the right of Z = 1.56 = (area to the right of Z = 0) – (area between Z = 0 and Z = 1.56)

$$= 0.5 - 0.44 = 0.06$$

Thus 0.06 is the area to the right of $Z = \dfrac{10}{\sigma}$ as well as to the right of Z = 1.56.

Hence $\dfrac{10}{\sigma} = 1.56$ or $\sigma = \dfrac{10}{1.56} = 6.41$

➤ EXERCISES ≺

6.1. Describe the distinction between a normal distribution and the standard normal distribution.

6.2. If a clinical variable X is normally distributed with a standard deviation of 8. What is the mean value of X, if 0.3413 of the values of X is greater than 58?

6.3. If z is normally distributed with $\mu = 0$ and $\sigma = 1$. Find (i) $P(Z \geq -1.64)$ (ii) $P(-1.96 \leq Z \leq 1.96)$ and (iii) $P(|Z| \geq 1)$.

6.4. Pulse rate of healthy male adults follow normal distribution with a mean of 75 per minute and a standard deviation of 4 per minute. Find out the percentage of individuals having pulse rate beyond 85 per minute.

6.5. For a normal distribution of 100 items, the lower quartile, Q_1 is 73 and σ is 15. Find (i) Median (ii) Limits for central 50% of the distribution.

6.6. Systolic B.P. readings of a large male population is normally distributed with $\mu = 100$ and $\sigma = 15$. What is the 90th percentile of systolic B.P. readings?

6.7. The mean weight of 200 students is 50 kg and the standard deviation is 4 kg. What percentage of students will have weight above 58 kg?

6.8. The average height of 100 students 160 cms with standard deviation of 5 cm. How many of the students will have height within the range of 165 to 175 cms?

6.9. Random sample of 600 school children showed mean Hb % of 12.5 gm % with standard deviation of 0.5. Find out the percentage of individuals having Hb % beyond 13.5 gm %.

6.10. If mean iron intake is 20 mg with standard deviation of 5 mg. Find out: (i) Z-value for individual iron intake of 30 mg, (ii) Percentage of individuals exceeding 30 mg of iron intake.

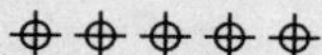

CHAPTER

7

Sampling Methods

• *Sampling*	• *Population*	• *Sequential*
• *Random Sample*	• *Strata*	• *Bias*
• *Cluster*	• *Standard Error*	• *Quota*

When information is collected in respect of every individual item or subject, the enquiry is said to be done by Complete Enumeration or Census; *e.g.*, during the Census of population, which is done every ten years in India, information is collected from each person residing in India. This method of collecting data from individuals involves a large number of investigators, huge amount of money, long time and much effort. In medical studies the data are collected from a population or universe sufficiently large and a portion (*i.e.*, a sample) or representative or the population under study chosen by a standard sampling technique. This process of partial enumeration is known as sample survey. The population or universe, must be clearly defined before drawing a sample. Population may be an entire group of defined persons such as all members of households, women of 15 to 49 years of age, all infants in a community or village(s), under 5 years of age children in city about whom information is required.

A value calculated from a defined population such as mean (μ), standard deviation (σ), or standard error mean, S.E. $(\overline{X})$ is called a parameter. It is a constant value, it covers all members of the population. A value calculated from a sample is called a statistic such as mean $(\overline{X})$ standard deviations (s.d.).

The two main objectives of sampling are:

(i) Estimation of population parameters from the sample statistics.

(ii) To test the hypothesis about the population from which the sample or samples are drawn.

Different Techniques of Sampling

Sampling techniques may be categorized into two main headings as:

(A) ***Random Sampling Techniques***

(i) Random Sampling (or Probability Sampling)

(ii) Multi-stage Sampling (Multi-stage Random Sampling)

(iii) Stratified Sampling (or Stratified Random Sampling)

(iv) Systematic Sampling (or Quasi-random Sampling)

(i) ***Random Sampling (or Probability Sampling):*** It is the process of drawing a sample from a population in such a way that each member of the population has an equal chance of being selected in the sample. This is also called simple random sampling. The sample obtained by the process of random sampling is called a random sample. Random sampling may be done either by adopting lottery method or by using a table of random numbers which consists of numbers of two or four or five digits compiled by some random process (refer to Appendix Table-II), commonly used in practice.

Random Sampling is the simplest among the various sampling techniques, and it is free from personal bias. Selection of items in a random sample depends entirely on chance. When the population is homogeneous in regard to a particular characteristics being, studied, random sampling is always expected to yield better results.

Random sampling is used in experimental medicine or cilinical trials like testing the efficacy of a particular drug. For example, suppose we want to put 20 patients on a clinical trial out of 120 available. To ensure randomness of selection of 20 patients we may adopt lottery method by numbering (serially) the total individual patients from 1 to 120, then we note down the serial number of patients on 120 slips of paper and shake them in a bowl so that all the slips get thoroughly mixed up, and pick out one. We would repeat the shaking and pick out another. Then we would continue this process until 20 slips (numbers) have been picked. The numbers contained on the slips of paper would identify the patients to be used in the sample and the 20 patients selected in this manner form the random sample.

A common method of drawing random sample is to use a table of random numbers (see Table II in Appendix). The table may be used as successive single digits, as successive two-digit numbers, as successive three-digit numbers, and so on. For example, in the table II if we begin at row one and move horizontally across the page the random order of single digits would be 3, 7, 5, 4, 2......... If we wish to use two digit numbers, the random order would be 37, 54, 20, 48,.........

Since the digits in the table are random, they may be used vertically in both directions and horizontally in both directions. To use the table properly, it should be entered randomly. One way would be to make slips of paper with row and column numbers and place the slips in a bowl, mix them up, and then pick a slip of one row number and other slip having a column number. The intersection of the row and column would be the location of the first random number. The remaining numbers would be located by moving from the first number in the direction specified prior to entering the table, *e.g.*, suppose we want to form a random sample of 10 subjects from a population of 30 subjects with the help of table of random numbers we may refer Table II in Appendix.

We first give serial numbers to all the 30 subjects at random, starting from any subject. This reduces the biasness at the very start. Total number of subjects or population from which desired number of subjects to be chosen is thirty, a two-digit number, *i.e.*, the numbers assigned are from 00 to 30. Numbers less than 30 may be chosen as they appear in the table, while numbers higher than 30 may be divided by 30 and the remainders may be noted as the numbers chosen for the sample. Next, the table would be entered randomly to locate the first number. Let us assume the entry occurs at the intersection of the first two-digit number of column 2 with row 10. The two-digit number located at this intersection is 17. Thus the first subject in the sample is the individual bearing the number 17. The next subject would be located by moving vertically down from 17.

Thus the second subject in the sample would be the individual bearing the number 05. This process would be continued until 10 subjects have been selected. The complete set of subject numbers would be 17, 05, (99/30, remainder 9) 09, (40/30, remainder 10) 10, (67/30, remainder 7) 07, (35/30, remainder 5) 05, 26, 20, 14 (94/30 remainder 4) 04. Note that the numbers 17 and 99 appeared twice in the table since the repeated number was not included and two more numbers have been taken from subsequent rows and the same column.

(ii) ***Multi-stage Sampling (Multi-stage Random Sampling):*** In this method, the sampling procedure is carried out in several stages. The population is first divided into large groups called first stage units. These first stage units are then divided into smaller groups, called second-stage units, and second-stage units are divided into third-stage units and so on until we come to the ultimate units or a sample of desired size. At first, a sample of the first stage units is chosen by any suitable methods. Then a sample of second-stage units is selected from each of the selected first stage units and the process is repeated from stage to stage until we reach the ultimate units.

EXAMPLE: In a tuberculosis survey, physical examination or Mantoux test may be done in all the cases of sample in the first stage, in the second stage X-ray of the chest may be done in Mantoux positive cases; while sputum may be examined in X-ray positive cases in the third-stage, number in the sub-samples in second and third stages will become successively smaller and smaller. Survey by such procedure will be less expensive and more purposeful.

(iii) ***Stratified Sampling (or Stratified Random Sampling):*** Stratified sampling is generally used when the population is heterogeneous. The population under study is first subdivided into several homogeneous groups or classes called strata (plural of stratum). Each stratum is called a subpopulation. Then a small sample (called sub-sample) is selected from each stratum at random in proportion to its size. All the sub samples combined together form the stratified sample. Stratified sampling is a process of giving representation to all strata of society or population such as selecting sample from defined areas, social classes, ages, sexes, education levels. If proper stratification can be made so that the strata differ from each other as much as possible, but there is much homogeneity within each stratum, than a stratified sample with give better estimates of the population characteristics than a random sample of the same size.

(iv) ***Systematic Sampling (or Quasi-Random Sampling):*** This is a technique of forming a sample in some systematic manner, usually by taking items at regular intervals. In this method, all the units of the population are arranged in some order (*i.e.*, alphabetically, ascending or descending order of magnitude). If the population size is finite, all the units are first serially listed and arranged in order. Then from the first K items, on unit is selected at random. This unit and every Kth unit of the serially listed population combined together constitute a systematic sample. K refers to the sample interval which is calculated by the formula:

$$K\text{ (sample interval)} = \frac{\text{Total population}}{\text{Sample size desired}}$$

e.g., if 20% sample is to be taken out of 1500 units of a population, then

$$K = \frac{1500}{20\%\text{ of }1500} = \frac{1500}{300} = 5$$

A number between 1 and 5, say 3, is selected at random with the help of lottery method by pulling out one card after shuffling, out of 5 cards serially numbered 1 to 5. Then the sample will consist of units with serial numbers 3, (3 + 5) = 8, (8 + 5) = 13, (13 + 5) = 18, ... till the 300 units.

Thus it is essential to have a complete list of population before a systematic sample is drawn.

(B) ***Non-random Sampling Techniques***

(i) Purposive Sampling (or Judgement Sampling)

(ii) Quota Sampling

(iii) Cluster Sampling (or Block Sampling)

(iv) Sequential Sampling

(i) ***Purposive Sampling (or Judgement Sampling):*** In this type, the individual units of a sample are chosen as according to convenience and personal choice of the investigator. Purposive selection is always subject to some kind of bias. This method is suitable for small sample.

(ii) ***Quota Sampling:*** In this type of sampling, the investigators are assigned definite quotas according to certain criteria. The investigators select the individuals, *i.e.*, sampling units for inteviews on their personal judgements within the quotas. When all or a part of the whole quota is not available or not approachable, the quota is completed by supplementing new respondents. It is very easy and time saving but it is open to various types of errors and bias.

(iii) ***Cluster Sampling (or Block Sampling):*** This method is used units of population are natural groups or clusters such as villages, wards, blocks, slum of a town, factories, children of a school. The technique of cluster sampling allows small number of the target population to be sampled while the data provided is statistically valid at 95% confidence limits. From the chosen clusters, 30 in number the entire population is surveyed. This method is easy to follow and very economical and time saving.

Cluster sampling technique is most often used to evaluate vaccination coverage under UIP (Universal Immunization Programme) conducted by World Health Organization, where only 210 children, taking 7 from each cluster in the age group below 24 months are to be examined (*i.e.*, 30 cluster sampling).

Indentification of Cluster for Collecting Data

(i) List all cities, towns, villages and wards of cities with their population falling in the target area under study for evaluation.

(ii) Calculate cumulative population and divide the same by 30. That gives the sampling interval.

(iii) Select a random number less than or equal to sampling interval having same number of digits.

(iv) Random number plus sampling interval gives the population of second cluster.

(v) Second cluster + Sampling interval = 3rd cluster, and so on, lastly.

30th cluster = 29th cluster + sampling interval

All houses with population are numbered and the first house for survey in each cluster should be randomly selected with the help of random number table. Before starting house to house survey, we define the age group and item which is to be studied *e.g.*, in the evaluation of immunization, we consider the children in the age group 12–17 months, fully immunized with 3 doses of DPT, 3 polio, 1 BCG and 1 measles vaccination.

Now we start doing house to house survey with the selected house till we get 7 children fully immunized. Thus 210 such children will be found in 30 clusters. Immunization coverage may also be calculated by the formula given below:

i.e., $$\text{Coverage} = \frac{210}{\text{Eligible children in surveyed house}} \times 100$$

(iv) *Sequential Sampling:* This method consists of a sequence of samples drawn one after another from the population depending on the results of previous samples. If the result of the first sample is not up to the mark for acceptance, the lot from which the sample was drawn is rejected and a second sample is drawn and, as before if required a third sample is drawn this process will be continued till we arrive at a decision to accept the sample. This method is widely used Quality Control.

Pilot Survey

Before conducting a large-scale statistical enquiry it is always better to do pilot survey (*i.e.*, a small exploratory) in the field of enquiry. Such a pilot survey will be useful in the following ways:

(i) It can reveal deficiencies in the sampling frame and sample design.

(ii) It can identify the main sources of non-response and indicate how they should be dealt with in the main survey.

(iii) It will analyse the first draft of the questionnaire and reveal the defects or short comings, if any.

(iv) It will provide insights into the problems faced by the interviewers.

(v) It can provide guidance as to the best form of administrative setup in conducting the survey.

⌖⌖⌖⌖⌖

CHAPTER

8

Sample Size Determination

- *Estimate*
- *Sampling Error*
- *Sample Size*
- *Parameters*
- *Sample Proportion*
- *Unbiased*

As we know that population (or universe) is the aggregate of statistical data forming a subject of investigation and a sample in a portion (or part) of the population which is examined with a view to estimating the characteristics of the population, *i.e.*, to estimate the true value of the population parameters, *e.g.*, population mean (μ), population standard deviation (σ) and population proportion (P) by using sample statistics such as sample mean, $\overline{X}$; sample standard deviation, s.d.; sample proponion; p. It is of fundamental importance to make a clear distinction between a distribution of sample means and the population distribution of observations. A distribution of sample means is the set of values of sample means obtained from all possible samples of the same size from a given population, *i.e.*, it is the population of all values of that statistic (sample mean).

EXAMPLE 8.1: A population consists of the four number 3, 4, 2, 5 consider all possible distinct samples of size two and verify that the population mean is equal to the mean of the sample means.

SOLUTION: The population mean, $\mu = \frac{3+4+2+5}{4} = 3.5$

All possible distinct samples of size two (*i.e.*, ${}^4C_2 = 6$), and the corresponding sample means are given below:

Sample No.	Samples	Sum of sample values	Sample Mean
1	3, 4	7	3.5
2	3, 2	5	2.5
3	3, 5	8	4.0
4	4, 2	6	3.0
5	4, 5	9	4.5
6	2, 5	7	3.5
Total	—	—	21.0

Mean of sample means $= \frac{21.0}{6} = 3.5$

Hence the population mean, 3.5 is equal to the sample means.

SAMPLING DISTRIBUTION OF A STATISTIC

Let us consider a population of size N (*i.e.*, a population containing N units) and we want to draw all possible random samples of a given size n, which can be known by ${}^NC_n = k$ (say), samples each of size n. For each of these k samples, we compute a statistic (*i.e.*, sample mean or sample standard deviation or sample proportion of defectives). The value of a statistic 't' may vary from sample to sample (as shown in the above example). Let $t_1, t_2, \ldots\ldots\ldots, t_k$ be the values of statistic t for the k samples. Each of these values occurs with a definite probability. Thus we can represent the set of values $t_1, t_2, \ldots\ldots\ldots, t_k$ with their respective probabilities in a tabular form. This probability distribution of a statistic, t is known as the sampling distribution of a statistic.

Note: A statistic has always a sampling distribution but a parameter has no sampling distribution.

Absolute and Relative Errors: In the field or experimental study area, errors may be occurred in measurement, counting, sampling, and approximation, etc.

To guard ourselves against getting wrong results due to errors occurring beyond certain limits, we should measure errors and express them in absolute and relative terms.

Absolute error: It is defined as the actual difference between the true value and the observed value, *i.e.*, Absolute error = True value – Observed (or estimated) value.

Relative error: It is defined as the ratio of the absolute error to the true value and expressed in percentage, *i.e.*,

$$\text{Relative error} = \frac{\text{Absolute error}}{\text{True value}} \text{ or } \frac{\text{Absolute error}}{\text{True value}} \times 100$$

For example, if 165.4 cms. is taken as 165 cms., then Absolute error will be

$$\left(\frac{165.4-165}{165.4} = \frac{0.4}{165.4}\right) = \frac{4}{1654} = 0.0024 \text{ (or } 0.24\%).$$

SAMPLING AND NON-SAMPLING ERRORS

Whatever be the sampling procedure or care taken while selecting the sample, the sample stastistic (*i.e.*, $\overline{X}$, s.d., or p) will differ from population parameters (*i.e.*, μ, σ or P) because of chance or biological variability. These differences between statistics and parameters are called sampling errors and cann be measured. Whereas in all surveys (sample survey or Census) some errors may occur during collection of the actual information. These errors are called non-sampling errors which can not be measured.

CENTRAL LIMIT THEOREM

It has two important sampling distribution:

(i) If $\overline{X}$ be the mean of a random sample of size n drawn from a population having mean, μ and standard deviation, (σ) then the sampling distribution of the sample mean $\overline{X}$ is approximately a normal distribution with mean μ and standard deviation, σ = Standard Error, S.E. of $\overline{X}$. Provided the sample size n is sufficiently large ($n \geq 30$).

(ii) If p be the proportion of defectives in a random sample of size n drawn from a population having the proportion of defectives P, then the sampling distribution of the sample proportion of defectives p is approximately a normal distribution with mean P and standard deviation = Standard Error, S.E. of p, provided the sample size n is sufficiently large ($n \geq 30$).

STANDARD ERROR (S.E.) OF A STATISTIC

The standard error of a statistic t (*i.e.*, S.E. sample mean, or sample standard deviation or sample proportion of defectives) is the standard deviation of the sampling distribution of the statistic, *e.g.*, S.E, $(\bar{X})$ = S.D. of sampling distribution of sample mean.

S.E. is used as a tool in tests of hypotheses or tests of significance. It helps in determining the limits (or confidence limits) within which the parameters are expected to lie.

The formulae for the standard errors (S.E.) of some well known statistics for random samples are given below:

(i) S.E. of sample mean $\bar{X} = \frac{\sigma}{\sqrt{n}}$

(ii) S.E. of sample proportion $p = \sqrt{\frac{PQ}{n}}$, where $Q = 1 - P$

(iii) S.E. of sample standard deviation (s.d.) $= \frac{\sigma}{\sqrt{2n}}$

(iv) S.E. of sample correlation coefficient $r = \frac{1 - R^2}{\sqrt{n}}$, where R is population correlation coefficient.

(v) S.E. of the difference of two sample means X_1, and X_2, *i.e.*, S.E. of $(\bar{X}_1 - \bar{X}_2) = \sqrt{\frac{\sigma_1}{n_1} + \frac{\sigma_2}{n_2}}$

(vi) S.E. of $(p_1 - p_2) = \sqrt{\frac{P_1Q_1}{n_1} + \frac{P_2Q_2}{n_2}}$, where p_1 and p_2 are the proportions of two random samples of size n_1 and n_2 drawn from two populations with proportions P_1 and P_2 respectively.

(vii) S.E. of $(s_1 - s_2)$ = S.E. of difference of two sample standard deviations

$$= \sqrt{\frac{\sigma_1^{\,2}}{2n_1} + \frac{\sigma_2^{\,2}}{2n_2}}$$

EXAMPLE 8.2: A random sample of size 64 is drawn from a finite population consisting of 122 units. If the population standard deviation is 16.8. Find the standard error of sample mean.

SOLUTION: Here $n = 64$, $\sigma = 16.8$

$$\therefore \quad \text{S.E. of sample mean} = \frac{\sigma}{\sqrt{n}} = \frac{16.8}{\sqrt{64}} = \frac{16.8}{8}$$

or $$\text{S.E. } (\bar{X}) = 2.1$$

EXAMPLE 8.3: A random sample of 800 articles is drawn from a large consignment containing 128 defective articles. Find the S.E. of the proportion of defective articles in a sample.

SOLUTION: Here n = 800, p = sample proportion of defectives,

i.e., $$p = \frac{128}{800} = 0.16$$

Since the population proportion, P is not known, we take the values of p for P,

$$\therefore \quad \text{S.E. of } p = \sqrt{\frac{PQ}{n}} = \sqrt{\frac{pq}{n}} \text{ (approximately)}, \qquad \text{where } q = 1 - p$$

$$= \sqrt{\frac{0.16 \times 0.84}{800}}$$

$$= 0.13 \text{ (approx.)}$$

For a finite population of size N, when a sample is drawn without replacement, we have

(i) Standard Error of sample mean $= \dfrac{\sigma}{\sqrt{n}}\sqrt{\dfrac{N-n}{N-1}}$

(ii) Standard Error of sample proportion $= \sqrt{\dfrac{PQ}{n}} \cdot \sqrt{\dfrac{N-n}{N-1}}$

EXAMPLE 8.4: A random sample of size 30 is drawn from a finite population consisting of 121 units. If the population standard deviation is 11.0. Find the standard error of sample mean when the sample is drawn (i) with replacement, and (ii) without replacement.

SOLUTION:

(i) When the sample is drawn with replacement, the standard error of sample mean, *i.e.,*

$$\text{S.E. }(\bar{X}) = \frac{\sigma}{\sqrt{n}} = \frac{11.0}{\sqrt{30}} = \frac{11.0}{5.5} = 2$$

(ii) When the sample is drawn without replacement, the

$$\text{S.E. of } \bar{X} = \frac{\sigma}{\sqrt{n}} \cdot \sqrt{\frac{N-n}{N-1}} = 2\sqrt{\frac{122-30}{122-1}} = 2\sqrt{\frac{92}{121}}$$

or $\quad$ S.E. of $\quad = 2 \times 0.87 = 1.74$

EXAMPLE 8.5: A sample of size 25 is drawn randomly (without replacement) from a population consisting of 100 units. If the number of defective units in the population be 10. Find the standard error of the sample proportion of defectives.

SOLUTION: S.E. of the sample proportion of defectives

$$= \sqrt{\frac{PQ}{n}}\sqrt{\frac{N-n}{N-1}}$$

Here $N = 100;\ n = 25$

$$P = \frac{10}{100} = \frac{1}{10}; \quad \text{and} \quad Q = (1-P) = 1 - \frac{1}{10} = \frac{9}{10}$$

$$\therefore \quad \text{S.E. of } p = \sqrt{\frac{\frac{1}{10} \times \frac{9}{10}}{25}}\sqrt{\frac{100-25}{100-1}} = \sqrt{\frac{9}{2500}}\sqrt{\frac{75}{99}}$$

$$= \frac{3}{50}\sqrt{\frac{75}{99}} = 0.06 \times 0.87 = 0.05 \text{ (or 5\%)}$$

SAMPLE SIZE DETERMINATION

As we know a population is a set of persons (or objects) having a common observable characteristic. A sample is a subset of a population. The primary reason for selecting a sample from a popula-tion is to draw inferences about the population. It is to be noted that the population may consist of persons, objects, or the observations of a characteristic. The set of observations may be summarized by a descriptive characteristic, called a parameter, when the same charac-teristic pertains to a sample, it is called a statistic. Sample statistics (summary values) help us draw inferences about population para-meters. The value of the population parameter is constant but usually unknown. The value of the statistic is known because it is computed from the sample. Observations differ from one sample to the next. Consequently, the value of the statistic varies from sample to sample. A representative sample will have its statistics almost equal to the parameters of entire population, still there will be a chance difference which can be reduced but not eliminated. The two main characteristics of a representative sample are:

(i) **Precision,** which implies the size of sample depending on the purpose. It is measured by the formula:

$$\text{Precision} = \frac{1}{\text{Standard error of mean}}$$

or $$\text{Precision} = \frac{\sqrt{n}}{\text{S.d.}}$$

or $\quad \text{Precision} = \dfrac{\sqrt{\text{Sample size}}}{\text{Standard deviation of sample}}$

Precision is directly proportional to the square root of sample size (n), *i.e.*, if n is increased 4 times, the precision will be double and if n is increased 9 times the precision will become treble.

(ii) **Unbiased character:** An appropriate sampling method (if utilized) in the random selection of sample size helps the sample to possess the representative characteristics of the parent (or entire) population. Differences in characteristics of samples and population will be negligible. For avoiding biasness in the investigations (or experiments), single or double blind clinical trials are suggested.

A suitable sample size depends on

(i) Effect size, *i.e.*, the amount of impact you expect the treatment to have on the dependent variable.

(ii) The significance level, *i.e.*, it determines the probability of making a type I error (rejecting a true null hypothesis), α. Generally, at 0.05 or 0.01.

(iii) The power of a test, *i.e.*, desired power of a test which describes as the likelihood of finding a true significance result (rejecting the null hypothesis when it is indeed false, *i.e.*, Type II error).

For the determination of sample size, the following methods are recommended:

For Quantitative data: If the standard deviation of population, σ is known from the past experience or records, then the sample size can be determined by the following formula with the desired permissble error, E at 5% risk, *i.e.*,

$$E = \frac{2\sigma}{\sqrt{n}} \quad \text{or} \quad E^2 = \frac{4\sigma^2}{n} \quad \text{or} \quad n = \frac{4\sigma^2}{E^2}$$

If E = 1 and σ^2 (variance) = 100, then, n (sample size)

$$= \frac{4 \times 100}{1^2} = 400.$$

Note: In case population standard deviation, σ is not known, a pilot survey or partial enumeration have to be carried out to estimate σ.

For Qualitative data: In this type of data we deal with proportions such as morbidity rates (*e.g.*, prevalence or incidence rate) and cure rates. The adequate sample size can be calculated by the formula given below with a desired permissible error (E) at 5% risk. In such data the permissible error should not exceed 20% of the positive character.

Sample size, $n = \frac{4pq}{E^2}$, where p is the positive character and q = (1–p) or (100 – p), E = permissible error of 'p'.

EXAMPLE 8.6: In a urban-slum community, the prevalence (rate) of hookworm was found to be 32% before the medical intervention and other preventive and curative measures. What should be the adequate sample size to find the prevalence rate now if permissible error is 10%?

SOLUTION: Here p = 32%; q = 100 – p = 100 – 32 = 68

and $$E = 10\% \text{ of } p = \frac{32 \times 10}{100} = 3.2$$

Adequate sample size at 5% risk is calculated by

$$n = \frac{4pq}{E^2} = \frac{4 \times 32 \times 68}{(3.2)^2} = \frac{4 \times 32 \times 68}{3.2 \times 3.2} = 850$$

EXAMPLE 8.7: Prevalence of diabetes in a community was found to be one diabetic case in 10 persons. Calculate the appropriate size of sample to find the prevalence rate now if permissible error is 20% or 10% at 5% risk.

SOLUTION: ∵ $n = \frac{4pq}{E^2} = \frac{4 \times 10 \times 90}{2 \times 2}$ where $E = \frac{10 \times 20}{100} = 2$

∴ n = 900 [if E = 20% of 'p']

and if $E = 10\% \text{ of 'p'} = \frac{10 \times 10}{100} = 1$

Then sample size at 5% risk is, $n = \frac{4pq}{E^2} = \frac{4 \times 10 \times 90}{1 \times 1} = 3600$

EXAMPLE 8.8: In a community, the mean serum cholesterol was found to be 180 mg% with a standard deviation of 42 mg%. Calculate the minimum size of the sample to verify the result if permission error is ± 2 at 5% risk.

SOLUTION: $$n = \frac{4\sigma^2}{E^2} = \frac{4 \times 42 \times 42}{2 \times 2} = 1764$$

If E = ± 4 at 5% risk

Then $$n = \frac{4 \times 42 \times 42}{4 \times 4} = 441$$

[**Note:** Larger the sample size, lesser will be the error.]

EXAMPLE 8.9: What should be the size of the sample for assessing prevalence rate of diabetes in an urban population where the prevalence as given as 3% in age group above 15 years. Permissible error, E is 20% of positive character at 5% risk.

SOLUTION: Here p = 3% ; q = 100 – 3 = 97%

and E at 5% risk $= \dfrac{3 \times 20}{100} = 0.6$

$$\text{Since } n = \frac{4pq}{E^2} = \frac{4 \times 3 \times 97}{0.6 \times 0.6} = 3233.$$

➤ EXERCISES ≺

8.1. Distinguish between a parameter and a statistic.

8.2. What is meant by sampling distribution of sample mean?

8.3. Differentiate the two terms: Standard deviation and standard error.

8.4. A simple random sample of size 5 is drawn without replacement from a finite population consisting of 41 units. If the population standard deviation is 6.25. Find the standard error of sample mean.

8.5. A sample of size 9 is drawn randomly without replacement from a population consisting of 25 units. If the number of defective units in the population be 5. Find the standard error of the sample proportion of defectives.

8.6. A random sample of the height of 100 students from a large population of students in a college having standard deviation of 22 cms has an average height of 168 cms. Find (i) 95% and (ii) 99% confidence limits for the average height of all the students of the college.

8.7. Following still birth rates per 1000 deliveries were reported by 20 villages in 1980: 15, 20, 22, 28, 30, 35, 25, 18, 30, 22, 32, 25, 30, 26, 24, 27, 33, 22, 25, 30.

Calculate standard error of mean for the above mentioned data.

8.8. Average height of Indian population is believed to be 165 cms with a standard deviation of 30 cms. What should be the sample size to verify this, if permissible error is ± 2 at 5% risk?

8.9. Mean systolic blood pressure in an urban community was found to be 120 mm of Hg with standard deviation of 20. Calculate the minimum size of sample to verify the result if permissible error is ± 1 at 5% risk.

8.10. In rural school age children, the prevalence rate of whooping cough was 11%. Estimate the sample size needed to conduct a similar study in another community with confidence of 95% if permissible error is 10%.

8.11. Hookworm prevalence rate in a community was found to be 20% before the specific treatment and adoption of other measures. Estimate the size of sample needed to find the prevalence rate now if permissible error is 10%.

8.12. On the basis of the following informations and constraints, estimate the sample size required:

(i) Attack rate of a disease in a community is 20%

(ii) Permissible error of 10%

(iii) Level of significance is 5% (or $\alpha = 0.05$).

8.13. What should be the size of sample required to obtain the estimate of weight of infants at one year of age when average population mean weight of infants at one year is 12 kg with standard deviation of 1.2 kg at 1% of accuracy?

8.14. In a district, prevailing mortality due to head injury is 60%. What should be the sample size if permissible error is 10% at 5% risk.

8.15. Estimate the sample size to obtain an estimatic of Hb % in a community where average Hb % is 9.6 with standard deviation of 2.2 at 5% permissible error.

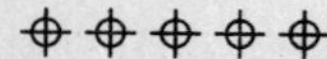

CHAPTER

9

Estimation

- *Confidence Interval*
- *Statistical Hypothesis*
- *Acceptance or Rejection*
- *Test Statistics*
- *Significance*
- *Test-statistic*
- *Estimator*
- *Critical Value*

Statistical estimation is a method by which we estimate the population parameters from sample values (*i.e.*, statistics). The sample value, *e.g.*, $\overline{X}$ or s.d. is called the estimator and the actual numerical value obtained by evaluating an estimator in a given instance is called estimate.

A statistic is called an unbiased estimator of the corresponding parameter if the mean of the sampling distribution of the statistic is equal to the corresponding population parameter, otherwise the statistic is called a biased estimator of the corresponding parameter. Analytically, a statistics 't' which is a function of the sample values $X_1, X_2, \ldots\ldots\ldots\ldots, X_n$ is an unbiased estimator of population parameter 'q' (say) if

$$E(t) = q, \textit{ i.e., } E(\text{statistics}) = \text{parameter}$$

Otherwise the statistic 't' is a biased estimator of q and the bias is given by, Bias = E (t) – q.

TYPES OF ESTIMATION

There are two types of estimation:

(i) Point Estimation

(ii) Interval Estimation

(i) Point Estimation: In point estimation a single statistic is used to provide an estimate of the population parameter, *i.e.*, the estimate of a population given by a single number is called the point estimation of the parameter. In point estimation we find a statistic which may be used for (or replace) an unknown parameter of the population for all practical purposes.

(ii) Interval Estimation: An interval estimation is the range of values used in making estimation of a population parameter. In other words, if an estimate of a population parameter be given by two distinct numbers between which the parameter may be considered to lie, then the estimate is called an interval estimate of the parameter.

For example, if the height of a student is measured as 175 cm. Then the measurement gives a point estimation, but if the height is given as (175 ± 10) cm, *i.e.*, the height lies between 165 cm and 185 cm, then the measurement gives an interval estimation.

CONFIDENCE INTERVAL ESTIMATES OF PARAMETERS

In an interval estimation of the population parameter θ, if we can find two quantities t_1 and t_2 based on sample observations drawn from the population such that the unknown parameter θ is included in the interval (t_1, t_2) in a specified percentage of cases, then this interval is called a confidence interval for the parameter θ. The lower limit t_1 and upper limit t_2 of this interval are called as confidence limits of θ. The confidence interval has a specified confidence or probability of correctly estimating the true value of the population parameter, *i.e.*, $P(t_1 \leq 0 \leq t_2) = C$, where C is a given (specified) probability.

We know that the sampling distribution of the sample mean $\overline{X}$ of a random sample of size n (≥ 30) drawn from a population having mean μ and standard deviation σ, is approximately a normal distribution with mean μ and standard deviation σ.

$$\text{S.E. of } \overline{X} = \frac{\sigma}{\sqrt{n}}$$

$$\therefore \qquad Z = \frac{\overline{X} - \mu}{\sigma/\sqrt{n}}$$

has a standard normal distribution with mean = 0 and $\sigma = 1$.

From the distribution of the area under a standard normal curve, it is known that 95.45% of the area lies between the ordinates $Z = \pm 2$,

i.e., $$P(-2 \le Z \le 2) = 95.45\% = 0.9545$$

or $$\overline{X} - 2\ (\text{S.E. of } \overline{X}) \le \mu \le \overline{X} + 2\ (\text{S.E. of } \overline{X})$$

This interval is called the 95.45% confidence interval for the population mean μ and $\overline{X} \pm 2$ (S.E. of $\overline{X}$) are called the 95.45% confidence limits for μ.

Again 99.73% of the area under the standard normal curve lies between the ordinates $Z = \pm 3$,

i.e., $P(-3 \le Z \le 3) = 0.9973$

$\therefore$ the 99.73% confidence interval and confidence limits for μ are respectively.

$\overline{X} - 3$ (S.E. of $\overline{X}$) $\le \mu \le \overline{X} + 3$ (S.E. of $\overline{X}$) and $\overline{X} \pm 3$ (S.E. of $\overline{X}$) respectively.

Some formulae for the confidence limits of well known statistics for large random samples are given below:

I. Confidence limits for the population mean μ

(i) 95% confidence limits are $\overline{X} \pm 1.96$ (S.E. of $\overline{X}$);

(ii) 95.45% confidence limits are $\overline{X} \pm 2$ (S.E. of $\overline{X}$);

(iii) 99% confidence limits are $\overline{X} \pm 2.58$ (S.E. of $\overline{X}$);

(iv) 99.73% confidence limits are $\overline{X} \pm 3$(S.E. of $\overline{X}$).

II. Confidence limits for population proportion P

(i) 95% confidence limits are $p \pm 1.96$ (S.E. of p);

(ii) 95.45% confidence limits are $p \pm 2$ (S.E. of p);

(iii) 99% confidence limits are $p \pm 2.58$ (S.E. of p);

(iv) 99.73% confidence limits are $p \pm 3$ (S.E. of p).

III. Confidence limits for the difference $\mu_1 - \mu_2$ of two population means μ_1 and μ_2

(i) 95% confidence limits are

$$(\overline{X}_1 - \overline{X}_2) \pm 1.96\ (\text{S.E. of } \overline{X}_1 - \overline{X}_2);$$

(ii) 95.45% confidence limits are

$$(\overline{X}_1 - \overline{X}_2) \pm 2\ (\text{S.E. of } \overline{X}_1 - \overline{X}_2);$$

(iii) 99% confidence limits are

$$(\overline{X}_1 - \overline{X}_2) \pm 2.58\ (\text{S.E. of } \overline{X}_1 - \overline{X}_2);$$

(iv) 99.73% confidence limits are

$$(\overline{X}_1 - \overline{X}_2) \pm 3\,(\text{S.E. of } \overline{X}_1 - \overline{X}_2).$$

IV. Confidence limits for the difference $P_1 - P_2$ of two population proportions

(i) 95% confidence limits are $(p_1 - p_2) \pm 1.96$ (S.E. of $p_1 - p_2$);

(ii) 95.45% confidence limits are $(p_1 - p_2) \pm 2$ (S.E. of $p_1 - p_2$);

(iii) 99% confidence limits are $(p_1 - p_2) \pm 2.58$ (S.E. of $p_1 - p_2$);

(iv) 99.73% confidence limits are $(p_1 - p_2) \pm 3$ (S.E. of $p_1 - p_2$).

Note: In calculating S.E., if population parameters are not known, corresponding statistics are used to find an approximate value of S.E.

EXAMPLE 9.1: Systolic blood pressure of 100 males was taken. Mean B.P. was found to be 128 mm. of mercury (Hg) and standard deviation 13 mm. of mercury. Find (i) 95% and (ii) 99% confidence limits of B.P. within which the population mean would lie.

SOLUTION: Here $\overline{X} = 128$ mm. of Hg; $n = 100$

Std. dev. = 13 mm. of Hg.

$$\therefore \text{S.E. of } \overline{X} = \frac{\sigma}{\sqrt{n}} = \frac{13}{\sqrt{100}} = \frac{13}{\sqrt{10}} = 1.3$$

(i) 95% confidence limits for the population mean are

$$\overline{X} \pm 1.96\,(\text{S.E. of } \overline{X}) = 128 \pm 1.96 \times 1.3$$
$$= (128 + 2.5) \text{ and } (128 - 2.5)$$
$$= 125.5 \text{ and } 130.5$$

(ii) 99% confidence limits for the population mean are

$$\overline{X} \pm 2.58\,(\text{S.E. of } \overline{X}) = 128 \pm 2.58 \times 1.3$$
$$= (128 + 3.4) \text{ and } (128 - 3.4)$$
$$= 131.4 \text{ and } 124.6$$

TESTING OF HYPOTHESIS (OR SIGNIFICANCE)

The testing of hypothesis, which was initiated by Neyman and Pearson, is a procedure that helps us to ascertain the likelihood of hypothesized population parameter being correct by making use of the sampling statistic. In testing of hypothesis a statistic is computed from a sample drawn from the parent population and on the basis of this statistic it is observed whether the sample so drawn has come from the population with certain specified characteristic.

Procedure of Testing a Hypothesis

There are following steps involved in the testing of a hypothesis:

I. Setting up of Hypothesis

In attempting to arrive at decision about the population on the basis of sample information, it is necessary to make assumptions about the population parameters involved. Such an assumption (or statement) is called a statistical hypothesis which may not be true. There are two hypothesis:

(i) Null hypothesis

(ii) Alternative hypothesis

(i) *Null Hypothesis:* In testing of hypothesis we always start with an assumption or hypothesis, *i.e.*, assumed value of a population parameter. This is known as Null hypothesis. It asserts that there is no difference between the sample statistic and population parameter and whatever observed difference is there is merely due to fluctuations in sampling from the same population. Null hypothesis is usually denoted by H_0.

Prof. R.A. Fisher defined Null Hypothesis as "The hypothesis which is tested for possible rejection under the assumption that it is true".

(ii) *Alternative Hypothesis:* Any hypothesis which is not a null hypothesis (*i.e.*, hypothesis of significant difference between the sample statistic and population parameter) is called an alternative hypothesis and is denoted by H_1.

The two hypotheses H_0 and H_1 are such that if one is true, the other is false or vice versa.

For example, if we have to test whether the average birth weight of new born (in Indian reference) is 2.5 kg (*i.e.*, $\mu_0 = 2.5$ kg), then the Null hypothesis is H_0: $\mu = \mu_0$ and the alternative hypothesis may be

(i) $H_1 : \mu \neq \mu_0$ (*i.e.*, $H_1 : \mu > \mu_0$ or $H_1 : \mu < \mu_0$)

(ii) $H_1 : \mu > \mu_0$ (iii) $H_1 : \mu < \mu_0$

The alternative hypothesis ($H_1 : \mu \neq \mu_0$) is known as a two tailed alternative and the alternative hypothesis ($H_1 : \mu > \mu_0$) and ($H_1 : \mu < \mu_0$) are known as right-tailed and left-tailed respectively.

II. Computation of Test Statistic

After setting up the null hypothesis and alternative hypothesis, we compute the test statistic. The test statistic is a statistic based on appropriate probability distribution. It is used to test whether the null hypothesis set up should be accepted or rejected.

The following are the most commonly used test statistic:

(i) Z-distribution test and (ii) Student t-test.

Z-distribution Test

We use Z-distribution under the normal distribution curve for large sample (*i.e.*, $n \geq 30$).

The Z-statistic, $Z = \frac{t - E(t)}{S.E.(t)} \sim N(0, 1)$ as $n \rightarrow \infty$

is a standard normal variate with a mean zero and standard deviation one, in which S.E. (t) is the standard error of the statistic t.

Student t-Test

It is also known as Student's t-statistic which is used for small sample (*i.e.*, $n < 30$).

$$t = \frac{\bar{X} - \mu}{S.E.(\bar{X})} = \frac{\text{Difference between sample and population means}}{\text{Standard error of mean}}$$

with (n – 1) degrees of freedom.

III. Errors of Sampling

Type – I and Type – II errors.

If a statistical hypothesis is tested, we may get the following four possible cases:

(i) the null hypothesis, H_0 is true but it is rejected by test procedure,

(ii) the null hypothesis, H_0 is false but it is accepted by test,

(iii) the null hypothesis, H_0 is true and it is accepted by test,

(iv) the null hypothesis, H_0 is false and it is rejected by test.

The first two cases lead to errors which are called errors of sampling. The error made in case (i) is called Type I error. The error committed in case (ii) is called Type II error. In either case a wrong decision is taken. The four possible cases that may arise in any test procedure are summarized below:

Inference	H_0 is rejected	H_0 is accepted
H_0 is true	Type I error (α)	Correct decision
H_0 is false	Correct decision	Type II error (β)

IV. Level of Significance and Critical Region

The level of significance is the maximum probability of making a type I error and it is denoted by α (*i.e.*, probability of rejecting H_0 when it is true). The probability of making correct decision is then $(1 - \alpha)$. The level of significance is generally specified before a test procedure so that the results may not influence the decision. In practice, we take either 5% (*i.e.*, 0.05) or 1% (*i.e.*, 0.01) level of significance. If we choose 5% level of significance ($\alpha = 0.05$) in a test procedure we shall mean that the probability of making type I error is 0.05 or 5%, *i.e.*, prob. [Rejecting H_0 when it is true] = 0.05.

This also means that we are 95% confident that a correct decision has been made. Similarly, if we choose 1% level of significance ($\alpha = 0.01$) in testing a hypothesis, then there is probability of making type I error is 0.01 or 1%, *i.e.*, we are 99% confident that we have made the correct decision.

The total area under the standard normal curve is 1 which is 100%. From the above figure we see that if the test statistic Z of a sample statistic – t lies between – 1.96 and 1.96, then we are 95% confident that the null hypothesis is true, *i.e.*, prob. $(-1.96 \leq Z \leq 1.96) = 0.95$. But if for a random sample the Z-score lies outside the range ± 1.96 (*i.e.*, if $|Z| > 1.96$) we say that such an event could happen with probaility of only 0.05. This concludes that Z-score differed significantly from the value expected under the null hypothesis and hence the hypothesis is to be rejected at 5% (or 0.05) level of significance.

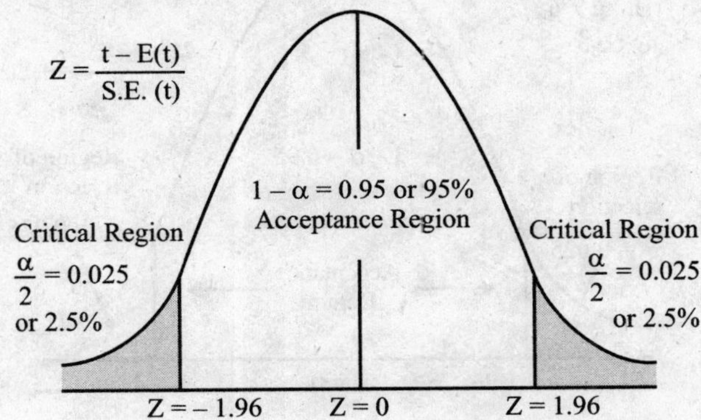

Fig. 9.1: Critical Region of a Test Statistic

Critical Region (or Rejection Region): It is the area under standard normal curve in which the test statistic value has to fall for the rejection of null hypothesis. While the set of Z-score inside the range ±1.96 (*i.e.*, area under the standard normal curve which is not covered by the rejection region) is called the region of acceptance of null hypothesis. The values – 1.96 and 1.96 are called critical values at 5% level of significance. Similarly, the values −2.58 and 2.58 are called critical values at 1% level of significance.

V. Two-Tailed Test and One-Tailed Test

The probability curve of the sampling distribution of the test statistic is a standard normal-curve. This curve has two ends which are known as two tails. When the test of hypothesis is made on the basis of rejection region represented by both sides (or ends) of the standard normal curve, it is called the two-tailed test. In other words, a test of statistical hypothesis where the alternative hypothesis H_1 is two sided or two tailed such as

$$\text{Null Hypothesis } H_0 : \mu = \mu_0$$

$$\text{Alternative Hypothesis } H_1 : \mu \neq \mu_0 \, (i.e., \, \mu > \mu_0 \text{ or } \mu < \mu_0)$$

Whereas if the alternative hypothesis H_1 in a test of a statistical hypothesis be one sided (or one tailed), either right-tailed or left-tailed, then the test is called a one-tailed test.

For example, to test whether the population mean $\mu = \mu_0$, we have $H_0 : \mu = \mu_0$ against the alternative hypothesis H_1 given by

$H_1 : \mu > \mu_0$ (Right-tailed)

or $H_1 : \mu < \mu_0$ (Left-tailed)

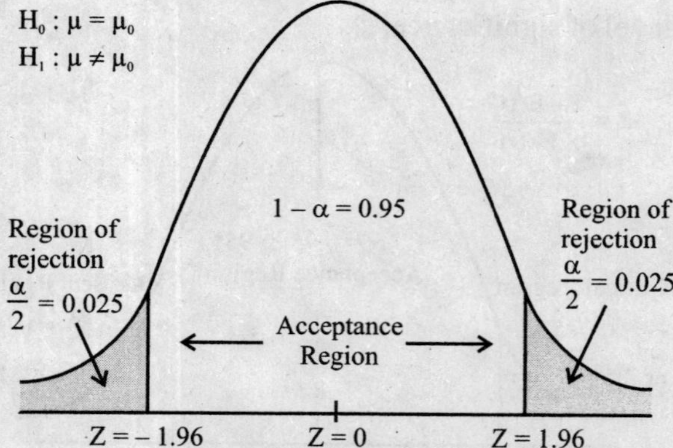

Fig. 9.2: Two-tailed Test at $\alpha = 0.05$

APPLICATION OF TWO-TAILED TEST

A two tailed test is applied in such cases when the difference between the sample mean and population mean is tending to reject the null hypothesis H_0 the difference is significant, it may be positive or negative.

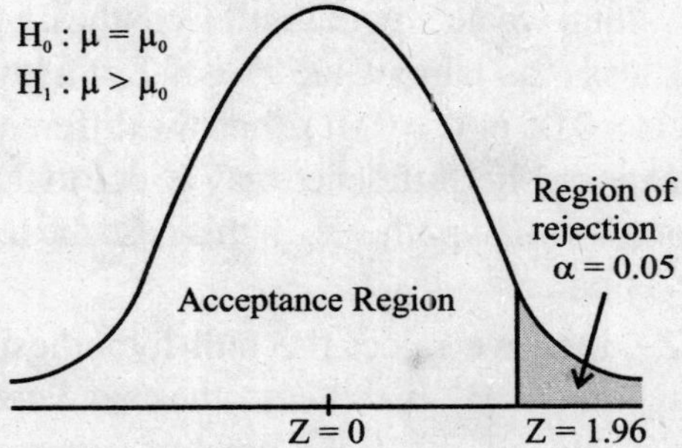

Fig. 9.3: Right-Tailed Test at $\alpha = 0.05$

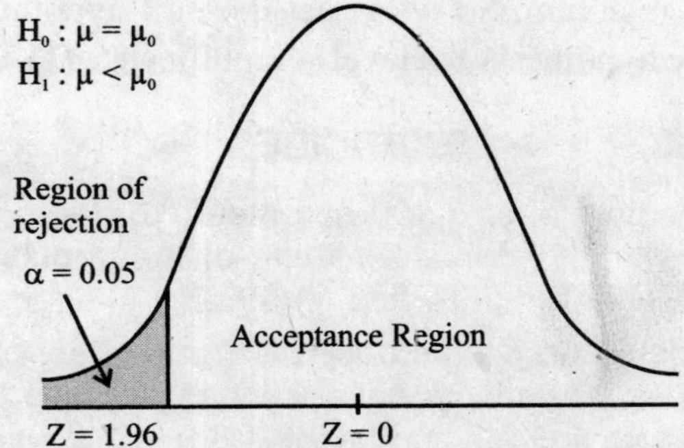

Fig. 9.4: Right-Tailed Test at $\alpha = 0.05$

APPLICATION OF ONE-TAILED TEST

A one tailed test is applied in such cases when it is considered to see whether the population mean is at least as large as some specified value of the mean or at least as small as some specified value of the mean. In the former case the right tailed test and in the later case a left tailed test are applied.

Critical values of Z for both two-tailed and one-tailed tests at 1% and 5% level of siginificance are given below:

Level of Significance (α)	1%	5%
Critical values for Two tailed test	$\|Z_\alpha\| = 2.58$	$\|Z_\alpha\| = 1.96$
Critical values for Right tailed test	$Z_\alpha = 2.33$	$Z_\alpha = 1.65$
Critical values for Left tailed test	$Z_\alpha = -2.33$	$Z_\alpha = -1.65$

VI. Decision Rule (Two-tailed Test)

The decision about null hypothesis, whether to accept it or reject it. The following rules to be followed as:

(i) If $|Z| < Z_\alpha$, then we accept the null hypothesis, *i.e.*, if the calculated value of Z is less than table value Z α of Z at a level of significance α, (practically, α = 0.05 or α = 0.01), then the difference between [t = E (t)] is not significant and this difference may be due to fluctuation of sampling. So we accept the null hypothesis. In this case the test statistic falls in the region of acceptance.

(ii) If $|Z| > Z_\alpha$, then we reject the null hypothesis H_0 and accept the alternative hypothesis H_1. In this case, the calculated value of Z is greater than the table value, Z_α of Z at a level of significance α, (practically, α = 0.05 or α = 0.01) and the calculated value of test statistics falls in the region of rejection. So we reject the null hypothesis and accept the alternative hypothesis at a level of significance (1 – α).

➤ EXERCISES ≺

9.1. A random sample of size 100 has mean 15, the population variance being 16. Find the Interval estimate of the population mean with a confidence level of (i) 95% and (ii) 99%.

9.2. Two hospitals A and B are cooperating in a study of hypertension. At the hospital A, 20 patients have a mean systotlic blood pressure of 160 mm-Hg with σ = 20, and hospital B has 30 patients having mean systolic B.P. of 170 mm of Hg with σ = 10 mm-Hg. Compute 95% and 99%. Confidence Intervals for the difference in means. Don't assume that the variances are equal.

9.3. In a random sample of 50 patients of liver diseases serum bilirubin was found abnormally raised in 30 patients. The point estimate of the proportion with such bilirubin level in liver diseases is p = 0.6. Find the 95% confidence Interval for the proportion of liver diseased cases.

9.4. Define standard error of mean. Mean Hb.% of the population is 14.3. Can a sample of 20 individuals with a mean of 14.8% and standard deviation 1.5 be from the same population?

9.5.

Sex	Number (n)	Mean height cms.	Std. dev. (σ)
Girls	55	152	8
Boys	170	168	14

Determine if height differs with sex.

9.6. Mean serum vitamin A level of 20 children was 24 mg/dl. Does this mean differ from a mean of population 28 mg/dl with variance of 40?

⊕⊕⊕⊕⊕

CHAPTER

10

Z–Test

- *Large Sample*
- *Levels of Significance*
- *Critical Region*
- *Critical Value*

For large samples (n ≥ 30), the sampling distributions of many statistics are approximately normal distributions. In such cases Z-statistic can be applied to test, the null hypothesis. Some special tests are given below:

(i) Test for a specified mean or test of significance of mean (Large sample).

(ii) Test for quality of two means or test of significance of difference between two means (Large samples).

(iii) Test for a specified proportion (Large samples).

(iv) Test for equality of two proportions or test of significance of difference between two sample proportions (Large samples).

(i) Test for a Specified Mean

A random sample of size $n \geq 30$ has a sample mean $\overline{X}$. To test the hypothesis that the population mean μ has a specified value μ_0.

The null hypthesis, $H_0: \mu = \mu_0$, *i.e.*, there is no significance difference between the sample mean and population mean.

The Alternative hypothesis is

$$H_1: \mu \neq \mu_0 \; (i.e., \; \mu > \mu_0 \text{ or } \mu < \mu_0)$$

Since n is large, the sampling distribution of $\overline{X}$ is approximately normal.

∴ If H_0 is true, the test statistic $Z = \dfrac{\overline{X} - \mu_0}{\text{S.E. of } \overline{X}}$ has approximately a standard normal distribution.

The critical region for Z depending on the nature of H_1 and level of significance α (*i.e.*, 1% or 5%). Critical values for two tailed test ($\mu \neq \mu_0$) are $|Z| = 2.58$ at 1% level of significance or $|Z| = 1.96$ at 5% level of significance. Critical values for right-tailed and left-tailed tests ($\mu > \mu_0$ or $\mu < \mu_0$) are $Z \pm 2.33$ at 1% level of significance and $Z = \pm 1.65$ at 5% level of significance respectively. Decision is taken according to:

(a) If the calculated value of $Z = |Z| >$ critical value Z_α at a level of significance α, then the null hypothesis is rejected and the alternative hypothesis is accepted.

(b) If the calculated value of $Z = |Z| <$ critical value Z_α at a level of significance α, then the null hypothesis H_0 is accepted. Here it is to be noted that without any reference to the level of significance, the null hypothesis, H_0 may be rejected when $|Z| > 3$.

EXAMPLE 10.1: A random sample of 500 persons is found to have a mean of 4.5 cms. Can it be reasonably regarded as a sample from a large population whose man is 5 cm and standard deviation is 2 cm?

SOLUTION: Here, $n = 500$ $\overline{X} = 4.5$ cm, $\mu = 5$ cm and $\alpha = 2$ cm

Null hypothesis, $H_0 = \mu = 5$ cm (*i.e.*, the sample has come from a large (normal) population with mean 5 and standard deviation 2).

∴ Alternative hypothesis $H_1 : \mu \neq 5$ cm.

Since H_1 is two-tailed ($\mu > 5$ or $\mu < 5$). So we apply two-tailed test.

Let us assume that H_0 is true. The test statistic Z is

$$Z = \frac{\overline{X} - \mu}{\text{S.E. of } \overline{X}} \qquad \text{where S.E. of } \overline{X} = \frac{\sigma}{\sqrt{n}} = \frac{2}{\sqrt{500}}$$

$$\text{S.E. of } \overline{X} = \frac{2}{22.4} = 0.09$$

$$\therefore \quad Z = \frac{4.5 - 5}{0.09} = \frac{-0.5}{0.09} = -5.56$$

or $|Z| = |-5.56| = 5.56 > 3$ (because α is not given)

we reject the null hypothesis and conclude that the given sample can not be regarded as a sample from the large (normal) population.

EXAMPLE 10.2: Suppose that chest circumference of presumably normal new born baby girls is normally distributed with $\mu = 35$ cm and $\alpha = 2$ cm. A sample of 50 new born baby girls from a population group living in a remote region and thought perhaps to contribute a genetic isolate are studied and found to have mean chest circumference of 32.5 cm. Is this evidence that the sample drawn from a normal population.

SOLUTION: Here $n = 50$, $\overline{X} = 32.5$, $\mu = 35$ and $\sigma = 2$

Null hypothesis H_0: $\mu = \mu_0 = 35$, then Alternative hypothesis H_1: $\mu \neq 35$

$$\therefore \quad \text{S.E. of } \overline{X} = \frac{\sigma}{\sqrt{n}} \frac{2}{\sqrt{50}} = \frac{2}{7.1} = 0.28$$

$$\text{S.E. of } (\overline{X}) = 0.28 \quad \text{Test statistic } Z = \frac{\overline{X} - \mu}{\text{S.E. of } \overline{X}}$$

$$Z = \frac{32.5 - 35}{0.28} = \frac{-2.5}{0.28} = -8.93$$

$$\therefore \quad |Z| = |-8.93| = 8.93 > 3$$

We reject the hypothesis and our conclusion is that the 50 new born baby girls can not be regarded to be a sample from the same population as the population is presumed normal.

(ii) Test for equality of two means or test of significance of difference between two means (large samples)

Let $\overline{X}_1$ and $\overline{X}_2$ be the sample means of two independent large random samples of sizes n_1 and n_2 drawn from two population having means μ_1 and μ_2 standard deviations σ_1 and σ_2. To test whether the two population means are equal. The null hypothesis is set in any one of the following forms:

H_0: $\mu_1 = \mu_2$ (*i.e.*, two sample have been drawn from different populations having the same means and equal standard deviations) or H_0: $\overline{X}_1 = \overline{X}_2$, *i.e.*, the two samples have been drawn from the same parent population.

Then the alternative hypothesis $H_1 : \mu_1 \neq \mu_2$ (Two-tailed test) or H_1: $\mu_1 > \mu_2$ or $H_1 : \mu_1 < \mu_2$ (One-tailed test)

$$\text{and} \qquad \text{S.E of } (\overline{X}_1 - \overline{X}_2) = \sqrt{\frac{\sigma_1^{\,2}}{n_1} + \frac{\sigma_2^{\,2}}{n_2}}$$

Assuming that H_0 is true, the test statistic

$$Z = \frac{\overline{X}_1 - \overline{X}_2}{\text{S.E. of } (\overline{X}_1 - \overline{X}_2)}$$

is approximately normally distributed with mean 0 and standard deviation 1.

Rejection Rule for H_0: $\mu_1 = \mu_2$

(a) If $|Z| > 1.96$, then reject H_0 at 5% level of significance

(b) If $|Z| > 2.58$, then reject H_0 at 1% level of significance otherwise accept the null hypothesis.

Note: If standard deviations, σ_1 and σ_2, of the two population are not given. In this case sample standard deviations S_1 and S_2 are taken as estimate of σ_1 and σ_2.

EXAMPLE 10.3: In a study on growth of children, one group of 70 children had a mean height of 65 cm and standard deviation of 2.5 cm. While another group of 80 children had a mean height of 68 cm and standard deviation of 3 cm. Is the difference between the two sample means statistically significant?

SOLUTION: Let μ_1 and μ_2 be means of the two populations, the null hypothesis H_0: $\mu_1 = \mu_2$, then the alternative hypothesis H_1: $\mu_1 \neq \mu_2$.

Assume that H_0 is true, *i.e.*, there is no difference between μ_1 and μ_2.

Since the sample sizes are large, the test statistic

$$Z = \frac{\overline{X}_1 - \overline{X}_2}{\text{S.E. of } (\overline{X}_1 - \overline{X}_2)}$$

where $\text{S.E. of } (\overline{X}_1 - \overline{X}_2) = \sqrt{\frac{\sigma_1^2}{n_1} + \frac{\sigma_2^2}{n_2}}$

Here $n_1 = 70$, $n_2 = 80$, $\overline{X}_1 = 65$, $\overline{X}_2 = 68$, $S_1 = 2.5$, $S_2 = 3$.

Since σ_1 and σ_2 are not known, we take the values of sample standard deviations S_1 and S_2 for σ_1 and σ_2 in calculating S.E. of $(\overline{X}_1 - \overline{X}_2)$.

$$\text{S.E. of } (\overline{X}_1 - \overline{X}_2) = \sqrt{\frac{S_1^2}{n_1} + \frac{S_2^2}{n_2}} = \sqrt{\frac{(2.5)^2}{70} + \frac{(3)^2}{80}}$$

$$= \sqrt{\frac{6.25}{70} + \frac{9}{80}} = \sqrt{0.09 + 0.11}$$

$$= \sqrt{0.2} = 0.45$$

$$\therefore \qquad Z = \frac{\overline{X}_1 - \overline{X}_2}{\text{S.E. of } (\overline{X}_1 - \overline{X}_2)} = \frac{65 - 68}{0.45} = \frac{-3}{0.45} = -6.67$$

$$|Z| = |-6.67| = 6.67 > 3$$

Hence we reject the null hypothesis and conclude that the difference between the means of two samples is significant, *i.e.*, the growth is more in the second group than in the first group of children.

EXAMPLE 10.4: A random of 50 male employees is taken at the end of a year and the mean number of hours of absenteeism for the years is found to be 63 hours. A similar sample of 50 female employees has mean of 66 hours. Could these samples be drawn from a population with the same mean and standard deviation 10 hours?

SOLUTION: Here $n_1 = 50$, $n_2 = 50$, $\overline{X}_1 = 63$, $\overline{X}_2 = 66$, $\sigma_1 = \sigma_2 = 10$

Null hypothesis $H_0: \mu_1 = \mu_2$, then, the alternative hypothesis $H_1: \mu_1 \neq \mu_2$, it is a case of two-tailed test.

Assuming that H_0 is true. The test statistic

$$Z = \frac{\overline{X}_1 - \overline{X}_2}{\text{S.E. of } (\overline{X}_1 - \overline{X}_2)}$$

where $\text{S.E. of } (\overline{X}_1 - \overline{X}_2) = \sqrt{\frac{\sigma_1^{\,2}}{n_1} + \frac{\sigma_2^{\,2}}{n_2}}$

is approximately normally distributed with mean 0 and standard deviation 1.

where $\text{S.E. of } (\overline{X}_1 - \overline{X}_2) = \sqrt{\frac{\sigma_1^{\,2}}{n_1} + \frac{\sigma_2^{\,2}}{n_2}} = \sqrt{\frac{10^2}{50} + \frac{10^2}{50}}$

$$= \sqrt{\frac{100}{50} + \frac{100}{50}} = \sqrt{4} = 2$$

and $$Z = \frac{\overline{X}_1 - \overline{X}_2}{\text{S.E. of } (\overline{X}_1 - \overline{X}_2)} = \frac{63 - 66}{2} = \frac{-3}{2} = -1.5$$

$\therefore$ $$|Z| = |-1.5| = 1.5 = 1.96$$

(Taking $\alpha = 0.05$, $Z_\alpha = 1.96$)

Hence we accept the null hypothesis and conclude that the difference between two sample means is insignificant, and two samples have been drawn from the same population.

(iii) Test for a specified proportion or test of significance for single proportion (large sample test)

A random sample of size $n \geq 30$ has sample proportion p of members possessing a certain attribute (*i.e.*, proportion of successes). To test the hypothesis that the proportion P in the population has a specified value P_0.

The null hypothesis H_0 is that the sample has been drawn from a population with population proportion P (*i.e.*, $H_0 : P = P_0$ where P_0 is a specified value of P).

The alternative hypothesis $H_1 : P \neq P_0 \Rightarrow$ Two-tailed test (*i.e.*, $H_1 : P > P_0$ or $H_1 : P < P_0$).

Since n is large, the sampling distribution of p (sample proportion) is approximately normal.

$$Z = \frac{p - P}{\text{S.E. of p}} = \frac{p - P_0}{\text{S.E. of p}}$$

is approximately normally distributed.

Standard Error of proportion (S.E. of p) $= \sqrt{\frac{PQ}{n}} = \sqrt{\frac{P(1-P)}{n}}$

where n is the sample size and P is population proportion and $Q = (1 - P)$.

The critical region for Z depending on the nature of H_1 and level of significance a, (*i.e.*, $|Z| > 2.58$ at 1% level of significance (l.s.) or $|Z| > 1.96$ at 5% level of significance for two-tailed test and $Z > 2.33$ at 1% 1.s. or $Z > 1.65$ at 5% 1.s. for right-tailed test; $|Z| < |-2.33|$ at 1% 1.s. or $|Z| < |-1.65|$ at 5% 1.s.).

EXAMPLE 10.5: A sample of size 600 persons selected at random from a large city shows that the percentage of male in the sample is 53%. It is believed that the ratio of male to the total population in the city is 1/2. Test whether this belief ratio in the city is 1/2. Test whether this belief is confirmed by the observation.

SOLUTION: Here $P = 50\%$, $Q = (100 - P) = (100 - 50) = 50\%$

$$p = 53\%, n = 600$$

Null Hypothesis H_0: $P = 1/2 = 50\%$

Alternative hypothesis $H_1 : P \neq 50\%$ (Two-tailed test) (*i.e.*, $H_1 : P > 50\%$ or $H_1 : P < 50\%$)

$$\text{S.E. (p)} = \sqrt{\frac{PQ}{n}} = \sqrt{\frac{50 \times 50}{600}} = \sqrt{\frac{2500}{600}} = 2.04$$

$$\therefore \quad \text{test statistic } Z = \frac{p - P}{\text{S.E. (p)}} = \frac{53 - 50}{2.04} = \frac{3}{2.04} = 1.5$$

Z_α at $\alpha = 0.05$ is 1.96

Thus $|Z| < Z_\alpha$ as $1.5 < 1.96$ $\Rightarrow$ Null hypothesis H_0 is accepted. So we conclude that male population is 59% (*i.e.*, male to the total population ratio in the city is 1/2).

EXAMPLE 10.6: In a hospital, 138 females and 162 males were born in a week. Do these figures confirm to the hypothesis that both (male and female) are born in the equal proportion?

SOLUTION: $P_0 = 1/2 = 0.5$ = Probability of equal proportion and p = proportion of females born $= \frac{138}{300} = 0.46$

Null hypothesis H_0: $P = P_0 = 1/2 = 0.5$

then Alternative hypothesis $H_1 : P \neq 1/2 = 0.5$

$$\text{S.E. of P} = \sqrt{\frac{PQ}{n}} = \sqrt{\frac{P(1-P)}{n}} = \sqrt{\frac{0.5 \times 0.5}{300}} = \sqrt{\frac{0.25}{300}} = 0.03$$

$$Z = \frac{P - P_0}{\text{S.E. of p}} = \frac{0.46 - 0.5}{0.03} = -1.33$$

Since $|Z| = 1.33 < Z_\alpha = 1.96$ at 5% l.s.

Thus H_0 is accepted $\Rightarrow$ both male and female are born in equal proportion.

(iv) Tests for equality of two proportions or test of significance of differnce between two sample proportions (large samples)

Let p_1 and p_2 be the proportions in two large random samples of sizes n_1 and n_2 drawn from two population having proportions P_1 and P_2. To test whether the two population proportions P_1 and P_2 are equal.

Null hypothesis $H_0 : P_1 = P_2$

Alternative hypothesis $H_1 : P_1 \neq P_2$

Sample proportion of two samples or estimated p

$$p = \frac{n_1 p_1 + n_2 p_2}{n_1 + n_2}$$

So that $q = 1 - p$

$$\text{Standard error of } (p_1 - p_2) = \sqrt{pq\left(\frac{1}{n_1} + \frac{1}{n_2}\right)}$$

Sinçe the sample sizes n_1 and n_2 are large, the test statistic

$$Z = \frac{p_1 - p_2}{\text{S.E. of } (p_1 - p_2)}$$

is approximately normally distributed with mean 0 and standard deviation 1.

Rejection Rule for $H_0 : P_1 = P_2$

(a) If $|Z| > 1.96$, then reject H_0 at 5% l.s.

(b) If $|Z| > 2.58$, then reject H_0 at 5% l.s.

Otherwise we accept H_0.

EXAMPLE 10.7: In an infantile paralysis epidemic 700 people contracted the disease. 400 received no serum treatment and of them 80 became paralysed. Of those who received serum treatment 70 became paralysed. Was the serum treatment effective ?

SOLUTION: Let p_1 and p_2 be the sample proportions of people who received no serum and received serum treatment respectively

$$\therefore \qquad p_1 = \frac{80}{400} = 0.02,\ p_2 = \frac{70}{300} = 0.23$$

Sample mean proportion of the two sample proportions

$$p = \frac{n_1 p_1 + n_2 p_2}{n_1 + n_2}$$

Here $\qquad n_1 = 400$ and $n_2 = 300$

$$\therefore \qquad p = \frac{400 \times 0.20 + 300 \times 0.23}{400 + 300} = \frac{80 + 69}{700}$$

or $$p = \frac{149}{700} = 0.21,\ q = 1 - q = 0.79$$

Let the Null hypothesis be $H_0 : P_1 = P_2$ (i.e., Serum was not effective).

Then the alternative hypothesis $H_1 : P_1 \neq P_2$

$$\text{Standard error of } (p_1 - p_2) = \sqrt{pq\left(\frac{1}{n_1} + \frac{1}{n_2}\right)}$$

$$= \sqrt{(0.21 \times 0.79)\left(\frac{1}{400} + \frac{0.03}{300}\right)}$$

$$= \sqrt{0.17 \times 0.006}$$

i.e., $\qquad$ S.E. of $(p_1 - p_2) = 0.03$

Assuming that H_0 is true, the test statistic is

$$Z = \frac{p_1 - p_2}{\text{S.E. of } (p_1 - p_2)}$$

or $$Z = \frac{0.20 - 0.23}{0.03} = \frac{0.03}{1} = 1.00$$

$$\therefore \qquad Z = 1.00$$

Since $|Z| = 1.00 < Z_\alpha = 1.96$ (at $\alpha = 0.05$), we accept the null hypothesis and conclude that the serum treatment was not effective.

EXAMPLE 10.8: In school A, tonsillectomy had been done in 25 students out of 60, while in the other school B it was done in 75 out of 400. Find if the difference observed in the two schools is by chance or due to some influence.

SOLUTION: Here $p_1 = \frac{25}{60} = 0.42$, $p_2 = \frac{75}{400} = 0.19$

Null hypothesis $H_0 : P_1, = P_2$, then alternative hypothesis $H_1 : P_1 \neq P_2$

$$\text{S.E. of } (p_1 - p_2) = \sqrt{pq\left(\frac{1}{n_1} + \frac{1}{n_2}\right)}$$

where $$p = \frac{n_1 p_1 + n_2 p_2}{n_1 + n_2} = \frac{60 \times 0.42 + 400 \times 0.19}{60 + 400}$$

$$p = \frac{25.6 + 76}{460} = \frac{101.2}{460} = 0.22$$

$\therefore$ $$q = (1 - p) = (1 - 0.22) = 0.78$$

$$\text{S.E. of } (p_1 - p_2) = \sqrt{(0.22 \times 0.78)\left(\frac{1}{60} + \frac{1}{400}\right)}$$

$$\text{S.E. of } (p_1 - p_2) = \sqrt{0.17 \times 0.02} = 0.06$$

Assuming that H_0 is true, the test statistic is

$$Z = \frac{p_1 - p_2}{\text{S.E. of } (p_1 - p_2)} = \frac{0.42 - 0.19}{0.06} = \frac{0.23}{0.06} = 3.83$$

Since $|Z| = 3.83 > Z_\alpha = 2.58$ at 1% level of significance.

Hence we reject the null hypothesis and conclue that there is a significant difference between the two schools as far as tonsillectomy is concerned which indicates that tonsillectomy is more common in school A. The factor, playing part in this, should be investigated.

➤ EXERCISES ➤

10.1. A die was thrown 900 times and of these 320 yielded 3 or 4. Is this consistent with the hypothesis that the die was unbiased ?

10.2. Find the significance of difference in the mean index of brightness of 30 boys and 30 girls with the following values:

Sex	Mean	Std. dev.
Boys	90.3	35.0
Girls	90.0	30.0

10.3. Constipation was considered to be a common feature as observed in 60% of typhoid patients. In a study of 300 typhoid patients 25% had consitpation. Can you consider constipation as a common feature of typhoid on this observation?

10.4. Two groups A and B consist of 100 patients each who have a disease. A serum is given to group A but not to group B. It is found that in groups A and B, 70 and 60 patients respectively recover from the disease. Test the hypothesis that the serum helps to cure the disease.

10.5. In an infantile paralysis epidemic 500 persons contracted the disease. 300 received no serum treatment and of those 75 became paralysed. Of these who did not received serum treatment 65 became paralysed. Was the serum treatment effective?

10.6. In rural school age children, the prevalence of whooping cough was 12%. Number of children studied were 100. Can you conclude that this rate is same as that of 14% observed in school age children of the earlier decade?

10.7. Mean ± SD values of height and weight of normal and PEM children are given below:

Children	Normal	PEM
Sample size	300	150
Height (cm)	95.5 ± 5.5	90.6 ± 6.4
Weight (kg)	15.6 ± 2.6	12.0 ± 3.5

Can we conclude that height and weight are significantly retarded in PEM children compared to normal children?

10.8. In two populations (Rural and Urban), proportion of nutritional deficiency among the under five children are 0.82 and 0.75 with sizes 300 and 250 respectively. Test whether proportions are significantly different in the two communities.

10.9. In a sample of 200 men from a certain city, 120 men are found to be smokers. In a sample of 500 from another city, 250 are found to be smokers. Do the data indicate that the two cities are significantly different with respect to the prevalence of smoking among men?

10.10. In a sample of 1200 people from a community, 650 persons are tea drinkers and the rest are coffee drinkers. Can we assume that both coffee and tea are equally popular in the community at 1% level of significance.

⌖⌖⌖⌖⌖

CHAPTER

11

Student t-Test

- *Degree of Freedom*
- *Paired*
- *Unbiased*
- *Unpaired*

Samples of size n<30 are called small samples. When the samples are small then the distribution of standardised variable Z of the statistic will be far from normality and as a result the normal test or Z-test can not be applied. In case of small samples (n<30) new technique or test of significance known as Student's t-distribution is applied which was developed by W.S. Gosset, writing under the pen name of "Student". This test is also known as t-test which involves an important expression, degrees of freedom.

DEGREES OF FREEDOM (D.F.)

It is a number which tells us how many of the values or (numbers) may be independently chosen. For example, if we are allowed to pick any three numbers, then there is no restriction on any of the three numbers (or values). Suppose we choose 5, 7, 10 or any other set of three numbers. Since all the three numbers have the freedom to vary. So the degrees of freedom is 3. If we impose a restriction on the numbers such as the mean is 8 (or the sum is 24), then we can no longer freely choose all the three numbers. We can choose the first two numbers independently but the third number must be such that the total is 24 (*i.e.,* if the first two numbers chosen freely be 5, 7, then the third number would be 12 so that the sum of all the three numbers to be 24). In this case, the degrees of freedom is (3–1) = 2. In general, if there are n values or numbers in a sample with a specified mean, then the degrees of freedom would be (n –1). But if there are two samples of sizes n_1 and n_2 with specified means $\overline{X}_1$ and $\overline{X}_2$, then the degrees of freedom would be $(n_1 + n_2 - 2)$.

STUDENT'S t-DISTRIBUTION

If $x_1, x_2, x_3, \ldots\ldots\ldots, x_n$ be any random sample of size n drawn from a normal (or approximately normal) population with mean μ and variance σ^2, then the Student's t-distribution is defined by the test statistic.

$$t = \frac{\overline{X} - \mu}{s/\sqrt{n}},$$

where s = Standard deviation of sample

and $s^2 = \frac{1}{(n-1)} \Sigma (X - \overline{X})^2$; $(n - 1)$ = degrees of freedom [*i.e.*, (sample size) –1]

is an unbiased estimate of σ^2

or

$$t = \frac{\overline{X} - \mu}{\text{S.E. of mean}}$$

$$= \frac{\overline{X} - \mu}{\sqrt{s^2/n-1}}$$

PROPERTIES OF t-DISTRIBUTION

(i) t-distribution is asymptotic to X-axis.

(ii) The shape of the curve or form of t-distribution varies with degrees of freedom.

(iii) t-distribution is a symmetrical distribution with mean zero.

(iv) t-distribution has a greater spread than normal distribution.

(v) t-distribution becomes closer to the Z distribution with increasing degrees of freedom. Theoretically, when d.f. approaches to ∞, then the t-distribution approaches the standard normal curve.

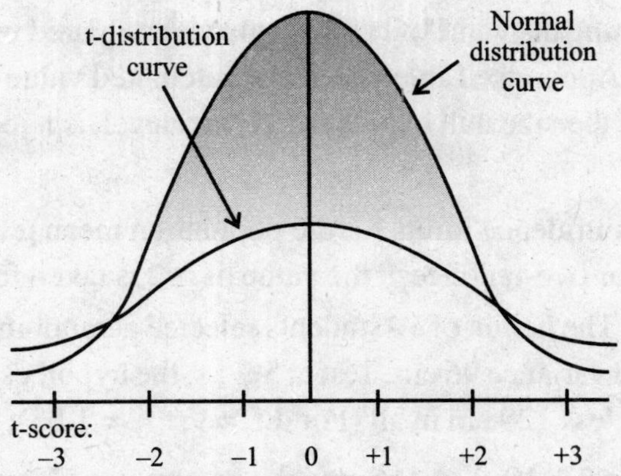

Application of t-distribution [For small sample (n<30)]

(a) To test the hypothesis that the population mean μ has a specified value μ_0 when population variance σ^2 is not known.

(b) To test whether the two population means are equal ($n_1 < 30$, $n_2 < 30$) when σ_1 and σ_2 are unknown.

INTERVAL ESTIMATE OF POPULATION MEAN

If $\overline{X}$ be the sample mean (n < 30) then the interval estimate of the population mean μ is given by $\overline{X} \pm t_\alpha$ S.E. $(\overline{X})$

where $$\text{S.E.}(\overline{X}) = \frac{s}{\sqrt{n}} \text{ and } s = \sqrt{\frac{\Sigma(X - \overline{X})^2}{n-1}}$$

The value of t at different level of significance (*i.e.,* 0.05, 0.01) are to be obtained from t-Table (see Appendix Table III) for the given degrees of freedom.

(a) Test for Specified Mean (when σ is not known)

A random sample of size (n < 30) has a sample mean $\overline{X}$. To test the hypothesis that the population mean μ has a specified value μ_0 when population standard deviation σ is not known.

Let the Null hypothesis be $H_0 : \mu = \mu_0$

The alternative hypothesis is $H_1 : \mu \neq \mu_0$

Assuming that H_0 is true, the test statistic, t is given by

$$t = \frac{\overline{X} - \mu}{s/\sqrt{n}} \quad \text{where} \quad s = \sqrt{\frac{\Sigma(X - \overline{X})^2}{n-1}}$$

Follows t-distribution with (d.f.), $\upsilon = n - 1$

After calculating the value of | t |, this value is compared with the Table value of t, Table III (see Appendix Table III). If the calculated value of t is greater than the table value of t, then the null hypothesis H_0 at α level, is rejected. Otherwise H_0 is accepted.

Note: 95% confidence limits for the population mean μ are $\overline{X} \pm t_{\alpha}$ S.E. $(\overline{X})$ where $\alpha = 0.025$ for two-tailed test, the value of $\alpha/2$ is taken for α.

EXAMPLE 11.1: The height of 10 students selected at random from a school had a mean 116 cm and variance 96 cm. Test at 5% l.s. the hypothesis that the students are on the average less 120 cm in all (For d.f. = 9, $t_{0.05} = 1.83$).

SOLUTION: Here n = 10, $\overline{X} = 116$ cm, $s^2 = 96$ cm, $\mu = 120$ cm.

Null hypothesis, H_0: $\mu = 120$ cm.

Alternative hypothesis $H_1 : \mu < 120$ (one tailed test)

Now $\quad$ S.E. of $\overline{X} = \dfrac{S}{\sqrt{n-1}} = \dfrac{9.79}{9} = \dfrac{9.79}{3} = 3.26$

$$\therefore \quad \text{Test statistic, } t = \frac{\overline{X} - \mu}{\text{S.E.}(\overline{X})} = \frac{116 - 120}{3.26} = \frac{-4}{3.26} = -1.23$$

$$\therefore \quad |t| = 1.23$$

The table value of t for 9 d.f. at 5% l.s. = 1.83

$\therefore \quad |t| = 1.23 < t_{0.05,\,9} = 1.83 \Rightarrow$ the null hypothesis. H_0 is accepted $\Rightarrow$ the average height of the students is not less than 120 cms.

EXAMPLE 11.2: A random sample of size 16 from a normal population give mean of 53 and a standard deviation of 3.16. Find 99% confidence interval for the population mean. ($t_{0.01,\,15} = 2.95$)

SOLUTION: Here n = 16, $\overline{X} = 53$, Std. Dev. = 3.16

99% confidence interval for $\overline{X}$ for 15 d.f. is given by $\overline{X} \pm t_{\alpha}$ S.E. $(\overline{X})$

$$= \overline{X} \pm t_{0.01,\,15} \frac{s}{\sqrt{n-1}}$$

$$= 53 \pm 2.95 \times \frac{3.16}{\sqrt{15}}$$

$$= 53 \pm \frac{9.32}{3.87}$$

$= 53 \pm 2.41$ (*i.e.*, 50.59 and 55.41)

Hence 99% C.I. for μ is $50.6 < \mu < 55.4$

(b) Test for equality for two means or test of significance of difference between two means (when σ_1 and σ_2 are not known):

Let $\overline{X}_1$ and $\overline{X}_2$ be the sample means of two independent random samples of sizes n_1 and n_2 drawn from two normal populations having means μ_1 and μ_2. To test whether the two population means are equal ($n_1 < 30, n_2 < 30$). Let the null hypothesis be $H_0 : \mu_1 = \mu_2$.

Then the Altermative Hypothesis $H_1 : \mu_1 \neq \mu_2$.

If the two population standard deviations σ_1 and σ_2 are equal, then $\sigma_1 = \sigma_2 = \sigma$ (suppose) and an unbiased estimate sample variance s^2 of the common variance σ^2 is given by

$$s^2 = \frac{n_1 s_1^2 + n_2 s_2^2}{n_1 + n_2 - 2}$$

where s_1^2 and s_2^2 are the two sample variances.

Assuming that H_0 is true, the test statistic t is given by the formula

$$t = \frac{\overline{X}_1 - \overline{X}_2}{\text{S.E. of } (\overline{X}_1 - \overline{X}_2)}$$

where $\text{S.E. of } (\overline{X}_1 - \overline{X}_2) = s\sqrt{\frac{1}{n_1} + \frac{1}{n_2}}$

Hence $t = \dfrac{\overline{X}_1 - \overline{X}_2}{s\sqrt{\frac{1}{n_1} + \frac{1}{n_2}}}$

Follows t distribution with $(n_1 + n_2 - 2)$ degrees of freedom. The calculated value of $|t|$ is compared with the table value of t (See Appendix Table III) at α level of significance at particular degrees of freedom. If $|t|$ calculated $>$ t-table value, (*i.e.*, $t_{\alpha,\, d.f.}$) then the null hypothesis is rejected, Otherwise accepted.

95% confidence limits for the difference of population means are

$$(\overline{X}_1 - \overline{X}_2) \pm t_\alpha\, s\sqrt{\frac{1}{n_1} + \frac{1}{n_2}}$$

where, $\alpha = 0.025$ (for two-tailed test, the value of $\alpha/2$ is taken for α).

EXAMPLE 11.3: A group of 15 normal children in a study had a mean serum iron level of 148 μg% and standard deviation of 44.03. Another group of 15 children with infantile cirrhosis of liver had mean serum iron level of 151 μg% and standard deviation of 49.04. Is the difference between the two serum means statistically significant ?

[Given $t_{0.05, 28} = 2.05$]

SOLUTION: Here $n_1 = 15$, $\bar{X}_1 = 148$, $s_1 = 44.03$

$$n_1 = 15, \ \bar{X}_2 = 151, s_2 = 49.04$$

$$\therefore \quad s^2 = \frac{n_1 s_1^{\ 2} + n_2 s_2^{\ 2}}{n_1 + n_1 - 2}$$

$$= \frac{15 \times (44.03)^2 + 15 \times (49.04)^2}{15 + 15 - 2}$$

$$= \frac{29079.61 + 36073.82}{28}$$

$$s^2 = \frac{65153.43}{28} = 2326.91$$

$$\therefore \quad s = \sqrt{2326.91} = 48.24$$

Let the null hypothesis be $H_0 : \mu_1 = \mu_2$. Then the alternative hypothesis $H_1 : \mu_1 \neq \mu_2$.

Assuming that H_0 is true, the test statistic is

$$t = \frac{\bar{X}_1 - \bar{X}_2}{s\sqrt{\dfrac{1}{n_1} + \dfrac{1}{n_2}}}$$

$$= \frac{148 - 151}{48.24\sqrt{\dfrac{1}{15} + \dfrac{1}{15}}}$$

$$= \frac{-3}{17.61}$$

$$= -0.17$$

$$\therefore \quad |t| = 0.17$$

Also $\quad$ $$\text{d.f.} = n_1 + n_2 - 2$$

$$= 15 + 15 - 2 = 28$$

$|t| = 0.17 < t_{0.05, 28} = 2.05 \Rightarrow$ the null hypothesis is accepted $\Rightarrow$ there is no significant difference between the two serum means.

EXAMPLE 11.4: A group of 7 patients treated with medicine 'A' weigh 35, 39, 40, 42, 51, 48, 60 Kg. Another group of 9 patients from the same ward of a hospital treated with medicine 'B' weigh 53, 56, 60, 62, 67, 43, 64, 45, 54 Kg. Do you agree with the claim that medicine 'B' increases the weight significantly? ($t_{0.05, 14} = 2.145$)

SOLUTION: Let the null hypothesis be $H_0 : \mu_1 = \mu_2$, the altrenative hypothesis is $H_1 : \mu_1 < \mu_2$ (left-tailed test) according to the condition, *i.e.*, Medicine 'B' increases the weight significantly. Assuming H_0 be true. We have

$$s^2 = \frac{n_1 s_1^2 + n_2 s_2^2}{n_1 + n_2 - 2}$$

and
$$t = \frac{\bar{X}_1 - \bar{X}_2}{s\sqrt{\frac{1}{n_1} + \frac{1}{n_2}}}$$

Calculation for s^2

X_1	$(X_1 - \bar{X}_1)$		X_2		
35	−10	100	53	−3	9
39	−6	36	56	0	0
40	−5	25	60	4	16
42	−3	9	62	6	36
51	6	36	67	11	121
48	3	9	43	−13	169
60	15	225	64	8	64
			45	−11	121
			54	−2	4
ΣX_1 = 315	—	Σ = 440	ΣX_2 = 504	—	Σ = 540

$$\bar{X}_1 = \frac{315}{7} = 45; \quad \bar{X}_2 = \frac{504}{9} = 56$$

$$n_1 s_1^2 = \Sigma (X_i - \bar{X}_1)^2 = 440$$

and
$$n_2 s_2^2 = \Sigma (X_2 - \bar{X}_2)^2 = 540$$

$\because$
$$s^2 = \frac{n_1 s_1^2 + n_2 s_2^2}{n_1 + n_2 - 2} = \frac{440 + 540}{7 + 9 - 2} = \frac{980}{14} = 70$$

$\therefore$
$$s = \sqrt{70} = 8.37$$

Since
$$t = \frac{\bar{X}_1 - \bar{X}_2}{s\sqrt{\frac{1}{n_1} + \frac{1}{n_2}}}$$

$$\therefore \quad t = \frac{45 - 56}{8.37\sqrt{\frac{1}{7} + \frac{1}{9}}} = \frac{-11}{8.37 \times 0.50} = -2.61$$

$$\therefore \quad |t| = 2.61$$

Since $|t| = 2.61 > t_{0.05,\,14} = 2.14$ (table value) $\Rightarrow$ the null hypothesis is rejected and we accept alternative hypothesis, H_1 which concluded that the medicine 'B' increases the weight significantly.

PAIRED t-TEST FOR THE DIFFERENCE OF MEANS

It is applied to paired data of independent observations from one sample only when each individual gives a pair of observation. Such situations are commonly faced in medical sciences, *e.g.*,

(i) To compare the effect of two drugs, given to same individuals in the sample at two different occasions. For example, adrenaline and noradrenaline on pulse rate, number of hours for which sleep is induced by two hypnotics.

(ii) To study the comparative accuracy of two different instruments, *e.g.*, two types of sphygmomanometers.

(iii) To study the role of a factor or cause when the observations are made before and after its play, *e.g.*, of exertion on pulse rate; of meals on leucocyte count; effect of a drug on blood pressure; of garlic on cholesterol levels in the blood.

(iv) To compare results of two different laboratory techniques, *e.g.*, estimation of haemoglobin by Tallquist and Sahli's methods; examination of stools for hookworm ova by zinc floatation and concentration methods.

Testing by this methods, eliminates individual sampling variations because the sample is one and the observations on each person in the sample are taken before and after the experiment.

For testing the significance diference

(a) Let $D = (X_1 - X_2)$ be the difference in each set of paired observations before and after the experiment.

(b) Calculate the mean of the difference, $\overline{D} = \frac{\Sigma D}{n}$

(c) Calculate $\Sigma (D - \overline{D})^2$ and $s = \sqrt{\frac{\Sigma (D - \overline{D})^2}{n - 1}}$

(d) Calculate estimated Standard Error of difference *i.e.*, S.E. $(\bar{D}) = \frac{s}{\sqrt{n}}$

Let the null hypothesis be $H_0 : \mu_1 = \mu_0$ or $\bar{D} = 0$, *i.e.*, there is no difference between the means of before and after observations.

Then the alternative hypothesis is $H_1 : \mu_1 \neq \mu_2$ (Two-tailed test) or $H_1 : \mu_1 < \mu_2$ or $H_1 : \mu_1 > \mu_2$ (one tailed test).

(e) Calculate 't' value with the help of test statistic

$$t = \frac{\bar{D}}{S.E.(\bar{D})} \quad \text{where S.E. } (\bar{D}) = \frac{s}{\sqrt{n}}$$

and
$$s^2 = \frac{1}{n-1}\left[\Sigma D^2 - \left(\frac{\Sigma D}{\sqrt{n}}\right)^2\right]$$

If the calculated value of $|t| < t_\alpha$, $(n - 1)$ d.f. then the null hypothesis is accepted and in case of calculated value of $|t| > t_\alpha$, $(n - 1)$ the null hypothesis is rejected and alternative hypothesis is accepted.

EXAMPLE 11.5: Systolic blood pressure of six hypertensive patients were 183, 179 165, 190, 175 and 180 m.m. of Hg. After administration of a particular drug for one week the B.Ps. were 187, 175, 150, 180, 180 and 170 m.m. of Hg respectively. Could such differences arise due to chance? [Given $t_{0.01,5} = 4.03$]

SOLUTION: Null hypothesis $H_0 : \mu_1 = \mu_0$ or $\bar{D} = 0$ then the Alternative hypothesis $H_1 : \mu_1 \neq \mu_2$.

Calculation for $\bar{D}$ and estimated variance s^2

Patients	B.P. before drug (X_1)	B.P. after drug (X_2)	Difference $D = X_1 - X_2$	D^2
1.	183	187	−4	16
2.	179	175	4	16
3.	165	150	15	225
4.	190	180	10	100
5.	175	180	−5	25
6.	180	170	10	100
			$\Sigma D = 30$	$\Sigma D^2 = 482$

Mean Difference $\bar{D} = \frac{\Sigma D}{n} = \frac{30}{6} = 5$

$$\text{Estimated variance, } s^2 = \frac{1}{n-1}\left[\Sigma D^2 - \left(\frac{\Sigma D}{\sqrt{n}}\right)^2\right]$$

$$= \frac{1}{6-1}\left[482 - \frac{30^2}{6}\right]$$

$$= \frac{1}{5}\left[482 - \frac{900}{6}\right] = \frac{1}{5}[482 - 150]$$

$$\therefore \qquad s^2 = \frac{1}{5} \times 332 = 66.4$$

or

$$s = \sqrt{66.4} = 8.15$$

$$\text{Standard Error of } \overline{D} = \frac{s}{\sqrt{n}} = \frac{8.15}{2.45} = 3.33$$

$$\text{Test statistic, } t = \frac{\overline{D}}{\text{S.E. of } \overline{D}} = \frac{5}{3.33} = 1.5$$

Since the calculated value of $|t| = 1.5$ is less than table value of $t_{0.04, 5} = 4.03$ (*i.e.*, Table value of t and 1% l.s. with 5 d.f.).

Hence we accept the null hypothesis and conclude that there is no significance difference between the means of before and after observations (*i.e.*, any difference one out of 100 is probably due to chance).

EXAMPLE 11.6: In order to determine the effect of certain oral contraceptive on weight gain, nine healthy females were weighed prior to the start of its use and again at the end of a 3 months period.

Subject No.	Initial weight (kg.)	Weight after 3 months (kg)
1.	48.0	49.2
2.	56.4	57.2
3.	52.0	56.0
4.	60.0	58.0
5.	54.0	56.0
6.	56.0	57.2
7.	48.0	47.2
8.	56.0	56.4
9.	52.0	52.8

Is there a sufficient evidence to conclude that females experience gain in weight following 3 months of the oral contraceptive use?

SOLUTION: Null hypothesis, $H_0 : \mu_1 = \mu_2$, *i.e.,* there is no weight gain after 3 months of the oral contraceptive use.

Alternative hypothesis, $H_1 : \mu_1 \neq \mu_2$ (Two Tailed test).

Subject No.	Initial weight (kg.)	Weight after 3 months (kg.)	Difference D	D^2
1.	48.0	49.2	– 1.2	1.44
2.	56.0	57.2	– 0.8	0.64
3.	52.0	56.0	– 4.0	16.00
4.	60.0	58.0	2.0	4.00
5.	54.0	56.0	– 2.0	4.00
6.	56.0	57.2	– 1.2	1.44
7.	48.0	47.2	0.8	0.64
8.	56.0	56.4	– 0.4	0.16
9.	52.0	52.8	– 0.8	0.64
Total	–	–	$\Sigma D = -7.6$	$\Sigma D^2 = 28.96$

Mean difference $\bar{D} = \frac{\Sigma D}{n} = \frac{-7.6}{9} = -0.84$

Estimated variance, $s^2 = \frac{1}{n-1}\left[\Sigma D^2 - \left(\frac{\Sigma D}{\sqrt{n}}\right)^2\right]$

$$= \frac{1}{9-1}\left[28.96 - \frac{57.76}{9}\right]$$

$$= \frac{1}{8}[28.96 - 6.42] = \frac{1}{8} \times 22.54$$

∴ $s^2 = 2.82$

or $s = \sqrt{2.82} = 1.68$

Standard Error of difference, S.E. $(\bar{D}) = \frac{s}{\sqrt{n}}$

∴ S.E. $(\bar{D}) = \frac{1.68}{\sqrt{9}} = \frac{1.68}{3} = 0.56$

Test statistic, $t = \frac{\bar{D}}{\text{S.E. of } (\bar{D})} = \frac{0.84}{0.56} = 1.5$

Since | t | = 1.5 < table value of $t_{0,01,8}$ = 3.3 ⇒ the null hypothesis is accepted, *i.e.*, there is no weight gain after 3 months of the oral contraceptive use.

➤ EXERCISES ≺

11.1. A random sample of 900 children was found to have mean skinfold thickness at triceps of 3.4 mm with a standard deviation of 2.3 mm. Can it be reasonably regarded as a representative sample of a population having a mean thickness of 3.2 mm ?

11.2. A random sample of 15 individuals with a mean Hb% of 13.5 and standard deviation of 1.5. Test the hypothesis that the mean Hb% of the population is 14.3.

11.3. In an infantile paralysis epidemic 500 persons contracted the disease. 300 received no serum treatment and of those 75 became paralysed. Of those who did receive serum treatment 65 became paralysed. Was the serum treatment effective ?

11.4. A college conducts both day and night classes intended to be identical. A sample of 100 day students yields examination results are given below:

$$\overline{X}_1 = 72 \text{ and } \sigma_1 = 14.$$

Another sample of 200 night students yields examination results as $\overline{X}_2 = 74$ and $\sigma_2 = 18$. Are the two means statistically equal to 5% level of significance?

11.5. The standard deviation of the height of students of a college is 4 cm. Two samples are taken. The standard deviation of 96 M.B.B.S.-II year students is 3.67 cm. and 54 M.B.B.S.-I year students is 4.2 cm. Test the significance of the difference of standard deviations of the samples.

11.6. In a random sample of 300 students from a medical college 120 are girls. Can it be said that boys and girls are in the ratio 5:3 in the college?

11.7. In the following table, the gain in weights (in kgs.) of cows fed on two diets A and B:

Diet A:	24	25	32	30	32	14	30			
Diet B:	40	24	40	22	34	31	34	42	35	30

Test at 5% level whether the two diets differ as regards their effect on mean increase in weight [$t_{0.05,15}$ = 2.13].

11.8. The erythrocyte sedimentation rate (mm/hour) of 20 male and 10 female T.B. patients before start of the treatment is given below.

Examine the siginificance of the difference in the means. The E.S.R. mm/hr. are as follows:

MALE : 60, 65, 82, 43, 68, 107, 115, 118, 75, 90, 95, 128, 120, 65, 82, 110, 84, 75, 105, 120.

FEMALE : 85, 90, 65, 100, 105, 125, 95, 98, 110, 65.

[$t_{0.01, 28} = 3.67$]

11.9. Serum digoxin levels were determined for 10 healthy males aged 20-45 years, following rapid intravenous injection of the drug. The measurements were made 4 hours after the injection and again at the end of an 8 hour period :

Serum digoxin concentration μg/ml		
Subject No.	**After 5 hrs.**	**After 8 hrs.**
1.	1.3	1.2
2.	0.9	0.7
3.	1.1	1.0
4.	1.3	1.3
5.	1.0	1.0
6.	1.1	1.0
7.	1.0	1.0
8.	0.9	0.8
9.	1.0	1.0
10.	1.3	1.2

Test the efficiency of the drug. [$t_{0.01, 9} = 3.25$]

11.10. A certain stimulus administered to each of the 10 patients resulted in the following increase of blood pressure.

2, – 1, 8, 5, 3, – 2, 5, 0, 4 and 6.

Can it be concluded that the stimulus will, in general, be accompanied by an increase in blood pressure?

[Given for 9 d.f., $t_{0.01} = 3.25$]

11.11. A group of 7 patients of RHD with distension of abdomen due to ascites, affecting breathing capacity were treated. Could the change noted in the breathing capacity given in the following table be attributed to treatment ? [Given $t_{0.01, 6} = 3.71$]

Max. breathing	Serial No. of patients						
Capacity (L/min)	1	2	3	4	5	6	7
Before treatment	102	88	32	82	36	56	80
After treatment	130	116	50	82	61	64	94

11.12. The soporific effect of drugs A and B was studied on 10 patients seperately. The results were assessed for the additional hours of sleep produced by the drugs. Compare soporific effects of the drugs from the following data :

Additional hours of sleep	Serial No. of patients									
	1	2	3	4	5	6	7	8	9	10
Drug A	0.8	1.6	0.2	1.2	0.2	3.4	3.8	0.9	0.1	2.2
Drug B	1.8	0.8	1.2	0.1	0.2	4.5	5.2	1.6	4.3	3.4

[Given $t_{0.05,\,9} = 2.26$]

11.13. In a clinical trial to assess the value of new tranquillizer on psychoneurotic patients with each patient being given a week's treatment with the drug, the drug was considered effective if it lowered anxiety score after treatment. Test the efficacy of drug on the following data:

Before treatement :	7	22	19	16	18	22	12	14	11	20
After treatment :	8	18	11	12	14	23	11	16	19	12

[Given $t_{0.05,\,9} = 2.26$]

11.14. The height (cms) of 10 males of a given community are found to be 162, 167, 172, 168, 170, 164, 166, 170, 168, 163. Is it reasonable to believe that the average height is greater than 164 cms? [Given $t_{0.05,\,9} = 1.83$]

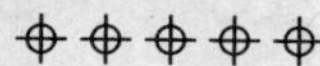

CHAPTER

12

Chi-Square Test

- *Non Parametric*
- *Contingency Table*
- *Distribution*
- *Goodness of Fit*
- *Experimental*
- *Expected*

Chi-square distribution is an important continuous probability distri-bution, first formulated by Helmert and then developed by Karl Pearson. Chi-square test is a non-parametric test not based on any summary values of population. This test is most commonly used when data are in frequencies such as in the number of responses in two or more categories. It can be used with any data which can be reduced to proportions or percentages. Chi-square test is denoted by Greek letter χ^2 and pronounced by 'kye square'. It is defined as:

$$\chi^2 = \sum \frac{(O-E)^2}{E}$$

where O is the observed frequency and E is the expected frequency of the same event (or for the same cell).

Values of Chi-square at various levels of significance with various degrees of freedom are given in (See Appendix Table IV).

OBSERVED AND EXPECTED FREQUENCIES

In many cases, it is seen that the results obtained in samples do not agree exactly with theoretical results expected according to rules of probability, *e.g.*, if we toss a fair coin 50 times, theoretically we may expect 25 heads and 25 tailes, but it is rare to obtain these results in practice. If, in a particular sample, a set of possible events $A_1, A_2, ..., A_n$ are observed to occur with frequencies $O_1, O_2, ..., O_n$ and according to probability rules $A_1, A_2, ..., A_n$ are expected to occur with frequencies $E_1, E_2, ..., E_n$ then frequencies $O_1, O_2, ..., O_n$ are called observed (or experimental) frequencies and $E_1, E_2, ..., E_n$ are called expected (or theoretical) frequencies. This is illustrated in the following table:

Event	A_1	A_2	A_3 .... A_n
Observed Freequency	O_1	O_2	O_3 .... O_n
Expected Freequency	E_1	E_2	E_3 .... E_n

Two-way classification table or h × k table in which observed frequencies occupy **h** rows and **k** columns is called contingency table.

Expected frequency in a contingency table is calculated by the formula :

$$\text{Expected frequency} = \frac{\text{Row total} \times \text{Column total}}{\text{Grand total}}$$

DEGREES OF FREEDOM

The number of degrees of freedom is defined as the total number of observations minus the number of independent constraints (*i.e.*, restrictions) imposed on the observations. It is denoted by υ (neu).

For a contingency table with **h** rows and **k** columns, the degrees of freedom (d.f.) = (h – 1) (k – 1).

Properties of χ^2 Distribution

1. Chi-square values increase with the increase in degrees of freedom.
2. The value of χ^2 lies between 0 and ∞.
3. Chi-square curve is always positively skewed.
4. The mean of χ^2 distribution is the number of degrees of freedom and the standard deviation = $\sqrt{2\upsilon}$, where υ is the degrees of freedom.

Applications of χ^2 Test: It is mainly applied

(a) to test the goodness of fit,

(b) to test the independence of attributes,

(c) to test the homogeneity of the attributes in respect of a particular characteristic or it may also be used to test the population variance.

Conditions of Validity of Chi-square Test

χ^2 test can be used only when

(i) the total number of observations is large, *i.e.*, $n > 30$.

(ii) the observations are independent.

(iii) the expected frequency of any item of cell should not be less than 5. If it is less than 5, then frequencies taking from the preceding or succeeding frequency be pooled together in order to make it 5 or more than 5.

(A) CHI-SQUARE TEST OF GOODNESS OF FIT

Chi-square is a measure of probabilities of association between the attributes. It gives an idea about the divergence between the observed and expected frequencies, *i.e.*, to test whether the difference between the theoretical and observed values can be attributed to chance or not.

Let the null hypothesis H_0 be that there is no significant difference between the observed (or experimental) values and the corresponding expected (or theoretical) values.

The alternative hypothesis H_1 is that the above difference is significant.

If $O_1, O_2, \ldots\ldots\ldots, O_n$ be a set of observed frequencies and $E_1, E_2, \ldots\ldots\ldots, E_n$ the corresponding set of expected frequencies, then Chi-square statistic is

$$\chi^2 = \sum_{i=1}^{n} \frac{(O_i - E_i)^2}{E_i} = \frac{(O_1 - E_1)}{E_1} + \frac{(O_2 - E_2)}{E_2} + \ldots\ldots\ldots + \frac{(O_n - E_n)^2}{E_n}$$

Assuming that the null hypothesis H_0 is true, the test statistic χ^2 follows Chi-square distribution with $(n-1)$ degrees of freedom, where

$$\sum_{i=1}^{n} O_i = \sum_{i=1}^{n} E_i, \quad \textit{i.e.,} \quad \sum_{i=1}^{n} (O_i - E_i) = 0$$

If the calculated value of χ^2 > tabulated value of χ^2 at α level of significance, then the null hypothesis H_0 is rejected, otherwise H_0 is accepted.

EXAMPLE 12.1: In a community survey of 300 families with 5 children each revealed the following distribution:

No. of girls:	0	1	2	3	4	5
No. of boys:	5	4	3	2	1	0
No. of families:	12	48	86	100	44	10

Is the result consistent with the hypothesis that the male and female births are equally probable? (or fit a Binomial distribution and test the goodness of fit).

SOLUTION: Null Hypothesis H_0 : Male and Female births are equally probable, *i.e.,* p = q = 1/2 and Alternative hypothesis H_1: Male and Female births are not equally probable.

The expected frequency r of female births is given by

$$f(r) = N.\ {}^nC_r\, p^r q^{n-r}$$

where N = 300, n = 5, r = 0, 1, 2, 3, 4, 5,

$\therefore$ $f(0) = 300 \times {}^5C_0 \times (1/2)^0 \times (1/2)^{5-0}$

$\therefore$ $f(0) = 300 \times 1 \times 1 \times 1/32 = 9.37 \sim 9$

$f(1) = 300 \times {}^5C_1 \times (1/2)^1 \times (1/2)^{5-1}$

$= 300 \times 5 \times 1/2 \times 1/16 = 46.87 \sim 47$

$f(2) = 300 \times {}^5C_2 \times (1/2)^2 \times (1/2)^{5-2}$

$= 300 \times 10 \times 1/4 \times 1/8 = 93.75 \sim 94$

$f(3) = 300 \times {}^5C_3 \times (1/2)^3 \times (1/2)^{5-3}$

$= 300 \times 10 \times 1/8 \times 1/4 = 93.75 \sim 94$

$f(4) = 300 \times {}^5C_4 \times (1/2)^4 \times (1/2)^{5-4}$

$= 300 \times 5 \times 1/16 \times 1/2 = 46.87 \sim 47$

$f(5) = 300 \times {}^5C_5 \times (1/2)^5 \times (1/2)^{5-5}$

$= 300 \times 1 \times 1/32 \times 1 = 9.37 \sim 9$

$\therefore$ The expected or theoretical (Binomial) frequencies of female births are:

r	:	0	1	2	3	4	5
f(r)	:	9	47	94	94	47	9

Now we apply χ^2 test to examine the goodness of fit of the given data to the above binomial distribution.

Calculation for χ^2:

No. of families				
Observed Freq., O	Expected Freq., E	(O – E)	$(O-E)^2$	$\frac{(O-E)^2}{E}$
12	9	3	9	1.00
48	47	1	1	0.02
86	94	– 8	64	0.68
100	94	6	36	0.38
44	47	– 3	9	0.19
10	9	1	1	0.11
Total	—	—	—	2.38

$$\chi^2 = \sum \frac{(O-E)^2}{E} = 2.38$$

d.f. (Degrees of freedom) is 6 – 1 = 5

Since the number of observation is 6 and the number of linear constraints is 1.

The Table IV (see Appendix) values of χ^2 at 5% level of significance with 5 d.f. is 11.07.

Here, the χ^2 calculated = 2.38 < χ^2 tabulated = 11.07 at $\alpha = 0.05$, d.f. = 5.

We accept the null-hypothesis and conclude that the male and female births are equally probable.

EXAMPLE 12.2: The following mistakes per page were observed in a book:

No. of mistakes per page	0	1	2	3	4	5	6
No. of pages	135	70	25	6	0	3	2

Fit a Poisson distribution and test the goodness of fit (where $e^{-0.68} = 0.5066$).

SOLUTION: Null hypothesis, H_0 : the mistakes are distributed according to Poisson Probability law and Alternative hypothesis, H_1 : the mistakes are not distributed according to Poisson Probability law.

Computation of Test Statistic:

If **r** be the random variable devoting the number of mistakes per page, then the observed frequency distribution of **r** is given below:

Here, $N = \Sigma f = 241, \Sigma fr = 165$

$$\therefore \text{Mean, } m = \frac{\Sigma fr}{\Sigma f} = \frac{165}{241} = 0.68$$

Now the expected frequency of r mistakes per page is obtained by applying the Poisson Probability distribution law *i.e.,*

r	*f*	*fr*
0	135	0
1	70	70
2	25	50
3	6	18
4	0	0
5	3	15
6	2	12
Total	241	165

$$p(r) = \frac{N_e^{-m}\, m^r}{r!}\text{; where } r = 0, 1, 2, 3, 4, 5, 6$$

$$\therefore \quad f(0) = \frac{241 \times e^{-0.68} \times (0.68)^\circ}{0!}$$

$$= \frac{241 \times 0.5060 \times 1}{1}\text{, since } 0! = 1$$

$$= 122.09$$

$$f(1) = \frac{122.09 \times 0.68}{1} = 83.02$$

$$f(2) = \frac{122.09 \times (0.68)^2}{2} = 28.23$$

$$f(3) = \frac{122.09 \times (0.68)^3}{6} = 6.40$$

$$f(4) = \frac{122.09 \times (0.68)^4}{24} = 1.09$$

$$f(5) = \frac{122.09 \times (0.68)^5}{120} = 0.15$$

$$f(6) = \frac{122.09 \times (0.68)^6}{720} = 0.02$$

No. of mistakes (r)	Observed frequency (O_i)	Expected frequency (E_i)	$(O_i - E_i)$	$(O_i - E_i)^2$	$\frac{(O_i - E_i)^2}{Ei}$
0	135	122.09	12.91	166.67	1.37
1	70	83.02	– 13.02	169.52	2.04
2	25	28.23	– 3.23	10.43	0.37
3	6 }	6.40 }			
4	0 } 11	1.09 } 7.66	3.34	11.16	1.46
5	3 }	0.15 }			
6	2 }	0.02 }			
Total	241	241.00	0	–	5.24

$$\therefore \quad \chi^2 = \sum_{i=1}^{n} \frac{(O_i - E_i)^2}{Ei}$$

$$\chi^2 = 5.24$$

and the table value of χ^2 for 7 – 1 = 6 degrees of freedom and $\alpha = 0.05$ level of significance is 12.59.

Since $\chi^2_{calculated} = 5.24 < \chi^2_{(0.05, 6)} = 12.59 \Rightarrow$ the null hypothesis is accepted $\Rightarrow$ that the mistakes are distributed according to Poisson probability law. Hence the Poisson distribution is a good fit to the given data.

(B) TEST FOR INDEPENDENCE OF ATTRIBUTES

Let the observations be classified according to two attributes and the frequencies O_i in the different categories be shown in a two-way table, called contingency table. To test on the basis of the cell frequencies whether the two attributes are independent or not.

Under the null hypothesis H_0 that the two attributes are independent, the expected frequencies E_i of any cell may be obtained by the formula as:

$$E_i = \frac{\text{Row total} \times \text{Column total}}{\text{Grand total}}$$

The test statistic $\chi^2 = \sum \frac{(O_i - E_i)^2}{E_i}$

approximately follows chi-square distribution with υ = d.f.
where d.f. = (Number of rows – 1) × (Number of columns – 1)

Decision

If the calculated value of χ^2 > the table value of χ^2 with υ, d.f. at α level of significance, we reject the null hypothesis, otherwise we accept H_0.

EXAMPLE 12.3: Naphropathy was observed in 100 cases of each class of diabetics, divided into 4 classes as per severity of disease.

Class:	I	II	III	IV
Observed: frequency	8	15	14	7

Is this inequality in different classes due to severity?

[Given $\chi^2_{0.05,3} = 7.81$]

SOLUTION: Let the null hypothesis, H_0 be that the severity of disease and incidence of nephropathy are independent.

The alternative hypothesis, H_1 is that the severity of disease in diabetics does affect the incidence of nephropathy.

Assuming that H_0 is true, the expected frequency in each class should be the same,

i.e., $$\frac{8+15+14+7}{4}=11$$

and test statistic is given by

$$\chi^2 = \sum \frac{(O_i - E_i)^2}{E_i}$$

Calculation for χ^2:

O_i	E_i	$(O_i - E_i)$	$(O_i - E_i)^2$	$\frac{(O_i - E_i)^2}{E_i}$
8	11	−3	9	9/11 = 0.82
15	11	4	16	16/11 = 1.45
14	11	3	9	9/11 = 0.82
17	11	−4	16	16/11 = 1.45
Total	—	—	—	= 4.54

Here d.f. = 4 – 1 = 3

$$\chi^2 = \sum \frac{(O\ - E_i)^2}{E_i} = 4.54$$

As the table value of χ^2 at $\alpha = 0.05$ with 3 d.f. is 7.81 (See Appendix Table IV).

Since χ^2 calculated $= 4.54 < \chi^2_{0.05,3} = 7.81 \Rightarrow H_0$ is accepted $\Rightarrow$ the severity of disease in diabetics does not affect the incidence of nephropathy.

Chi-square Test for 2 × 2 Table

For 2 × 2 contingency table, *i.e.*, two rows and two columns; the χ^2 value can be calculated directly without finding out the expected frequencies.

For illustration, 2 × 2 contingency table is given below:

Disease status	Male	Female	Total
With disease	a	b	(a + b)
Without disease	c	d	(c + d)
Total	(a + c)	(b + d)	a + b + c + d = N

where a, b, c, and d are the frequencies in the respective cells and N = (a + b + c + d) is the total sample size.

Now, $$\chi^2 = \frac{N(ad - bc)^2}{(a+b)(c+d)(a+c)(b+d)}$$

With d.f. $= (R-1)(C-1) = (2-1)(2-1) = 1$

Since, the χ^2 distribution in 2 × 2 table is discrete (*i.e.*, qualitative data), a correction for continuity is required which is called Yate's correction. Thus

$$\chi^2 = \frac{N(|ad - bc| - N/2)^2}{(a+b)(c+d)(a+c)(b+d)}$$

Note:

(i) Yate's correction for continuity is not used for larger than 2 × 2 contingency tables.

(ii) In 2 × 2 contingency table, if the frequencies in some of the cells are very small (*i.e.,* less than 5), Fisher's exact probability test should be applied.

EXAMPLE 12.4: Can we conclude with the data given below that growth status and exposure to infection are associated?

Growth status	Infected	Non-infected
Good	20 (a)	75 (b)
Poor	80 (c)	25 (d)

SOLUTION: Let the Null hypothesis, H_0 be that there is no association between growth status and exposure to infection. The alternative hypothesis, H_1 is that the exposure to infection is associated with growth status.

χ^2 is calculated by substituting the above values (*i.e.,* frequencies) in the formula as follows:

$$\chi^2 = \frac{N(ad - bc)^2}{(a+b)(c+d)(a+c)(b+d)}$$

$$= \frac{200(20 \times 25 - 75 \times 80)^2}{(20+75)(80+25)(20+80)(75+25)}$$

$$= \frac{200(500 - 6000)^2}{95 \times 105 \times 100 \times 100}$$

$$= \frac{200 \times 5500 \times 5500}{9500 \times 10500} = \frac{605000}{9975} = 60.7$$

The table value of χ^2 at $\alpha = 0.05$ with 1 degree of freedom is 3.84.

Since χ^2 calculated = 60.7 > $\chi^2_{(0.05, 1)}$ = 3.84 which implies that the null hypothesis is rejected and concluded that there is significant association between growth status and exposure to infection ($p < 0.05$).

Now by applying Yate's correction,

$$\chi^2_{\text{corrected}} = \frac{N(|ad - bc| - N/2)^2}{(a+b)(c+d)(a+c)(b+d)}$$

$$= \frac{200\,(|20\times25 - 75\times80| - 200/2)^2}{95\times105\times100\times100}$$

$$= \frac{200\,(5500 - 100)^2}{9500\times10500}$$

$$\therefore\ \chi^2_{\text{corrected}} = \frac{200\times5400\times5400}{9500\times10500} = \frac{583200}{9975}$$

$$\chi^2_{\text{corrected}} = 58.5 > \chi^2_{(0.05, 1)} = 3.84$$

also includes a significant association [$p < 0.05$].

Note: Yate's correction for continuity reduces the χ^2 value (*i.e.*, from χ^2 = 60.7 to χ^2_c = 58.5) but the conclusion is revealed the same.

FISHER'S EXACT PROBABILITY TEST

χ^2 test in 2 × 2 table relies on a large sample assumption and in such situations where a large sample assumptions is not valid, Fisher's exact test provides exact p-values for a given frequency table. Fisher's exact test computes the probability for occurrence of exactly the same frequencies as observed in each cell under null hypothesis. If the probability is less than 0.05, the null hypothesis is rejected. For example, if a, b, c, and d are the frequencies in the four cells of 2 × 2 contingency table. (a + b), (c + d) are the row totals and (a + c), (b + d) are the column totals, then the probability of observing the respective number of observation (*i.e.,* observed frequency) in each cell is given by:

$P = [\{(a+b)!\,(c+d)!\,(a+c)!\,(b+d)!\}] \div \{N!\,a!\,b!\,c!\,d!\}]$, where sign ! is used for factorial.

EXAMPLE 12.5: The number of boys and girls who are regular in their physical exercises is distributed as given below:

Habit	Boys	Girls	Total
Exercise regularly	2 (a)	7 (b)	9
Do not exercise regularly	8 (c)	3 (d)	11
Total	10	10	20 (N)

SOLUTION: Since the observed frequencies in some of the cells are less than 5, Chi-square will not yield correct probability, p-value as such. So in this case Fisher's exact probability test is appropriate to apply.

$$P = \frac{(9)!(11)!(10)!(10)!}{20!2!7!8!3!}$$

$$\therefore \quad P = \frac{(10)(9)(10)(9)(8)(9)(8)(7)(6)(5)(4)}{(20)(19)(18)(17)(16)(15)(14)(13)(12)}$$

$$= \frac{(9)(5)(3)}{(19)(17)(13)} = 0.032$$

Decision: P = 0.032 which is less then 0.05, it indicates that the differance between boys and girls in physical exercise habits is significant ($p < 0.05$).

EXAMPLE 12.6: From the following data, use χ^2-test and conclude whether inoculation is effective in preventing tuberculosis:

bit

Group	Attacked	Not Attacked	Total
Inoculated	10	90	100
Not inoculated	26	74	100
Total	36	164	200

SOLUTION: Let the Null hypothesis be that inoculation is not effective. The Alternative Hypothesis is that inoculation is effective. The expected frequencies are tabulated as below:

Group	Attacked		Not Attacked		Total
	O	E	O	E	
Inoculated	10(A)	18	90(C)	82	100
Not inoculated	26(B)	18	74(D)	82	100
Total	36		164		200

$\because$ Expected frequency $= \dfrac{\text{Row total} \times \text{Column total}}{\text{Grand total}}$

$\therefore$ Expected frequency of cell (A) $= \dfrac{100 \times 36}{200} = 18$

$\therefore$ Expected frequency of cell (B) $= \dfrac{100 \times 36}{200} = 18$

$\therefore$ Expected frequency of cell (C) $= \dfrac{100 \times 164}{200} = 82$

$\therefore$ Expected frequency of cell (D) $= \dfrac{100 \times 164}{200} = 82$

Calculation of χ^2:

Cell	Observed Frequency (O)	Expected Frequency (E)	$(O-E)^2$	$\dfrac{(O-E)^2}{E}$
A	10	18	$(-8)^2$	$64/18 = 3.555$
B	26	18	8^2	$64/18 = 3.555$
C	90	82	8^2	$64/82 = 0.780$
D	74	82	$(-8)^2$	$64/82 = 0.780$
Total	—	—		$\sum \dfrac{(O-E)^2}{E} = 8.67$

Assuming that H_0 is true, the test statistic is

$$\chi^2 = \sum \frac{(O-E)^2}{E} = 8.67$$

and $\upsilon = \text{d.f.} = (2-1)(2-1) = 1$

The table value of χ^2 at $\alpha = 0.05$ with 1 degree of freedom is 3.84 (See Appendix IV).

Since $8.67 > 3.84$, *i.e.*, $\chi^2(\text{calculated}) = 8.67 > \chi^2\ (\text{Table value}) = 3.84 \Rightarrow$ the null hypothesis is rejected and conclude that inoculation is effective.

EXAMPLE 12.7: A certain drug is claimed to be effective in curing colds. In an experiment of 164 people with cold, half of them were given the drug and half of them given sugar pills. The patients' reactions to the treatment are recorded in the following table. Test the hypothesis that the drug is not better than sugar pills for curing colds.

	Helped	Harmed	No effect
Drug:	52	10	20
Sugar Pills:	44	12	26

SOLUTION: Null hypothesis, H_0 is that the drug is not better than sugar pills. The alternative hypothesis, H_1 is that the drug is better than sugar pills.

The expected frequencies are tabulated as below:

	Helped		Harmed		No effect		Total
	O	E	O	E	O	E	
Drug	52	(48)	10	(11)	20	(23)	82
Sugar Pills	44	(48)	12	(11)	26	(23)	82
Total	96		22		46		164

$$\because \quad \text{Expected frequency} = \frac{\text{Row total} \times \text{Column total}}{\text{Grand total}}$$

$\therefore$ Expected frequency corresponding to each cell is given by

$$E_1 = \frac{82 \times 96}{164} = 48,$$

$$E_2 = 96 - 48 = 48,$$

$$E_3 = \frac{82 \times 22}{164} = 11,$$

$$E_4 = 22 - 11 = 11,$$

$$E_5 = \frac{82 \times 46}{164} = 23,$$

$$E_6 = 46 - 23 = 23.$$

Calculations for χ^2

Cell	Observed Frequency	Expected Frequency	$(O-E)^2$	$\frac{(O-E)^2}{E}$
1	52	48	4^2	16/48 = 0.33
2	10	11	$(-1)^2$	1/11 = 0.09
3	20	23	$(-3)^2$	9/23 = 0.39
4	44	48	$(-4)^2$	16/48 = 0.33
5	12	11	1^2	1/11 = 0.09
6	26	23	3^2	9/23 = 0.39
Total	—	—	—	$\frac{(O-E)^2}{E} = 1.62$

Assuming that H_0 is true, the test statistic

$$\chi^2 = \sum \frac{(O-E)^2}{E} = 1.62$$

and d.f. = (2 – 1) (3 – 1) = 2

$\chi^2 = 1.62$ and $\chi^2_{(0.05,\,2)} = 5.99$

Since $\chi^2_{calculated} = 1.62 < \chi^2_{(0.05,\,2)} \Rightarrow$ the null hypothesis is accepted $\Rightarrow$ the drug is not better than sugar pills.

(C) TEST FOR A SPECIFIED POPULATION VARIANCE

Suppose that a random sample $X_1, X_2, \ldots\ldots\ldots\ldots, X_n$ is drawn from a normal population with mean μ and variance σ^2. To test the hypothesis that the population variance σ^2 has a specified value σ_0^2.

Let the Null Hypothesis be $H_0 : \sigma^2 = \sigma_0^2$ (or $\sigma = \sigma_0$)

Then the Alternative hypothesis $H_1 : \sigma^2 \neq \sigma_0^2$ Two-tailed test or

$H_1 : \sigma^2 > \sigma_0^2$ (or $\sigma > \sigma_0$) One-tailed test

The test statistic is $\chi^2 = \sum \frac{(X_i - \bar{X})^2}{\sigma_0^2} = \frac{ns^2}{\sigma_0^2}$

where s^2 = Sample variance = $\frac{\Sigma(X_i - \bar{X})^2}{n}$

Assuming that H_0 is true, the test statistic χ^2 follows Chi-square distribution with (n – 1) degrees of freedom. If the calculated value of χ^2 > the tabulated value, we reject the null hypothesis H_0. Otherwise we accept H_0.

EXAMPLE 12.8: Weight in kg of 10 students are given below: 47, 42, 40, 52, 39, 45, 54, 49, 50, 44. Can we say that variance of the distribution of weights of all students from which the above sample of 10 students was drawn is equal to 20 kg? [$\chi^2_{0.05,\,9} = 16.92$]

SOLUTION: The Null hypothesis $H_0 : \sigma^2 = 20$

and the Alternative hypothesis $H_1 : \sigma^2 \neq 20$ (Two tailed test)

Here $\sigma_0^2 = 20$; sample mean $\bar{X} = \frac{\Sigma xi}{n} = \frac{462}{10} = 46.2$

Calculation for sample variance, s^2:

X_i	47	42	40	52	39	45	54	49	50	44
$(X_i - \bar{X})$	0.8	– 4.2	– 6.2	5.8	– 7.2	–1.2	7.8	2.8	3.8	– 2.2
$(X_i - \bar{X})^2$	0.64	17.64	38.44	33.64	51.84	1.44	60.84	7.84	14.4	4.84

Here $s^2 = \frac{\Sigma (X_i - \bar{X})^2}{n} = \frac{231.6}{10} = 23.16$

Assuming that H_0 is true,

$$\chi^2 = \frac{ns^2}{\sigma^2} = \frac{10 \times 23.16}{20} = 11.58$$

Degrees of freedom = (n – 1) = 10 – 1 = 9

Since the calculated value of χ^2 is 11.58 which is less than the table value of χ^2 at $\alpha = 0.05$ with 9 d.f. (*i.e.*, $\chi^2_{0.05, 9} = 16.92$).

Hence we accept the null hypothesis that the variance of the distribution of weights of all students in the population is 20 kg.

SNEDECOR'S F-DISTRIBUTION

It is a continuous probability distribution, first organised by G.W. Snedecor and named as F in honour of R.A. Fisher. It is used to test the equality of two population variances. It is defined as the ratio of two independent Chi-square variates divided by their respective degrees of freedom, *i.e.*,

$$F = \frac{\chi_1^2}{\upsilon_1} \div \frac{\chi_2^2}{\upsilon_2}$$

where υ_1 and υ_2 are degrees of freedom.

Test for Equality of Two Population Variances

Let two independent random samples of sizes n_1 and n_2 be drawn from two normal populations. To test the hypothesis that the two population variances σ_1^2 and σ_2^2 are equal.

The Null hypothesis $H_0 : \sigma_1^2 = \sigma_2^2$ and the alternative hypothesis $H_1 : \sigma_1^2 \neq \sigma_2^2$

The estimates of σ_1^2 and σ_2^2 are given by

$$\hat{\sigma}_1^2 = \frac{n_1 s_1^2}{n_1 - 1} \text{ and } \hat{\sigma}_2^2 = \frac{n_2 s_2^2}{n_2 - 1}$$

where s_1^2 and s_2^2 are the variances of the two samples. Assuming that H_0 is true, the test statistic

$$F = \hat{\sigma}_1^2 \div \hat{\sigma}_2^2 \quad \text{if } \hat{\sigma}_1^2 \geq \hat{\sigma}_2^2$$

or

$$F = \hat{\sigma}_2^2 \div \hat{\sigma}_1^2 \quad \text{if } \hat{\sigma}_2^2 \geq \hat{\sigma}_1^2$$

Follows F-distribution with $(n_1 - 1)$ and $(n_2 - 1)$ degrees of freedom.

Generally $\hat{\sigma}_1^2$ is greater than $\hat{\sigma}_2^2$ but if $\hat{\sigma}_2^2$ is greater than $\hat{\sigma}_1^2$, then in such cases the two variances should be interchanged so that the value of F is always greater than 1.

If the calculated value of F > the table value of F at 5% level of significance and respective d.f., we reject the null hypothesis H_0 and conclude that the variances σ_1^2 and σ_2^2 are not equal. Otherwise we accept the null hypothesis H_0.

EXAMPLE 12.9: In a sample of 10 observations, the sum of the squares of the deviations of items from their mean is 95. In another sample of 12 observations, the sum of the squares of the items is found to be 102. Test whether the difference is significant at 5% level. [Given, $F_{0.05,(9,11)} = 2.90$]

SOLUTION: Let the $H_0 : \sigma_1^2 = \sigma_2^2$, where σ_1^2 and σ_2^2 are the variances of two populations from which the samples are drawn.

$$H_1 : \sigma_1^2 \neq \sigma_2^2$$

We have
$$\hat{\sigma}_1^2 = \frac{\Sigma(x_i - \bar{x})^2}{n_1 - 1}$$

and
$$\hat{\sigma}_2^2 = \frac{\Sigma(y_i - \bar{y})^2}{n_2 - 1}$$

Here,
$$n_1 = 10,\ \Sigma(x_i - \bar{x})^2 = 95$$

and
$$n_2 = 12,\ \Sigma(y_i - \bar{y})^2 = 102$$

$\therefore$
$$\hat{\sigma}_1^2 = \frac{95}{(10-1)} = 10.56$$

and
$$\hat{\sigma}_2^2 = \frac{102}{(12-1)} = 9.27$$

Assuming that H_0 is true.

Since, $\hat{\sigma}_1^2 > \hat{\sigma}_2^2$, the test statistic is

$$F = \hat{\sigma}_1^2 \div \hat{\sigma}_2^2 = \frac{10.56}{9.27} = 1.14$$

Decision: The table value of F at 5% level for $\upsilon_1 = 9$ and $\upsilon_2 = 11$ degrees of freedom is $2.8962 \cong 2.9$ [see Appendix Table V(a)] and F calculated is 1.14 (*i.e.*, 1.14 is less than 2.90), we accept the H_0 and conclude that the difference is not significant ($p > 0.05$).

EXAMPLE 12.10: Two samples were drawn from two normal populations and their values are:

A: 66 67 75 76 82 84 88 90 92

B: 64 66 74 78 82 85 87 92 93 95 97

Test whether the two populations have the same variance at 5% level of significance.

SOLUTION: Let the Null hypothesis be $H_0 : \sigma_1^2 = \sigma_2^2$, where σ_1^2 and σ_2^2 are the variances of the two populations.

The alternative hypothesis is $H_1 : \sigma_1^2 \neq \sigma_2^2$ (Two tailed test)

Calculation for sample variance:

Sample A			Sample B		
X	$(X-\bar{X})$	$(X-\bar{X})^2$	Y	$(Y-\bar{Y})$	$(Y-\bar{Y})^2$
66	−14	196	64	−19	361
67	−13	169	66	−17	289
75	−5	25	74	−9	81
76	−4	16	78	−5	25
82	2	4	82	−1	1
84	4	16	85	2	4
88	8	64	87	4	16
90	10	100	92	9	81
92	12	144	93	10	100
			95	12	144
			97	14	196
$\Sigma X = 720$	—	$\Sigma(X-\bar{X})^2 = 734$	$\Sigma Y = 913$	—	$\Sigma(Y-\bar{Y})^2 = 1298$

$$\bar{X} = \frac{\Sigma x}{n_1} = \frac{720}{9} = 80, \qquad \bar{Y} = \frac{\Sigma y}{n_2} = \frac{913}{11} = 83$$

$$\hat{\sigma}_1^2 \text{ or } s_1^2 = \frac{\Sigma(X-\bar{X})^2}{n_1 - 1}; \qquad \hat{\sigma}_2^2 \text{ or } s_2^2 = \frac{\Sigma(Y-\bar{Y})^2}{n_2 - 1}$$

$$s_1^2 = \frac{734}{8} = 91.75; \qquad s_2^2 = \frac{1298}{10} = 129.8$$

Assuming that H_0 is true, the test statistic is -

$$F = \frac{s_2^2}{s_1^2} \text{ because } s_2^2 > s_1^2$$

$$\therefore F = \frac{129.8}{91.75} = 1.41 \text{ and d.f. are } (n_2 - 1) \text{ and } (n_1 - 1), \textit{ i.e.}, (10, 8)$$

The table value of F at 5% l.s. with 10 and 8 degrees of freedom is 3.35 [See Appendix Table V (a)].

Since the calculated value of F = 1.41 is less than the table value of F = 3.35, *i.e.*, F calculated = 1.41 < $F_{0.05}$ = 3.35 for 10 and 8 d.f. ⇒ H_0 is accepted ⇒ the two populations have the same variance.

➤ EXERCISES ≺

12.1. Determine if there is any association between whooping cough and tonsillectomy when in a random sample of 100 children of a school, 25 had a history of tonsillectomy and 60 of whooping cough and 10 had both while 25 had one. ($\chi^2_{0.005,\,1}$ = 3.84)

12.2. Ratio of male to female births in universe is expected to be 1:1. In one village it was found that male children born were 52 and female 48. Is this difference due to chance?

12.3. From the data given in the following table test whether the prevalence of Scabies in two sexes is significantly different:

Sex	Patients with Scabies	Patients without Scabies
Male	117	1041
Female	55	764

($\chi^2_{0.01,1}$ = 6.64)

12.4. The following table gives the results of neomycin prophylaxis in cross-infection of burns during first 14 days.

Dressing with	Staphylococcal Infection Acquired	Staphylococcal Infection Not acquired	Total
Penicillin cream plus neomycin	5	28	33
Penicillin cream alone	18	12	30
Total	23	40	63

What conclusions will you draw from this data?

12.5. To test the efficacy of a new drug a controlled experiment was conducted wherein 300 patients were administered the new drug and 200 other patients were not given the drug. The patients were monitored and the results were obtained as follows:

	Cured	Condition worsened	No effect	Total
Given the drug	200	40	60	300
Not given the drug	20	30	50	200

Use χ^2-test for finding the effect of the drug. [Given ($\chi^2_{00.5,\,2}$ = 5.99]

12.6. For a sterilization program to be really effective in controlling the birth rate, suppose it is desired that the acceptors must be in accordance with the following pattern:

Parity:	1	2	3	4 and above
Percentage:	15	55	25	5

In a sample of 200 acceptors, the distribution by parity was 30, 76, 52 and 42 respectively. Is this pattern significantly different from the desired?

12.7. The following table gives the classification of 100 workers according to sex and the nature of work. Test whether the nature of work is independent of the sex of the work:

	Male	Female
Skilled	40	20
Unskilled	10	30

12.8. Two groups of 100 people each were taken for testing the use of a vaccine. 15 persons contracted the disease out of the inoculated persons, while 25 contracted the disease in the other group. Test the efficiency of vaccine using χ^2-test. [Given $\chi^2_{0.05.1} = 3.84$].

12.9. There is a general belief that high income families and their children to public schools and low income families send their children to Govt. Schools. The following results are obtained :

Income	Public Schools	Govt. Schools
Low	100	200
High	500	200

Use χ^2 test to determine whether income level and the type of schooling are associated.

12.10. A dice is tossed 120 times with the following results:

Number turned up:	1	2	3	4	5	6
Frequency:	28	35	15	10	18	14

Test the hypothesis that the dice is unbiased. [Given $\chi^2_{0.05,\,5} = 11.07$]

12.11. A study is made of the relationship between a certain disease and the healing of wounds among certain hospital patients. The results are as follows:

	Normal Healing	Prolonged Healing
Diseased	10	4
Not diseased	8	2

Is there any evident relationship between the disease and healing time?

12.12. In a sample of 13 observations, the sum of the squared deviations of items from the mean was 105.5 whereas another sample of 15 observations, the value was found to be 115.2. Test whether the difference is significant at 5% level. [Given, $F_{(11,\ 14)\ \text{at}\ \alpha = 0.05} = 2.53$]

12.13. Two random samples are drawn two normal populations and the following results were obtained:

Sample A: 116 119 120 122 125 127 128 130

Sample B: 101 105 111 112 116 118

Test whether the two populations have the same variance at 5% level of significance. [Given, $F_{0.05\ (5,\ 7)} = 3.97$]

CHAPTER

13

Correlation and Regression

- *Relationship*
- *Multiple*
- *Prediction*
- *Partial*
- *Logistic*
- *Linear*

Sometimes two continuous characters (or variables) are measured in the same person such as height and weight, temperature and pulse rate, age and weight, age and height, circulating protein (in gms.) and surface area (in meter^2), etc. At other times the same character is measured in two related groups such as tallness in parents and tallness in children, intelligent quotient (IQ) in brothers and in corresponding sisters (siblings). The relationship or association between two quantitatively measured or continuous variables is called correlation. Correlation is a statistical measure for finding out degree (or strength) of association between two variables. By 'association' we mean the tendency of the variables to move together. If two variables X and Y are so related that movements (or variations) in one tend to be accompanied by the corresponding movements (or variations) in the other, the X and Y are said to be correlated. The movements may be in the same direction (*i.e.*, either both X and Y increase or both of them decrease) or in opposite direction (*i.e.*, one, X increases and other, Y decreases). Correlation is said to be positive or negative according as these movements are in the same or in the opposite directions. If Y is unaffected by any change in X, then X and Y are said to be uncorrelated.

Correlation may be linear or non-linear. If the amount of variation in X bears a constant ratio to the corresponding amount of variation in Y, then correlation between X and Y is said to be linear. Otherwise it is non-linear.

The degree or extent of linear relationship between two variables is measured by Karl Pearson's coefficient of correlation or simply correlation coefficient and denoted byt 'r'.

The extent or degree of correlation varies between –1 and +1, *i.e.*, $-1 \leq r \leq 1$.

There are five types of correlation depending on its extent and direction.

(i) *Perfect positive correlation*: In this, the two variables X and Y are directly proportional and fully correlated with each other (*i.e.*, r = + 1, both variables rise or fall in the same proportion).

(ii) *Perfect negative correlation*: When one variable, X rises and other variable, Y falls in the same proportion (*i.e.*, two variables X and Y are inversely proportional to each other). In this case r = –1.

(iii) *Partial positive correlation*: In this case, $0 < r < 1$ (*i.e.*, non-zero values of coefficient of correlation lie in between 0 and +1).

(iv) *Partial negative correlation*: The non-zero values lie between –1 and 0 (*i.e.*, $-1 < r < 0$).

(v) *Absolutely no correlation*: In this case, r = 0 indicating no linear relationship exists between two variables.

Correlation between two variables may be determined by any one of the following methods:

(i) Scatter Diagram

(ii) Co-variance method or Karl Pearson's method

(iii) Rank method

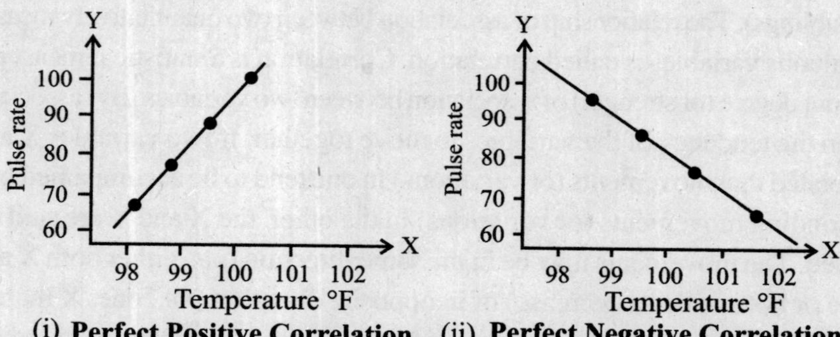

(i) **Perfect Positive Correlation** (ii) **Perfect Negative Correlation**

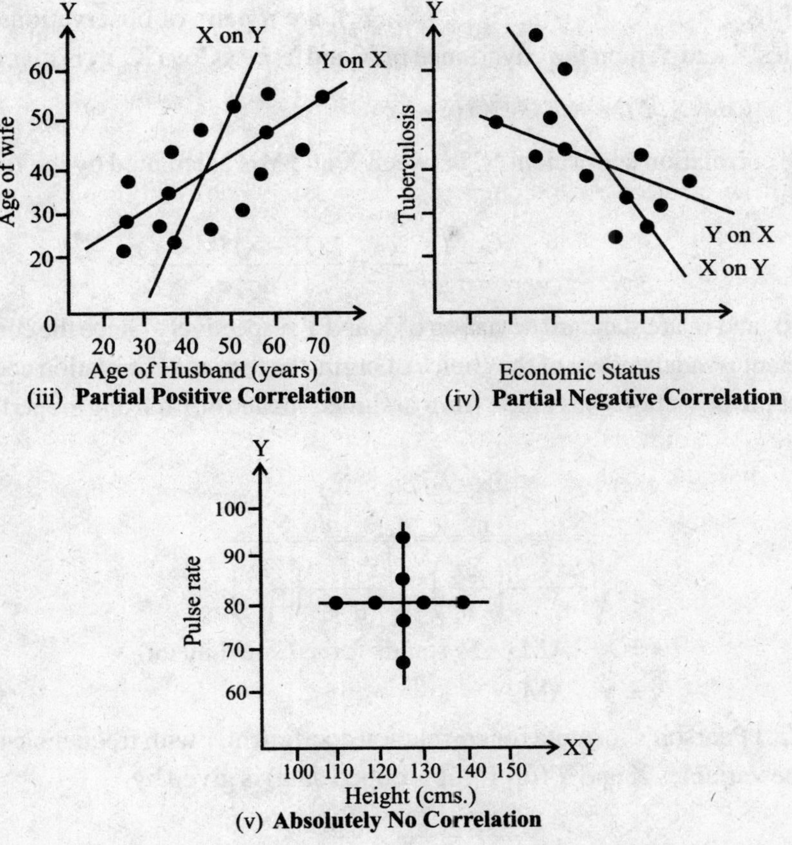

(iii) **Partial Positive Correlation**

(iv) **Partial Negative Correlation**

(v) **Absolutely No Correlation**

Fig. 13.1: The above scatter diagrams are based on Hypothetical data for illustration purpose

(i) Scatter Diagram

The existence of correlation can be shown graphically means of a scatter diagram. Statistical data relating to simultaneous movements (or variations) of two variables can be represented by dots. One of the two variables, say X, is taken along the horizontal axis and the other variable, say, Y is taken along the vertical axis. All the pairs of values of X and Y are shown by dots on the graph paper. This diagramatic representaion of bivariate data is known as scatter diagram (see Fig. 13.1).

(ii) Correlation Coefficient (r) by Covariance Method (or Karl Pearson's method)

When associated variables are normally distributed such as height and weight, the correlation coefficient 'r' is calculated by covariance method.

If $(X_1, Y_1), (X_2, Y_2), \ldots\ldots\ldots, (X_n, Y_n)$, are n pairs of observations on two variables X and Y, then the covariance of X and Y, *i.e.*, Cov (X, Y) is given by

$$\text{Cov}(X, Y) = \frac{1}{n}\Sigma(X - \overline{X})(Y - \overline{Y})$$

and the correlation coefficient 'r' between X and Y is calculated by the following formula:

$$r = \frac{\text{Cov}(X, Y)}{\sigma_x \sigma_y} = \frac{\Sigma(X - \overline{X})(Y - \overline{Y})}{n\sigma_x\sigma_y}$$

where σ_x and σ_y are standard deviation of X and Y respectively. Since the correlation coefficient is independent of the choice of orgin, the formula correlation coefficient r, when the deviations are taken from assumed mean (or r for ungrouped data) is given by

$$r = \frac{\frac{\Sigma xy}{n} - \frac{\Sigma x}{n} \times \frac{\Sigma y}{n}}{\sqrt{\frac{\Sigma x^2}{n} - \left(\frac{\Sigma x}{n}\right)^2}\sqrt{\frac{\Sigma y^2}{n} - \left(\frac{\Sigma y}{n}\right)^2}}$$

where $x = X - AM$ (AM stands for assumed mean)

$y = Y - AM$

I. Karl Pearson's formula for correlation coefficient, r with frequencies of both the variables X and Y (or 'r' for grouped data) is given by

$$r = \frac{\frac{\Sigma xy}{n} - \frac{\Sigma x}{n} \times \frac{\Sigma y}{n}}{\sqrt{\frac{\Sigma x^2}{n} - \left(\frac{\Sigma x}{n}\right)^2}\sqrt{\frac{\Sigma y^2}{n} - \left(\frac{\Sigma y}{n}\right)^2}}$$

II. Karl Pearson's formula for correlation coefficient, r is given by

$$r = \frac{\Sigma\, dx\, dy}{\sqrt{\Sigma\, dx^2\, \Sigma\, dy^2}}$$

where $dx = X - \overline{X}$ and $dy = Y - \overline{Y}$

Interpretation of 'r':

(i) The correlation coefficient is also subjected to sampling variation and hence observed value of 'r' is to be tested for its significance.

(ii) The standard error of 'r' is given by $\sqrt{(1 - r^2)/(n-2)}$.

(iii) The test of significance for 'r' is given by $t = r/\sqrt{[(1 - r^2)/(n-2)]}$ with (n – 2) degrees of freedom.

EXAMPLE 13.1: On entry to a school, an intelligence test was given to a small group of children. The following results obtained in that test and in a subsequent examination are:

Children Number	Intelligence Test Score	Marks in examination
1	7	10
2	6	7
3	5	4
4	7	5
5	8	4
6	9	7
7	6	4
8	8	7

Calculate the coefficient of correlation as a measure of closeness of association between the two variables.

SOLUTION: Calculation for 'r'

X	Y	$x = (X - \bar{X})$	$y = (Y - Y)$	x^2	y^2	xy
7	10	0	4	0	16	0
6	7	−1	1	1	1	−1
5	4	−2	−2	4	4	4
7	5	0	−1	0	1	0
8	4	1	−2	1	4	−2
9	7	2	1	4	1	2
6	4	−1	−2	1	4	2
8	7	1	1	1	1	1
$\Sigma X = 56$	$\Sigma Y = 48$	0	0	$\Sigma x^2 = 12$	$\Sigma y^2 = 32$	$\Sigma xY = 6$

$$\bar{X} = \frac{\Sigma X}{n} = \frac{56}{8} = 7$$

$$\bar{Y} = \frac{\Sigma X}{n} = \frac{48}{8} = 6$$

$$\therefore \quad r = \frac{\Sigma xy}{\sqrt{\Sigma x^2}\,\sqrt{\Sigma y^2}} = \frac{6}{\sqrt{12}\,\sqrt{32}} = \frac{6}{19.6} = 0.31$$

EXAMPLE 13.2: Calculate correction coefficient to show association between the following two variables:

No. of subject :	1	2	3	4	5	6	7	8	9	10
X :	2.0	3.0	4.5	5.0	6.0	7.0	7.5	8.5	9.5	10.0
Y :	1.5	2.0	3.5	3.5	3.5	4.0	3.0	4.5	4.5	5.0

SOLUTION: Calculation for coefficient correlation 'r'

X	Y	$x = (X - \overline{X})$	$y = (Y - \overline{Y})^2$	x^2	y^2	xy
2.0	1.5	−4.3	−2.0	18.5	4.0	8.6
3.0	2.0	−3.3	−1.5	10.9	2.3	5.0
4.5	3.5	−1.8	0	3.2	0	0
5.0	3.5	−1.3	0	1.7	0	0
6.0	3.5	−0.3	0	0.1	0	0
7.0	4.0	0.7	0.5	0.5	0.3	0.4
7.5	3.0	1.2	−0.5	1.4	0.3	−0.6
8.5	4.5	2.2	1.0	4.8	1.0	2.2
9.5	4.5	3.2	1.0	10.2	1.0	3.2
10.0	5.0	3.7	1.5	13.7	2.3	5.6
X = 63	ΣY = 35	—	—	$\Sigma x^2 = 65$	$\Sigma y^2 = 11.2$	Σxy=24.4

$$\overline{X} = \frac{\Sigma x}{n} = \frac{63}{10} = 6.3, \qquad \overline{Y} = \frac{\Sigma y}{n} = \frac{35}{10} = 3.5$$

$$r = \frac{\Sigma xy}{\sqrt{\Sigma x^2}\ \sqrt{\Sigma y^2}}$$

$$\therefore\ r = \frac{24.4}{\sqrt{65}\ \sqrt{11.2}} = 0.9$$

(iii) Rank Correlation (or Correlation by Rank Method)

Simple correlation coefficient is based on the magnitudes of the variable. But in many situations it is not possible to find the magnitude of the variable at all. Such as beauty and intelligency can not be measured in quantity. In such cases, it is possible to rank the individuals in some order. Rank correlation is based on the rank or the order of the variable. It is more suitable if the individuals (or variables) can be arranged in order of merit or proficiency. If the rank assigned to individuals range from 1 to N, then the correlation coefficient between two series of ranks is called Rank correlation coefficient, ρ (Rho).

The Spearman's Rank correlation coefficient is given by the formula:

$$\rho = 1 - \frac{6\Sigma D^2}{N\,(N^2 - 1)}$$

where D = difference between ranks of two series and N = Number of pairs of observations.

To ascertain rank: If in a series two or more individuals (or items) have the same score, then we find the average of the ranks of these individuals and allot this average rank to each of them. (See example).

EXAMPLE 13.3: Ten students got the following percentage of marks in Anatomy and Physiology:

% marks (X) in Anatomy	78	45	36	78	62	90	65	75	39	41
% marks (Y) in Physiology	84	55	50	60	82	86	58	60	47	51

Find the rank correlation coefficient.

SOLUTION:

X	Y	Rank (R_X)	Rank (R_Y)	Rank difference $D = (R_X - R_Y)$	D^2
78	84	2.5	2	0.5	0.25
45	55	7	7	0	0
36	50	10	9	1	1
78	60	2.5	4.5	– 2	4
62	82	6	3	3	9
90	86	1	1	0	0
65	58	5	6	– 1	1
75	60	4	4.5	– 0.5	0.25
39	47	9	10	– 1	1
41	51	8	8	0	0
Total	—	—	—	—	$\Sigma D^2 = 16.5$

$$\because \quad \rho = 1 - \frac{6\Sigma D^2}{N(N^2 - 1)}$$

$$\therefore \quad \rho = 1 - \frac{6 \times 16.5}{10\,(100 - 1)} = 1 - \frac{99}{990} = 0.9$$

EXAMPLE 13.4: Calculate the rank correlation coefficient (ρ) between X and Y for the following data:

X	92	89	87	86	83	77	71	63	53	50
Y	86	83	91	77	68	85	52	82	37	57

SOLUTION:

X	Y	Rank (R_X)	Rank (R_Y)	Rank difference $D = (R_X - R_Y)$	D^2
92	86	1	2	−1	1
89	83	2	4	−2	4
87	91	3	1	2	4
86	77	4	6	−2	4
83	68	5	7	−2	4
77	85	6	3	3	9
71	52	7	9	−2	4
63	82	8	5	3	9
53	37	9	10	−1	1
50	57	10	8	2	4
Total	—	—	—	–	$\Sigma D^2 = 44$

$$\because \quad \rho = 1 - \frac{6\Sigma D^2}{N(N^2-1)} = 1 - \frac{6 \times 44}{10(100-1)} = 1 - 0.27$$

$$\therefore \quad \rho = 0.73$$

PARTIAL CORRELATION

Partial correlation is the degree of relationship between dependent variable and one particular independent variable when all other variables involved are kept constant, *i.e.*, when the effect of all other variables are removed. Partial correlation is measured by partial correlation coefficient.

Partial correlation coefficient between two variables x_1 and x_2, keeping x_3 constant is denoted by $r_{12.3}$ which refers to partial correlation between x_1 and x_2 holding the influence of x_3 constant. The formula for $r_{12.3}$ is given by

$$r_{12.3} = \frac{r_{1.2} - r_{1.3}\, r_{2.3}}{\sqrt{(1 - r_{1.3}^2)(1 - r_{2.3}^2)}}, \quad \text{where } -1 \le r_{12.3} \le 1$$

Similarly, $r_{13.2} = \dfrac{r_{1.3} - r_{1.2}\, r_{2.3}}{\sqrt{(1-r_{1.2}^2)(1-r_{2.3}^2)}}$ and $r_{23.1} = \dfrac{r_{2.3} - r_{1.2}\, r_{1.3}}{\sqrt{(1-r_{1.2}^2)(1-r_{1.3}^2)}}$

where $r_{13.2}$ is the coefficient of partial correlation between x_1 and x_3 keeping x_2 constant and $r_{23.1}$ is the coefficient of partial correlation between x_2 and x_3 keeping x_1 constant.

EXAMPLE 13.5: The correlation coefficient between weight (x_1), serum cholesterol (x_2) and diastolic BP (x_3) among 12 adult males are:

$r_{1.2} = 0.47$, $r_{1.3} = 0.62$ and $r_{2.3} = 0.92$. Determine the partial correlation coefficient between weight (x_1) and cholesterol (x_2) by keeping diastolic BP (x_3) constant.

SOLUTION: We have

$$r_{12.3} = \frac{r_{1.2} - r_{1.3}\, r_{2.3}}{\sqrt{(1-r_{1.3}^2)(1-r_{2.3}^2)}}$$

$$= \frac{0.47 - (0.62)(0.92)}{\sqrt{\{1-(0.62)^2\}\{1-(0.92)^2\}}}$$

$$= \frac{0.47 - 0.57}{\sqrt{(1-0.38)(1-0.85)}}$$

$$r_{12.3} = \frac{-0.10}{\sqrt{(0.62)(0.15)}} = \frac{-0.10}{\sqrt{0.093}} = \frac{-0.10}{0.30}$$

$\therefore \quad r_{12.3} = -0.33$

MULTIPLE CORRELATION

The degree of relationship existing between three or more variables is called multiple correlation. For example, if the weight a baby at birth is considered, the birth weight may be related to many factors such as age of the mother, period of gestation, gravida, health condition of the mother etc. The overall correlation of all these independent factors with the dependent factor is considered as multiple correlation. The multiple correlation is measured by coefficient of multiple correlation denoted by 'R'. For example, $R_{1.23}$ indicates that the variable x_1 is associated with the variables x_2 and x_3. The formula for $R_{1.23}$ is given by

$$R_{1.23} = \frac{\sqrt{r_{1.2}^2 + r_{1.3}^2 - 2r_{1.2}\, r_{1.3}\, r_{2.3}}}{1 - r_{2.3}^2}, \text{ where } 0 \le R_{1.23} \le 1$$

and $r_{1.2}$ is the correlation coefficient between x_1 and x_2,

$r_{1.3}$ is the correlation coefficient between x_1 and x_3,

and $r_{2.3}$ is the correlation coefficient between x_2 and x_3.

Similarly $$R_{2.34} = \sqrt{\frac{r_{2.3}^2 + r_{2.4}^2 - 2r_{2.3}^2\, r_{2.4} + r_{3.4}}{1 - r_{3.4}^2}}$$

and $$R_{1.24} = \sqrt{\frac{r_{1.2}^2 + r_{1.4}^2 - 2r_{1.2}\, r_{1.4}\, r_{2.4}}{1 - r_{2.4}^2}}$$

EXAMPLE 13.6: In a three-variate multiple correlation analysis the following results are as follows:

$$r_{1.2} = 0.82; \quad r_{1.3} = 0.2 \text{ and } \quad r_{2.3} = 0.45$$

Find the multiple correlation coefficient $R_{1.23}$.

SOLUTION: Since

$$R_{1.23} = \sqrt{\frac{r_{1.2}^2 + r_{1.3}^2 + 2r_{1.2}\, r_{1.3}\, r_{2.3}}{1 - r_{2.3}^2}}$$

$$R_{1.23} = \sqrt{\frac{(0.82)^2 + (0.68)^2 - 2(0.82)\,(0.68)\,(0.45)}{1-(0.45)^2}}$$

or $$R_{1.23} = \sqrt{\frac{0.67 + 0.46 - 0.50}{1 - 0.20}} = \sqrt{\frac{0.63}{0.80}}$$

∴ $$R_{1.23} = 0.89$$

REGRESSION

After having understood the correlation between two variables it is necessary to estimate or predict the value of one character (variable say Y) from the known value of the other character (variable say X) such as to estimate height when weight is known. This is possible when the two (variables) are linearly correlated. The variable (Y, *i.e.*, height) to be estimated is called dependent variable and the variable (X, *i.e.*, weight) which is known, is called independent variable. This is done by means of regression line or equation.

According to M.M. Blair: "Regression is the measure of the average relationship between two or more variables in terms of the original units of the data". The prediction or estimation of most likely values of one variable for specified values of the other is done by using suitable equations involving the two variables. Such equations are known as Regression Equations.

In linear regression the relationship between the two variables X and Y is linear (*i.e.*, straight line of the type $X = a + bY$ or $Y = a' + b'X$). In order to estimate the best average values of the two variables, two regression equations are required. One equation is used for estimating the value of X variable for a given value of Y variable and the second equation is used for estimating the value of Y variable for a given value of X variable. Therefore, the two lines of regression are:

(i) Regression equation of X on Y is

$$X - \overline{X} = r\frac{\sigma_x}{\sigma_y}(Y - \overline{Y})$$

(ii) Regression equation of Y on X is

$$Y - \overline{Y} = r\frac{\sigma_y}{\sigma_x}(X - \overline{X})$$

where X = Value of X; $\overline{X}$ = Mean of X values

Y = Value of Y; $\overline{Y}$ = Mean of Y values

σ_x = Std. Dev. of X values or series

σ_y = Std. Dev. of Y values or series

r = Correlation coefficient betwen X and Y

REGRESSION COEFFICIENTS

Regression coefficient of Y on X is denoted by b_{yx} and regression coefficient of X on Y is denoted by b_{xy}. These are found by either of the following three formulae:

(i) If correlation coefficient, r is already calculated, the regression coefficients are derived as $b_{yx} = \frac{r\sigma_y}{\sigma_x}$ and $b_{xy} = \frac{r\sigma_x}{\sigma_y}$

(ii) If means are already calculated, the regression coefficients are derived by the least-sqares method:

$$b_{yx} = \frac{\Sigma(X - \overline{X})(Y - \overline{Y})}{\Sigma(X - \overline{X})^2} = \frac{\Sigma xy}{\Sigma x^2}$$

and

$$b_{xy} = \frac{\Sigma(X - \overline{X})(Y - \overline{Y})}{\Sigma(Y - \overline{Y})^2} = \frac{\Sigma xy}{\Sigma y^2}$$

(iii) If means are not to be calculated, then a simple and direct method is adopted to find regression coefficient as

$$b_{yx} = \frac{\Sigma xy - \frac{\Sigma x \Sigma y}{n}}{\Sigma x^2 - \frac{(\Sigma x)^2}{n}} \text{ and } b_{yx} = \frac{\Sigma xy - \frac{\Sigma x \Sigma y}{n}}{\Sigma y^2 - \frac{(\Sigma y)^2}{n}}$$

EXAMPLE 13.7: The following results of the height and weight of 1000 students:

$\overline{Y} = 170$ cm; $\overline{X} = 60$ kg; $r = 0.6$, $\sigma_y = 6.5$ cm, $\sigma_x = 5$ kg. Anil weighs 45 kg. Sunil is 165 cm tall. Estimate the height of Anil from his weight and the weight of Sunil from his height.

SOLUTION: Here, Height = Y Weight = X

$$\overline{Y} = 170 \text{ cm}, \quad \overline{X} = 60 \text{ kg.}, \quad r = 0.6,$$
$$\sigma_y = 6.5 \text{ kg.}, \quad \sigma_x = 5 \text{ kg.}$$

(i) The regression equation of Y on X is

$$Y - \overline{Y} = r\frac{\sigma_y}{\sigma_x}(X - \overline{X})$$

or
$$Y - 170 = 0.6 \times \frac{6.5}{5}(X - 60)$$

$$\Rightarrow \quad Y = 170 = 0.78\,(X - 60)$$

$$\Rightarrow \quad Y = 170 + 0.78\,X - 46.8$$

$$\therefore \quad Y = 0.78\,X + 123.2$$

When Anil's weight $X = 45$ kg

Then his height Y will be $= 0.78 \times 45 + 123.2$

$= 35.1 + 123.2 = 158.3$ cms.

∴ Required height of Anil = 158.3 cms.

(ii) The regression equation of X and Y is

$$X - \overline{X} = r\frac{\sigma_x}{\sigma_y}(Y - \overline{Y})$$

or
$$X - 60 = 0.6 \times \frac{5}{6.5}(Y - 170)$$

$$\Rightarrow \quad X - 60 = 0.46\,(Y - 170)$$

$$\Rightarrow \quad X - 60 = 0.46\,Y - 78.2$$

$$\Rightarrow \quad X = 0.46\,Y + 60 - 78.2$$

$$\therefore \quad X = 0.46\,Y - 18.2$$

When Sunil's height $Y = 165$ cms.

Then his weight X will be $= 0.46 \times 165 - 18.2$

$= 75.9 - 18.2 = 57.7$ kg

∴ Required weight of Sunil = 57.7 kg.

REGRESSION LINE

Since in most instances of linear regression the points (dots) representing the individual pairs of values for the two variables will not all fall in such a way that every dot will fit on a straight linge (perfect correlation), the problem resolves itself into determining the equation of the straight line that best fits the dots, or in other words, the line around which the dots have the least scatter. This line is called a regression line and its equation can be found by a method known as least squares. This involves finding the line for which the sum of the squares of the distances of each observed point from the line shall be as small as possible. Let us consider a case, see Fig. 13.2, where for simplicity only three points, R, S and T have been plotted. If the distance from point R to the line be measured by d_R, that from S by d_S, and that from T by d_T, the problem is to find the equation of the line which will make $d_R^2 + d_S^2 + d_T^2$ a minimum. The general form of a straight line is $Y = a + bX$, where Y and X are two variables, 'a' the Y intercept (or the distance between the X-axis and the point where the line crosses the Y-axis) and 'b' the slope of the line (or the increase in the Y value per unit change in the X value).

The equation $Y = a + bX$ can also be written as

$$\Sigma Y = na + b\Sigma X$$

or

$$\sum \frac{Y}{n} = a + b\frac{\Sigma X}{n}$$

or

$$\overline{Y} = a + b\overline{X}$$

Therefore, knowing b, $\overline{X}$ and $\overline{Y}$ it becomes easy to find the value of 'a'. Thus it represents that the regression line will always pass through the mean of the X values and the mean of the Y values.

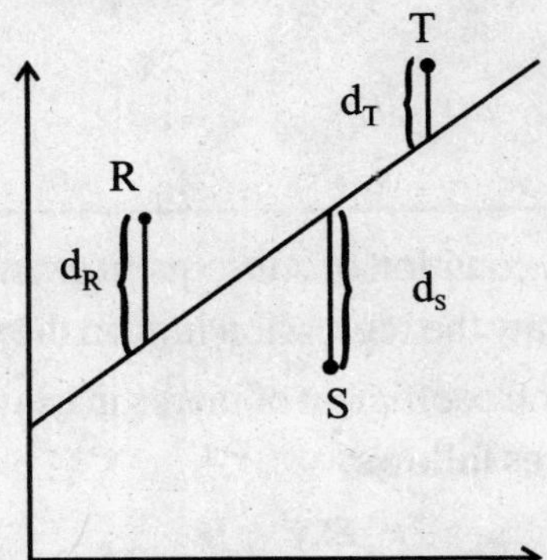

Fig. 13.2: Deviations from the line in the Y-axis direction.

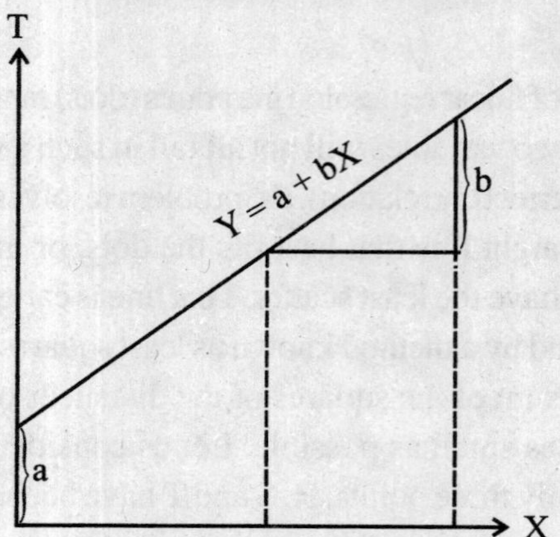

Fig. 13.3: Intercept (a) and slope (b) for the regression line.

EXAMPLE 13.8: On entry to a school, a new intelligence test was given to a small group of children. The result obtained in that test and in a subsequent examination are tabulated as follows:

Child Number	Intelligence Test score (X)	Marks in examination (Y)
1	7	10
2	6	7
3	5	4
4	7	5
5	8	4
6	9	7
7	6	4
8	8	7

Derive the regression equation of subsequent examination performance (Y) on initial test result (X). Draw the regression line on the scatter diagram.

SOLUTION: The regression coefficient of marks in examination (b_{YX}) for one unit of intelligence is calculated as follows:

$$b_{YX} = \frac{\Sigma xy}{\Sigma x^2} = \frac{6}{12} = 0.5$$

Regresion line for character Y can be drawn on a graph paper by finding expected or calculated values of Y, *i.e.*, Y_C corresponding to oberved values of X from the regression coefficient (b or b_{YX}) and same can be done X and Y.

Now we plot these calculated values of marks, *i.e.*, Y_C, corresponding to observed values of intelligence test scores, *i.e.*, 7, 6, 5, 7, 8, 9, 6, 8, on the graph paper. A straight line called regression line of Y on X, is formed as shown in figure below:

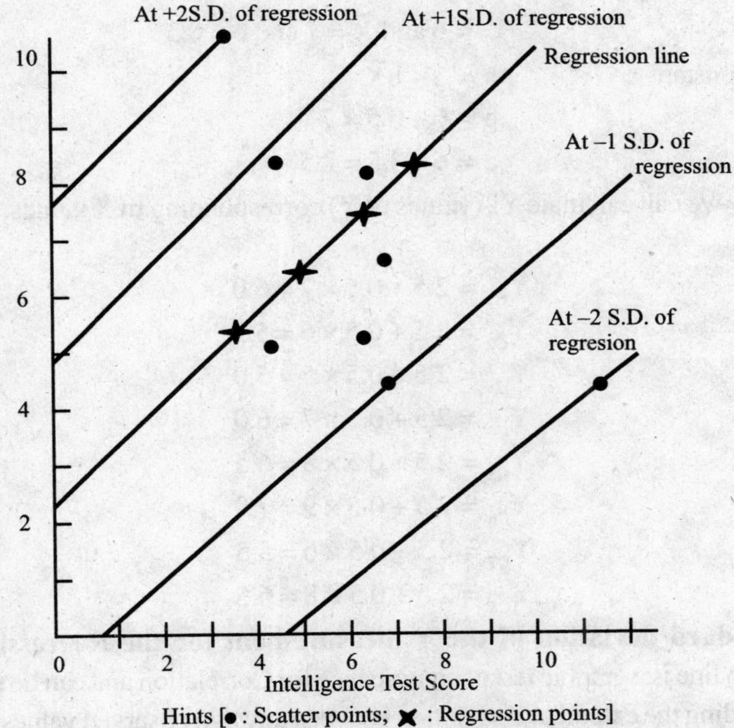

Fig. 13.4: Shows the scatter points and regression line

The above regression line is the mean line of X and Y lines and it will pass through the scatter diagram, about half the points lying on one side and other half on the other side of the line. Any expected value of Y can be known on the regression line for the given value of X.

Calculated value of Y, *i.e.*, Y_C, will be equal to mean of Y, *i.e.*, $\overline{Y}$ plus the regression coefficient, b multiplied by X, *i.e.*, $(X-\overline{X})$, because if X moves by one unit beyond $\overline{X}$, then Y_C moves 1b beyond $\overline{Y}$ and if X moves by X unit then Y_C beyond $\overline{Y}$ moves by bX, *i.e.*, bX units. Thus calculated value of Y, *i.e.*, Y_C corresponding to any value of X is equal to $\overline{Y} + bX$.

$$Y_C = \overline{Y} + bX$$

or $$Y_C = \overline{Y} + b(X - \overline{X}) = \overline{Y} + bX - b\overline{X}$$

where $$= \overline{Y} - b\overline{X} \text{ is a constant and denoted by 'a'}$$

then $$Y_C = a + bX \text{ represents a regression line}$$

To calculate Y_C for the marks corresponding to intelligence test scores, we have

$$\overline{Y} = 6 \text{ and } \overline{X} = 7 \text{ and } b = 0.5$$

So constant $$a = Y - b\overline{X}$$

or $$a = 6 - 0.5 \times 7$$

$\therefore$ $$a = 6 - 3.5 = 2.5$$

Now we can calculate Y_C (values of Y) corresponding to X values, *i.e.*, $Y_C = a + bX$

$$Y_{C1} = 2.5 + 0.5 \times 7 = 6.0$$
$$Y_{C2} = 2.5 + 0.5 \times 6 = 5.5$$
$$Y_{C3} = 2.5 + 0.5 \times 5 = 5.0$$
$$Y_{C4} = 2.5 + 0.5 \times 7 = 6.0$$
$$Y_{C5} = 2.5 + 0.5 \times 8 = 6.5$$
$$Y_{C6} = 2.5 + 0.5 \times 9 = 7.0$$
$$Y_{C7} = 2.5 + 0.5 \times 6 = 5.5$$
$$Y_{C8} = 2.5 + 0.5 \times 8 = 6.5$$

Standard deviation of the Y measurement for the Regression line: Regression line is a graphic test of significance for Correlation and can be made use of it, in finding the extend of correlation between any two observed values from the normal distribution of scatter points around the regression line.

Standard deviation of the Y measurements from the regression line can be calculated by any of the following three formulae:

$$\text{Std. dev. of regression} = \sqrt{\frac{\Sigma(Y - Y_C)^2}{n}} \quad \text{.........(1)}$$

or $$\text{Std. dev. of regression} = \sqrt{\frac{\Sigma(y - y_C)^2}{n}} \quad \text{.........(2)}$$

or $$\text{Std. dev. of regression} = \sqrt{\frac{\Sigma y^2 - \frac{(\Sigma xy)^2}{\Sigma x^2}}{n}} \quad \text{.........(3)}$$

Y_C is taken instead of $\overline{Y}$ to find standard deviation because the calcuated values (Y_C) are assumed to be mean values of Y corresponding to specified values of X. The actural values of Y are assumed to have a normal distribution around the mean values of Y_C. We may find the standard deviation of regression for Y_C (*i.e.*, expected marks in examination) from the previous example as shown below:

Y	y	Y_c	$Y-Y_c$	$(Y-Y_c)^2$	$y_c = (Y_c - \overline{Y})$	$y - Y_c$	$(y-y_c)^2$
10	4	6.0	4.0	16.00	0	4.0	16.00
7	1	5.5	1.5	2.5	−0.5	1.5	2.25
4	−2	5.0	−1.0	1.00	−1.0	−1.0	1.00
5	−1	6.0	−1.0	1.00	0	−1.0	1.00
4	−2	6.5	−2.5	6.25	0.5	−2.5	6.25
7	1	7.0	0	0	1.0	0	0
4	−2	5.5	−1.5	2.25	−0.5	−1.5	2.25
7	1	6.5	−0.5	0.25	0.5	0.5	0.25
48	–	–	0.5	29.00	–	—	29.00

Std. dev. of regression by using formula (1)

$$= \sqrt{\frac{\Sigma(Y - Y_C)^2}{n}} = \sqrt{\frac{29}{8}} = 1.9$$

Std. dev. of regression by using formula (2)

$$= \sqrt{\frac{\Sigma (y - y_C)^2}{n}} = \sqrt{\frac{29}{8}} = 1.9$$

Note: Formula (1) and (2) are the same because $(Y - Y_C) = (y - y_C)$.

Std. dev. of regression by using formula (3)

$$= \sqrt{\frac{\Sigma y^2 - \frac{(\Sigma xy)^2}{\Sigma x^2}}{n}} = \sqrt{\frac{32 - \frac{6\times 6}{12}}{8}} = \sqrt{\frac{29}{8}} = 1.9$$

In this case the sample size is small (*i.e.*, n = 8) so getting more accurate results we take (n – 1) instead of n in the above formulae.

$$\text{Std. dev. of regresion} = \sqrt{\frac{\Sigma y^2 - \frac{(\Sigma xy)^2}{\Sigma x^2}}{n-1}} = \sqrt{\frac{29}{8-1}} = \sqrt{\frac{29}{7}} = 2$$

Now we draw two parallel lines on a graph paper at a distance of one standard deviation of regression (*i.e.*, 2) from the regression line on either sides 68% of the scatter points will lie within these lines. Similarly we can draw two more parallel lines at a distance of 2 standard deviation of regression (*i.e.*, $2 \times 2 = 4$), 95% of scatter points of two variables will lie within these lines. This is shown graphically in the Fig. 13.4. It concludes that the marks falling outside $\pm$ 2 std. dev. lines, will not be proportional to the corresponding intelligence test score at 95% confidence limits. If X line represents the heights and Y line the weights and regression lines are also drawn as in Fig. 13.4, the weight of any person can be predicted corresponding to any specified height and it can also be estimated whether a given weight of a person is proportional to his height or not.

DIFFERENCE BETWEN CORRELATION AND REGRESSION

Correlation coefficient shows the degree or strength of relationship between two variables X and Y whereas the regression enables us to predict the values of one variables (say Y) on the basis of the other variable (say X). Thereby the cause and effect relationship between two variables is understood precisely (i) when there is a perfect correlation (*i.e.*, $r = +1$ or $r = -1$), the two regression lines $Y = a + bX$ and $X = a' + b'$ will coincide, (ii) when correlation is zero (*i.e.*, $r = 0$), the variable are independent and the two regression lines intersect at 90°, (iii) if correlation coefficient is closer to '1' strength of the regression for prediction is very good.

EXAMPLE 13.9: Calculate the coefficient of correlation and obtain the lines of regression for the following data:

X:	1	2	3	4	5	6	7	8	9
Y:	8	9	11	10	12	14	13	15	16

Obtain an estimate of Y which should correspond on the average to $X = 5.5$.

SOLUTION: Calculation of coefficient of correlation, r

X	dx = x – 5	dx²	Y	dy = Y – 12	dy²	dxdy
1	–4	16	8	–4	16	16
2	–3	9	9	–3	9	9
3	–2	4	11	–1	1	2
4	–1	1	10	–2	4	2
5	0	0	12	0	0	0
6	+1	1	14	+2	4	2
7	+2	4	13	+1	1	2
8	+3	9	15	+3	9	9
9	+4	16	16	+4	16	16
N = 9	$\Sigma dx = 0$	$\Sigma dx^2 = 60$	N = 9	$\Sigma dy = 0$	$\Sigma dy^2 = 60$	$\Sigma dxdy = 58$

Here, assumed Mean for X-series is 5 and Assumed Mean for Y-series is 12.

Since $$r = \frac{\Sigma dxdy - \Sigma dx\, \Sigma dy/N}{\sqrt{\Sigma dx^2 - (\Sigma dx)^2/N}\ \sqrt{\Sigma dy^2 - (\Sigma dy)^2/N}}$$

$$\therefore \quad r = \frac{58-0}{\sqrt{60-0}\ \sqrt{60-0}} = \frac{58}{60} = +0.97$$

Now Regression coefficient of Y on X, *i.e.*,

$$b_{YX} = \frac{\Sigma dxdy - \Sigma dxdy/N}{\Sigma dx^2 - (\Sigma dx)^2/N} = \frac{58-0}{60-0} = \frac{58}{60} = +0.97$$

and Regression coefficient of X on Y, *i.e.*,

$$b_{YX} = \frac{\Sigma dxdy - \Sigma dxdy/N}{\Sigma dy^2 - (\Sigma dy^2)/N} = \frac{58-0}{60-0} = \frac{58}{60} = +0.97$$

Regression equation of Y on X is given by

$$Y - Y = byx\,(X - \overline{X})$$

or $$Y - 12 = 0.97\,(X - 5)$$

or $$Y = 0.97\,X - 4.85 + 12$$

or $$Y = 0.97\,X + 7.15$$

and Regression equation of X on Y is given by

$$X - \overline{X} = bxy\,(Y - \overline{Y})$$

or $$X - 5 = 0.97\,(Y - 12)$$

or $$X = 0.97\,Y - 11.64 + 5$$

or $$X = 0.97\,Y - 6.64$$

By putting X = 5.5 in the regression equation of Y on X, we have

$$Y = 0.97\,(5.5) + 7.15 = 5.34 + 7.15$$

or $$Y = 12.49 = 12.5 \text{ approximately}$$

Thus the estimate of Y corresponding to (X = 5.5) is 12.5.

MULTIPLE REGRESSION

Multiple regression is used for predicting the dependent variable on the basis of two or more independent variables.

The multiple regression equation of x_1 on x_2 and x_3 is

$$x_1 = \overline{x}_1 + b_{12.3}\,(x_2 - \overline{x}_2) + b_{13.2}\,(x_3 - \overline{x}_3)$$

and the multiple regression equation of x_2 on x_1 and x_3 is

$$x_2 = \overline{x}_2 + b_{21.3}\,(x_1 - \overline{x}_1) + b_{23.2}\,(x_3 - \overline{x}_3)$$

Similarly, the multiple regression equation of x_3 on x_1 and x_2 is

$$x_3 = \bar{x}_3 + b_{31.2}(x_1 - \bar{x}_1) + b_{32.2}(x_2 - \bar{x}_2)$$

where $$b_{12.3} = \frac{r_{1.2} - r_{1.3}\, r_{2.3}}{1 - r_{2.3}^2}\left(\frac{s_1}{s_2}\right)$$

and $$b_{13.2} = \frac{r_{1.3} - r_{1.2}\, r_{2.3}}{1 - r_{2.3}^2}\left(\frac{s_1}{s_3}\right)$$

are the partial regression coefficients where s_1, s_2 and s_3 are standard deviations of x_1, x_2 and x_3 respectively.

EXAMPLE 13.10: The correlation coefficient between weight (x_1), serum cholesterol (x_2) and diastolic BP (x_3) among 12 adult males are: $r_{12} = 0.47$, $r_{13} = 0.62$ and $r_{23} = 0.92$.

Determine the multiple correlation coefficient $R_{1.23}$ and also estimate the diastolic BP of a person whose weight is 70 kg and serum cholesterol is 250. [Given that $\bar{x}_1 = 55$, $\bar{x}_2 = 230$, $\bar{x}_3 = 80$, and $s_1 = 0.68$, $s_2 = 3.2$ and $s_3 = 2.4$]

SOLUTION:

Since $$R_{1.23} = \sqrt{\frac{r_{1.2}^2 + r_{1.3}^2 - 2\, r_{1.2}\, r_{1.3}\, r_{2.3}}{1 - r_{23}^2}}$$

We have $$R_{1.23} = \sqrt{\frac{0.22 + 0.38 - 0.54}{1 - 0.85}} = \sqrt{\frac{0.06}{0.15}} \doteq 0.63$$

Now the multiple regression equation of x_3 (diastolic BP) on x_1 (weight) and x_2 (cholesterol) is

$$x_3 = \bar{x}_3 + b_{31.2}(x_1 - \bar{x}_1) + b_{32.1}(x_1 - \bar{x}_2)$$

$$b_{31.2} = \frac{r_{1.3} - r_{2.3}\, r_{1.2}}{1 - r_{1.2}^2}\left(\frac{s_3}{s_1}\right) = \frac{0.62 - 0.92\,(0.47)}{1 - (0.47)^2}\left(\frac{2.4}{0.68}\right)$$

$$b_{31.2} = \frac{0.62 - 0.43}{0.78} \times 3.53$$

or $$b_{31.2} = \frac{0.19\,(3.53)}{0.78} = \frac{0.67}{0.78} = 0.86$$

and $$b_{32.1} = \frac{r_{2.3} - r_{1.3}\, r_{1.2}}{1 - r_{1.2}^2}\left(\frac{s_3}{s_2}\right)$$

$$= \frac{0.92 - 0.62\,(0.47)}{1 - (0.47)^2}\left(\frac{2.4}{3.2}\right)$$

or $$b_{31.2} = \frac{(0.92 - 0.29)\,0.75}{1 - 0.22} = \frac{0.63\,(0.75)}{0.78} = \frac{0.47}{0.78} = 0.60$$

Thus, $$x_3 = 55 + 0.86\,(70 - 55) + 0.60\,(250 - 230)$$

or $$x_3 = 55 + 12.9 + 12 = 80$$

Conclusion

The diastolic BP of a person whose weight is 70 kg and serum cholesterol level is 250, is estimated as 80 mm of Hg.

LOGISTIC REGRESSION ANALYSIS

Logistic regression analysis enables data to elicit influence of several independent variables on dependent variable when the dependent variable is in dichotomous form (*i.e*., in the form of 'Yes' or 'No'). It also enables to control the influence of extraneous factors. Ordinary regression analysis seeks to measure the degree of influence of different independent variables on dependent variable while logistic regression analysis the odds that an event will or will not occur in relation to different values of independent variable.

Examples:

(a) Study on the probability of family planning adoptation on para 1, 2, 3, and so on.

(b) Study of CHD occurrence associated with age, sex, serum cholesterol level, and so on.

(c) Study of survival Cohort of cancer cervix associated with stages of cancer, time of detection of cancer, and so on.

Illustration 1

Logistic regression is suitable in situations where the response or the dependent variable is dichotomous observed, *i.e*., the response is binary. For example, occurrence of prostate cancer is dichotomous (Yes or No) and may be investigated to depend on (say) vasectomy status (Yes or No) as a primary variable of interest. Possible confounding factors such as smoking index and age at vasectomy can be other explanatory (or independent) variables in the model.

Logistic Model

$$\lambda = \text{logit}\ \frac{p}{1 - p}$$

[Note: The dependent variable is actually the proportion (or probability) of subjects falling into a specified category.]

$p \div (1 - p)$ represents the odds for presence of the response in the subjects. Logistic transformation, $\lambda = p \div (1 - p)$ also helps to linearize the relationship between dependent and independent variables, whereas the relationship between untransformed probability and other factors in general non-linear. $p = \dfrac{1}{1+e^{-\lambda}}$. The function $\hat{\lambda} = \dfrac{p}{1-p}$ is called the logistic of p (or logit of p). The functional form of relationship between λ and its possible predictors is called a logistic regression (or logistic regression model). A useful application of logistic regression is in case control studies. λ is estimated by a linear combination of the levels of various predictors, *i.e.*,

$$\hat{\lambda} = b_0 + b_1x_1 + b_2x_2 + b_3x_3 + \ldots + b_kx_k$$

The constants b_1, b_2, b_3 ,....., b_k are called regression coefficients and b_0 is called the intercept.

Illustration 2

Consider a case control study of male patients who are HIV positive. To assess the associated risk factors. For the convenience of illustration we restrict risk factors to only three: heterosexual promiscuity, blood transfusion received or not, and injectable drug used or not. The controls are non-HIV male patients matched for age and socio-economic status. Let there be 20 subjects in each group. Suppose heterosexual promiscuity (x_1) is measured in terms of number of casual sex partners ever in life and the other two (x_2, x_3) receive values 1 for 'yes' and zero for 'No'. The data are entered into a complete and the logistic regression for matched data is obtained. Suppose the estimated value of intercept is –2.42 and the regression coefficients are 0.50, 0.82 and 2.18 for x_1, x_2 and x_3 respectively.

Thus, the following logistic regression is obtained:

$$\hat{\lambda} = -2.42 + 0.50\,(x_1) + 0.82\,(x_2) + 2.18\,(x_3)$$

For a person with $x_1 = 7$ sex partners who received blood transfusion ($x_2 = 1$) but never on injectable drug ($x_3 = 0$), we have

$$\hat{\lambda} = -2.42 + 0.50 \times 7 + 0.82 \times 1 + 2.18 \times 0 = 1.9$$

Since $\hat{\lambda} = \text{logit}\ \dfrac{p}{1-p}$ we get the estimate of the odd $\dfrac{p}{1-p} = e^{1.9} = 6.7$

For a person $x_1 = 0$, $x_2 = 0$, and $x_3 = 0$

We get $\hat{\lambda} = 2.42$ and odd $= e^{-2.42} = 0.0906$

$\therefore$ The odd ratio $= \dfrac{6.7}{0.0906} = 74$

Thus, that person is nearly 74 times as likely to be HIV positive as a person with no sex partner, no blood transfusion, and no drug use. The estimated probability using $p = \dfrac{1}{1+e^{-1\,9}} = 0.86$.

It concludes that there is 86% chance that this person belongs to the HIV positive group (*i.e.*, a person with those values of x_1, x_2, x_3 has an 86% chance of contracting the disease).

➤ EXERCISES ➤

13.1. Find the coefficient of correlation from the following data:

X:	1	2	3	4	5
Y:	3	2	5	4	6

13.2. The rankings of 10 individuals at the starts and on the finish of a course of training are as follows:

Individuals:	A	B	C	D	E	F	G	H	I	J
Rank before:	1	6	3	9	5	2	7	10	8	4
Rank after:	6	8	3	7	2	1	5	9	4	10

Calculate the rank correlation coefficient.

13.3. From the following data, find the two regression equations:

X:	1	2	3	4	5
Y:	2	3	5	4	6

Find also the most probable value of Y when X = 2.5.

13.4. Find the correlation coefficient and the equation of the regression line of the following values of x and y:

$$\{(x,y)\} = \{(1,2), (2,5), (3,3), (5,8), (5,7)\}$$

13.5. Calculate the rank correlation coefficient 'r' for the following data:

X:	43	82	85	86	80	75	71	60	53	50
Y:	86	80	90	77	68	85	52	72	37	55

13.6. Find the correlation coefficient between the heights of fathers and adults sons from the given data:

Height of father (cms)	178	180	182	176	188	184	172	186	176	174
Height of adult son (cms)	162	160	166	162	168	170	160	174	168	160

13.7. Calculate the coefficient of correlation and obtain the lines of the regression for the following data:

Marks obtained: in Paper I	55	60	45	56	80	65	68	70	85
Marks obtained: in Paper II	50	58	56	60	70	55	65	70	76

Also estimate the most probable marks in Paper II for the students who secured 70 marks in Paper I.

13.8. Given: $\overline{X} = 40$, $\overline{Y} = 36$, $\sigma_X = 6$, $\sigma_Y = 8$, and $r = 0.8$. Find the two lines of regression. Predict Y when X = 21, and predict X when Y = 45.

13.9. What is regression? From the following data, obtain the regression coefficients and equations:

X:	1	2	3	4	5
Y:	166	184	142	180	338

13.10. Estimate the value of Y, when X = 36 from the following data; $\overline{X} = 30$, $\overline{Y} = 45$, $\sigma_X = \sigma_Y = 10$, and $r = + 4/5$.

13.11. In a certain trivariate distribution: $r_{12} = 0.67$; $r_{23} = r_{21} = 0.55$ and $s_1 = 5$, $s_2 = s_3 = 7$. Find, (i) Partial correlation coefficient, $r_{12.3}$, (ii) Multiple correlation coefficient, $R_{1.23}$ and (iii) Partial regression coefficient, $b_{12.3}$.

13.12. Calculate the Karl Pearson's coefficient of correlation (r) for the following data:

SBP (mm of Hg):	120	140	128	142	110	148	132	126	158	100
Pulse per minute:	70	78	72	74	66	76	80	68	84	60

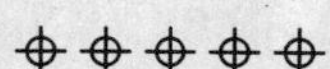

CHAPTER

14

Analysis of Variance (ANOVA)

- *Assumptions*
- *Homogeneity*
- *Mutually Exclusive*
- *Sampling Variation*
- *Variance Ratio*
- *Correction Factor*

INTRODUCTION

The analysis of variance is one of the most powerful tools of statistical methods and this technique is used to test whether the difference (or variation) between the means of three or more populations is significant or not. This statistical technique was originally developed by R.A. Fisher and the F-distribution was named in his honour. Earlier this technique was used in agricultural experiments. Now analysis of variance is widely used in diverse fields. Some examples where comparison of several groups is of interest are:

(i) Whether different varieties of seeds or manures or soils differ significantly or not as regards average yields of land.

(ii) Energy intakes of individuals engaged in different activity levels.

(iii) The differences in various types of drugs manufactured by a company to cure a particular disease.

DEFINITION

According to R.A. Fisher: The analysis of variance is the separation of the variance ascribable to one group of causes from the variance ascribable to other groups.

Thus, analysis of variance is a statistical method of partitioning the total variance into parts (*i.e.,* between the groups and within the groups) so as to yield independent estimate of the population variance.

Assumptions

The analysis of variance is based on the following assumptions:

(i) The samples (or groups) should be mutually exclusive, *i.e.,* independent to each other;

(ii) All the populations from which samples are drawn should be normally distributed;

(iii) The samples (or groups) should have equal variances, *i.e.,* homogeneity of variance.

The observations may be classified according to one factor (criterion) or two factors (or criteria). The classifications according to one factor and two factors are called one way classification and two way classification respectively.

ONE WAY CLASSIFICATION (OR ONE WAY ANOVA)

In one way classification, the observations (or data) are classified according to one factor (or criterion). For example,

(i) The yields of several plots of land may be classified according to one or more types of fertilizers.

(ii) The different types of drugs which are to be compared for their effectiveness in controlling or cure a particular disease.

(iii) Iron intake of antenatal mothers in four villages.

TWO WAY CLASSIFICATION (OR TWO WAY ANOVA)

Two way analysis of variance is utilized when there is a need to study the impact of two different factors (or criteria) on variations in a specific variable. For example,

(i) The yield of a crop in several plots of land may be classified according to different varieties of seeds and different types of manures;

(ii) The effect of age and sex on variations in height;

(iii) The effect of grades of socio economic status and literacy levels of mothers on variations in protein quality or dietary adequacies of the children.

Variances and its different components may be computed in each of the two types of classifications by

(i) Direct Method and (ii) Short-cut Method.

One Way ANOVA : The computational procedures involved in such an analysis is illustrated in the following steps:

Direct Method: Let the Null hypothesis be $H_0: \mu_1 = \mu_2 = ... = \mu_k$, where $\mu_1, \mu_2, ..., \mu_k$ are the means of populations from which is k samples are randomly drawn.

The Alternative hypothesis is H_1 : all μ_i (i = 1, 2, ..., k) are not equal.

Now the steps in carrying out the analysis are as follows:

I. Calculation of Variance Between the Samples (or Groups)

(*i.e.*, calculation of the sum of the squares of variations between the samples)

(i) Calculate the sample means $\overline{x}_1, \overline{x}_2, ..., \overline{x}_k$

(ii) Calculate the grand mean $\overline{x}$, *i.e.*, $(\overline{x}_1, \overline{x}_2 + ... + \overline{x}_k) \div k$ or T/N, where T is grand total of all observations, and N is total number of observations in all k samples.

(iii) Find the deviations of the means of the different samples from the grand mean, $\overline{x}$, *i.e.*, $(\overline{x}_1 - \overline{x})$, $(\overline{x}_2 - \overline{x})$, ..., $(\overline{x}_k - \overline{x})$.

(iv) Find the sum of squares of the deviations for variances between the samples (or between the columns) and it is denoted by SSB (or SSC), *i.e.*, SSB = $\sum_{i=1}^{k} n_i(\overline{x}_i - \overline{x})^2$.

Variance or Mean Square between samples (MSB or MSC). If we divide the total obtained in Step (iv) by the degrees of freedom, *i.e.*, $\upsilon_1 = (k - 1)$, we get the Mean Square between the samples which is denoted by MSB or MSC.

Note: MSB indicates sampling variation.

II. Calculation of Variance within the Samples (or Groups)

(*i.e.*, calculation of the sum of the squares of variances within the samples)

Variance within the samples is the total of the sum of squares of the deviations of the various items (observations) from the mean values of the respective samples and its calculation is done in the following steps:

(i) Calculate the sample means $\overline{x}_1, \overline{x}_2, \ldots, \overline{x}_k$ of all the k samples.

(ii) Find the deviations of the various items of k samples from the mean values of the respective samples, *i.e.*,

$$(x_i - \overline{x}_1), (x_i - \overline{x}_2), \ldots\ldots, (x_i - \overline{x}_k)$$

(iii) Find the sum of squares of deviations within the samples (or sum of squares due to error) and it is denoted by SSW or SSE, *i.e.*,

$$SSW = \Sigma(x_i - \overline{x}_1)^2 + \Sigma(x_i - \overline{x}_2)^2 + \ldots + \Sigma(x_i - \overline{x}_k)^2$$

Variance or Mean Square within the samples (MSW or MSE). If the total obtained in Step (iii), *i.e.*, SSW is divided by the degrees of freedom, $\upsilon_2 = (N - k)$, we get the Mean Square within the samples which is denoted by MSW or MSE.

Note: MSW indicates chance variation.

III. Calculation of the Test Statistic F (Variance Ratio)

$$F = \frac{\text{Mean sum of squares between samples (or groups)}}{\text{Mean sum of squares within samples (or groups)}}$$

i.e.,

$$F = \frac{MSB}{MSW} \text{ or } \frac{MSC}{MSE}$$

which follows F-distribution with degrees of freedom υ = k – 1) and $\upsilon_2 = (N - k)$.

Note: Generally, MSB > MSW. But if MSB < MSW, we shall take the inverse ratio for F, *i.e.*, F = MSW ÷ MSB.

IV. Decision

Compare the calculated value of F with the critical (Tabulated) value of F for (k – 1, N – k) degrees of freedom at α-level (generally at 5% or 1%). If the calculated value of F is more than critical (tabulated) value then reject the H_0 and conclude that all the population means are not equal, otherwise accept H_0 and conclude that the population means are all equal.

All the above mentioned steps for the calculation of variances between and within the samples (or groups) can be summarised in a tabular form called the analysis of variance table (ANOVA Table).

ANOVA Table

Source of variation	Sum of squares (SS)	Degrees of freedom	Mean Squares (MS)	Test Statistic
Between	SSB	k – 1	$MSB = \frac{SSB}{k-1}$	$F = \frac{MSB}{MSW}$
Within	SSW	N – k	$MSW = \frac{SSW}{N-k}$	
Total	SST	N – 1	—	—

EXAMPLE 14.1: The following table gives the yields of three varieties of wheat in four plots of agricultural land:

	Plot yield			
Variety	**I**	**II**	**III**	**IV**
A	12	18	14	16
B	19	17	15	13
C	14	16	18	20

Test the significance of difference between the yields of the three varieties.

SOLUTION: H_0 : There is no significant difference in thelaverage yields under the three varieties.

H_1 : The difference is significant.

I. Calculation for Sample Means:

	Variety		
Plot yield	**A**	**B**	**C**
I	12	19	14
II	18	17	16
III	14	15	18
IV	16	13	20

$\bar{x}_1 = 15; \quad \bar{x}_2 = 16; \quad \bar{x}_3 = 17$

Grand $= \frac{\bar{x}_1 + \bar{x}_2 + \bar{x}_3}{3} = \frac{15+16+17}{3} = 16$

SSB = Sum of the squares between the samples

$= \Sigma n_i (\bar{x}_i - \bar{x})^2$

$= n_1 (\bar{x}_1 - \bar{x})^2 + n_2 (\bar{x}_2 - \bar{x})^2 + n_3 (\bar{x}_3 - \bar{x})^2$

$$= 4\,(15-16)^2 + 4\,(16-16)^2 + 4\,(17-16)^2$$

$$SSB = 4 + 0 + 4 = 8$$

and υ_1 = degree of freedom = $k - 1 = 3 - 1 = 2$

$\therefore$ MSB = SSB ÷ (k − 1) = 8 ÷ 2 = 4

II. Calculation for SSW (Sum of squares within the samples)

Variety A Sample 1		Variety B Sample 2		Variety C Sample 3	
x_1	$(x_1 - \bar{x}_1)^2$	x_2	$(x_2 - \bar{x}_2)^2$	x_3	$(x_3 - \bar{x}_3)^2$
12	$(12-15)^2 = 9$	19	$(19-16)^2 = 9$	14	$(14-17)^2 = 9$
18	$(18-15)^2 = 9$	17	$(17-16)^2 = 1$	16	$(16-17)^2 = 1$
14	$(14-15)^2 = 1$	15	$(15-16)^2 = 1$	18	$(18-17)^2 = 1$
16	$(16-15)^2 = 1$	13	$(13-16)^2 = 9$	20	$(20-17)^2 = 9$
Total	$\Sigma(x_1 - \bar{x}_1)^2 = 20$	–	$\Sigma(x_2 - \bar{x}_2)^2 = 20$	–	$\Sigma(x_3 - \bar{x}_3)^2 = 20$

SSW = Sum of squares within the samples

$$= \Sigma(x_1 - \bar{x}_1)^2 + \Sigma(x_2 - \bar{x}_2)^2 + \Sigma(x_3 - \bar{x}_3)^2$$

SSW = 20 + 20 + 20 = 60

and υ_2 = degrees of freedom = $N - k = 12 - 3 = 9$

MSW = Mean square within the samples

$\therefore$ MSW = SSW ÷ (N − k) = 60 ÷ 9 = 6.7

ANOVA Table

Source of variation	Sum of squares	d.f.	Mean square	Test statistic
Between samples	8	2	4	$F = \frac{6.7}{4} = 1.67$
Within samples	60	9	6.7	
Total	SST = 68	(N − 1) = 11	–	

Here, $F_{calculated} < F_{tabulated,\ at\ 0.05\ (2,\ 9)}$, *i.e.*, $1.67 < 4.26$ [see Appendix Table V (a)].

Hence, we accept the H_0 at 5% level and conclude that there is no significant difference in the average yield of three varieties ($p > 0.05$).

EXAMPLES 14.2: Anxiety scores across groups on MAACL are as follows:

Experimental Group I (Relaxation)	Experimental Group II (Procedure information)	Control Group III
5	7	12
8	9	13
7	7	12
9	12	8
5	10	11
8	8	14
4	7	10
3	11	10
5	9	15
4	7	9

Is there any significant difference in the groups scores?

SOLUTION: H_0 : There is no significant difference in groups scores

H_1 : The difference is significant

I. Calculation for Samples (Groups) Means and Variances between the Samples

Experimental Group I	ExperimentaB Group II	Central Group III
5	7	12
8	9	13
7	7	12
9	12	8
5	10	11
8	8	14
4	7	10
3	11	10
5	9	15
4	7	9
$\bar{x}_1 = 5.8$	$\bar{x}_2 = 8.7$	$\bar{x}_3 = 11.4$

Grand Mean, $\bar{x} = \dfrac{\bar{x}_1 + \bar{x}_2 + \bar{x}_3}{3}$

$$= \frac{5.8 + 8.7 + 11.4}{3} = 8.6$$

$\because$ SSB = Sum of squares Between the samples (groups)

$= \Sigma n_i \ \Sigma(\bar{x}_i - \bar{x})^2$

$= 10(5.8-8.6)^2 + 10(8.7-8.6)^2 + 10(11.4-8.6)^2$

$\therefore$ SSB $= 78.4 + 0.1 + 78.4 = 156.9$

and $\upsilon_1 = k - 1 = 3 - 1 = 2$

MSB = SSB ÷ (k − 1)

$\therefore$ MSB $= 156.9 \div 2 = 78.5$

II. Calculation for Sum of Squares Within the Samples (Groups)

Experiment Group I	Experiment Group II	Experiment Group II
x_1 $(x_1 - \bar{x}_1)^2$	x_2 $(x_2 - \bar{x}_2)^2$	x_3 $(x_3 - \bar{x}_3)^2$
5 $(5-5.8)^2 = 0.6$	7 $(7-8.7)^2 = 2.9$	12 $(12-11.4)^2 = 0.4$
8 $(8-5.8)^2 = 4.8$	9 $(9-8.7)^2 = 0.1$	13 $(13-11.4)^2 = 2.6$
7 $(7-5.8)^2 = 1.4$	7 $(7-8.7)^2 = 2.9$	12 $(12-11.4)^2 = 0.4$
9 $(9-5.8)^2 = 10.2$	12 $(12-8.7)^2 = 10.9$	8 $(8-11.4)^2 = 11.6$
5 $(5-5.8)^2 = 0.6$	10 $(10-8.7)^2 = 1.7$	11 $(11-11.4)^2 = 0.2$
8 $(8-5.8)^2 = 4.8$	8 $(8-8.7)^2 = 0.5$	14 $(14-11.4)^2 = 6.8$
4 $(4-5.8)^2 = 3.2$	7 $(7-8.7)^2 = 2.9$	10 $(10-11.4)^2 = 2.0$
3 $(3-5.8)^2 = 7.8$	11 $(11-8.7)^2 = 5.3$	10 $(10-11.4)^2 = 2.0$
5 $(5-5.8)^2 = 0.6$	9 $(9-8.7)^2 = 0.1$	15 $(15-11.4)^2 = 13.0$
4 $(4-5.8)^2 = 3.2$	7 $(7-8.7)^2 = 2.9$	9 $(9-11.4)^2 = 5.8$
– $\Sigma(x_1 - \bar{x}_1)^2 = 37.2$	– $\Sigma(x_2 - \bar{x}_2)^2 = 30.2$	– $\Sigma(x_3 - \bar{x}_3)^2 = 44.8$

$\because$ SSW = Sum of squares Within the samples (groups)

$= \Sigma(x_1 - \bar{x}_1)^2 + \Sigma(x_2 - x_2)^2 + \Sigma(x_3 - \bar{x}_3)^2$

$\therefore$ SSW $= 37.2 + 30.2 + 44.8 = 112.2$

and $\upsilon_2 = N - k = 30 - 3 = 27$

MSW = Mean square Within the samples (groups)

or MSW = SSW ÷ N − k = 112.2 ÷ 27 = 4.2

ANOVA Table

Source of variance	Sum of squares	d.f.	Mean square	Test statistic
Between groups	156.9	2	78.5	$F = \frac{78.5}{4.2}$
Within groups	112.2	27	4.2	= 18.7
Total	SST = 269.1	(N − 1) = 29	–	

The Table value of F for $\upsilon_1 = 2$ and $\upsilon_2 = 27$ at 5% level of significance is 3.35 [Appendix Table V(a)]. Since $F_{calculated} = 18.7 > F_{tabulated} = 3.35$ at 5% level. Hence, we reject the H_0 and conclude that the three groups of scores are significantly different ($p < 0.05$).

Short cut method: This method is based on the sum of squares of individual values. The various steps are followed in this method.

Step I: Calculate the total, T of all the observations in all k samples (or groups), *i.e.,*

$$T = \Sigma x_1 + \Sigma x_2 + ... + \Sigma x_k$$

Step II: Then, find out the correction factor *i.e.,* C.F. = $T^2 \div N$.

Stept III: Calculate the sum of squares of all the values (or observations) in k samples and subtract the correction factor ($T^2 \div N$) from the sum to obtain the total sum of the squares of deviations, SST. Thus

$$SST = \Sigma x_1^2 + \Sigma x_2^2 + ... + \Sigma x_n^2 - (T^2 \div N)$$

Step IV: Find the sum of squares of deviations Between the samples, *i.e.,*

$$SSB = \frac{(\Sigma x_1)^2}{n_1} + \frac{(\Sigma x_2)^2}{n_2} + ... + \frac{(\Sigma x_k)^2}{n_k} - \frac{T^2}{N}$$

Step V: After this, calculate SSW, *i.e.,* the sum of squares Within the samples by subtracting SSB from SST.

Thus, $SSW = SST - SSB$

Step VI: Finally, obtain MSB, MSW, and F-ratio to arrive at the conclusion by summarising all these steps for the calculations in ANOVA table.

EXAMPLE 14.3 : Gain in weight of albino rats by four diets are given below:

	Weight (gm) gain by albino rates				
Diet	**1**	**2**	**3**	**4**	**5**
A	20	24	26	30	32
B	19	23	25	27	29
C	18	22	23	26	26
D	17	20	19	22	24

Test whether the diets differ significantly.

SOLUTION: H_0 : There is no significant difference in the mean values of gain in weights under the four diets.

H_1 : The difference is significant.

Diet	A (X_1)	X_1^2	B (X_2)	X_2^2	C (X_3)	X_3^2	D (X_4)	X_4^2	Total
1	20	400	19	361	18	324	17	289	74
2	24	576	23	529	22	484	20	400	89
3	26	676	25	625	23	529	19	361	93
4	30	900	27	729	24	576	22	484	103
5	32	1024	29	841	26	676	24	576	111
Total	132 $= \Sigma X_1$	3576 =	123 $= \Sigma X_2$	3085 =	113 $= \Sigma X_3$	2589 =	102 $= \Sigma X_4$	2110 =	470

T = Sum of all the values of the four samples

$= \Sigma X_1 + \Sigma X_2 + \Sigma X_3 + \Sigma X_4$

$= 132 + 123 + 113 + 102 = 470$

Correction factor $= T^2 \div N = (470)^2 \div 20 = 11045$ (Here N = 20)

SST = The total sum of squares

$$= \Sigma X_1^2 + \Sigma X_2^2 + \Sigma X_3^2 + \Sigma X_4^2 - (T^2 \div N)$$

$$= 3576 + 3085 + 2589 + 2110 - (11045)$$

$\therefore$ SST $= 11360 - 11045 = 315$

$\because$ SSB = Sum of squares Between the samples (*i.e.*, diets)

$$= \frac{(\Sigma X_1)^2}{n_1} + \frac{(\Sigma X_2)^2}{n_2} + \frac{(\Sigma X_3)^2}{n_3} + \frac{(\Sigma X_4)^2}{n_4} - \frac{T^2}{N}$$

$$= \frac{(132)^2 + (123)^2 + (113)^2 + (102)^2}{5} - \frac{T^2}{N}$$

(Here $n_1 = n_2 = n_3 = n_4 = 5$)

$\therefore$ SSB $= 11145.2 - 11045 = 100.2$

and $\upsilon_1 = k - 1 = 4 - 1 = 3$

$\because$ SSW = Sum of squares Within the samples

= SST – SSB

$\therefore$ SSW $= 315 - 100.2 = 214.8$

and $\upsilon_2 = N - k = 20 - 4 = 16$

ANOVA Table

Source of variation	Source of squares	d.f.	Mean squares	Test statistic
Between samples	100.2	3	100.2 ÷ 3 = 33.4	$F = \frac{33.4}{13.4} = 2.5$ = 2.5
Within samples	214.8	16	214.8 ÷ 16 = 13.4	
Total	SST = 315.0	(N – 1) = 19	–	–

$F_{calculated} = 2.5$ is less than the critical value of $F_{0.05, (3, 16)} = 3.24 \Rightarrow H_0$ accepted $[p > 0.05]$ (*i.e.*, there are no significant differences in the mean values of gain in weights under four diets).

CODING METHOD

As the test statistics F in the analysis of variance is the variance ratio, its value does not alter if all the given values are coded (*i.e.*, values are either multiplied or divided by a common factor or if a common factor is either added to or subtracted from each of the given value).

EXAMPLE 14.4: Systolic blood pressure (SBP) in mm of Hg of three groups of individuals in three occupations are given below. Test whether the mean systolic blood pressures in three groups differ or not.

Labour group SBP mm of Hg	Official Job SBP mm of Hg	MRs (Medical Representatives) SBP mm of Hg
120	112	126
122	116	124
114	124	118
116	120	130
128	118	128
124	114	120
126	128	132
118	125	127
125	130	122
112	126	125

SOLUTION: H_0 : The mean systolic BP in three groups are equal

H_1 : The mean systolic BP in three groups are not equal

Let us subtract 120 from each of the given values for making calculations easy. The revised data are as follows:

Calculations for Analysis of Variance:

Labour group			Official work			Medical representatives		
SBP	(X_1)	$(X_1)^2$	SBP	(X_2)	$(X_2)^2$	SBP	(X_3)	$(X_3)^2$
120	0	0	112	−8	64	126	6	36
122	2	4	116	−4	16	124	4	16
114	−6	36	124	4	16	118	−2	4
116	−4	16	120	0	0	130	10	100
128	8	64	118	−2	4	128	8	64
124	4	16	114	−6	36	120	0	0
126	6	36	128	8	64	132	12	144
118	−2	4	125	5	25	127	7	49
125	5	25	130	10	100	122	2	4
112	−8	64	126	6	36	125	5	25
–	$\Sigma X_1 = 5$	$\Sigma X_1^2 = 265$	–	$\Sigma X_2 = 13$	$\therefore \Sigma X_2^2 = 361$	–	$\Sigma X_3 = 52$	$\Sigma X_3^2 = 442$

T = Sum of all the values in the three groups

$T = \Sigma X_1 + \Sigma X_2 + \Sigma X_3 = 5 + 13 + 52 = 70$

C.F. = Correction factor = $T^2 \div N = (70)^2 \div 30 = 163.3$

$\because$ SST = Total sum of the squares

$= \Sigma X_1^2 + \Sigma X_2^2 + \Sigma X_3^2 - \text{C.F.}$

$\therefore$ SST $= 265 + 361 + 442 - (163.3) = 904.7$

SSB = Sum of squares Between the groups

$$= \frac{(\Sigma X_1)^2}{n_1} + \frac{(\Sigma X_2)^2}{n_2} + \frac{(\Sigma X_3)^2}{n_3} - \text{C.F.}$$

$$= \frac{(25 + 169 + 2704)}{10} - 163.3 \quad (\text{Here } n_1 = n_2 = n_3 = 10)$$

$\therefore$ SSB $= 289.8 - 163.3 = 126.5$

and $\upsilon_1 = \text{d.f.} = k - 1 = 3 - 1 = 2$

SSW = Sum of squares Within the groups

$= \text{SST} - \text{SSB} = 904.7 - 126.5$

$\therefore$ SSW $= 878.2$ and $\upsilon_2 = \text{d.f.} = N - k = 30 - 3 = 27$

Now, $\quad MSB = \dfrac{SSB}{\upsilon_1} = \dfrac{126.5}{2} = 63.2$

and $\quad MSW = \dfrac{SSW}{\upsilon_2} = \dfrac{878.2}{27} = 32.5$

ANOVA Table

Source of variation	Sum of squares (SS)	d.f.	Mean squares (MS)	Test statistic
Between groups	126.5	2	63.2	$F = \dfrac{63.2}{32.5} = 1.94$
Within groups	878.2	27	32.5	
Total	1004.7	29	–	–

Since F calculated = 1.94 is less than F tabulated value for $\upsilon_1 = 2$ and $\upsilon_2 = 27$ at 5% level is 3.35 [see Appendix Table V(a)]. Hence H_0 is accepted and conclude that the mean systolic BPs in three groups are equal (*i.e.*, $p > 0.05$).

TWO-WAY CLASSIFICATION

Two-way classification of variance is utilised when there is a need to study the impact of two different factors on variations in a specific variable. For example,

(i) The yield of a crop in several plots of land may be classified according to different varieties of seeds and different types of fertilizers.

(ii) The effect of age and sex on variations in height among the children.

Assumptions are to be made in Two-way classification as follows:

(a) The subjects must be chosen at random.

(b) The variable under study must have normality characteristic.

(c) There is no interaction between the two factors.

Procedure for Two-Way Classification or ANOVA

The total variance or the sum of squares of variances in a Two-way classification consists of three parts:

(i) SSC, *i.e*, the same of squares Between the columns,

(ii) SSR, *i.e*, the sum of squares Between the rows, and

(iii) SSE, *i.e*, the sum of squares for the residuals (or due to errors).

Thus, SST = SSC + SSR + SSE

Calculations for Two-Way ANOVA

(i) $T = \Sigma X_1 + \Sigma X_2 + ... + \Sigma X_k$

(ii) $C.F. = T^2 \div N$

(iii) $SST = \Sigma X_1^2 + \Sigma X_2^2 + ... + \Sigma X_k^2 - (T^2 \div N)$

(iv) $SSC = \frac{\Sigma(\Sigma X_c)^2}{n_c} - \frac{T^2}{N}$, where n_c = No. of units in each column

(v) $SSR = \frac{\Sigma(\Sigma X_r)^2}{n_r} - \frac{T^2}{N}$, where n_r = No. of units in each row

(vi) $SSE = SST - (SSC + SSR)$

(vii) The total number of degrees of freedom = (N – 1) = Cr – 1, where c and r are the number of columns and the number of rows respectively.

- d.f. between columns = c – 1
- d.f. between rows = r – 1
- d.f. between residuals = (c – 1) (r – 1)

Two-Way ANOVA Table

Source of variation	Sum of squares (SS)	d.f.	Mean squares (MS)	Test statistic
Between columns	SSC	C – 1	MSC = SSC ÷ C – 1	$F = \frac{MSC}{MSE}$ and
Between rows	SSR	r – 1	MSR = SSR ÷ r – 1	$F = \frac{MSR}{MSE}$
Residual	SSE	(C – 1) (r – 1)	MSE = SSE ÷ (C – 1) (r – 1)	
Total	SST	N –1	–	–

Conclusion

Calculated value of F is then compared with F tabulated at 5% (or 1%) for C–1, (C–1, r – 1) and for r –1, (C–1, r – 1). If the F calculated > F tabulated, then reject the null hypothesis otherwise accept.

EXAMPLE 14.5: The following data showing the yield of three varieties of a crop from four different blocks:

Variety of a crop	Blocks			
	I	II	III	IV
A	5	9	7	9
B	9	7	5	5
C	8	7	9	4

Test whether (i) the mean yields of the varieties are equal or not and (ii) the quality of the block means.

SOLUTION: H_0 : The mean yields of the varieties of crop are equal and the blocks means are not different.

First of all we subtract 5 from each values then classify the data according to two factors (*i.e.*, Blocks and Varieties).

Calculations for Two Way ANOVA

Variety of crops	Blocks				
	I	II	III	IV	Total
A	0	4	2	4	10
B	4	2	0	0	6
C	3	2	4	– 1	8
Total	7	8	6	3	24

$$\text{C.F.} = T^2 \div N = (24)^2 \div 12 = 48 \qquad \text{(Here N = 12)}$$

SSC = Sum of squares Between blocks (*i.e.*, between Columns)

$$= \frac{7^2}{3} + \frac{8^2}{3} + \frac{6^2}{3} + \frac{3^2}{3} - \frac{T^2}{N}$$

$$\therefore \quad \text{SSC} = (16.3 + 21.3 + 12.0 + 3) - 48 = 4.6$$

and $\text{d.f.} = (c - 1) = 4 - 1 = 3$

SSR = Sum of squares Between varieties (*i.e.*, between Rows)

$$= \frac{10^2}{4} + \frac{6^2}{4} + \frac{8^2}{4} - \frac{T^2}{N} = (25 + 9 + 16) - 48 = 2$$

and $\text{d.f.} = (r - 1) = 3 - 1 = 2$

SST = Total sum of squares

$$= [0^2 + 4^2 + 3^2 + 4^2 + 2^2 + 2^2 + 2^2 + 0^2 + 4^2 + 4^2 + 0^2 + (-1)^2] - \frac{T^2}{N}$$

$\therefore$ SST = 86 – 48 = 38

and d.f. = N – 1 = 12 – 1 = 11

$\therefore$ SSE = SST – (SSC + SSR) = 38 – (4.6 + 2) = 31.4

and d.f. = (C – 1) (r – 1) = 3 × 2 = 6

Two-Way ANOVA Table

Source of variation	Sum of squares (SS)	d.f.	Mean squares (MS)	Variance ratio
Between Blocks	4.6	3	$\frac{4.6}{3} = 1.53$	$F = \frac{5.23}{1.53} = 9.42$
Between Varieties	2.0	2	2 ÷ 2 = 1.00	$F = \frac{5.23}{1.00} = 5.23$
Residual	31.4	6	$\frac{31.4}{6} = 5.23$	
Total	38.0	11	—	

Since the calculated value of $F = 9.42 > F_{0.05,(6,3)} = 8.94$ (see Appendix Table Va). We conclude that the block means are not equal. Again the calculated value of $F = 5.23 < F_{0.05,(6,2)} = 19.33$ implies that there is no significant difference between the varieties ($p > 0.05$).

Note: At 1% level for (6, 3) d.f. the tabulated value of F is 27.9 and $F_{0.01,(6,2)} = 99.3$ [see Appendix Table V(b)] both tabulated values are greater than their respective calculated values of F and hence there is no significant difference between the blocks and varieties ($p > 0.01$).

➤ EXERCISES ➤

14.1. The following data is related to production (in kg) of three varieties:

A :	16	15	18	19
B :	14	15	20	22
C :	18	16	16	19

Is there any significant difference in the production of three varieties?

14.2. The following data showing the iron intake (in mg) of antenatal mothers of four villages:

Village	Iron intake (in mg) by Antenatal mother									
A	12.0	18.5	14.5	20.0	22.0	24.5	16.0	28.0	21.5	19.0
B	16.5	22.0	24.0	19.0	18.5	30.0	24.5	15.0	22.5	17.0
C	29.0	18.0	30.0	16.5	24.5	17.5	19.0	28.5	18.5	14.5
D	25.5	27.0	30.0	22.0	28.0	34.0	27.5	32.0	22.0	29.0

Test whether the differences in the mean iron intake between villages are significant or not.

14.3. Following table gives the number of items sold by four salesmen in three months:

	Salesmen			
Months	**A**	**B**	**C**	**D**
October	500	400	700	800
November	400	700	500	300
December	300	500	400	600

Is there any significant difference in the sales made by the four salesmen?

14.4. Diastolic BP (mm of Hg) of three occupational groups of individuals are recorded in the following table:

Business class	Technical group	Labour class
84	98	82
88	96	92
90	102	86
98	90	98
82	95	94
78	100	90
100	92	88
95	94	96
92	104	95
86	88	84

Test whether the mean diastolic BP in three groups differs.

14.5. The protein content of five varieties of leafy vegetables estimated in three regions are given in the following table:

	Region		
Variety of vegetable	**I**	**II**	**III**
A	1.00	1.22	2.62
B	1.72	0.74	1.11
C	1.53	1.46	2.19
D	0.85	1.90	0.94

Test the variation due to regions and varieties.

14.6. A company sales manager appoints four salesmen and observes their selling ability in three seasons. The figures (in lakhs) are given in the following table:

Season	**Salesmen**			
	A	B	C	D
Summer	25	28	26	28
Monsoon	16	18	20	19
Winter	26	24	22	25

Perform the analysis and draw your conclusion.

14.7. The following data pertaining to the experiment for testing four test materials for their action in reducing blood sugar levels. Each test material was given to each of the five individuals through randomization and without any interaction between them:

	Test materials			
Person	**Test I**	**Test II**	**Test III**	**Test IV**
1	85	110	89	110
2	92	106	94	118
3	102	98	98	106
4	96	100	78	126
5	92	112	86	100

Test whether the differences between test materials and individuals are significant or not.

14.8. The following data give the yields on 12 plots of an agriculture land in three samples under three types of fertilizers A, B, and C

A	B	C
24	20	30
26	19	28
21	18	26
25	16	—
22	—	—

Is there any significant difference in the average yields of land under the three varieties of fertilizers?

14.9. The following table gives the data of a randomised block design on the bacterial counts in milk made by four observers on each of six plates:

	Observer			
Plate No.	**A**	**B**	**C**	**D**
I	342	250	245	280
II	228	180	155	198
III	130	70	82	125
IV	248	210	206	212
V	240	324	300	315
VI	126	72	66	98

Prepare the ANOVA table and record your conclusions.

14.10 The following data show the birth-weight (kgs) of new borns, classified according to the age of mother and the order of gravida:

	Age of mother (yrs.)					
Order of gravida	**15-19**	**20-24**	**25-29**	**30-34**	**35-39**	**40 and above**
1	2.5, 2.2, 2.4	2.2, 2.4, 2.6	2.4, 2.4, 2.6	2.2, 2.4, 2.5	2.5, 2.5, 2.6	2.2, 2.4, 2.3
2	2.6, 2.6, 2.7	2.5, 2.5, 2.6	2.5, 2.6, 2.8	2.6, 2.4, 2.5	2.6, 2.6, 2.8	2.3, 2.4, 2.5
3.	2.8, 2.8, 2.9	2.7, 2.5, 2.8	2.8, 2.7, 2.6	2.7, 3.0, 2.8	2.5, 3.0, 3.2	2.5, 2.6 2.6
4.	2.9, 2.8, 2.9	2.8, 2.9, 2.8	2.8, 2.8, 2.7	2.9, 3.0, 3.0	2.8, 3.0, 3.2	3.0, 2.9 2.8
5 and above	2.7, 2.5, 2.5	2.8, 2.8, 2.6	2.5, 2.8, 2.7	2.6, 2.5, 2.8	2.6, 2.6, 2.5	2.5, 2.7 2.6

Test whether the age of mother and order of gravida significantly affect the birth-weight.

CHAPTER

15

Non-Parametric Test

- *Heterogeneity*
- *Sign Test*
- *Rank Test*
- *Run Test*

A relatively extreme situation occurs when it is possible to use methods of testing significance which do not make restrictive assumptions about the shape of population distribution. These are known as distribution-free, or more commonly, non-parametric methods or tests.

Definition of Non-Parametric Methods

"Methods which do not involve hypothesis concerning specific values of parameters or which are based on some functions of the sample observations whose sampling distribution can be determined without knowledge of the specific distribution function of the underlying population."

Uses of Non-Parametric Tests

There are four situations in which of a distribution free or non-parametric technique is indicated:

(i) When the assumptions of a parametric procedure are not satisfied and the consequences of this are either unknown or known to be serious.

(ii) When quick or preliminary data analysis is needed.

(iii) When data are only roughly scaled, *e.g.*, when only comparative rather than absolute magnitudes are available. In dealing with clinical data, perhaps patients can only be classified as better, unchanged (stable), or worst.

(iv) When the basic question of interest is distribution-free or non-parametric in nature.

Types of Non-Parametric Tests

1. The Sign Test

The sign test is the simplest of all statistical tests. It focuses on the median rather than the mean as a measure of central tendency. It is called the sign test because we use (+) and (–) signs as the new data is performing the calculation. The sign test can be used with a single sample and a paired sample.

Single Sample

In a single sample, we test the null hypothesis, H_0 that the sample median is equal to population median. For this purpose, we assign (+) sign to observations that fall above the population median and (–) sign to those that fall below the population median. A tie (similar observations) is given a zero and is not counted. If the null hypothesis, H_0 is true, *i.e.*, the medians are the same and then we expect an equal number of (+) and (–) signs.

EXAMPLE 15.1 : In an anesthetic used for major surgery, the median number of hours it takes for the anesthesia to wear off is 6. A new agent has been suggested that supposedly provides relief much sooner. In a series of 10 surgeries using the new anesthetic, the following times for recovery were recorded:

Recovery time :	3	4	4	4	5	5	6	6	7	8
Sign :	(–)	(–)	(–)	(–)	(–)	(–)	0	0	(+)	(+)

Null Hypothesis (H_0)

The median recovery time for the new anesthetic is 6 hours.

Since the suggestion is made that the new anesthetic is better. Here, six outcomes are less than the median of the standard anesthetic and two are more. We exclude the two scores since they are equal to the median of 6.

Thus, we observe only two (+)s when we expected 4 (+)s under the null hypothesis.

To determine the probability that the two (+) positives occur randomly, we use the table of critical values for the Sign Test (see Appendix Table VI). From this table, we can see, for $n = 8$ and $\alpha = 0.05$ one tailed test, that $q = 1$ or 7. Therefore, for this sample to have a significantly better recovery time than 6 hours, it will require 7 negatives (–)s or one (+). Since we observed six (–)s, so we cannot reject H_0, *i.e.*, there is no significant difference between the recovery time from the sample and that of the population median.

Paired Samples

The sign test is also suitable for experiments with paired data such as before and after (or treatment and control). The only assumption we make in the sign test is that the different pairs are to be independent, *i.e.*, only the direction of change in each pair is recorded as a (+) or (–) signs. We expect an equal number of (+) and (–) sign if there is no treatment effect. The null hypothesis tested by the paired samples sign test is that the median of the observations listed first is the same as that of the median of the observations listed second in each pair. If the observations of a pair are same (in tie), *i.e.*, the difference is zero which has no sign. Such differences should be discarded from the sample.

EXAMPLE 15.2 : Nine blood samples were sent to two reference laboratories for serum cholesterol determination. The result are as follows:

Patient	1	2	3	4	5	6	7	8	9
Lab. A	240	246	262	266	272	260	272	295	268
Lab. B	245	248	285	288	276	282	276	318	280
Sign of difference	(–)	(–)	(–)	(–)	(–)	(–)	(–)	(–)	(–)

H_0: The median serum cholesterol determination of both laboratories is equal.

Since, there are no ties in the data, so the number of paired observations (n = 9) and the number of (–) differences is also 9. What should be the chances of obtaining such a result by chance, it can be seen from the sign test table (see Appendix Table VI) for n = 9; the critical value of q is either 1 or 8 for $\alpha = 0.05$ two tailed test. Consequently, we have 9 (–)s as a result, which is greater than 8. Hence we reject the H_0 of no difference in medians at 5% level and conclude that there is a significant difference in the investigation procedures of the two laboratories in determining cholesterol levels ($p < 0.05$).

Note: The significance of difference between the two procedures can also be tested by the usual Chi-square test, *i.e.*,

$$\chi^2 = \frac{(|a - b| - 1)^2}{n} \text{ with one d.f.}$$

where 'a' and 'b' are the number of (+) and (–) respectively and n = (a + b).

If χ^2 calculated is more than χ^2 Tabulated, it signifies the rejection of null hypothesis at $p < 0.05$.

EXAMPLE 15.3: The following data are obtained on 12 male adults of age group 45 to 55 years. The values are serum cholesterol readings taken after 12 hours of fasting and repeated 1 hour after eating:

Participants	Fasting	After eating	Difference
A	200	195	(+)
B	210	220	(–)
C	240	225	(+)
D	220	230	(–)
E	180	185	(–)
F	210	200	(+)
G	190	180	(+)
H	225	235	(–)
I	250	255	(+)
J	260	265	(+)
K	245	240	(+)
L	195	190	(+)

Test to see if the difference may come from a population having median zero by the sign test.

SOLUTION: H_0: The differences come from a population having median zero.

There are no ties in the data, so $n = 12$ and the number of (+) difference ($n_+ =$ 8). This is larger than the value of 6 that would be expected if both readings come from a population having the same median (*i.e.*, number of (+)s should be equal to the number of (–)s differences). The critical value of n_+ for $n = 12$ at 5% level two tailed sign test is 2, 10 (see Appendix Table VI). Since $n_+ = 8$ is between the values of 2 and 10, we accept the H_0 of no difference in medians at 5% level ($p > 0.05$).

2. Wilcoxon Signed Rank Test:

This test is useful for testing the significance of differences in paired observations when the data is quantitative in nature. Again the tested hypothesis is that the first and second members of the pairs come from populations having the same median or that the pair differences come from a population having median zero.

The following procedure is adopted:

(i) To obtain the difference (d) between individual pairs of observations. It is to be noted that the pairs yielding a difference of zero are eliminated from the calculation and the sample size is reduced accordingly.

(ii) To perform the test, we rank the absolute differences by assigning ranks of '1' for the smallest to 'n' for the largest. In case, ties occur among the differences; the tied differences are each given the average of the ranks that would have been assigned if the differences had differed slightly. The signs of the original differences are then restored to each rank.

(iii) We obtain the sum of the positive ranks, T_+, which serves as the test statistic. If the null hypothesis (H_0) is true, we would expect to have an equal number of positive and negative ranks.

(iv) If T_+ is less than the critical value given in (see Appendix Table VII) for the given n pairs of observations at 5% level two tailed test, the null hypothesis is rejected at $p > 0.05$.

If there is only one sample and we want to compare the location of the distribution with that of a specified one, we may use this test. In this situation we first calculate the difference from the specified value (say median), rank all the absolute (without sign) differences together and then treat them as two groups according to whether the difference is positive or negative.

For Large Samples: Although non-parametric methods are specially suited for small samples but sometimes it is preferred for large samples also. For large samples, T_+ is approximately normally distributed with mean = [n (n + 1)] ÷ 4 and variance

$$= \frac{n\,(n+1)\,(2n+1)}{24}$$

$$\text{Thus,} \quad z = \frac{(T_+) - n\,(n+1) \div 4}{\sqrt{n\,(n+1)\,(2n+1) \div 24}}$$

If calculated value of $z > 1.96$ then it signifies rejection of the null hypothesis of $P < 0.05$.

EXAMPLE 15.4: A group of 10 hypertensive individuals determined to find out if they could lower their systolic blood pressure (mm of Hg) through a systematic physical fitness program. They observed their blood pressure (SBP) before they began their program and then again six month later. The following results were found:

Subjects	Systolic Blood Pressure (mm of Hg)									
	1	2	3	4	5	6	7	8	9	10
Before the program program	170	152	156	136	128	130	144	155	140	160
After six months of the program	158	156	146	150	120	124	128	160	137	162

Test whether there is any significant difference in the SBP values before and after physical fitness program.

SOLUTION: H_0 : There is no significant difference is the SBP values before and after physical fitness program.

Now we perform Wilcoxon Signed Rank Test on the above data.

Subjects	Systolic Blood Pressure (mm of Hg)									
	1	2	3	4	5	6	7	8	9	10
Before the program (b)	174	152	156	154	142	130	146	155	140	163
After six month of program (a)	168	156	146	140	130	132	138	160	137	170
Difference (a – b)	– 6	+4	– 10	– 14	– 12	+2	– 8	+5	– 3	+7
| a – b |	6	4	10	14	12	2	8	5	3	7
Signed Rank	5 (–)	3 (+)	8 (–)	10 (–)	9 (–)	1 (+)	7 (–)	4 (+)	2 (–)	6 (+)

Since there are no ties in the data, so $n = 10$.

Sum of (+) ranks = 3 + 1 + 4 + 6 = 14, and

Sum of (–) ranks = 5 + 8 + 10 + 9 + 7 + 2 = 41

From the Wilcoxon's signed rank test table (see Appendix Table VII) it is observed that for 10 pairs, a rank sum of less than or equal to 8 is required for rejection of the null hypothesis at 5% level. Since the calculated $T_+ = 14$ is more that the tabulated value of 8. Thus we accept the null hypothesis and conclude that the difference is not significant ($p > 0.05$).

EXAMPLE 15.5: The following data shows consumption of Bidis/Cigarettes (usually smoked per day) before and after pregnancy among the female workers:

Subjects	Number of Bidis/Cigarettes per day	
	Before pregnancy	After pregnancy
1	07	04
2	12	14
3	14	04
4	10	16
5	20	12
6	16	10
7	20	15
8	15	04
9	06	10
10	07	04
11	15	06
12	12	12
13	04	04
14	20	08
15	05	06
16	12	10
17	16	20
18	06	06
19	10	10
20	04	02
21	08	01
22	06	04
23	12	03
24	02	02
25	02	03

Apply Willcoxon Signed Rank Test. Is there any significant reduction in the smoking habit consequent to pregnancy?

Solution: H_0: There is no difference between smoking status before and after pregnancy.

Subjects **Number of Bidis/Cigarettes per day**

	Before pregnancy (x_b)	After pregnancy (x_a)	($x_a - x_b$)	$\lvert x_a - x_b \rvert$	Signed Rank Test
1	07	04	− 3	3	7.5 (–)
2	12	14	+ 2	2	4.5 (+)
3	14	04	− 10	10	18 (–)
4	10	16	+ 6	6	13 (+)
5	20	12	− 8	8	16 (–)
6	16	10	− 6	6	13 (–)
7	20	15	− 5	5	11 (–)
8	15	04	− 11	11	19 (–)
9	06	10	+ 4	4	9.5 (+)
10	07	04	− 3	3	7.5 (–)
11	15	06	− 6	6	13 (–)
12	12	12	0	0	—
13	04	04	0	0	—
14	20	08	− 12	12	20 (–)
15	05	06	+ 01	01	1.5 (+)
16	12	10	− 2	2	4.5 (–)
17	16	20	+ 4	4	9.5 (+)
18	06	06	0	0	—
19	10	10	0	0	—
20	04	02	− 2	2	4.5 (–)
21	08	01	− 7	7	15 (–)
22	06	04	− 2	2	4.5 (–)
23	12	03	− 9	9	17 (–)
24	02	02	0	0	—
25	02	03	+ 1	1	1.5 (+)

Sum of (+) ranks, $T_+ = 4.5 + 13 + 9.5 + 1.5 + 9.5 + 1.5 = 39.5$

Sum of (–) ranks, $T_- = 7.5 + 18 + 16 + 13 + 11 + 19 + 7.5 + 13 + 20 + 4.5 + 4.5 + 15 + 4.5 + 17$

$= 170.5$

As a check, the sum of $T_{(+)}$ and $T_{(-)}$ should be equal to [n (n +) ÷ 2], *i.e.*, Sum of all ranks is $[20\,(21) \div 2] = 210 = [T_{(+)} + T_{(-)} = 39.5 + 170.5] = 210$.

Under the H_0, we assume that the sum of the (+) ranks is equal to the sum of negative (–) ranks, *i.e.*, each will be the half of the total sum of the ranks. Therefore, the expected sum of the ranks will be $\frac{1}{2}[n(n+1) \div 2]$ which $[20(21) \div 4] = 105$.

The test statistic, T_+ is 39.5 is smaller of sum of all ranks. Since T_+ is approximately normally distributed with mean of $[n(n+1) \div 4]$ and variance of $[n(n+1)(2n+1) \div 24]$.

We can apply Z-test for the difference between the sums of matched ranks as

$$Z = \frac{T_+ - [n(n+1) \div 4]}{\sqrt{[n(n+1)(2n+1) \div 24]}}$$

$$= \frac{39.5 - 105}{\sqrt{105 \times 6.83}} = \frac{-65.5}{\sqrt{717.15}}$$

$$\therefore \quad |Z| = \frac{65.5}{26.5} = 2.44$$

This result indicates that the difference between the observed and expected rank sums is significant ($p < 0.05$). Thus, we reject the null hypothesis and conclude that there is a significant reduction in the smoking habit consequent to pregnancy.

3. Mann-Whitney Test

This test is useful for testing the difference between unpaired observations, *i.e.*, the observations in one sample are independent to those in the other sample. The test is performed in following steps:

(i) Combine all the observations from both the samples and arrange the entire combined set of observations in order of their magnitude from the smallest to the largest observation.

(ii) Give ranks to all combined observations according to their magnitude. If tied values occur, average of the ranks is given to them as in the case of Wilcoxon's signed rank test.

(iii) Proper identification mark is made to differentiate the observations of the two samples separately.

(iv) Calculate the sum of ranks of each of the samples separately.

(v) The test statistic is T_s, the smaller rank sum is compared with the critical values in the Table (see Appendix Table VIII) for Mann- Whitney test.

(vi) If the value of T_s is equal of less than the tabulated value, the null hypothesis is rejected; otherwise accepted at 5%.

Notes:

1. When two samples are of unequal in size, the smaller rank sum is calculated by $T_s = n_1 (n_1 + n_2 + 1) - T_1$, where T_1 is the rank sum of the sample with smaller number of observations and while n_1 and n_2 are the number of observations in the first and second sample respectively.
2. In case, when the values of n_1 and n_2 are greater than 20, the Z-test is preferred for testing the hypothesis.

$$Z = (|\mu - T_s| - 0.05) \div \sigma$$

where $\mu = n_1 (n_1 + n_2 + 1) \div 2$

and $\sigma = \sqrt{n_2 \mu \div 6}$

while n_1 and n_2 are the smaller sample size and the bigger sample size respectively.

The Z calculated is compared with Z table value of if Z calculated is more than 1.96, the null hypothesis is rejected, otherwise accepted at 5% level.

EXAMPLE 15.6: The following data represent the total histidine excretions (mg) per 24-hour urine sample for 7 men and 10 women on unrestricted diets:

Men :	180	172	235	220	432	266	436			
Women:	198	220	116	135	142	204	200	138	210	86

Is there any significant difference between men and women in the total histidine excretions through urine?

SOLUTION: H_0: There is no significance difference between men and women urine samples with total histidine excretions.

The combined set of values are arranged in the order of magnitude with assigned ranks, *i.e.*,

Values:	86	116	135	138	142	172	180	198	200	204	210	220	220
Ranks:	1	2	3	4	5	6	7	8	9	10	11	12.5	12.5
Values:		235		266	432	436							
Ranks:		14		15	16	17							

Since the size of two samples are different (*i.e.*, $n_1 = 7$ and $n_2 = 10$) first, the sum of ranks of the smaller sample is found out

$$T_1 = 6 + 7 + 12.5 + 14 + 15 + 16 + 17 = 87.5$$

and $T_s = n_1 (n_1 + n_2 + 1) - T_1$

where n_1 is the smaller sample size (*i.e.*, $n_1 = 7$) and n_2 is the bigger sample size (*i.e.*, $n_2 = 10$).

$$T_s = 7 (7 + 10 + 1) - 87.5$$

$$\therefore \quad T_s = 7(18) - 87.5 = 126 - 87.5 = 38.5$$

Since 38.5 is smaller than 87.5, we refer to this value in the Mann-Whitney T-Table (see Appendix Table VIII) for $n_1 = 7$ and $n_2 = 10$. The table value of T corresponding to these degrees of freedom is 42 at 5% level which is more than the calculated value of 38.5. Thus, we reject the null hypothesis and conclude the difference is significant at 5% level.

4. Kruskal-Wallis Test

A rank test for 'k' independent samples is Kruskal-Wallis test. This is a non-parametric analysis of variance in one way classification. This test is used to test whether or not the groups of independent samples have been drawn from the same population. It does not require assumptions concerning the population probability distribution to compare the 'k' samples.

The test statistics is given by $H = \frac{12}{n(n+1)} \sum_{i=1}^{k} \frac{R_i^2}{n_i} - 3(n+1)$

where, n is the total number of observations in all the samples together, R_i is the sum of ranks in the *i*th sample and n_i is the number of observations in the *i*th sample. 'H' is interpreted as Chi-square with degrees of freedom equal to one less than the number of samples compared, *i.e.*, k–1.

EXAMPLE 15.7: Scores obtained by three occupational groups of patient-attendants on the disease burden felt by them in a tertiary care hospital, are given below:

Agriculture		Service		Business	
Score	Ranks (R_1)	Score	Rank (R_2)	Score	Rank (R_3)
12	03	20	11	10	01
14	05	30	22.5	22	13
15	06	18	09	32	25.5
29	21	33	27.5	26	17
31	24	28	20	33	27.5
16	07	11	02	35	30
21	12	23	14	27	18.5
27	18.5	32	25.5	13	04
17	08	34	29	24	15
19	10	25	16	30	22.5
$n_1 = 10$	$\Sigma R_1 = 114.5$	$n_2 = 10_3$	$\Sigma R_2 = 176.5$	$n_3 = 10$	$\Sigma R_3 = 174$

Test the randomness of the sequence of scores.

SOLUTION: Here $n_1 = n_2 = n_3 = 10$

n = Total number of observations = 30

All the observations are ranked in ascending order of their magnitudes irrespective of their groups.

H_0 : All the three groups (or samples) have been drawn from the same population.

The rank sums are $R_1 = 114.5, R_2 = 176.5$, and $R_3 = 174$

Thus, Test statistic $H = \frac{12}{n(n+1)} \sum_{i=1}^{3} \frac{R_i^2}{n_i} - 3(n+1)$

$$= \frac{12}{30(31)}\left[\frac{(114.5)^2}{10} + \frac{(176.5)^2}{10} + \frac{(174)^2}{10}\right] - 3(31)$$

$$= \frac{12}{930}\left[\frac{13110.25 + 31152.25 + 30276}{10}\right] - 93$$

$$= \frac{12}{930}(7453.85) - 93$$

∴ $H = 96.2 - 93 = 3.2$

The degrees of freedom $= (k-1) = 3 - 1 = 2$

The approximate distribution of the test statistic, H is a Chi-square distribution with $(k-1) = (3-1) = 2$ degrees of freedom. Since the calculated value of $H = 3.2$ is less than $\chi^2_{0.05,2} = 5.99$ (tabulated value), we accept the null hypothesis and conclude that the samples (groups) have not been drawn from the same population ($p > 0.05$).

EXAMPLE 15.8: The following table shows the number of workers in nine companies representing each of three different business classifications, *i.e.*, technical, sales and purchases, and official:

Number of workers in nine different companies

Technical		Sales and purchase		Official	
I	Ranks (R_1)	II	Rank (R_2)	III	Rank (R_3)
5	1	155	25	20	7
105	22	90	21	15	5
10	2	80	19	18	6
25	10	30	12	75	18
12	4	62	16	22	8
110	23	145	24	38	14
35	13	85	20	11	3
65	17	180	26	28	11
23	9	202	27	55	15
$n_1 = 9$	$\Sigma R_1 = 101$	$n_2 = 9$	$\Sigma R_2 = 190$	$n_3 = 9$	$\Sigma R_3 = 87$

Test whether there is any significant difference amount three samples.

SOLUTION: H_0 : Three is no difference among the samples (*i.e.*, they have identical probability distributions).

H_1 : At least two of the three samples are differ in location the test-statistic.

$$H = \frac{12}{n(n+1)} \sum_{i=1}^{3} \frac{R_i^2}{n_i} - 3(n+1)$$

where $n = (n_1 + n_2 + n_3) = 27\ (n_1 = n_2 = n_3 = 9)$

and rank sums are : $\Sigma R_1 = 101$; $\Sigma R_2 = 190$; and $\Sigma R_3 = 87$

Thus
$$H = \frac{12}{27(28)}\left[\frac{(101)^2}{9} + \frac{(190)^2}{9} + \frac{(87)^2}{9}\right] - (27+1)$$

$$= \frac{12}{756}\left[\frac{10201 + 36100 + 7569}{9}\right] - 3(28)$$

$$= \frac{12}{756}(5985.5) - 84$$

$$\therefore \quad H = 95 - 84 = 11$$

The degree of freedom = (k – 1) = (3 – 1) = 2

The approximate distribution of the test statistic, H is a Chi-square distribution with $(k-1) = (3-1) = 2$ degrees of freedom. Since the calculated value of $H = 11$ is more than $\chi^2_{0\,05,2} = 5.99$ (Tabulated value), we reject the null hypothesis and conclude that there is a significant difference among the samples or at least two probability distributions are different $(p < 0.05)$.

5. Runs Test for Randomness

A Run is considered as a sequence of identical occurrences preceded and followed by different occurrences or by none at all. For example,

(a) If women and men enter in a hall as follows:

$$\underbrace{W, W}_{1},\ \underbrace{M, M, M}_{2},\ \underbrace{W}_{3},\ \underbrace{M, M, M, M}_{4},\ \underbrace{W, W, W}_{5},\ \underbrace{M}_{6}$$

Then this sequence contains six Runs. Also in this case, we have two types of occurrences n_1 and n_2 (*i.e.*, $n_1 = 6$ = number of women and $n_2 = 8$ = number of men). The total number of runs, r = 9. The test statistic, r for a Run-test is based on the idea that too low or two many Runs show that the items (or observations) were not chosen randomly.

(b) Consider the following sequence of (+) and (–) signs:

+, +, –, –, –, +, –, –, –, –, +, –, –, –, –, +, +, +

The sequence begins with a Run of two plus signs followed by runs of three minus signs, one plus sign, and so on, lastely a run of three pluses. So that there are seven runs in the sequence and the total number of observed events ($N = n_1 + n_2$) is 18 where n_1 = the number of (+) signs and n_2 = the number of (–) signs.

Procedure of Performing Runs Test (First Method)

(i) Firstly, find the median of the sample and for each observation record a plus sign if it is above the median, a minus sign if it is below the median.

(ii) If the sample size is odd, one observation will be equal to median because this observation will produce neither a plus nor minus sign and it must be discarded, thereby reducing the sample size by one.

(iii) The critical values of 'r' in the Table (see Appendix Table IX) are such that if total number of runs, r is between the critical values, the randomness hypothesis, H_0 is accepted and if it falls outside the values or equals one of them, then null hypothesis is rejected at the corresponding level of significance for a two tailed test.

EXAMPLE 15.9 : Following table shows the aggression scores for each child in the order in which those scores occurred:

Aggression scores in order of occurrence

Child	Score	Child	Score
1	12	8	86
2	23	9	15
3	36	10	18
4	43	11	78
5	51	12	24
6	44	13	13
7	31	14	27

Test the randomness of the data by using the Runs test.

SOLUTION: H_0: The pluses and minuses occur in random order. First we calculate median of the given data. The median of the data is the average of $\frac{N}{2}$th and $\left(\frac{N}{2}+1\right)$th term of the arrange data, since N is 14 (even) 12, 13, 15, 18, 23, 24, 27, 31, 36, 43, 44, 51, 78, 86.

$\therefore \qquad \text{Median} = \dfrac{27+31}{2} = 29$

Now we have the sequence of plus sign (above the median) and minus sign (below the median) for the given data (*i.e.*, ungrouped data) as follows:

$$\underbrace{-,-}_{1}, \underbrace{+,+,+,+,+,+}_{2}, \underbrace{-,-}_{3}, \underbrace{+}_{4}, \underbrace{-,-,-}_{5}$$

The total number of runs, $r = 5$ and n_1 = number of plus signs = 7, n_2 = number of minus signs = 7. Since the total number of runs, $r = 5$ falls in between the critical values of 3 and 13 (see Appendix Table IX) for $n_1 = n_2 = 7$ at 5% level in two tailed test.

Thus, the null hypothesis of randomness is accepted.

Runs Test for Large Samples (Second Method): If either n_1 or n_2 is larger than 20, for such large samples, a good approximation to the sampling distribution of r is the normal distribution, with

Mean of the r-statistic,

$$\mu_r = \frac{2\,n_1 n_2}{n_1 + n_2} + 1$$

and standard deviation,

$$\sigma_r = \sqrt{\frac{2n_1 n_2\,(2n_1 n_2 - n_1 - n_2)}{(n_1 + n_2)^2\,(n_1 + n_2 - 1)}}$$

Therefore, null hypothesis may be tested by

$$Z = \frac{r - \mu_r}{\sigma_r} = \frac{r - (2n_1 n_2 / n_1 + n_2) + 1}{\sqrt{\dfrac{2n_1 n_2\,(2n_1 n_2 - n_1 - n_2)}{(n_1 + n_2)^2\,(n_1 + n_2 - 1)}}}$$

Decision: If Z calculated > 1.96, then H_0 is rejected; otherwise accepted at 5% of significance.

Note: The null hypothesis of randomness of scores in runs test may also be test by knowing the limits of the acceptance region at 5% level of significance, ***i.e.***, for normal distribution of r.

Upper limit $= \mu_r + 1.96\sigma_r$

and Lower limit $= \mu_r - 1.96\sigma_r$

If the observed 'r' falls within the acceptance region, it concludes that H_0 is to be accepted at 5% level (*i.e.*, sequence appears to be random).

EXAMPLE 15.10: Test for randomness of the following sample using the 5% level of significance: M, F, M, M, M, F, F, M, F, F, F, M, M, F, M, F, F, M, F, M, M, F, M, M, M, F, F, F, M, F, M, F, M, M, F, M, M, M, M, F.

SOLUTION: H_0 : The order of Males and Females is random

Here n_1 = number of males = 22

n_2 = number of females = 18

r = number of runs = 24

To determine whether $r \geq 24$ might readily have occurred under H_0 we compute the value of z by the following formula:

$$Z = \frac{r-[2n_1n_2 \div (n_1+n_2)-1]}{\sqrt{\frac{2n_1n_2\,(2n_1n_2-n_1-n_2)}{(n_1+n_2)^2(n_1+n_2-1)}}}$$

$$Z = \frac{24-[2(22)\,(18) \div (22+18)+1]}{\sqrt{\frac{2\,(22)\,(18)\,[2\,(22)(18)-22-18]}{(22+18)^2\,(22+18-1)}}}$$

$$Z = \frac{24-(19.8+1)}{\sqrt{\frac{792\,(752)}{1600\,(39)}}} = \frac{3.2}{\sqrt{\frac{595584}{62400}}}$$

$$\therefore \quad Z = \frac{3.2}{\sqrt{9.5}} = \frac{3.2}{3.1} = 1.03$$

Since, Z calculated is less than 1.96 at 5% level of significance hence, we accept the null hypothesis that the sequence of scores is random ($p > 0.05$).

Note: H_0 may be tested by the limits of acceptance region at 5% level of significance, *i.e.*, for normal distribution of r.

Since, Mean of r-statistic, $\mu_r = \frac{2n_1n_2}{n_1+n_2}+1$

Here $n_1 = 22$, and $n_2 = 18$

Therefore $$\mu_r = \left(\frac{2\times22\times18}{22+18}\right)+1 = 20.8$$

and $$\sigma_r = \sqrt{\frac{2n_1n_2\,(2n_1n_2-n_1-n_2)}{(n_1+n_2)^2\,(n_1+n_2-1)}}$$

$$\therefore \quad \sigma_r = \sqrt{\frac{792\,(752)}{1600\,(39)}} = \sqrt{9.5} = 3.1$$

Now Upper limit $= \mu_r + 1.96\,\sigma_r$

$= 20.8 + 1.96\,(3.1) = 20.8 + 6.1 = 26.9$

and Lower limit $= \mu_r - 1.96\,\sigma_r$

$= 20.8 - 1.96\,(3.1) = 14.7$

Decision: The observed value of r = number of runs = 24 falls within the acceptance region (*i.e.*, between 14.7 and 26.9), so we accept the null hypothesis and conclude that the sequence of scores is random.

➤ EXERCISES ➤

15.1: The following table shows serum cholesterol readings on ten patients aged between 40 years and 60 years:

Patients	1	2	3	4	5	6	7	8	9	10
12 years of fasting	210	180	190	200	195	220	230	200	240	210
Repeated one hour after eating	200	190	175	195	200	225	240	190	245	225

Test whether the differences come from a population having median zero by using sign test.

15.2: Ten patients had supine systolic BP taken at the onset and conclusion of a half hour rest period. The readings are recorded in the following table:

Patients	1	2	3	4	5	6	7	8	9	10
Sys. BP Before	152	138	128	154	140	136	160	172	146	150
Sys. BP After	144	142	122	148	134	132	164	170	138	154

Test whether the differences occurred from a population having median zero by using the signed rank test.

15.3: The following data represent age at immunization in months for infants during a certain month by two paediatrician practising in the same community:

Age at Immunization (in months)

Paediatrician A	9.2	14.2	11.7	17.2	12.7	13.2	18.4
Paediatrician B	12.4	8.2	12.6	14.9	16.2	9.4	

Apply the rank sum test to verify whether or not these samples come from population with identical distributions.

15.4: The following table shows the weight gain by a mother during pregnancy:

Weight gain during pregnancy

Mother with no dietary restrictions	3.7	4.2	2.9	3.3	3.7	3.1	2.7
Mother restricted to 7 kg	3.1	3.0	3.8	4.6	4.1	2.7	

Test whether these samples come from populations with same distribution by using the rank sum test.

15.5: The following table shows serum cholinesterase indices in normal population. Test whether the data are arranged in random order by using the runs test.

1.44, 1.55, 1.22, 2.60, 1.16, 1.91, 1.70, 1.75, 2.17, 1.27, 1.89, 2.14, 2.27, 1.35, 2.59, 1.93, 2.26, 2.60, 1.83, 1.91, 1.16, 2.60, 1.22, 1.55, 1.16, 2.13, 1.96, 1.15, 1.32, 2.52.

15.6: In an experiment, 15 obese employees are randomly assigned to three conditions, with 5 subjects per condition. The data presented below are the number of kg loss or gain by each subject over a period of six month. Analyse the data by using Kruskal-Wallis test.

	A	B	C
Condition Subject	**Diet**	**Diet + Exercise**	**Control**
1	− 1.0	− 5.5	− 4.0
2	− 4.5	− 5.2	− 2.2
3	− 3.0	− 7.0	+ 1.2
4	− 2.5	− 6.5	+ 3.5
5	− 6.0	− 7.2	+ 4.0

15.7: The haemoglobin levels of 12 anaemic patients were noted (before and after therapy) in the following table:

Patient No. :	1	2	3	4	5	6	7	8	9	10	11	12
Hb gm % Before :	4.8	7.5	5.6	7.2	6.5	4.4	6.7	7.6	6.2	3.5	7.5	6.4
Hb gm % After :	9.4	8.0	10.2	7.2	10.0	8.0	8.2	8.5	9.5	6.0	8.5	7.0

Test whether differences occurred from a population having median zero by using signed rank test.

❖❖❖❖❖

CHAPTER

16

Demography

- *Fertility*
- *Mortality*
- *Migration*
- *Fecundity*
- *Population growh*
- *Urbanization*

The word demography (Demo + graphy) stands for 'Demo' means population and 'graphy' means study (*i.e.*, **Demography** is the study of human populations). It can be applied to any kind of dynamic human population, *i.e.*, one that changes over time or space. It encompasses the study of the size, structure, and distribution of populations, and spatial and/or temporal changes in them with respect to fertility (births), mortality (deaths) and migration (marriage registrations).

Demographic analysis can be applied to populations, *i.e.*, whole societies or to groups defined by criteria such as education, nationality, religion and ethnicity.

Demography limits its object of study to the measurement of populations processes, while the more broad field of social demography (population studies) also analyze the relationships between economic, social, cultural and biological processes influencing a population.

POPULATION DENSITY

It is defined as number of people living in one square kilometer area. It is an indicator of assessing the slow or rapid increase in congestion due to population growth over different periods of time.

Population density in a town may be calculated as persons per room to determine overcrowding. Density ratio of over 2 persons per room is indicative of overcrowding.

DATA AND METHODS

There are two methods of data collection: (i) direct, and (ii) indirect. Direct data is obtained from vital statistics registries which include all births and deaths as well as certain changes in legal status such as marriage, divorce, and migration.

A census (*i.e.*, total enumeration) is the other common direct method of collecting demographic data. A census is usually conducted by a central government and attempts to enumerate every person in a country at 10 years of interval. However, in contrast to vital statistics data, which are typically collected continuously and summarized on an annual basis. Analysis is conducted after a census to estimate how much over or under reported taking place.

Census does more than just count people. The informations about families (or households) in addition to individual characteristics such as age, gender, marital status, literacy/education, employment status, occupation, and geographical location are collected. The data on migration (or place of birth or of previous residence), language, religion, nationality, and citizenship are also collected. Countries in which the vital registration system may be incomplete, the census data is also used as a direct source of information about fertility and mortality.

Indirect methods of collecting data are required in countries where complete data is not available. One of these techniques is the sister method, where survey investigators ask women how many of their sisters have died or had children and at what age. With these surveys, investigators can then indirectly estimate birth or death rates for the entire population. Other indirect methods include asking people about siblings, parents, and children.

There are a variety of demographic methods for modeling population processes. They include models of mortality (including the life table, Gompertz models, hazards models, Cox proportional hazards models, multiple decrement life tables, Brass relational logits), fertility (Hernes model, Coale-Trussell models, parity progression ratios), marriage (Singulate Mean at Marriage, Page model), disability (Sullivan's method, multistate life tables), population projections (Lee Carter, the Leslie Matrix), and population momentum (Keyfitz).

DEMOGRAPHIC INDICATORS

As demography is interested in changes in human populations, that is why demographers focus on specific indicators of change. Two of the most important indicators are birth and death rates, which are also referred to as fertility (including fecundity) and mortality. Additionally, demographers are interested in migration trends or the movement of people from one location to another.

FERTILITY AND FECUNDITY

Fertility, in demography, refers to the ability of females to produce healthy offspring in abundance. Whereas fecundity is the potential reproductive capacity of a female. Some of the more common demographic measures used in relation to fertility and/or fecundity include:

CBR: The Crude Birth Rate, the annual number of live births per 1,000 people.

GFR: The General Fertility Rate, the annual number of live births per 1,000 women of childbearing age (often taken to be from 15 to 49 years old).

ASFR: Age-Specific Fertility Rates, the annual number of live births per 1,000 women in particular age groups (usually age 15-19, 20-24 etc.)

GRR: The Gross Reproduction Rate, the number of daughters who would be born to a mother completing her reproductive life at current age-specific fertility rates.

NRR: The Net Reproduction Ratio is the expected number of daughters, per newborn prospective mother, who may or may not survive to and through the ages of childbearing.

TFR: The Total Fertility Rate, the number of live births per woman completing her reproductive life, if her childbearing at each age reflected current age-specific fertility rates.

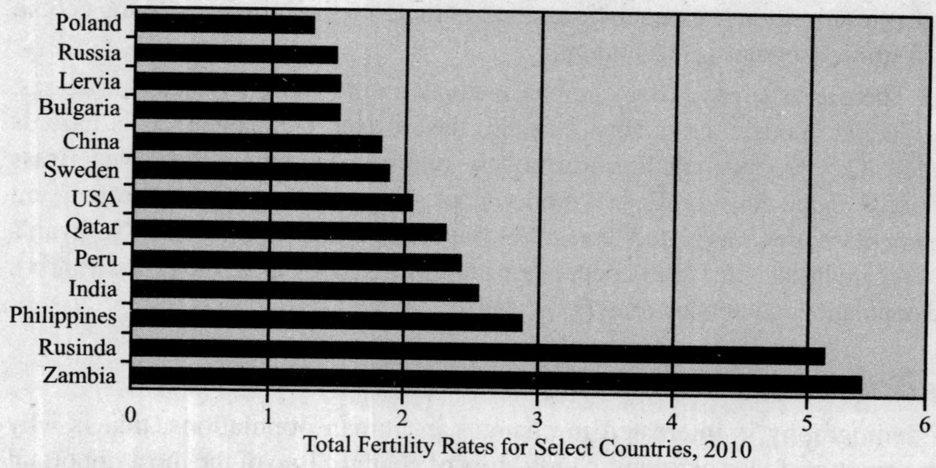

Fig. 16.1: Highlights the varied fertility rates of specific countries as some have very low fertility rates, many have moderate rates, and some have very high rates.

Another important demographic concept relating to fertility is replacement level. Replacement level fertility (RLF) refers to the number of children that a woman must have in order to replace the existing population. Sub-replacement fertility is a fertility rate that is not high enough to replace an existing population. Replacement level fertility is generally set at 2.1 children in a woman's lifetime (this number varies by geographic region given different mortality rates). Sub-replacement fertility is below approximately 2.1 children in a woman's life time. The reason the number is set to 2.1 children per woman is because two children are needed to replace the parents and an additional one-tenth of a child is needed to make up for the mortality of children and women who do not reach the end of their reproductive years. Of course, women do not have one-tenth of a child; this results from statistical averaging between women who have more than two children and those who have two or fewer children.

RLF: The Replacement Level Fertility, the average number of children a woman must have in order to replace herself with a daughter in the next generation. For example, let the replacement level fertility of a country be 3.51. It means that 100 women will bear 351 children, 175 of which will be females. About 3% of the alive female infants are expected to decease before they bear children, thus producing 170 women in the next generation.

One of the strongest predictors of fertility rates is women's educational attainment. Almost globally, higher levels of educational attainment result in lower fertility rates. It is not; however, education itself that causes decline in fertility but rather its association with other factors that reduce fertility such as women with higher levels of education delay marriage, have improved job opportunities are more likely to use contraceptive methods.

MORTALITY

Mortality refers to the number of deaths in a given time or place or the proportion of deaths in relation to a population. Some of the more common demographic measures of mortality include:

CDR: The Crude Death Rate, the annual number of deaths per 1,000 people.

IMR: The Infant Mortality Rate, the annual number of deaths of children less than 1 year old per 1,000 live births.

Life expectancy: The number of years which an individual at a given age could expect to live at present mortality rates.

Note that the crude death rate as defined above and applied to a whole population can give a misleading impression. For example, the number of deaths per 1000 people can be higher for developed nations than in less-developed countries, despite standards of health being better in developed countries. This is because developed countries have relatively more older people, who are more likely to die in a given year, so that the overall mortality rate can be higher even if the mortality rate at any given age is lower. A more complete picture of mortality is given by a life table which summarizes mortality separately at each age.

The best predictors of longevity (*i.e.*, a long life) is education, even when other factors are controlled: the more educated you are, the longer you can expect to live. Education also increases the probability of people engaging in healthy behaviors, like frequently exercising.

Other factors associated with greater longevity include:

Wealth: money increases access to good healthcare, which improves health and increases longevity

Race: whites live longer than blacks, though this is due to other social disparities, like income and education, and not to race itself

Ability to delay gratification: with the ability to delay gratification people live healthier lives and engage in healthier behaviors (*e.g.*, exercise)

Larger social networks: having a large group of friends and close relationships with relatives increases your social support, which positively influences health

Job satisfaction: people in more powerful and more satisfying jobs tend to be healthier than people in less satisfying jobs.

A **stable population,** one that has had constant crude birth and death rates for such long time that the percentage of people in every age class remains constant, or equivalently, the population pyramid has an unchanging structure. A stable population does not necessarily remain fixed in size, it can be expanding or shrinking.

A **stationary population,** one that is both stable and unchanging in size (the difference between crude birth rate and crude death rate is zero).

THE DEMOGRAPHIC TRANSITION

The **demographic transition** is a model and theory describing the transition from high birth rates and death rates to low birth and death rates that occurs as part of the economic development of a country. In pre-industrial societies, population growth is relatively slow because both birth and death rates are high. In most post-industrial societies, birth and death rates are both low. The transition from high rates to low rates is referred to as the demographic transition.

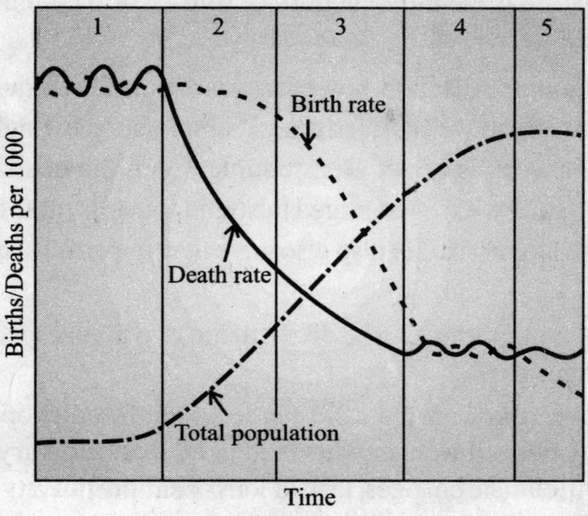

Fig. 16.2

The beginning of the demographic transition in a society is indicated when death rates drop without a corresponding fall in birth rates (usually the result of improved sanitation and advances in healthcare). Countries in the second stage of the demographic transition (see Fig. 16.2) experience a large increase in population. This is depicted in the Fig. when death rates fall in stage two but birth rates do not fall until stage three. The line begins its rapid upward growth in stage two and begins to level off at the end of stage three. By the end of stage three, birth rates drop to fall in line with the lower death rates.

MIGRATION

Migration is the movement of people from one region or society to another for the purpose of settlement.

There are two main types of migration: first, internal migration, *i.e.*, migration within one country, and secondly international migration, which means the movement from one country to another.

Migration into an area, called immigration, is measured as the immigration rate, which is the number of people entering a region per each 1,000 people in the population. Migration out of an area, or emigration, is measured as the emigration rate, which is the number leaving per each 1,000 people in the population. Internal migration is the movement from one area to another within a country's borders.

A good example of internal migration is the movement from East Germany to West Germany, which causes big problems for East Germany. A good example of international migration is the movement from third-world countries to Europe or America.

The spread of industrialization, however, was drastically to transform migration pattern within the country as well as international immigration to England. The growth of opportunities for work is urban areas coupled with the decline of household production in the countrywide encouraged the trend towards rural-urban migration. Demands within the labour market also also gave new impetus to immigration from abroad.

The reasons for migration can be divided into two main aspects, the so-called "push" and "pull" factors.

Push factors are those in their old place which force people to move. For example, there may be civil wars or wars in general in the country, but political or religious oppression, climate changes, lack of jobs or simply poverty are all important push factors.

Pull factors are factors in the target country which encourage people to move; these include peace and safety, a chance of a better job, better education, social security, a better standard of living in general as well as political and religious freedom.'

The crude net migration rate can be obtained by applying the corresponding rates in the inter-censal period to the balancing equation as follows:

$$\text{Population Growth} = \text{CBR} - \text{CDR} + \text{Net Migrants}$$

Therefore, $\text{Net migrants} = \text{Population Growth} - \text{CBR} + \text{CDR}$

BASIC DEMOGRAPHIC EQUATION

Suppose that a country (or other entity) contains population persons at time t. What is the size of the population at time t + 1?

Population at (t + 1) = Population at t + Natural increase at t + Net migration at t

i.e., $P_{t+1} = P_t + \text{Natural increase}_t + \text{Net migration}_t$

Natural increase from time t to (t + 1)

Natural increase at t = Births at t – Deaths at t

Net migration from time t to (t + 1)

i.e., $\text{Net migration}_t = \text{Immigration}_t - \text{Emigration}_t$

This basic equation can also be applied to subpopulations. For example, the population size of ethnic groups or nationalities within a given society or country is subject to the same sources of change. However, when dealing with ethnic groups, "net migration" might have to be subdivided into physical migration and ethnic reidentification. Individuals who change their ethnic self-labels or whose ethnic classification in government statistics changes over time may be thought of as migrating or moving from one population subcategory to another.

Generally, while the basic demographic equation holds true by definition, in practice the recording and counting of events (births, deaths, immigration, emigration) and the enumeration of the total population size are subject to error. So allowance needs to be made for error in the underlying statistics when any accounting of population size or change is made.

POPULATION GROWTH AND OVERPOPULATION

Population Growth (Natural Increase)

The difference between fertility and mortality, which is known as the 'natural' increase. It is found by subtracting the deaths per 1000 population from the births per 1000 population, resulting in a natural increase or decrease per 1000 population. The figure is divided by 10 as the natural increase rate is usually presented as percentage figure. Growth rate determines the population doubling time which is the number of years in which a country can double its population, the higher the growth rate, the lesser the population doubling time (Table 16.1).

TABLE 16.1: Population Growth Rate and its Impact

Annual growth rate (%)	Population doubling time	Rating of growth
< 0.5	> 139 years	Slow growth
0.5 – 1.0	139 – 70 years	Moderate growth
1.0 – 1.5	70 – 47 years	Rapid growth
1.5 – 2.0	47 – 35 years	Very rapid growth
> 2.0	< 35 years	Explosive growth

TABLE 16.2: Annual Death rate, Birth rate, and Rate of growth of the Indian Population

Year	Population (millions) as per census	Crude birth rate	Crude Death rate	Crude rate of Natural increase
1941	318.6	39.9	27.4	12.5
1951	361.0	41.7	22.8	18.9
1961	439.2	41.2	19.0	22.2
1971	548.1	37.2	15.0	22.2
1981	685.2	33.7	12.3	21.4
1991	844.3	29.5	9.8	19.7
2001	1027.0	26.1	8.7	17.4
2011	1210.2	21.3	7.5	13.8

Source: Health Statistics of India, Ministry of Health & Family Welfare, Govt. of India.

The Table 16.2 shows that there was no change in the Growth rate of 1961 and 1971 census.

Fertility, mortality, and migration all influence the size of a society's population. Poorer countries tend to grow almost completely from internal causes (for example, high birth rates due to the absence of reliable contraception), while richer countries tend to grow from both internal causes and migration. Demographers determine a population's natural growth rate by subtracting the crude death rate from the crude birth rate. The world's low-growth nations tend to be more industrialized, such as the United States and Europe. The high-growth countries tend to be less industrialized, such as Africa and Latin America.

Malthusian Theory

The field of demography arose two centuries ago in response to the population growth of that day. Thomas Robert Malthus (1766 – 1834), English economist and clergyman, argued that increases in population, if left unchecked, would eventually result in social chaos. Malthus predicted that the human population would continue to increase exponentially (1, 2, 4, 16, 256 ...) until the situation is out of control. He also warned that food production would only increase arithmetically (1, 2, 3, 4, 5 ...) because of limitations in available farmland. To say the least, Malthus provided a disturbing vision of the future that included massive, global starvation as a consequence of unrestrained population growth.

As it turned out, Malthus' predictions were mistaken because he failed to account for technological advancements and ingenuity that would increase agricultural and farm production, not to mention the increasing development and acceptance of birth control methods. Yet Malthus' forebodings do not lack merit. As noted by the New Malthusians, a group of demographers, assets such as habitable and fertile land, clean air, and fresh water are finite resources. And with medical advances increasing fertility and lowering death rates, the global population continues to grow exponentially with no end in sight.

Demographic Transition Theory

Replacing Malthus' ideas today, demographic transition theory defines population growth in an alternating pattern of stability, rapid growth, and then stability again. This theory proposes a three-stage model of growth.

- **Stage 1:** Stable population growth. In this stage, birth and death rates roughly balance each other. Most societies throughout history have stayed at this stage.
- **Stage 2:** Rapid population growth. Death rates fall sharply while birth rates remain high in Stage 2. Most poor countries today fit into this stage. Malthus formed his ideas during one such high-growth period.
- **Stage 3:** Stable population growth. In this stage, fertility falls because high living standards make raising children expensive. Women working outside the home also favor smaller families, brought about by widespread use of birth control. Death rates drop because of technological advances in medicine. With low birth rates and death rates, the population only grows slowly, if at all. It may, in fact, witness population shrinkage, in which deaths outnumber births in a society.

Stage 3 suggests that technology holds the key to population control. Instead of the out-of-control population explosions that Malthus predicted, demographic transition theory claims that technology will ultimately control population growth and ensure enough food for all.

OVERPOPULATION

Overpopulation indicates a scenario in which the population of a living species exceeds the carrying capacity of its ecosystem. Overpopulation is not a function of the number or density of the individuals, but rather the number of individuals compared to the resources they need to survive. In other words, it is a ratio: *population* over *resources*. If a given environment has a population of 10, but there is food and drinking water enough for only 9 people, then that environment is overpopulated, while if the population is 100 individuals but there are food and water enough for 200, then it is not overpopulated. Resources to be taken into account when estimating if an ecosystem is overpopulated include clean water, food, shelter, warmth, etc. In the case of human beings, there are others such as fertile land and, for all but tribes with primitive lifestyles, lesser resources such as jobs, money, education, fuel, electricity, medicine, proper sewage and garbage management, and transportation.

Presently, every year the world's human population grows by approximately 80 million. About half the world lives in nations with sub-replacement fertility and population growth in those countries is due to immigration. The United Nations projects that the world human population will stabilize in 2075 at nine billion due to declining fertility rates.

Some of the other characteristics of overpopulation include:

- Child poverty
- High birth rates
- Lower life expectancies
- Lower levels of literacy
- Higher rates of unemployment, especially in urban
- Insufficient arable land
- Little surplus food
- Poor diet with ill health and diet-deficiency diseases (*e.g.* rickets)
- Low per capita GDP
- Increasingly unhygienic conditions
- Government is stretched economically
- Increased crime rates resulting from people stealing resources to survive
- Mass extinctions of plants and animals as habitat is used for farming and human settlements

Underpopulation

Once countries pass through the demographic transition, some experience fertility rate decreases so substantial that they fall well below replacement level and their populations begin to shrink. A new fear for many governments, particularly those in countries with very low fertility rates, is that a declining population will reduce the GDP and economic growth of the country, as population growth is often a driving force of economic expansion. To combat extremely low fertility rates, some of these governments have introduced pro-family policies, that include things like payments to parents for having children and extensive parental leave for parents. Such policies may reverse the low fertility rates, but they also seem to be shortsighted in light of the concerns associated with overall world population growth.

POPULATION CONTROL

Historically, many groups and societies have discouraged contraception (the prevention of conception, or birth control) to assure survival of its members and humanity as a whole. Certain religious groups strongly disapprove of sexual activity that does not culminate in coitus and the possibility of conception. Other groups place little importance on the matter of contraception. The Yanomamo of South America, for instance, harbor little or no concept of contraception. Instead, they parent as many children as possible, and then kill off those they view as the undesirable, such as some females and deformed infants.

Modern medicine has spread throughout different parts of the world, and people of all ages now live longer, causing the world's population to explode in growth. In fact, at five billion today, the world's population doubles, on average, every 35 years, with most of this growth occurring in developing countries. Given this population crisis, certain governments, like that of China, regulate the number of births allowed per household.

Besides the issue of controlling overpopulation, other benefits to practicing contraception exist. For example, a young couple may want to postpone having children until their finances improve. Or an unmarried, sexually active teenager may wish to finish her education or get married before starting a family, thereby reducing her chances of eventually relying on the government for financial support.

Family planning also plays an important role in protecting the physical health of both mother and child. The older or younger a woman is, and the closer together she bears children (that is, more frequently than every two years), the greater the risk of pregnancy and birth complications, early infant mortality, and maternal death. For example, women over age 40 or under age 19 have an increased risk of bearing a child of low birth weight, and thus a variety of birth defects and even outright death. Estimates say that approximately one million teenage women in the United States become pregnant each year.

URBANIZATION

Urbanization is the physical growth of urban areas as a result of global change. Urbanization is also defined by the United Nations as movement of people from rural to urban areas with population growth equating to urban migration. Urbanization is closely linked to modernization, industrialization, and the sociological process of rationalization.

As more and more people leave villages and farms to live in cities, urban growth results. The rapid growth of cities like Chicago in the late 19th century and Mumbai a century later can be attributed largely to rural-urban migration and the demographic transition.

Causes

People move into cities to seek economic opportunities. A major contributing factor is known as "rural flight". In rural areas, often on small family farms, it is difficult to improve one's standard of living beyond basic sustenance. Farm living is dependent on unpredictable environmental conditions, and in times of drought, flood or pestilence, survival becomes extremely problematic. In modern times, industrialization of agriculture has negatively affected the economy of small and middle-sized farms and strongly reduced the size of the rural labour market. Cities, in contrast, are known to be places where money, services and wealth are centralized. Cities are where fortunes are made and where social mobility is possible. Businesses, which generate jobs and capital, are usually located in urban areas. Whether the source is trade or tourism, it is also through the cities that foreign money flows into a country. Thus, as with immigration generally, there are factors that push people out of rural areas and pull them into urban areas.

There are also better basic services as well as other specialist services in urban areas that aren't found in rural areas. There are more job opportunities and a greater variety of jobs. Health is another major factor. People, especially the elderly are often forced to move to cities where there are doctors and hospitals that can address their health needs. Other factors include a greater variety of entertainment (*e.g.*, restaurants, movie theaters, theme parks, etc.) and better quality of education in the form of universities. Due to their high populations, urban areas can also have much more diverse social communities allowing others to find people like them when they might not be able to in rural areas. These conditions are heightened during times of change from a pre-industrial society to an industrial one.

⌖⌖⌖⌖⌖

CHAPTER

17

Vital Statistics
(Life Table)

• *Crude Birth Rate*	• *Crude Death Rate*
• *MMR*	• *IMR*
• *ASFR*	• *TFR*
• *NRR*	• *Sex Ratio*

VITAL STATISTICS

According to Benjamin, "Vital Statistics are conventional numerical records of marriages, births, sickness and deaths by which the health and growth of a community may be studied".

Measures of Vital Statistics

The raw data of vital statistics are given in the from of frequencies of vital events such as births and deaths. These absolute numbers are converted into rates and ratios for comparison of vital statistics from place to place or year to year, *e.g.*, infant deaths in two different states in a country.

Rate: It is a proportion with a defined denominator termed as population. The numerator is occurrence of an event which is counted in the same population. The fraction is generally multiplied by a constant, which for most rates is 1000. When occurrence of an event is rare such as Cancer multiplied by 1,00,000. Therefore, the rate describes the rapidity with which new events are occurring in a community. For example, the rate of admissions to the hospital represents how rapidly persons are entering the hospital per year.

In general,

$$\text{Rate of a vital event} = \frac{\text{Number of cases of the vital event}}{\text{Total number of persons exposed to the risk of occurrence of the event}}$$

The rates are generally of two types, Crude and Specific.

Sex Ratio: This is also an index of fertility and it is defined by

$$\text{Sex Ratio} = \frac{\text{No. of females}}{\text{No. of males}} \times 1000$$

The sex ratio at birth is a better index of fertility then the overall sex ratio. It is defined by

$$\text{Sex Ratio at birth} = \frac{\text{No. of female live birth}}{\text{No. of male live birth}} \times 1000$$

Measures of Fertility

Fertility is the actual bearing of children by a women during her child-bearing age, *i.e.*, 15-49 years.

Fecundity is the inherent capacity of woman to reproduce.

Reproduction is the ability of a population to replace itself and to grow.

(i) Crude Birth Rate (CBR): The simplest way of measuring fertility is to relate the number of births to the total population (specifically mid-year population). Since it is only a five birth that signifies an addition to the existing population, five births alone are considered in measuring fertility, thus excluding still births. The formula is, therefore,

$$\text{CBR} = \frac{B}{P} \times 1000$$

where B = Number of five births which occurred in the given region the given period

P = Mid-year population of the given region during the given period.

Crude birth rate of India in 1991 was 29.5 and in 1996 it was 27.5 (in Rural 29.3 and in Urban 21.6).

The measure is a crude one because total population taken as denominator is not exposed to births, only ever married women (15-49) years of age are exposed.

(ii) General Fertility Rate (GFR): By relating the number of live births to the number of women in the child bearing ages, *i.e.*, (15 to 49) years, the general fertility rate (GFR) is obtained. The formula is

$$\text{GFR} = \frac{\text{Number of live births in the given region during the given period}}{\text{Number of women aged 15-49 years in the given region during the given period}} \times 1000$$

(iii) Total Fertility Rate (TFR): It gives an estimate of the average number of children that would be born alive to a women throughout her reproductive age span as per prevailing specific fertility rates.

The TFR is a hypothetical figure: It shows how many children would be born alive to 1000 women if none of them died before reaching the end of the reproductive period and if all were subject to the observed specific fertility rates throughout this period, *i.e.*, TFR = Sum of ASFRs

Table 17.1: General Fertility Rate (GFR), Total Fertility Rate (TFR) and General Reproduction Rate (GRR) in India (2005-2009)

Indicators	Area	2005	2006	2007	2008	2009
General Fertility Rate (GFR)	Rural	106.2	103.4	98.6	96.9	94.9
	Urban	70.9	69.1	67.3	66.5	65.9
	Combined	95.8	93.3	89.5	88.0	86.5
Total Fertility Rate (TFR)	Rural	3.2	3.1	3.0	2.9	2.9
	Urban	2.1	2.0	2	1.9	1.9
	Combined	2.9	2.8	2.7	2.6	2.6
Gross Reproduction Rate (GRR)	Rural	1.5	1.5	1.4	1.4	1.4
	Urban	1.0	1.0	0.9	0.90	0.9
	Combined	1.4	1.3	1.3	1.2	1.2

Source: Family Welfare Statistics in India – 2011. Ministry of Health and Family Welfare, Govt. of India, New Delhi.

(iv) Age-Specific Fertility Rate (ASFR): To form a better idea as to the fertility situation obtaining in a community, it is necessary to complete a fertility rate for each age-group of mothers separately.

$$\text{ASFR} = \frac{\text{Number of live births to mothers of a specified age group}}{\text{Mid-year female population of the same age-group}} \times 1000$$

Table 17.2: Age Specific Fertility Rates (ASFR) in India, 2004 to 2009

Age Groups	Rural					
	2004	2005	2006	2007	2008	2009
15-19	58.6	52.4	52.6	47.3	47.8	44.3
20-24	240.6	246.2	227.7	235.5	218.6	44.3
25-29	184.0	171.2	180.9	169.4	169.7	166.0
30-34	96.5	99.1	87.5	83.0	80.7	82.7
35-39	45.6	41.4	42.5	37.5	39.2	34.8
40-44	21.1	21.5	18.8	15.3	15.3	14.5
45-49	10.7	8.1	8.0	5.5	6.3	6.3

Age Groups	Urban					
	2004	2005	2006	2007	2008	2009
15-19	33.6	28.4	25.7	23.7	24.5	21.7
20-24	164.9	170.0	159.7	161.7	154.4	153.7
25-29	140.7	134.6	138.2	132.1	132.3	135.9
30-34	59.6	60.0	58.2	56.3	55.0	56.8
35-39	20.2	20.1	20.3	18.0	17.8	18.2
40-44	7.3	5.9	5.9	5.3	5.1	4.5
45-49	2.2	2.1	1.7	1.2	1.9	1.2

Source: Sample Registration System, Registrar General of India.

MEASUREMENT OF MORTALITY

(i) Crude Death Rate (CDR): It measures the decline in population due to mortality in general without specifying the factors that influence the deaths such as age sex composition of population, occupation, cause of death, etc.

$$\text{CDR} = \frac{D}{P} \times 100$$

where D = Number of deaths (from all causes) which occurred in the population of a given area during a year,

P = Mid-year total population of the given area during the same year.

(ii) Specific Death Rates (SDRs): These rates are calculated to find the mortality experience in different sections of the population with respect to age and sex or mortality due to different causes.

Age specified death rate

$$= \frac{\text{Number of deaths in the specified age group}}{\text{Mid-year population of the same age group}} \times 1000$$

(iii) Sex Specific Death Rate (SSDR): Death rates can be had specifically for males as well as for femailes, *i.e.*,

$$\text{Male death rate} = \frac{\text{No. of male deaths}}{\text{Mid-year population of males}} \times 1000$$

$$\text{Female death rate} = \frac{\text{No. of female deaths}}{\text{Mid-year population of females}} \times 1000$$

(iv) Case Fatality Rate (CFR): It is the ratio of deaths due to a particular disease in a certain period to the number of cases of the same disease reported during the same period, the quotient being multiplied by 100.

$$\text{CFR} = \frac{\text{No. of deaths due to a particular disease}}{\text{No. of cases of the same disease}} \times 1000$$

(v) Cause of death rate: This rate is used to measure the contribution to the total mortality of a community that is made by a specified cause of death. Therefore, the (Crude) cause-of-death rate for specified cause.

$$= \frac{\text{Total number of deaths from (any) specified cause occuring in the given period in the given community}}{\text{Total population of the given community in the given period}} \times 100000$$

(vi) Maternal Mortality Rate (MMR): It is defined as the number of deaths assigned to puerperal causes (*i.e.*, those related to child bearing) in a calendar year, divided by the number of live births in that year, the quotient being multiplied by 100,000. Thus,

$$\text{MMR} = \frac{\text{No. of deaths due to puerperal causes in women}}{\text{No. of live births}} \times 100{,}000$$

(vii) Perinatal Mortality Rate (PNMR): It includes

(i) Foetal deaths after 28 weeks of gestation,

(ii) Deaths during labour, and

(iii) Deaths within 7 days of neonatal life.

$$\text{PNMR} = \frac{\text{Late foetal deaths after 28 weeks + deaths under one week}}{\text{Total No. of Deliveries (live births + still births)}} \times 1000$$

(viii) Neonatal Mortality Rate (NNMR): The number of deaths of infants under 28 days of age in a given year per 1000 live births in that year, *i.e.*,

$$\text{NNMR} = \frac{\text{No. of deaths under 28 days during a given year}}{\text{No. of live births during the same year}} \times 1000$$

(ix) Post Neonatal Mortality Rate (PNNMR): It is defined as the number of deaths 28 days of life up to one year, divided by the number of live births, the quotient being multiplied by 1000.

$$\text{PNNMR} = \frac{\text{No. of deaths after 28 days of life upto one year}}{\text{No. of live births during the year}} \times 1000$$

(x) Infant Mortality Rate (IMR): The number of deaths to infants under one year of age in a given year per 1000 live births in that year, *i.e.*,

$$\text{IMR} = \frac{\text{No. of deaths under 1 year of age in a year}}{\text{No. of live births in that year}} \times 1000$$

(xi) Proportional Mortality Rate (PMR): It is the ratio of the number of deaths due to a specific cause or in specific age or in specific sex or region to the total number of deaths and this ratio is multiplied by 100.

$$\text{PMR} = \frac{\text{No. of deaths in a specific age / sex / region}}{\text{Total No. of deaths in a year}} \times 100$$

Reproductive Rate

The reproduction depends on the number of female children born. There are two indices of reproduction:

Gross Reproduction Rate (GRR)

$$= \frac{\text{Total No. of female children born alive to women in the cohort}}{\text{Total No. of women in the same cohort}} = i\sum_{15}^{49} \frac{B_f}{P_f}$$

where B_f = No. of daughter born

P_f = No. of mothers

i = Class interval

Net Reproductive Rate (NRR)

NRR is a sophisticated measure of population growth. It indicates how many daughters would be born to a group of mothers (cohort) beginning lives together and all were subject to the levels of observed ASDRs and ASFRs at each age during their child bearing ages.

$$\text{NRR} = \frac{\text{No. of daughters survived after the mortality experience}}{\text{No. of cohort mothers survived at the end of reproductive period as per their mortality experience}} = i\sum_{15}^{49} F_r \times S_r$$

where S_r = Survival rate

This rate indicates how mwny future mothers woujld be born to present mothers according to the current levels fo fertility and mortality. If the NRR = 1, then the population is maintaining itself (*i.e.*, remains constant in size) and if NRR> or <1, it means the population is increasing or decreasing. The NRR is a good index of population growth.

Measure of Morbidity

In a given population, morbidity (*i.e.*, sickness) for a given period may be measured in terms of new cases of sickness (incidence) or in terms of new plus old cases of sickness (Prevalence).

(i) Morbidity Incidence Rate:

The term 'incidence' to the emergence of new cases of sickness and this rate is defined as the number of newly reported cases of a given disease (sickness) in a calendar year, divided by the population on July 1st of that year (*i.e.*, mid-year population) and the quotient being multiplied by convenient factor, usually 1000, or 100,000.

Thus, the (Mordibity) Incidence rate is given by

$$\text{IR} = \frac{I}{P} \times 1000$$

where I = Total number of new cases of sickness in a calendar year

P = Total popuation on July 1st of that year

(ii) Morbidity Prevalence Rate:

Here the term 'prevalence' relates to cases of sickness prevalent or existing during the given period and it is of two kinds:

(a) Period prevalence and (b) Point prevalence

(a) **Period prevalence:** It is applied to measure the frequency of a sickness in existence during a specified period (it amy be a day, week, month or year). It is thus defined by

$$\text{Period prevalence} = \frac{\begin{array}{c}\text{Total number of new and}\\ \text{old cases observed to exist}\\ \text{during a specified period}\end{array}}{\begin{array}{c}\text{Total population exposed to}\\ \text{risk in the same period}\end{array}} \times 100$$

(b) **Point prevalence:** This term is used to measure the number of cases (old and new) of sicknes, existing at a particular point of time such as at 10 a.m. on Wednedsay, the 15th of September, 2007.

$$\text{Point prevalence} = \frac{\begin{array}{c}\text{Number of new \& old cases of sicknes}\\ \text{occurred at a particular point of time}\end{array}}{\begin{array}{c}\text{Total population exposed to risk at}\\ \text{same point of time}\end{array}} \times 100$$

(iii) Secondary Attack Rate (SAR):

This rate measures the occurrence of a contagious disease among susceptible persons who have been exposed to a primary case and is defined by

$$\text{SAR} = \frac{\begin{array}{c}\text{No. of additional cases among contacts of primary}\\ \text{case within the maximum incubation period}\end{array}}{\text{Total No. of susceptible contacts}} = k$$

where k = 100 or 1000

(iv) Still birth rate:

It is defined as

$$\text{Still birth rate} = \frac{\text{Foetal deaths after 28 weeks of gestation}}{\text{Number deliveries in a year}} \times 1000$$

EXAMPLE: 17.1: The mid-year population of a city was 6,50,000 there were 20500 live births, 400 still births, 850 deaths within one week after birth and 1600 deaths in the first month of life and 2400 deaths in the first year of life, in a particular year. Calculate still birth, perinatal, neonatal and post neonatal mortality rates.

SOLUTION:

$$\text{Still birth rate} = \frac{\text{Foetal deaths after 28 weeks of gestation}}{\text{Live births + Still births}} \times 1000$$

$$= \frac{400 \times 1000}{20900} = 19.12 \text{ per } 1000$$

Perinatal Mortality Rate (PNMR)

$$\text{PNMR} = \frac{\begin{array}{c}\text{Foetal deaths after 28 weeks +}\\ \text{deaths under one week of age}\end{array}}{\text{Total births (Live + Still)}} \times 1000$$

$$= \frac{400 + 850}{20500 + 400} \times 1000 = \frac{1250 \times 1000}{20900}$$

$= 59.8$ per 1000

Neonatal Mortality Rate (NNMR)

$$= \frac{\text{Number of deaths under 28 days of age}}{\text{Number of live births}} \times 1000$$

$$= \frac{1600}{20500} \times 1000 = 78.05 \text{ per } 1000$$

Post Neonatal Mortality Rate (PNNMR)

$$= \frac{\text{No. of deaths occuring from 28 days of life to under 1 year of age in a given year}}{\text{Number of live births in the same year}} \times 1000$$

$$= \frac{(2400 - 1600)}{20500} \times 1000 = 39 \text{ per } 1000$$

EXAMPLE 17.2: Calculate the proportional mortality rate in pre school children of two investigations conduct in Kerala and U.P.

Age group (years)	No. of deaths Kerala	No. of deaths U.P	% of population Kerala	% of population U.P.
Upto 5	32	68	10.47	16.86
6 and above	96	90	89.53	83.14

SOLUTION:

PMR in the the children of age 0-5 years

$$= \frac{\text{No. of deaths in the age 0 - 5 years}}{\text{Total No. of deaths}} \times 100$$

$$\text{PMR in Kerala} = \frac{32}{128} \times 100$$

$= 25\%$

$$\text{PMR in U.P.} = \frac{68}{158} \times 100$$

$= 43\%$

Thus, the proportional mortality rate is higher in U.P. than in Kerala. PMR and population composition (%) with children upto 5 years are lower in Kerala than in U.P.

EXAMPLE 17.3: The mid-year population of a city was 4,00,000. In the same year the number of live births were 12,000; number of deaths 6,400 and the number of infant deaths 1500. Calculate the crude birth rate, crude death rate and infant mortality rates.

SOLUTION:

$$\text{Since CBR} = \frac{\text{Number of live births during a year}}{\text{Mid-year population of the year}} \times 1000$$

$$\therefore \quad \text{CBR} = \frac{12000}{400000} \times 1000 = 30 \text{ per } 1000$$

$$\because \quad \text{CDR} = \frac{\text{No. of deaths during a year}}{\text{Mid-year population of the year}} \times 1000$$

$$\therefore \quad \text{CDR} = \frac{6400}{400{,}000} \times 1000$$

$$= 16 \text{ per } 1000$$

$$\text{and} \quad \text{IMR} = \frac{\text{Number of deaths under 1 year of age}}{\text{Number of live births during the year}} \times 1000$$

$$\text{or} \quad \text{IMR} = \frac{1500}{12000} \times 1000$$

$$= 125 \text{ per } 1000$$

EXAMPLE 17.4: Calculate the General Fertility Rate, Total Fertility and the Gross Reproduction Rate from the following data, assuming that for every 100 girls 104 boys are born.

Age Group Women	No. of	Age specific Fertility Rate
15-19	21,000	92.0
20-24	19,000	165.0
25-29	16,500	152.0
30-34	14,500	140.0
35-39	12,300	90.0
40-44	10,200	45.0
45-49	4,500	16.0

SOLUTION: Calculation of G.F.R., and T.F.R:

Age group	No. of women	ASFR	No. of births = $\frac{(2)\times(3)}{1000}$
15 – 19	21,000	92.0	$\frac{21000\times 92}{1000}=1932$
20 – 24	19,000	165.0	$\frac{19000\times 165}{1000}=3135$
25 – 29	16,500	152.0	$\frac{16500\times 152}{1000}=2508$
30 – 34	14,500	140.0	$\frac{145000\times 140}{1000}=2030$
35 – 39	12,300	90.0	$\frac{123000\times 90}{1000}=1107$
40 – 44	10,200	45.0	$\frac{10200\times 45}{1000}=459$
45 – 49	4,500	16.0	$\frac{4500\times 16}{1000}=72$
Total	98,000	700.0	11243

$$\text{G.F.R.} = \frac{\text{Total number of births}}{\text{Total number of women age group (15 – 49) years}}\times 1000$$

$$= \frac{11243}{98000}\times 1000 = 114.7$$

and $$\text{T.F.R.} = \text{i}\times \sum_{15}^{49}\text{ASFR}$$

where i, is the class interval (class width), *i.e.*, (i = 5), and

ASFR = Age Specific Fertility Rate

$\therefore$ T.F.R. = 5 × 700 = 3500 per 1000

Since it is given that for every 100 girls 104 boys are born, an approximation of G.R.R is given by

$$\text{G.R.R.} = \frac{\text{Number of female births}}{\text{Total births}}\times \text{T.F.R.} = \frac{100}{204}\times 3500$$

$$= 1715.7$$

EXAMPLE 17.5: The number of live births occuring in a city in the year 2007 is given below, classified according to age of mother, together with the number of women in each age-group of the reproductive period.

Age group (Years)	Number of Women	Number of Live births
15-19	22000	750
20-24	28000	2850
25-29	26500	2200
30-34	20500	1550
34-39	15000	500
40-44	7500	120
45-49	5500	30
Total	125000	8000

If the total population of the city during the year was 500,000 then with the above data, determine (i) CBR (ii) GFR (iii) ASFR and (iv) TFR.

SOLUTION:

(i) $$\text{CBR} = \frac{\text{Total live births during a year}}{\text{Total population of the year (mid year population)}} \times 1000$$

$$= \frac{8000}{500000} \times 1000 = 16 \text{ per } 1000$$

(ii) $$\text{GFR} = \frac{\text{Total live births during a year}}{\text{Total number of women in the age group (15 – 49) during the year}} \times 1000$$

$$= \frac{8000}{125000} \times 1000 = 64 \text{ per } 1000$$

(iii) $$\text{ASFR} = \frac{\text{No. of live births to women of specific age group during a year}}{\text{No. of women of the specific age group during the year}} \times 1000$$

Computation of ASFR:

Age-Group (Years)	No. of women (Pw)	No. of Live Births (Bl)	Age-Specific Fertility Rate ASFR =Bl/Pw ×1000
15 – 19	22000	750	$\frac{750}{22000} \times 1000 = 34.10$
20 – 24	28000	2850	101.79
25 – 29	26500	2200	83.02
30 – 34	20500	1550	75.61
35 – 39	15000	500	33.33
40 – 44	7500	120	16.00
45 – 49	5500	30	5.45
Total	125000	8000	349.30

(iv) Total Fertility Rate (TFR) = $\sum_{15}^{49} \text{ASFR}$

Since the data are given in 5 yearly groups (*i.e.*, the width of each class (Age-group) is 5. So we have TFR = 5 × ASFR

$$= 5 \times 349.30 = 1746.5 \text{ per thousand}$$

also TFR per Woman = $\frac{1746.5}{1000} = 1.75$

STANDARDIZATION OF DEATH RATES

Standardized rates, which are also called adjusted rates, are crude rates that have been modified (adjusted) to control for the effects of age, sex or other characteristics and thereby allow for valid comparison of rates. Standardization is usually applied to death rates but may be used to adjust any type of rate. In case of death rates, the comparison of many age specific death rates (ASDR) can become unwieldy. Therefore, to obtain a summary death rate that is free from age bias, investigations can age-standardize (age-adjust) the crude death rates by a direct or an indirect method.

I. Direct Standardization

In the direct method of Standardization, the ASDRs of the two (or more) populations to be compared are applied to a single standard population. This is done by multiplying each ASDR from a population to be compared by the number of persons in the corresponding age group in the standard population. Becausee the age structure of the standard population is the same for all of the death rates applied to it, the distorting effect of having different real populations is estimated. Overall death rates can then be compared without age bias.

The standard population may be any real (or any realistic) population, and it is often a larger population of which the populations to be compared are a part. Thus, the death rates of two cities in a state can be compared using the state's population as the standard population. Likewise, the death rates of states may be standardized using the population of the country. The direct method may be applied to compare incidence rates of disease or injury as well as deaths.

II. Indirect Standardization

This is done when ASDRs are not known in the population whose crude death rate is to be adjusted. The indirect method uses standard rates and applies them to the known age-groups in the population to be standardized.

The method has following steps:

(i) Index Death Rate of Local population should be calculated as

$$\text{Index D.R} = \frac{(\text{Px} \times \text{Ds})}{\text{Px}}$$

where Px = Local Population

Ds = Age-specific death rate of standard population.

(ii) C.D.R. of standard population is calculated by the formula

$$\text{CDR (Standard)} = \frac{\text{Total deaths}}{\text{Total populatiopn}} \times 1000$$

(iii) $\text{Correction Factor} = \dfrac{\text{CDR of standard population}}{\text{Index DR of Local population}}$

(iv) SDR of local population = CDR of Local population × CF.

The computation of the standardized death rate (or adjusted death rate) by adjusting the C.D.R. in this manner is called Indirect standardized of specific death rates. In general, the indirect method leads to almost the same value for the standardized death rate as the direct method would.

EXAMPLE 17.6: The population and the number of deaths of two localities, according to age groups, are given below:

Age roup (yrs)	Locality A		Locality B	
	Population	No. of Deaths	Population	No. of Deaths
<5	7000	215	85000	1404
5 – 15	15000	250	125000	1506
15 – 35	12500	295	180000	2850
35 – 40	5500	210	80000	1650
50+	6500	320	64400	1430

Compute (i) crude death rate (ii) standardized death rates taking population of locality A as standardized population, and (iii) compare their health conditions.

SOLUTION: **Table for compution of CDRs**

Age group (Years)	Locality A			Locality B			
	Population (Ps)	Deaths	Death Rates (Ds)	Population (Px)	Death	Death Rates (Dx)	Ps × Dx
<5	7000	215	30.7	85000	1404	16.5	115500
5 – 15	15000	250	16.7	125000	1506	12.0	180000
15 – 35	12500	295	23.6	180000	2850	15.8	197500
35 – 50	5500	210	38.2	80000	1650	20.6	113300
50+	6500	320	49.2	64400	1430	22.2	144300
Total	46500	1290	—	534400	8840	-	750600

(i) C.D.R. for locality A

$$= \frac{\text{Total number of deaths in locality A}}{\text{Total population of locality A}} \times 1000$$

$$= \frac{1290}{46500} \times 1000 = 27.7$$

and, C.D.R. for locality B

$$= \frac{\text{Total deaths occured in Locality B}}{\text{Total Population of Locality B}} \times 1000$$

$$= \frac{8840}{534400} \times 1000 = 16.5$$

(ii) Since the population of locality A is taken as standardized population, therefore,

S.D.R. of locality A = CDR of Locality A = 27.7

$$\text{S.D.R. of Locality B} = \frac{\Sigma PsDx}{\Sigma Ps} = \frac{750600}{46500} = 16.1$$

(iii) Here SDR of locality B is less than the SDR of locality A which indicates that the locality B is healthier than the locality A.

Standardized Death Rate of Locality B by Indirect method:

$$\text{Index Death Rate of Locality B} = \frac{\Sigma PxDs}{\Sigma Px}$$

$$= \frac{(8500 \times 30.70) + (125000 \times 16.7) + (180000 \times 23.6) + (80000 \times 38.2) + (64400 \times 49.2)}{534400}$$

$$= \frac{15169480}{534400} = 28.4$$

$$\text{Correction Factor (C.F.)} = \frac{\text{CDR of Locality A (Standard)}}{\text{Index death rate of Locality B}}$$

$$= \frac{27.7}{28.4} = 0.98$$

Now SDR of Locality B = CDR of locality B × C.F.

= 16.5 × 0.98 = 16.1

Here we see that the SDR of locality B, *i.e.*, 16.1 calculated by Direct Method of standardization of death rate is same as SDR of locality B calculated by Indirect Method of standardization of death rate.

EXAMPLE 17.7: Calculate the crude and standardized death rates of the local population from the following data and compare them with the crude death rate of the standard population:

Age group (Yrs)	Standard Population		Local Population	
	Population	Deaths	Population	Deaths
0 – 15	6000	140	5000	150
15 – 30	25000	250	24000	300
30 – 45	35000	455	31000	403
45 – 60	24000	360	20000	310
60+	5000	125	6000	127
Total	95000	1330	86000	1290

SOLUTION: Calculation of the CDR & SDR:

Age group (Years)	Standard Population			Local Population		
	Population (Ps)	Deaths	Death Rates (Ds)	Population (Px)	Deaths	Death Rates (Dx)
0 – 15	6000	140	23.3	5000	150	30.0
15 – 30	25000	250	10.0	24000	300	12.5
30 – 45	35000	455	13.0	31000	403	13.0
45 – 60	24000	360	15.0	20000	310	15.5
60+	5000	125	25.0	6000	127	21.2
Total	95000	1330	—	86000	1290	—

Crude Death Rate of Local Population $= \dfrac{\text{Total deaths}}{\text{Total population}} \times 1000$

or C.D.R. (Local) $= \dfrac{1290}{86000} \times 1000 = 15$

and crude death rate of standard population

$$= \frac{\text{Total deaths}}{\text{Total population}} \times 1000$$

(*i.e.*, standardized death rate of standard population)

$\therefore$ C.D.R. (Standard) $= \dfrac{1330}{95000} \times 1000 = 14$

Standardized death rate of Local Population $= \dfrac{\Sigma PsDx}{\Sigma Ps}$

$$= \frac{(6000 \times 30) + (25000 \times 12.5) + (35000 \times 13) + (24000 \times 15.5) + (5000 \times 21.2)}{6000 + 25000 + 3500 + 24000 + 5000} = \frac{1425500}{95000}$$

$= 15$

Here, we see that standardized death rate of local population is greater than the standardized death rate of standard population (*i.e.*, crude death rate of standard population). Thus the standard population is healthier than local population.

Example 17.8: Calculate the Gross and Net reproduction rates from the following data:

Age (yrs):	15-19	20-24	25-29	30-34	35-39	40-44	45-49
Fertility rate:	0.011	0.066	0.068	0.041	0.022	0.006	0.001
Survival rate:	0.969	0.967	0.963	0.958	0.952	0.942	0.928

Solution: Calculation of G.R.R. and N.R.R.:

Age (yrs)	Fertility rate per woman (F_r)	Survival rate (S_r)	Female offspring of survivors ($F_r \times S_r$)
15-19	0.0110	0.969	0.01066
20-24	0.0660	0.967	0.06382
25-29	0.0680	0.963	0.06548
30-34	0.0410	0.958	0.03928
35-39	0.0220	0.952	0.02094
40-44	0.0060	0.942	0.00565
45-49	0.0011	0.928	0.00093
Total	0.2151	—	0.20676

Since Gross Reproduction Rate (GRR)

$$= i\sum_{r=15}^{49} F_r$$

Here $\sum_{r=15}^{49} F_r = 0.2151$ and $i = 5$

$\therefore$ $\quad$ $G.R.R. = 5\Sigma F_r = 5 \times 0.2151 = 1.0755$

and Net Reproduction Rate (NRR)

$$= i\sum_{r=15}^{49} (F_r \times S_r)$$

Here $\Sigma(F_r \times S_r) = 0.20676$ and $i = 5$

$$\therefore \quad N.R.R. = 5\sum_{r=15}^{49} (F_r \times S_r) = 5 \times 0.20676 = 1.0338$$

LIFE TABLE OR MORTALITY TABLE

The life table gives the life history of a hypothetical group or cohort as it is gradually diminished by deaths. It is a conventional method of expressing the most fundamental and essential facts about the age distribution of mortality in a tabular form and is a powerful tool for measuring the probability of life and death of various age sectors.

A life table provides answers to the following questions:

1. How will a group of infants all born at the same time and experiencing unchanging mortality conditions throughout the life time, gradually die out?

2. When in the course of time all these infants die, what would be the average longevity per person?
3. What is the probability that persons of specified age will survive a specified number of years?
4. How many persons, out of selected number of persons living at some initial age, survive on the average to each attained age?

The life table thus gives a summary of the mortality experience of any population group during a given period and is a very effective and comprehensive method for providing concise measures of the longevity of that population. The data used for constructing a life table are the census data and death registration data. Life tables are generally constructed for various sections of the people which, as experience shows, have sharply different patterns of mortality. Thus, there are life tables constructed for different races, occupational groups and sex. Life tables are as well constructed on regional basis and other factors accounting differential mortality.

NOTATIONS AND TERMINOLOGY

l_x: represents the number of persons living at any specified age x in any year out of an assumed number of births, say, l_0 usually called the cohort or radix of the life table.

d_x: is the number of persons among the l_x persons (attaining a precise age x) who die before reaching the age (x + 1), *i.e.*,

$$d_x = l_x - l_{x+1} = -\Delta l_x$$

where Δ is the difference operator.

np_x: is the probability that a person aged x survives up to age x + n. Thus, if l_{x+n} is the number of persons living at age (x + n) in any year, then

$$np_x = \frac{l_{x+n}}{l_x} \Rightarrow l_{x+n} = l_x . np_x$$

In particular if we take n = 1, we have

$$p_x = \frac{l_{x+1}}{l_x}$$

which gives the probability that a person aged x will survive till his/her next birthday.

$q_x = 1 - p_x$: is the complementary probability of survival, *i.e.*, q_x is the probability that a person of exact age x will die within one year following the attainment of that age. Thus we have $q_x = \dfrac{d_x}{l_x}$

It is also by definition $l_{x+1} = l_x - d_x$

$$= l_x - q_x l_x$$

$$= l_x (1 - q_x)$$

$$= l_x p_x$$

L_x: is the number of years lived in the aggregate by the cohort of l_0 persons between age x and (x + 1). Thus, if deaths are assumed to be uniformly distributed over the whole year or equivalently, if we assume the linearity of l_{x+1} for $t \in [0,1]$, then we get

$$L_x = \int_0^1 l_{x+t} dt \quad \text{and} \quad l_{x+1} = l_x - td_x$$

$$\therefore \qquad L_x = \int_0^1 (l_x - td_x) dt$$

$$= l_x \,|t|_0^1 - d_x \left|\frac{t^2}{2}\right|_0^1$$

$$= l_x - \frac{1}{2} dx = l_x - \frac{1}{2}(l_x - l_{x+1})$$

$$L_x = \frac{1}{2}(l_x + l_{x+1})$$

T_x: is the total number of years lived by the cohort l_x after attaining the age x, *i.e.*, T_x is the total future life time of the l_x persons who reach age x. Thus, we have

$$T_x = L_x + L_{x+1} + L_{x+2} + \ldots$$

Thus if w is the highest age at which any survivors are recorded in the mortality table, *i.e.*, if l_w=0, then

$$T_x = \sum_{i=0}^{w-x-1} L_{x+i}$$

$$T_x = L_x + T_{x+1}$$

The following theorems establish the relationship between the various quantities defined above:

Theorem 1: $\qquad np_x = p_x p_{x+1} \cdots p_{x+n-1}$

Theorem 2: $\qquad nq_x = \dfrac{d_{x+n-1}}{l_x}$

Theorem 3: If w is the last age at which l_x vanishes, *i.e.*, if $l_w = 0$, then

$$l_x = \sum_{i=x}^{w\ 1} di$$

Theorem 4: $$T_x = \frac{1}{2} l_x + l_{x+1} + l_{x+2} + ...$$

Expectations of Life

The curate expectation of life, usually denoted by e_x gives the average number of complete years of life lived by the cohort l_0 after age x by each of l_x persons attaining that age. The complete expectation of life, usually denoted by e_x^0 measures the average number of years a person of given age can be expected to live under the prevailing mortality conditions. It gives the number of years of life entirely completed and includes the fraction of the year survived in the year in which death occurs, which on the average can be taken to be half year. Thus, we have

$$e_x^0 = e_x + \frac{1}{2}$$

Since total number of years lived by l_x persons of age x is given by

$$T_x = \int_0^{\infty} l_{x+t}\, dt$$

the complete expectation of life of a person attaining age x is obtained from the following relation

$$e_x^0 = \frac{T_x}{l_x}$$

e_0^0, is the expectation of life at age 0, is the average age at death or the average longevity of a person belonging to a given community.

Theorem 5: $$e_x = \frac{\sum_{n=1}^{\infty} l_{x+n}}{l_x}$$

i.e., e_x = Average number of years lived by persons of the given age x.

Stationary Population

A population is said to be stationary if it is of constant size and constant age and sex composition over time. Such a population may be conceived of under the following conditions:

1. If every year, the number of births is exactly l_0 (say) and is equal to the number of deaths and these are distributed uniformly throughout the year, and
2. If the population is not affected by emigration or immigration.

Under these conditions, in each year, the number of persons between the ages x and (x + 1) denoted by L_x will always be the same. Thus, the columns L_x and T_x of the life table may be interpreted as giving respectively the age-distribution and the number of persons with age x or more in a stationary population.

Stable Population

A population is said to be stable

1. If it has a fixed age and sex distribution,
2. If constant mortality and fertility rates are experienced at each age, and
3. If the population is closed to emigration or immigration.

For a stable population, the overall rates of births and deaths remain constant and consequently such a population increases at a constant rate. In particular, if the constant overall birth and death rates are equal, then the population size remains fixed and in this case stable population becomes stationary population.

Central Mortality Rate

The central mortality (or death) rate is the probability that a person whose exact age is not known but lies in between x and (x + 1) will die within one year following the attainment of that age. It is denoted by m_x and is given by the mathematical expression as

$$m_x = \frac{\text{No. of deaths within age interval x to (x + 1)}}{\text{Average } l_x \text{ of the cohort in that interval}}$$

or $$m_x = \frac{d_x}{L_x}$$

or $$m_x = \frac{d_x}{l_x - \frac{1}{2}d_x}, \text{ where } L_x = l_x - \frac{1}{2}d_x$$

or $$m_x = \frac{2\frac{d_x}{l_x}}{2 - \frac{d_x}{l_x}} = \frac{2q_x}{2 - q_x}, \quad \text{Since } \frac{d_x}{l_x} = q_x$$

and $$q_x = \frac{2m_x}{2 + m_x}$$

Here, it is to be noticed that the results $\left(\text{i.e., } m_x = \frac{2q_x}{2 - q_x} \text{ and } q_x = \frac{2m_x}{2 + m_x}\right)$ have been obtained under the assumption that deaths are uniformly distributed over the age interval (x, x + 1). This assumption is not satisfied for early ages especially for x = 0. Since the death rate is generally very high in the first few weeks after birth, *i.e.*, neonatal period and then declines sharply.

Force of Mortality

Since deaths occur at all ages and at every fraction of time of the year, l_x is a continuous function of x. At any age x, the rate of decrease is l_x is given by

$$\lim_{t \to 0} \frac{l_x - l_{x+1}}{t} = -\lim_{t \to 0} \frac{l_{x+1} - l_x}{t}$$

$$= -\frac{dl_x}{d_x}$$

where $\frac{dl_x}{d_x}$ is the differential coefficient of l_x w.r.t. x.

The force of mortality at age x is defined as the ratio of instantaneous rate of decrease in l_x to the value of l_x.

It is denoted by μ_x and expressed by

$$\mu_x = -\frac{1}{l_x} \cdot \frac{dl_x}{d_x} = -\frac{d}{d_x} \log l_x$$

Assumptions, Descriptions and Constructions of Life Table

Assumptions

The following assumptions are useful in the construction of the life tables:

1. The cohort is closed for emigration or immigration, *i.e.*, there is no change in the census except the losses due to deaths.
2. Individuals die at each age according to pre-determined schedule which is fixed and does not change.
3. The cohort originates from some standard number of births, say 10,000 or 1,00,000 which is called the radix of the table.
4. The deaths are distributed uniformly over the period (x, x+1) for each x (expect for first few years). In other words, deaths are uniformly distributed between one birthday and the next.

Description of a Life Table

A typical life table has the following columns:

1	2	3	4	5	6	7	8	9	10	11
x	l_x	d_x	q_x	p_x	m_x	μ_x	L_x	T_x	e_x^0	e_x

For x = 0, 1, 2, ..., we have

1. $d_x = l_x - l_{x+1}$

2. $q_x = \dfrac{d_x}{l_x}$

3. $p_x = 1 - q_x = \dfrac{l_{x+1}}{l_x}$

4. $m_x = \dfrac{2q_x}{2 - q_x}$

5. $\mu_x + \dfrac{1}{2} = m_x$

6. $L_x = l_x - \dfrac{1}{2} d_x = \dfrac{1}{2}(l_x + l_{x+1})$

7. $T_x = L_x + L_{x+1} + L_{x+2} + ...$

8. $e_x^0 = \dfrac{T_x}{l_x}$

9. $e_x = e_x^0 - \dfrac{1}{2}$

The columns 5, 6, 7 do not occur in all the life tables. However, the remaining columns are necessary in any life table.

Construction of Life Table

The complete life table can be constucted if we can compute the quantities q_x (or p_x) for all $x \geq 0$. The only other data which is needed is the radix, l_0. The q_x column is thus called the pivotal column of the life table.

Starting with radix l_0 and q_x (x = 0, 1, 2, ...), we have

$$d_0 = l_0 q_0 \quad \Rightarrow \quad l_1 = l_0 - d_0$$

$$d_1 = l_1 q_1 \quad \Rightarrow \quad l_2 = l_1 - d_1$$

and so on

From these values of l_x $(x = 0, 1, 2, ...)$ the columns L_x, T_x and e_x^0 of the table can be completed as follows:

$$L_x = \frac{1}{2}(l_x + l_{x+1})$$

$$T_x = \sum_{i=x}^{\infty} L_i$$

$$e_x^0 = \frac{T_x}{l_x}$$

For reference, Life Table (Males/Females) can be shown below:

Age in yrs.	Number living at at x	Survival ratio	Mortality rate	Number living between ages x and x + 1	Number living above age x	Expectation of life
x	l_x	p_x	q_x	L_x	T_x	e_x^0
1	2	3	4	5	6	7
0	100000	0.75600	0.24400	79170	3806540	48.2
1	75600	0.85945	0.14055	76430	3718360	52.6
2	72400	0.94315	0.05685	74658	3649335	53.8
.						
.						
.						
5	70130	0.93110	0.07890	70990	3411780	53.0
6	70225	0.99170	0.00830	70351	3407187	52.3
7	69115	0.99135	0.00865	70020	3391405	51.0
.						
.						
20	62300	0.99100	0.00900	69120	3210055	40.2
.	.	.	.	.	.	.
.	.	.	.	.	.	.
.	.	.	.	.	.	.
60+	15990	0.95416	0.04584	20150	2083350	7.4

Uses of Tables

The basic objective of life tables is to give a clear picture of the age distribution of mortality in a given population group. It has been used widely in a large number of spheres. Life table has its important place in demography and public health.

According to William Farr, Life Table is the 'Biometer of the population'.

Following are the important applications of life tables:

1. Life tables are indispensable for the solution of all questions concerning the duration of human life. These tables are based on the scientific use of statistical methods and form the basis for determining the rates of premiums necessary to various amount of life assurance.
2. Life tables are used by demographers to devise measures such as 'Net Reproductive Rate' to study the rate of growth of population.
3. Life tables are used in preparation of population projections by age and sex.
4. Life tables for two or more different groups of population may be used for the relative comparison of various measures of mortality such as death rate, life expectancy at various ages, etc.
5. Life tables are well used by the government and the private establishments for determining the rates of retirement benefits to be given to its employees.
6. Life tables are also used for predicting the school going population in connection with school building programmes.
7. Life tables are used for estimating the probable number of future windows and orphans in a community and computing the approximate size of future labour force etc.

EXAMPLE 17.9: Complete the following life table:

x:	0	1	2	3	4	5	6
l_x:	90	80	70	65	50	25	0

R_1, R_2, and R_3 are three rabbits of age 1, 2, and 3 years respectively. Find the probability that (i) at least one of three rabbits will be alive for one year more (ii) all the three rabbits will be alive for two years time.

SOLUTION: The complete life table for the given data is

Age	l_x	$d_x = l_x - l_{x+1}$	$q_x = \frac{d_x}{l_x}$	$L_x = \frac{l_x + l_{x+1}}{2}$	$T_x = \sum_{i=0}^{x} L_i$	$e_x^0 = \frac{T_x}{l_x}$
1	2	3	4	5	6	7
0	90	10	0.11	85.0	335.0	3.72
1	80	10	0.13	75.0	250.0	3.13
2	70	5	0.07	67.5	175.0	2.50
3	65	15	0.23	57.5	107.5	1.65
4	50	25	0.50	37.5	50.0	1.00
5	25	25	1.00	12.5	12.5	0.50
6	0	–	–	–	–	–

(i) Let p_1 = Probability that R_1 will die in one year $= \frac{d_1}{l_1} = \frac{10}{80}$

p_2 = Probability that R_2 will die in one year $= \frac{d_2}{l_2} = \frac{5}{70}$

p_3 = Probability that R_3 will die in one year $= \frac{d_3}{l_3} = \frac{15}{65}$

Hence the probability that all three rabbits will die in one year is given by the compound probability theorem by the expression

$$p = p_1.p_2.p_3 = \frac{10}{80}.\frac{5}{70}.\frac{15}{65} = \frac{750}{364000} = 0.002$$

$\therefore$ p[at least one rabbit will survive for one year more]

= 1 – p[none will survive for one year more]

= 1 – p = 1 – 0.002 = 0.998

(ii) Let E_1, E_2, and E_3 denote the events that R_1, R_2, and R_3 survive for two years more respectively.

Then $P(E_1) = \frac{l_3}{l_1} = \frac{65}{80} = 0.81 \Rightarrow P(\bar{E}_1) = 1 - 0.81 = 0.19$

$P(E_2) = \frac{l_4}{l_2} = \frac{50}{70} = 0.71 \Rightarrow P(\bar{E}_2) = 1 - 0.71 = 0.29$

$P(E_3) = \frac{l_5}{l_3} = \frac{25}{65} = 0.38 \Rightarrow P(\bar{E}_3) = 1 - 0.38 = 0.62$

Hence the required probability that all the three rabbits will survive for two years is given by the compound probability theorem by the expression

$$P(E_1 \cap E_2 \cap E_3) = P(E_1)P(E_2)P(E_3) = 0.81 \times 0.71 \times 0.38 = 0.22$$

EXAMPLE 17.10: Complete the following table of the population of a certain type of insects, x being the age in days and l_x=1000 for x = 0:

x :	0	1	2	3	4	5	6	7
q_x :	0.122	0.005	0.012	0.052	0.100	0.500	0.800	0.950

SOLUTION: Since we are given the values of q_x, in order to complete the life table, first of all we shall find the values of l_x (x = 0, 1, 2, ..., 7) by using the relations $q_x = \frac{d_x}{l_x}$ and $l_{x+1} = l_x - d_x$

Since $l_0 = 1000$

Hence $d_0 = l_0 q_0 = 1000 \times 0.122 = 122$

$l_1 = l_0 - d_0 = 1000 - 122 = 878$

$d_1 = l_1 q_1 = 878 \times 0.005 = 4.39$

$l_2 = l_1 - d_1 = 878 - 4.39 = 873.61$

$d_2 = l_2 q_2$, $l_3 = l_2 - d_2$ and so on

The values of l_x and d_x (x = 0, 1, 2, ..., 7) can be obtained by using the above relations in the following table:

x	q_x	l_x	$d_x = l_x q_x$	$L_x = \frac{l_x + l_{x+1}}{2}$	$T_x = \sum_{i=0}^{x} L_i$	$e_x^0 = \frac{T_x}{l_x}$
0	0.122	1000	1000 × 0.122 = 122	939.00	5074.46	5.07
1	0.005	1000 – 122 = 878	878 × 0.005 = 4.39	875.81	4135.46	4.71
2	0.012	878 – 4.39 = 873.61	873.61 × 0.012 = 10.48	868.37	3259.65	3.73
3	0.052	873.61 – 10.48 = 863.13	863.13 × 0.052 = 44.88	840.69	2391.28	2.77
4	0.100	863.13 – 44.88 = 818.25	818.25 × 0.100 = 81.83	777.34	1550.59	1.90
5	0.500	818.25 – 81.83 = 736.42	736.42 × 0.500 = 368.21	552.32	773.25	1.05
6	0.800	736.42 – 368.21 = 368.21	368.21 × 0.800 = 294.57	220.93	220.93	0.60
7	0.950	368.21 – 294.57 = 73.64	73.64 × 0.950 = 69.96	–	–	–

EXAMPLE 17.11: Fill in the blanks in a portion of a life table given below:

Age (yrs.)	l_x	d_x	p_x	q_x	L_x	T_x	e_x^0
4	85,000	400	?	?	?	3,750,200	?
5	?	300	?	?	?	?	?

SOLUTION: In the usual notations, we have

$$l_5 = l_4 - d_4 = 85000 - 400 = 84600$$

$$p_4 = \frac{l_5}{l_4} = \frac{84600}{85000} = 0.9953$$

$$q_4 = (1 - p_4) = 1 - 0.9953 = 0.0047$$

$$l_6 = l_5 - d_5 = 84600 - 300 = 84300$$

$$p_5 = \frac{l_6}{l_5} = \frac{84300}{84600} = 0.9965$$

$$q_5 = (1 - p_5) = 1 - 0.9965 = 0.0035$$

$$L_4 = \frac{l_4 + l_5}{2} = \frac{85000 + 84600}{2} = 84800$$

$$L_5 = \frac{l_5 + l_6}{2} = \frac{84600 + 84300}{2} = 84450$$

$$e_4^0 = \frac{T_4}{l_4} = \frac{3750200}{85000} = 44.12$$

$$T_5 = T_4 - L_4 = 3750200 - 84800 = 3665400$$

$$e_5^0 = \frac{T_5}{l_5} = \frac{3665400}{84600} = 43.33$$

EXAMPLE 17.12: The complete expectation of life at ages 40 and 41 for a particular group are respectively 20.4 and 19.5 years and that the number living at age 40 is 40,550. Find (i) the number that attains the age 41 and (ii) the number that will die without attaining the age 41.

SOLUTION: (i) Here we need the value of l_{41} and we are given

$$e_{40}^0 = 20.4,\ e_{41}^0 = 19.5 \text{ and } l_{40} = 40{,}550$$

$$\therefore \quad e_{40} = e_{40}^0 - \frac{1}{2} = 20.4 - 0.5 = 19.9$$

and
$$e_{41} = e_{41}^0 - \frac{1}{2} = 19.5 - 0.5 = 19.0$$

Now we have the formula

$$p_x = \frac{l_{x+1}}{l_x} = \frac{e_x}{1+e_{x+1}}$$

By taking $x = 40$, we get $\frac{l_{41}}{l_{40}} = \frac{e_{40}}{1+e_{41}}$

$$l_{41} = \frac{l_{40}e_{40}}{1+e_{41}} = \frac{40550 \times 19.9}{20} = 40347$$

(ii) The number of persons who die without attaining the age 41 is equal to the numbers of persons dying between the age period 40 and 41 which is given by

$$d_{40} = l_{40} - l_{41}$$
$$= 40550 - 40347 = 203$$

EXAMPLE 17.13: The number of persons dying at age 70 is 455 and the complete expectation of life at 70 and 71 years are 3.72 and 3.46 years. Find the numbers living at ages 70 and 71.

SOLUTION: Here, we are given $e^0_{70} = 3.72$, $e^0_{71} = 3.46$ and $d_{70} = 455$

Now, we get $e_{70} = e^0_{70} - 0.50 = 3.22$

and $e_{71} = e^0_{71} - 0.50 = 2.96$

again $l_{71} = \frac{l_{70}e_{70}}{1+e_{71}} = l_{70}\frac{3.22}{3.96}$

also $d_x = l_x - l_{x+1}$

$$d_{70} = l_{70} - l_{71} = 455 \text{ (given)}$$

$$l_{70} - l_{70}\frac{3.22}{3.96} = 455$$

$$l_{70}\left(1 - \frac{3.22}{3.96}\right) = 455$$

$$\therefore \quad l_{70} = \frac{455 \times 198}{37} = 2435$$

ABRIDGED LIFE TABLE

As we know a complete life table is one in which the age interval is a year throughout the table with life table functions such as l_x, d_x, q_x, m_x, etc., are given for all integral values of x. Whereas in abridged life table, the values of these functions are as follows:

(i) either for some integral values of x which are at some distance apart,usually 5 years or 10 years.

(ii) or they are given for age groups of values of x, usually of width 5 years or 10 years.

Methods used for the construction of abridged life table are:

1. Reed-Merrell Method
2. Greville's Method

Reed-Merrell Method

This method is based on the following fundamental result which is the form of a lemma:

$$ {}_n q_x^z = \frac{2n\left({}_n m_x^z\right)}{2 + n\left({}_n m_x^z\right)} $$

Where ${}_n p_x^z$ and ${}_n d_x^z$ are respectively the average number of persons and the number of deaths between ages x to (x + n) in the calender year z and ${}_n m_x^z = \frac{{}_n d_x^z}{{}_n p_x^z}$ is the central rate of mortality in the calender year z, n being the length of the age group.

Description of the Method

For each possible value of x, the values of ${}_n p_x^z$ and ${}_n d_x^z$ are known from the census and registration data respectively. Using these values we can find ${}_n m_x^z$ by the relation

$$ {}_n m_x^z = \frac{{}_n d_x^z}{{}_n p_x^z} $$

and finally the values of ${}_n q_x^z$ from the relation, *i.e.*,

$$ {}_n p_x^z = \frac{2n({}_n m_x^z)}{2 + n({}_n m_x^z)} $$

Thus starting with given radix l_x, we can find other values l_{x+n}, l_{x+2n} and so on by the relation

$$ l_{x+n} = l_x \cdot {}_n p_x $$
$$ l_{x+2n} = l_x \cdot {}_n p_{x+n} $$

and so on where ${}_n p_x = 1 - {}_n q_x$. Other functions of the life table can be obtained in usual way.

Greville's Method

As in the construction of complete life table, the values of ${}_nq_x$ for early ages (x = 0, 1, 2, ...) are obtained by any one of the method involving birth and death statistics. From these probabilities we can get a value l_x which will serve as a radix for the construction of the abridged life table. We have

$$ {}_nd_x = l_x \cdot {}_nq_x $$

and
$$ {}_np_x = \frac{l_{x+n}}{l_x} = 1 - {}_nq_x $$

∴
$$ l_{x+n} = l_x(1 - {}_nq_x) = l_x - {}_nd_x $$

where ${}_nd_x$ is the total number of deaths in the life table stationary population in the age sector x to (x + n).

Now starting with the radix l_x and computing the ${}_nq_x$ values from the relation

$$ {}_nq_x = \frac{2n({}_nm_x)}{1 + {}_nm_x\left[n + \frac{n^2}{6}({}_nm_x - \log_e C)\right]} $$

we can obtain the values of l_{x+n}, l_{x+2n} and so on.

After this we compute the ${}_nL_x$ column for the abridged life table. If we assume that central rate of mortality, ${}_nm_x$ in the observed population is same as in the life table stationary population then by definition, we get

$$ {}_nm_x = \frac{{}_nd_x}{{}_nL_x} $$

and
$$ {}_nL_x = \frac{{}_nd_x}{{}_nm_x} $$

where ${}_nm_x$ are given values and ${}_nd_x$ are computed from the relation ${}_nd_x = l_x \cdot {}_nq_x$

If w + n is the terminal age, *i.e.*, the age at which l_x vanishes which implies that $l_{w+n} = 0$, then we get

$$ {}_nL_w = \frac{nd_w}{nm_w} = \frac{l_w}{nm_w} $$

The next column of the table, viz.,

$T_x = {}_nL_x + {}_nL_{x+n} + \ldots\ldots + {}_nL_w$ is obtained from the ${}_nL_x$ column by taking cumulative totals starting from the bottom of the table. The calculations may be simplified by using the relation

$$ T_x = {}_nL_w + T_{w+n} $$

Finally the last column giving the expectation of life is obtained from the relation

$$e_x^0 = \frac{T_x}{l_x}$$

EXAMPLE 17.14: The following table gives the population and deaths for ages 0 to 4 years. Make a life table for 10,000 children who start life and find the number of survivors at each successive birthday till the 5th year of age.

Age(x)	Population	Deaths
0-1	5600	60
1-2	6392	16
2-3	6396	8
3-4	6598	4
4-5	6399	2

SOLUTION: In the first year of life, all the 60 deaths did not occur on the first day. Probably 7/10th died by mid-year. Therefore mid year population of first year would have been $5600 + \frac{7}{10} \times 60 = 5642$. Then the probability of dying per person, *i.e.*, d_x $= \frac{60}{5642} = 0.0106$. Thus, 106($d_x$) out of 10 000 would actually die, so the number of survivors entering life for 2nd year is $10{,}000 - 106 = 9894$. After the first year, we presume that half of deaths occurred before and half after six months. When 16 deaths occured, they lived 8 years more. These 8 years are to be added to those that reached 2nd year, *i.e.*, $6392 + 8 = 6400$. The chance of dying per person $= \frac{16}{6400}$ $= 0.0025$. By multiplying 9894×0.0025 we get the number died in the 2nd year, *i.e.*, 25. The population surviving to start the 3rd year of life will be $9894 - 25 = 9869$ and similarly the number of those starting life in 4th and 5th years of life. Thus, in this way, life table upto the age of 100 years can be constructed and seen when all in the population of 10,000 that started life disappear at the death rates of chosen year.

Age	Mid year population	Prob. of dying	Prob. of surviving	Popn. that died out of 10,000 at the rate, q_x	Popn. that started life
x	l	q_x	$p_x = 1 - q_x$	d_x*	l_x
0-1	$5600 + \frac{7}{10} \times 60$ $= 5642$	$\frac{60}{5642}$ $= 0.0106$	0.9894	10000×0.0106 $= 106$	10,000
1-2	$6392 + \frac{1}{2} \times 16$ $= 6400$	$\frac{16}{6400}$ $= 0.0025$	0.9975	9894×0.0025 $= 24.7$ (25)	$10000 - 106$ $= 9894$
2-3	$6396 + \frac{1}{2} \times 8$ $= 6400$	$\frac{8}{6400}$ $= 0.0013$	0.9987	9869×0.0013 12.8 (13)	$9894 - 25$ $= 9869$
3-4	$6598 + \frac{1}{2} \times 4$ 6600	$\frac{4}{6600}$ $= 0.0006$	0.9994	9856×0.0006 $= 5.9$ (6)	$9869 - 13$ $= 9856$
4-5	$6399 + \frac{1}{2} \times 2$ $= 6400$	$\frac{2}{6400}$ $= 0.0003$	0.9997	$9850 \times .0003$ $= 2.9$ (3)	$9856 - 6$ $= 9850$

*It is assumed that the deaths occurred uniformly throughout the year.

The expectation of life is a very popular measure of health on the one hand and of socioeconomic development on the other. It is considered a very comprehensive indicator because many aspects of development seem to reflect on the longevity of people.

LIFE EXPECTANCY

The average number of years expected to be lived by individuals in a population is called expectation of life. This can be calculated at birth or at any other age. The expectation of life at birth (ELB) can be crudely interpreted as the average age at death.

The ideal method for computing the expectation of life is by observing a large cohort (called a radix) of live births as long as any individual of the cohort is alive. This may take more than 100 years and thus is impractical unless records for over a hundred years are complete. As a shortcut, it is assumed that the individuals at different ages are exposed to the current risks of mortality.

Thus, the current age-specific death rates are used on a preassumed cohort of, say, 100,000 persons. The average of life so obtained is the number of years a newborn is expected to live if the current levels of mortality continue.

The computation of expectation of life at birth or at any other age becomes convenient by preparing what is called a life table. It utilizes the information regarding people alive at different ages, the age-specific death rates, and the years lived by segments of population of different ages. It is desirable to do the computation for each year of age, say for age 46 years, 47 years, etc., but the mortality rates are generally available for age groups such as 45-49 years. When such groups are used, this is called an abridged life table.

EXAMPLE 17.15: Following table is an abridged life table for Indian urban females for the Block years 2000-2005.

Age (yrs.) interval $(t, t+n_t)$	Prob. of death in the interval, q_t	Expected surviving age t, l_t	Person-years lived in the interval, L_t	Person-years lived beyond age t, T_t	Expectation of life at age t, e_t
0-1	0.04989	100,000	96508	6214374	62.14
1-5	0.02453	95011	375149	6117866	64.39
.	.	.	.	.	.
.	.	.	.	.	.
.	.	.	.	.	.

where n_t = Length of the age interval beginning with age t

q_t = Probability of death in the age interval $(t, t+n_t)$ when the person is alive at age t

$$= \frac{n_t m_t}{1+(1-a_t)n_t m_t},$$

where m_t is the age-specific death rate for the age interval $(t, t+n_t)$ and a_t is the average length of life lived per year in that interval by those who die in the interval.

When $a_t = \frac{1}{2}$, $q_t = \dfrac{n_t m_t}{1+\frac{1}{2}n_t m_t}$

This assumes that the risk of death is same throughout the interval. This is generally true for age intervals (5 – 10), (10 – 15), ... , (65 – 70) years but not for the younger and higher age intervals, *e.g.*, infant deaths are highly concentrated in the neonatal period.

In low-mortality areas, those who survive the neonatal period tend to live almost as long as anybody else. In that case, for $t = 0$, the convention is to use $a_0 = 0.1$. For high-mortality areas, $a_0 = 0.3$ is used.

For age interval (1-5) years, $t = 1$ and $a_1 = 0.475$ can be used for all areas.

$$l_t = \text{Expected number of persons surviving the age t.}$$

The radix is 100,000 which survives age $t = 0$. The survivors at age $(t + n_t)$ are

$$l_{t+nt} = (\text{Survivors at t}) - (\text{Dying in the interval } t, t + n_t)$$

or

$$l_{t+nt} = l_t - q_t l_t$$

For example, the expected survivors at age 40 years

$$l_{40} = 88276 - 0.01168 \times 88276 = 87245$$

$$L_t = \text{Expected number of person-years lived in the interval } (t, t + n_t)$$

$$= (n_t/2)\,(I_t + I_{t+nt})$$

Finally e_t = Expectation of life at age $t = T_t/l_t$

(i) All life tables assume that there are no sudden deaths due to calamities.

(ii) Males and females in general have differential mortality patterns and, therefore, separate life tables are drawn for the two genders. A similar distinction may also be needed between other groupings such as rural-urban, low income-high income, and skilled and non skilled.

(iii) Age-specific mortality may change from year to year. The rates in the year 2000 are not necessarily the same as in the year 2005. Thus, a life table is prepared every year or at least once in 5 years.

(iv) Expectation of life at birth (ELB) is severely affected by infant mortality. That is, if a child survives the infantile period, his remaining period life is expected to be longer than the whole period of life expected for a new born. The expectation of life is a very popular measure of health on the one hand and of socio-economic development on the other.

Other Forms of Life Expectancy

1. **Potential Years of Life Lost (PYLL):** The death of a person at 55 years due to, say, a vehicular accident, who otherwise was expected to live for another 30 years amounts to a loss of 30 potential years of life, Thus,

$$\text{PYLL} = (\text{Life expectancy at the age of premature death}) - (\text{Actual age at death})$$

$$= e_t - t$$

where t is the age at death and e_t is expectation of life at age t.

2. **Disability Adjusted Life Years (DALYs):** DALYs lost are a combination of the potential years of life lost due to premature mortality and the equivalent years for duration of restricted activity, weighted for severity of various causes. Death is given weight 1.0, and a state of complete restriction of movements (bedridden) but no other restriction (as in the case of fracture) can be given a weight of 0.6. A separate weighting scheme depending on age is also incorporated. This is the value of a year of life at that age. The most valuable years are considered between 20 and 30 years of age and get the highest weight, 1.4 compared with 1.0 at the ages of 10 years and 55 years, and 0.4 at the age of 90.
3. **Global Burden of Disease (GBD):** DALYs lost are used to measure the global burden of disease. It was estimated by World Bank that 45.8% of DALYs lost in the world in the year 1990 were due to communicable diseases, 42.2% to non-communicable diseases, and 11.9% to injuries. Respiratory infections were the single most important factor and contributed 9.0% of the burden. In India, diarrhoea and respiratory infections together are responsible for more than 1/5th of the burden. India lost 344 DALYs per 1000 population in the year 1990, while China lost 178.

SURVIVAL ANALYSIS

Survival data arise when the aim is to study the time elapsed from some particular starting point to the occurrence of an event. Thus, a follow-up is an integral part of survival studies. The term 'survival' presumes that the event is death, but, in practice, this could be any failure such as occurrance of metastasis, toxicity or relapse or any success such as recovery, discharge from the hospital. In case of survival studies, not all the subjects of a cohort necessarily begin at the same point of time. The subjects can join and leave at any point. The joining time is considered time zero and all durations are measured from this point. The interest in survival studies basically is in the expected duration from a beginning point to an end point. This is studied in terms of probability of the outcome within a specified time interval.

For example, the chance of recurrence of sputum positivity in TB within a six-months period after its treatment was discounted in the middle of its course. Another example is the median duration elapsed in appearance of the outcome.

There are two methods used in survival studies:

1. Life table method.
2. Kaplan-Meier method

Life Table Method

In this method, survival time is grouped into intervals, the lost-to-followup subjects are considered to have been lost at the mid point of the interval. This is equivalent to half a subject going through the full interval. This is a crude adjustment to lost-to-followup subjects but works very well in situations in which the dropouts are uniform over the interval. Therefore, in this case the following expression is applicable if there are K intervals:

$$p_k = \frac{n_k - d_k - C_k/2}{n_k - C_k/2}, \quad k = 1, 2, ..., K$$

where p_k is the proportion surviving the kth interval among those who survived (k – 1)th interval,

n_k is the number of subjects known alive at the beginning of kth interval,

d_k is the number of deaths in the kth interval,

and C_k is the number of subjects with incomplete segments in the kth interval.

The numerator of the formula is the number of survivors and the denominator is the number of subjects at risk.

The estimated probability of surviving the kth interval is (*i.e.*, survival function)

$$S_k = p_k p_{k-1} \ldots\ldots. p_2 p_1$$

where $k = 1, 2, 3, ..., K$

This can be obtained for each of the k intervals. Now S_k is the estimated unconditional probability obtained by the product rule.

EXAMPLE 17.16: Consider the following data on survival time of 15 patients after having radical mastectomy for breast cancer. The study started in January 2002 and continued upto December 2005. The maximum follow-up was 4 years, and many patients joined after January 1992 as and when radical mastectomy was done.

Survival time (months): 6 8 20 20 20+ 24+ 25+ 30+ 35+ 37 37 38+ 40+ 42 45+

where + means that the patients are lost to follow-up or not followed up after this period. They are the incomplete segments. Their exact survival time is not known but it is at least as many months as shown.

In life table method, the duration of survival is grouped which is given in the following table for 12 month grouping (see Table 17.3).

Table 17.3: Life Table Method for Calculation of Survival

Interval No. (k)	Duration after surgery (months)	Known alive at the start of the interval (n_k)	Died during the interval d_k	Patients with incomplete segments C_k	At risk in the interval $n_k - C_k/2$	Survivors $n_k - d_k - C_k/2$	Proportion surviving the interval p_k	Proportion surviving since the beginning S_k
1	0-11	15	2	0	15.0	13.0	$\frac{13}{15} = 0.87$	0.87
2	12-23	13	2	1	12.5	10.5	$\frac{10.5}{12.5} = 0.84$	0.73
3	24-35	10	0	4	8.0	8.0	$\frac{8.0}{8.0} = 1.0$	0.73
4	36-47	6	3	3	4.5	1.5	$\frac{1.5}{4.5} = 0.33$	0.24

Kalpan-Meier Method

In this method, each time of death is considered as such without grouping it into intervals. The probability of survival is computed for each duration in place of each interval. For this, first we should arrange the subjects according to the known duration of survival, including the censored duration.

Now corresponding to formula used in life table method $\left(i.e., \ p_k = \frac{n_k - d_k - C_k/2}{n_k - C_k/2}, k = 1, 2, ..., K \right)$, we have the following formula for I distinct time points:

$$p_i = \frac{n_i - d_i}{n_i} \quad \text{where } i = 1, 2, ..., I$$

p_i is the proportion surviving the ith time point among those who survived the (i – 1)th time point,

n_i is the number of subjects at risk of death at the ith time point, *i.e.*, those who are still being followed up excluding the incomplete segments,

k_i is the number of subjects with incomplete segments, and d_i is the number who died on the ith time point.

The proportion surviving the ith time point is $S_i = p_i p_{i-1} \ldots\ldots p_2 p_1$; i = 1, 2, ..., I

This is the survival function and it is computed for each time point instead of the time interval. It is to be noted that only unique time points are considered. If a time point is applicable to two or more subjects, it is counted only once.

We would prefer the same example to illustrate the Kaplan-Meier Method.

Table 17.4: Kaplan-Meier Method for Calculation of Survival

Patient No.	Months of survival	Time point (i)	No. of patients at risk (at the beginning) n_i	No. with incomplete segments k_i	Deaths at the ith time point d_i	No. of known survivors $n_i - k_i - d_i$	Proportion survived ith time point p_i	Proportion survived since the beginning S_i
1	6	1	15	0	1	14	14/15 = 0.93	0.93
2	8	2	14	0	1	13	13/14 =0.93	0.87
3, 4, 5	20	3	13	1	2	10	11/13 = 0.85	0.73
6	24^+	4	10	1	0	9	10/10 = 1.00	0.73
7	25^+	5	9	1	0	8	9/9 = 1.00	0.73
8	30^+	6	8	1	0	7	8/8 = 1.00	0.73
9	35^+	7	7	1	0	6	7/7 = 1.00	0.73
10, 11	37	8	6	0	2	4	4/6 = 0.67	0.49
12	38^+	9	4	1	0	3	4/4 = 1.00	0.49
13	40^+	10	3	1	0	2	3/3 = 1.00	0.49
14	42	11	2	0	1	1	1/2 = 0.50	0.24
15	45^+	12	1	1	0	0	1/1 = 1.00	0.24

Note: Patients with complete segments do not contribute to the calculation of S_i after they are lost.

Salient Features of Survival Analysis

❖ It is important in all survival studies to exactly define the entry point or the starting point. This could be the day of diagnosis, the day of starting therapy, the day of onset, or the day of any such event.

❖ To define the exit point or the end point. In many cases this could be death. However, in some cases, as mentioned earlier, the interest could be in recurrence, occurrence of a particular complication, recovery etc.

❖ To decide whether or not the intervening period between entry and exit has to be event free and whether or not the occurrence of other events is to be disregarded.

❖ Some subjects can always be lost to followup due to moved out of the area or stopped cooperating or one just untraceable. It is, however, desirable that there are not too many such losses.

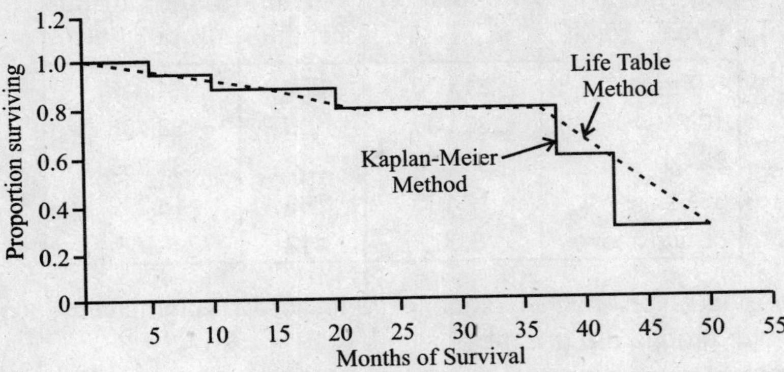

Fig. 17.1: Survival function curve(s) by Life Table Method and Kaplan-Meier Method.

➤ EXERCISES ➤

17.1. The population of a district as per census – 2001 was 22,58,480 and as per census – 1991 was 18,98,880. Calculate the mid-year population in 1994 and 2005.

17.2. According to census, population of a city on 1st March 1991 and 2001 was 8,86,200 and 12,66,440 respectively. Estimate the mid-year population of the city for the year 1996 and 2006.

17.3. Calculate the CBR, CDR and IMR of a city whose mid-year population is 8,40,000; live births in a year were 14,000; number of deaths 6,500 and the number of infant deaths 1680.

17.4. The mid-year population of a city was 12,48,500. In the same year, the number of attacks from Cholera was 1360 and the number of deaths was 340. Calculate the morbidity rate due to Cholera, and the case fatality rate.

17.5. The mid-year population of a district was 32,36,800. There were 18,560 live births, 510 still births, 950 deaths within one week after birth and 1650 deaths in the first month of life and 1920 deaths in the first year of life in a particular year. Calculate still birth, perinatal and infant mortality rates.

17.6. The populations of two cities are given as 16,78,000 and 8,98,000 respectively and their respective death rates as 16.2 and 18.6 per 1000. Find the combined death rate for the two cities.

17.7. Calculate the CDR for the following data:

Age-group (Yrs.)	Population	No. of deaths	Standardized population
0-9	21,000	350	24,315
10-24	30,000	105	32,785
25-54	36,820	230	31,355
55-64	17,180	353	16,392
65 and above	5,000	412	5,168

17.8. The population and the number of deaths of two communities, according to age groups are given below:

Age group (Yrs.)	Community A		Community B	
	Population	No. of deaths	Population	No. of deaths
< 5	7,500	250	85,000	780
5-15	14,200	265	1,22,100	600
15-35	15,000	290	1,68,400	720
35-50	5,500	300	73,000	1,200
50 +	7,100	415	68,000	1,400

Compute (i) CDRs (ii) Standardized death rates taking population of community A as standardized population.

17.9. Which of the two localities A and B is healthier?

Age group (Yrs.)	Locality A		Locality B	
	Population	Deaths/1000	Population	Deaths/1000
0-10	700	35	550	42
10-20	1200	5	1800	4
20-60	3500	8	3000	10
60 +	400	52	600	22

17.10. Calculate the GFR, TFR from the following data:

Age group (Yrs.)	Number of Woman	Number of Live births
15-19	26,000	780
20-24	22,000	2,420
25-29	18,000	1,998
30-34	15,000	1,425
34-39	12,000	480
40-44	6,000	120
45-49	4,000	12

17.11. Calculate the GRR and NRR from the following data:

Age-group (Yrs.)	No. of Woman	No. of female children born	Survival rate
15-19	10,000	300	0.898
20-24	9,000	630	0.889
25-29	7,990	478	0.877
30-34	7,000	280	0.868
34-39	6,000	152	0.849
40-44	4,980	34	0.826
45-49	2,930	12	0.790

17.11. Calculate the Gross Fertility Rate (GFR) and Gross Reproduction Rate (GRR) from the following data:

Age group (Yrs.)	Number of Woman	Number of Live births
15 – 19	16,000	260
20 – 24	16,400	2140
25 – 29	15,800	1980
30 – 34	15,200	1400
34 – 39	14,800	900
40 – 44	14,000	280
45 – 49	13,500	120

[**Hint:** Sex ratio being, Male : Female = 52:48.]

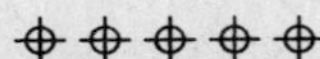

CHAPTER

18

Research Methods (Clinical)

- *Research Protocol*
- *Medical Ethics*
- *Matching*
- *Clinical Trial*
- *Study Design*
- *Data Management*

INTRODUCTION

Research is either discovery of new facts, enunciation of new principles, or fresh interpretation of the known facts. The basic concept of research is to answer Why? What? and How? of a phenomenon.

Clinical research or clinical trial is a scientific investigation in which a drug or therapy is applied with diagnostic or therapeutic or prophylactic intention to patients.

The objective of clinical research is to progress from a state of 'no knowledge' to 'complete knowledge ' after a course of time. Before trying a new drug to human, it should be tried on animal and the animal toxicity data have to be examined carefully. On the basis of these results, human pharmacology has to be investigated to see the toxicity effects of new drug in human being.

The different phases of clinical research are as follows:

Research is a systematic search for answers to questions about facts and relationship between facts. It has been described in different phases.

1. The Research Question

The research question is the uncertainty about something in the population that the investigator wants to resolve by making measurements on the study subjects. Research questions often begin with a general concern that must be narrowed down to a concrete research issue.

The characteristics of a good research question are described as (FINE-R): It should be

(i) Feasible,
(ii) Interesting,
(iii) Novel,
(iv) Ethical and
(v) Relevant.

2. Selection of Study Subjects

All clinical research is based on the use of a sample to represent a population (or universe). In designing a study the first step is to conceptualize the target population, formulating a specific set of inclusion criteria that establish the demographic and clinical characteristics of subjects well suited to the research question and a parsimonious set of exclusion criteria that eliminate subjects who are unethical or inappropriate to study.

The next step is to design an approach to sampling the population. A convenience sample is often a good choice in clinical research. Simple random sampling can be used to reduce the size of a convenience sample if necessary, and other probability samples, *i.e.,* stratified and cluster are useful in certain situations. A sample must be large enough to meet the study needs.

3. Planning the Measurements

Variables are either continuous, discrete, or categorical. Categorical variable are further classified as nominal or ordinal. Variables which have only two categories are called dichotomous. It is good to prefer continuous variables because they contain additional information that improves efficiency and therapy permit smaller sample size. The precision of a measurement is another major determinant of power and sample size. Precision is reduced by random error from three sources of variability: the observer, the instrument, and the subject. Whereas the accuracy of a measurement is increased by calibration, by unobtrusive measures, and by blinding.

HYPOTHESES

The primary purpose of the hypothesis is to establish the basis for tests of statistical significance. Hypotheses are not needed in descriptive studies which describe how characteristics are distributed in a population. Hypotheses are needed for studies that will use tests of statistical significance to compare findings among group. Most observational studies and all experiments address research questions that involve making comparisons.

Null and Alternative Hypothesis

The null hypothesis states that there is no association between the predictor and outcome variables in the population. The proposition that there is an association is called the alternative hypothesis.

Estimation of Sample Size

The sample size should be estimated in the beginning of a research design so that appropriate modifications can be made.

Analytical and experimental studies need a hypothesis that specifies for the purpose of subsequent tests of significance, the anticipated association between the main predictor and outcome variables.

The null hypothesis, which proposes that the predictor and outcome variables are not associated, is the basis for tests of significance. The alternative hypothesis proposes that they are associated. Statistical tests attempt to reject the null hypothesis of no association in favour of the alternative hypothesis that there is an association.

For analytical studies and experiments, the sample size is an estimate of the number of subjects required to detect an association of a given effect size and variability at a specified likelihood of making a type I (false-positive) and type II (false-negative) errors.

Cohort Studies

In Cohort studies, subjects are followed overtime to describe the incidence or natural history of a condition and to analyze predictors (risk factors) for various outcomes. Measuring the predictor before the outcome occurs establishes the sequence of events and helps control bias in that measurement.

Prospective Cohort Studies

May require large numbers of subjects followed for long periods of time.

Cross-sectional Study

In a cross-sectional study, the variables are all measured at a single point in time, with no structural distinction between predictors and outcomes. Cross sectional studies are valuable for providing descriptive information about prevalence.

In a Case Control Study

The prevalence of risk factors in a sample of subjects who have a disease or other outcome of interest (the cases) is compared with that in a sample who do not (the controls). This design, in which people with and without the disease are sampled separately, is relatively inexpensive and uniquely efficient for studying rare diseases.

A **confounding variable** is one that is associated with the predictor variable and is a cause of the outcome variable, *e.g.,* cigarette smoking is a likely confounder in the coffee and MI because smoking is associated with coffee drinking and is a cause of MI. If this is the actual explanation, then the association between coffee and MI does not represent cause-effect even though it is perfectly real; the coffee is an innocent bystander. Aside from bias, confounding is often the only likely alternative explanation to cause-effect and the most important one to try to rule out, it is also the most challenging.

Clinical Trial

A research activity that involves the administration of a test regimen to human to evaluate its efficacy and safety. The term is subject to wide variation in usage, from the first use in human without any control treatment to a rigorously designed and executed experiment involving test and control treatments and randomization. The different phases of clinical trial are as follows:

Phase-I trial safety and pharmacologic profiles. The first introduction of a candidate vaccine or a drug into a human population to determine its safety and mode of action. In drug trials, this phase may include studies of dose and route of administration.

Phase-II trial pilot efficacy studies. Initial trial to examine efficacy usually in 200 to 500 volunteers (participants), with vaccines, the focus is on immunogenicity, and with drugs, on demonstration of safety and efficacy in comparison to other existing regimens. Usually subjects are randomly allocated to study and control groups.

Phase-III trial extensive clinical trial. This phase is intended for complete assessment of safety and efficacy. It involves larger numbers perhaps thousands, of volunteers, usually with random allocation to study and control groups.

Phase-IV trial with drugs, this phase is conducted after the national drug registration authority has approved the drug for distribution or marketing. These trials may include research designed to explore a specific pharmacologic effect to establish the incidence of adverse reactions or to determine the effects of long term use. Ethical review is essential for conducting the clinical trials.

Ethics are integral part of clinical trial. Ethics have following aspects which are very important for a clinical research:

(a) Whether a new treatment be ethically withheld from a patient under physician's supervision.

(b) Type of patients to be included under randomized control trial.

(c) Necessary to obtain informal consent of patient for inclusion in a clinical trial.

(d) Whether blinding is necessary for an investigator with regard to administering the new drug or placebo.

(e) Justification for use of placebo from ethical point of view.

RESEARCH PROTOCOL

The research protocol consists of the following steps:

1. **The Conceptual Phase**
   (a) Formulation of the research problem
   (b) Review of literature
   (c) Establishing the hypothesis.
2. **The Empirical Phase**
   (a) Preparation of research design
   (b) Determination of sampling design and sample size
   (c) Collection of data.
3. **The Analytical Phase**
   (a) Analysis of data
   (b) Testing of hypothesis
   (c) Discussion of results
   (d) Report writing
   (e) References or Bibliography.

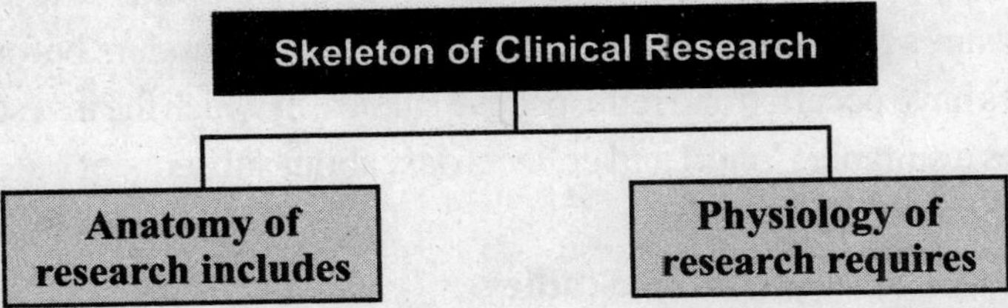

- The research question, design, study subjects, measurements, sample size calculation, etc.

- To estimate population parameters with the help of sample statistic (i.e., to draw inferences about actually happened in study sample and about in the universe outside).
- To minimize the errors (random and systematic) that affect conclusions based on the inferences.

4. Sample Size Estimation

Sample size estimation for

(a) Analytical studies, the following steps need to be considered:

(i) State the null hypothesis, specifying the number of sides.

(ii) Select a statistical test that could be used to analyse the data, based on the types of predictor and outcome variables.

(iii) Estimate the effect size and its variability from the results of previous similar studies (or a Pilot study).

(iv) Specify appropriate values for α and β, based on the importance of avoiding type I and type II errors.

(b) The steps for estimating sample size for descriptive studies, which do not have hypotheses are:

(i) Estimate the proportion of subjects with a dichotomous outcome or the standard deviation of a continuous outcome.

(ii) Specify the desired precision, *i.e.,* width of the confidence interval.

(iii) Specify the level of significance (usually 95%).

5. Study Designs

(a) Designing an Observational study: Cohort Studies

In Cohort studies a group of subjects are followed over time to describe the incidence or natural history of a condition and to analyse predictors (risk factors) for various outcomes. Cohort studies are of two types:

(i) Prospective Cohort Studies and

(ii) Retrospective Cohort Studies.

Prospective Cohort studies, in which the investigator defines the sample and measures predictor variables and potential confounders before any outcomes have occurred and retrospective studies, in which the investigator identifies a suitable Cohort and collects data about subsequent outcomes that occurred at a later time.

(b) Designing Cross-sectional Studies

In a cross-sectional study, the variables are measured at a single point in time (*i.e.,* all measurements are made on a single occasion) with no structural distinction between predictors and outcomes. Cross-sectional studies can also be used for examining associations, although the choice of which variables to level as predictors and which as outcomes depends on the cause and effect hypotheses of the investigator rather than on the study design. A major strength of cross-sectional studies is there is no waiting for the outcome to occur which makes them fast and inexpensive. Cross-sectional studies can be performed for rare diseases if the sample is drawn from a population of diseased patients rather than from a general population. Cross-sectional studies can only measure prevalence (and not incidence) of disease.

(c) Designing Case-control Studies

In a case control study, the prevalence of risk factors in a sample of subjects who have a disease or other outcome of interest (the cases) is compared with that in a sample who do not (the controls). This design, in which people with and without the disease are sampled separately is relatively inexpensive and efficient for studying rare diseases. The information available in case control studies is limited, *i.e.,* there is no direct way to estimate the incidence or prevalence of the disease, nor the attributable risk. The biggest weakness of case control studies is their increased susceptibility to sampling bias. The likelihood of sampling bias depends on both the disease and risk factor in question. There are four approaches to reducing sampling bias in case control studies:

(i) To sample controls and cases in the same way.

(ii) To match the cases and controls.

(iii) To do a population-based study.

(iv) To use several control groups, sampled in different ways.

The other major problem with case control studies is their retrospective design which makes them susceptible to differential measurement bias between cases and controls. Such bias can be reduced by blinding the subjects and observers.

6. Coping with Confounders in the Design Phase

As we know a confounding variable is one that is associated with the predictor variable and is a cause of the outcome variable.

In observational studies, most strategies for coping with confounding variables require that an investigator be aware of and able to measure them. (This is not true of experiments, which can control unmeasured confounders by randomization.) The first step is to list the variables (like age and sex) that may be associated with the predictor variable of interest and that may also be a cause of the outcome. The investigator must then choose between the design and analysis strategies for controlling the influence of these potential confounding variables.

The two design-phase strategies, specification and matching, involve changes in the sampling scheme. Cases and controls (in a case-control study) or exposed and unexposed subjects (in a Cohort study) are sampled in such a way that they have comparable values of the confounding variable. This removes the confounder as an explanation for any association that is observed between predictor and outcome.

(a) **Specification:** The simplest strategy is to design inclusion criteria that specify a value of the potential confounding variable and exclude everyone with a different value, *e.g.*, the investigator studying coffee and MI could specify that only non-smokers would be included in the study. If an association was observed in between coffee and MI it obviously could not be due to smoking. Specification is an effective strategy.

(b) **Matching:** In a case control study, matching involves selecting cases and controls with matching values of the confounding variable. Matching and specification are both sampling strategies that prevent confounding by allowing comparison only of cases and controls that share comparable levels of the confounder.

Matching is usually done individually (pairwise matching). In the study of coffee drinking as a predictor to MI, *e.g.*, each case (a patient with an MI) could be individually matched to one or more controls that smoked roughly the same amount as the case the coffee drinking of each case then would be compared with the coffee drinking of the matched control of that case.

Matching is an effective way to prevent confounding by constitutional factors such as age and sex that are strong determinants of outcome, are not susceptible to intervention.

7. Ethical Issues

Research with human participants raises ethical concerns because people accept risks and inconvenience primarily to advance scientific knowledge and to benefit others. Investigators must ensure that their projects observe the ethical principles of respect for people, beneficence, and justice.

(i) The principle of respect for people requires investigator to obtain informed consent from research participants to protect participants with impaired decision-making capacity and to maintain confidentiality.

(ii) The principle of beneficence requires that the research design be scientifically sound and that the risks of the research be acceptable in relation to the likely benefits. Risks to participants include not only physical harm from tests or treatments but also psychosocial harm.

(iii) The principle of justice requires that the benefits and burdens of research be distributed fairly. Vulnerable populations such as people with poor access to health care, those with impaired decision making capacity may lack the capacity to make informed (or free choices) about participating in research. Justice also requires equitable access to the benefits of research.

Investigators must have ethical integrity. They must not commit scientific misconduct including fabrication, falsification.

8. Questionnaires and Data Collection Instruments

Investigators should make sure the instruments are as valid and reproducible as possible before conducting the study. Open ended questions leave the respondents free to answer with fewer limits imposed by the researcher whereas closed ended questions are easier to answer and analyse. The response options to a closed-ended questions should be exhaustive and mutually exclusive. Closed ended questions ask respondents to choose from one or more preselected answers, therefore, they are quicker and easier to answer questions should be simple, neutral, clear and appropriate for the respondents. Investigators should examine potential questions from the view point of potential participants, looking for ambiguous terms and common pitfalls like double-barreled questions, and hidden assumptions. The whole set of measurements to be used in a study should be pretested. Self-administered questionnaires are more economical than interviews, they are more readily standardized, and the added privacy can enhance the validity of the responses.

The protocol is the detailed written plan of the study. It is the scientific component of a proposal for funding, which also contain administrative and supporting information required by the funding agency.

A proposal is a document written for the purpose of obtaining funds from granting agencies. It contains the study protocol, the budget, and other administrative as supporting information that is required by the specific agency. The proposal must provide a realistic work plan and time table, including dates when each major phase of the study will be started and completed.

9. Data Management

It can be described in the following steps:

(i) **Define or code each variable:** Investigator should assign a name (by using abbreviations) and define the variable format and the range of permitted responses.

(ii) **Setting up the data base and data dictionary:** Investigator should set up the database before the study begins. This includes determining the hardware and software that are used to manage the data, the format of the database, and how data will be entered and edited. The data dictionary includes a description of study variables and data management procedures (*i.e.,* variable names, format, permissible values, logic checks, derived variables, and any other data management rules).

(iii) **Test data management procedures before the study begins:** The entire data base system (*i.e.,* forms, coding, data entry and editing, query and data transfer) should be tested by using dummy data. It is important to document the reason for changes in the original data at this point, the edited data is declared 'frozen' so that no further changes are permitted. The accuracy of data entry can be improved by using double data entry. After ensuring accurate entry, data are edited. Data editing includes checking to make sure that the variables are not missing, are within the permitted range, and are logically consistent with other variables. The final step in editing data is to examine extreme values.

(iv) **Entering the data and correcting errors:** Data should be recorded directly on the forms at the time the measurements are made to minimize the possibility of losses or transcription errors. Errors in the data base should be identified and corrected during each step of creating and analyzing the database.

(v) **Backup the dataset regularly:** Datasets should be backed up regularly and stored in more than one location.

(vi) **Creating a dataset for analysis:** Generally, a copy of the data base is transferred to statistical analysis software. All procedures used to create an analysis ready data set should be clearly defined in the data dictionary and in a well documented data management program.

At the end of the study the original data, data dictionary, final database, and the study analysis should be archived and stored for several years. Such archives allow the investigator to respond to questions about the integrity of the data analysis.

Flow Chart for Data Management

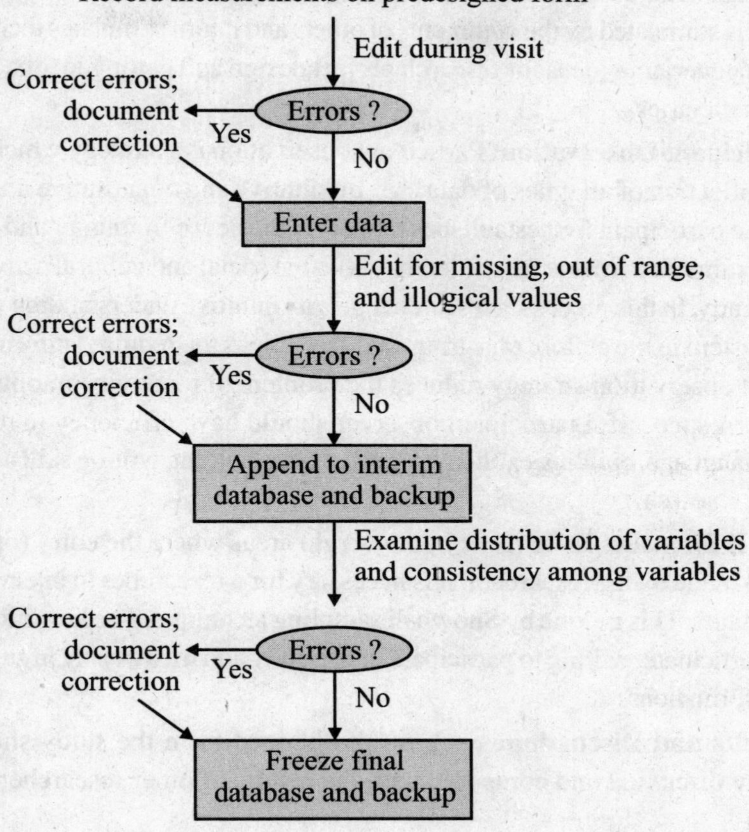

QUALITATIVE RESEARCH METHODS

Qualitative research is a formative research for obtaining indepth responses about what the people think ad feel. Qualitative research is usually undertaken to answer the question 'why' rather than 'what'. It identifies a number of related variables that give insight into the nature and causes of some problems and its consequences for those affected. Qualitative research is also undertaken to quantify the distribution and association of certain variable in the population under study.

The following qualitative methods are commonly used in health and demographic research studies:

(i) FGD (Focus Group Discussion)

(ii) PO (Participant Observation)

(iii) KI (Key Informants) interview.

Focus Group Discussion: It is a group situation in which the participants talk with each other on some topic or issue under the guidance of a facilitator. Each participant is stimulated by the comments of others and inturn stimulates them. FGD is useful in generating ideas for research project design and getting feedback from project beneficiaries.

Participant Observation: Participant observation is a strategy which facilitates the collection of all types of data, *i.e.*, qualitative and quantitative under this strategy, the participant first establishes rapport in the new community and mix-up with the community. So that he/she learns about the social and cultural activities of the community. In this process, a researcher gets an intuitive understanding with the ongoing system in the culture of a group and then elicits the required informations. Participant observation strategy reduces the problem of reactivity among the respondents. A successful participant observer should have efficiency in the local (regional) language, building explicit awareness, and building writing skill about the qualitative research.

Key Informants Interview: In the vergin areas where the entry (or study) has not yet made by the researcher, it is necessary for a researcher to interview the key informants. This is done by Snowball sampling technique. The key informants should be articulate, willing to participate in the study and trustworthy in supplying detailed informations.

Results and Discussion: Each result obtained from the study should be exclusively discussed and compared with the results of other researchers in the same field.

Report Writing: Report writing is an important task of the researcher because no research can be completed without its report. It is the end product of a research activity. An exhaustive report of research study should contain the following components under the following categories:

(i) **Preliminary Pages:** Preliminary pages should contain the title, place of work, data acknowledgement and foreword. Then there should be an index containing table of contents, list of tables, graphs, diagrams, etc. in accordance with the pages.

(ii) **Main Text:** It should start with introduction containing the aims and objectives of the research, methodology used, scope of the research and limitation if any, in the study. The report should be presented in a logical sequence. There should be a statement of finding and recommendations as concluding remark. Constraints experienced during research may as well be stated.

(iii) References: There should be a complete list of books, journals, reports that the researcher has consulted while doing research. The list should contain essential information such as: the authors, title of publication, publisher and year of publication. In case of a journal-article, additional information regarding the name of the journal, volume number, month and year of publication and pages become relevant.

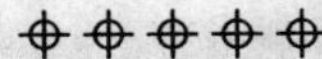

CHAPTER

19

Health Survey Protocol

• *Planning*	• *Bias*	• *Participants*
• *Response*	• *Evaluation*	• *Questionnaire*

In this chapter, we discuss two fundamental research tools, the health survey and the research protocol which are inseparable parts of the same process: that of aiding scientists, managers, and public officials in their decision making.

Health surveys are conducted for a number of reasons, but most often, they are undertaken to determine the health needs of a community. Subjects of a health survey are general public, *i.e.,* who are the users of health services. They are regarded as consumers of health services. Health surveys may entail inquiries into the consumers's knowledge, attitudes, and practices (KAP), utilization of health services, past history of disease, and satisfaction (or dissatisfaction) with health service delivery or they may involve research directed toward elucidating the etiology of a disease or evaluation of a health programme.

PLANNING A HEALTH SURVEY

A public health researcher is always keen to conduct a survey that clearly and accurately describes some health related phenomenon. A health survey can be a tricky business. Unless it follows a prescribed stepwise systematic procedure, a survey could produce faulty information leading to bad consequences.

A brief protocol for planning a health survey has been described below:

1. A written statement of the purpose of the survey.
2. Formulation of objectives and hypotheses.
3. To specify the target population.
4. Listing of variable or parameters to be measured.
5. Reviewing the existing pertinent data.
6. To specify the methodology adopted for data collection.
7. To establish the time frame.
8. Designing the survey tools, *i.e.,* questionnaire.
9. Pretesting the questionnaire.
10. Selection of adequate sample.
11. Data collection.
12. Editing, coding, and entering the data on a computer and verifying the data entries.
13. Analysing the data by appropriate statistical methods.
14. Report writing (*i.e.,* results and conclusions).

1. **A Written Statement of the Purpose:** The purpose of survey should be well thought out and clearly defined. This initial step will aid up proper thinking and will help in carrying out further steps.
2. **Formulation of Objectives and Hypotheses:** A descriptive survey seeks to estimate one or more characteristics of a target population, whereas an analytical survey seeks to examine relationship among some specified characteristics. To carry it out, there is a need to define the hypotheses to be tested.
3. **To Specify the Target Population:** The target population is the group of persons or subjects from whom reliable informations are to be collected for the purpose. This may be restricted to one from which the investigator may feasibly draw a sample. To test a hypothesis, it is essential to estimate certain characteristics of individual persons of the target population. An individual number of a target population is often referred to as an element. In health surveys the element may be a person, a mother-child pair, or a household. Measurements are taken on the element. Once target population is defined and elements are identified, list the variables that are to be assessed on each element (or subject).
4. **Listing of Variable:** In general, researcher focuses on personal characteristics of individual members of the target population. For example, characteristics

could be a person's height, weight, age, religion, blood pressure, marital status, etc. The variable considered should be potentially measurable on each element. All the variables related to the survey should be clearly defined during the planning stages.

5. **Reviewing the Existing Pertinent Data:** It is important to review current literature on the subject being surveyed so that one can determine the state of art, current hypotheses, variables regarded as pertinent. It is advisable to use standardized questions with standard working so that results may be compared with standard or well-known studies.
6. **Methodology to Collect Data:** In collecting data, the person to person interview is often regarded as the standard because of the high response rate. The interviewer, being at the scene, can make additional observations regarding subtle aspects of the interviewer's behavior. An alternative is the telephone interview by using random digit dialing but telephoning introduces a new potential bias which excludes approximately 10% of the households those do not have telephone lines. There is still another approach to collect data is the mailed questionnaire which rules out the problem of interviewer bias. The respondent is less likely to be defensive about answering socially sensitive questions. But this approach has poor response rates. Other problems include uncertainty as to whether the respondents are truly representative of the target population.
7. **To Establish the Time Frame:** It is necessary to establish a time frame to realistically schedule survey events. Plan for back up procedures and personnel to avoid major delays. It is better to have some trained interviewers on standby basis.
8. **Designing the Questionnaire:** Questions to be made in simple and local language so as not to confuse the respondent or arouse extraneous attitudes. The questions should provide a clear understanding of the information sought. Be precise, avoid ambiguity and wording that might be perceived to elicit a specific response.

   Questions may be open-ended, multiple choice, completion, or a variation of these. Questionnaire should have the following characteristics:

   (i) It should be easy for the respondent to read, understand, and answer,

   (ii) It should motivate the respondent to answer,

   (iii) It should be designed for efficient data processing,

   (iv) It should have a well-designed professional appearance, and

   (v) It should be designed to minimize missing data.
9. **Pretesting the Questionnaire:** It is never possible to anticipate in advance all the potential problems that may occur when a questionnaire is adminis-

tered. So it is important to pretest the questionnaire before exercising it among the respondents. In pretesting, we identify questions that respondents tend to misinterpret, omit, or answer inappropriately. It should be done on few individuals similar to, but not included in, the target population by applying the same methodology that will be applied in the survey. This technique is called Pilot study.

10. **Selection of an Adequate Sample:** A random sample is selected in such a way that valid inferences can be drawn regarding the target population. A representative sample is one that minimizes sampling bias and economic in operation. There are various types of sampling methods viz., simple random, systematic random, stratified random and multistage sampling. By applying an appropriate sampling technique, one can select a representative sample for the survey.
11. **Data Collection:** After a completed and pretested questionnaire, it is ready for data collection. This procedure needs to attain the following objectives:
    (i) To maximize the response rate by minimizing non-responses.
    (ii) To avoid duplication.
    (iii) To avoid failing to contact part of the sample.
    (iv) To protect confidentiality of the data.
    (v) To provide anonymity.
    (vi) To maintain a cooperative spirit in the target population.
12. **Editing and Coding of Data:** In editing the data. The researcher is intended to make sure that the text meets certain standards and that errors are corrected. It needs a proper checking for missing data, for inconsistencies, and for problems that can be solved. Editing of data should be done urgently after the data collection. For computerized analysis of data, it is essential that the variables be reduced to a form in which a numerical value may be assigned to each possible choice. The process is referred to as coding. It is carried out simultaneously with editing. Coding may be done either by use of an ad hoc coding system or by use of a standard coding system. A well-accepted technique for the coding of diseases or causes of death is the ICD (International Classification of Diseases) published by W.H.O.
13. **Analysing the Data:** The well collected, edited and coded data is ready for analysis. Analysis of the data is done by using appropriate statistical techniques. A preliminary step for data analysis is needed: to search out possible outliers,

to look at the distribution of various variables, to provide an item analysis for the variables of special interest, and finally to assess the amount of missing data.

14. **Report Writing:** The report should begin with background information that provides a rationale for the study. It should indicate the specific objectives that the survey seeks to accomplish. A 'material and methods' section should describe the target population, the sampling design and the test instrument, *i.e.,* statistical test applied. Lastly, the 'results and conclusion' section should discuss the findings and possible further implications.

EVALUATION OF A RESEARCH REPORT

Research literature is seen in many forms: journal articles, monographs, books, administrative documents, programme evaluations etc. A valuable skill to develop is the ability to critically read and evaluate research literature. A top-grade report stands unshaken under the critical process of peer view. It is well-known fact that some research literature is of poor quality (*i.e.,* inconsistencies, poor grammar, and some muddy logic). Researcher must exercise constant vigilance to avoid bias while working towards a rewarded objective. Bias may creep in-usually inadvertently perhaps subconsciously, and often as a consequence of some aspect of the research design. It is important to know about various types of bias usually come across in the research article.

Observer Bias

When the observer (or interviewer) is fully aware that the person being interviewed has a certain disease, the observer may subconsciously attribute certain characteristics to the subject. The result of this observer bias is that those characteristics are more likely to be recorded for cases than for controls. The solution of choice is to 'blind' the observer as to whether the subject is a case or a control.

Sampling Bias

Bias may enter whenever samples are chosen in a non-random fashion; convenience sampling in which subjects are choosen by observer' or investigator's convenience, *i.e.,* subjects who are easy to find in the population. It leads almost biased results. Systematic sampling (choosing every Kth subject from a list) carries the potential of subtle error, especially if the list has some cyclical pattern.

Selection Bias

Selection bias may lead to a false association between a disease and some factor because of different probabilities of selecting persons with and without the disease, and with and without the variable of interest.

Response Bias

When participation in a study is voluntary, response bias (or non-respondent bias) is important. Owing to their psychological makeup, internal motivation, educational background, concern for their own health, and many other reasons, persons who choose voluntarily to participate are known to differ from those who decline. A way to control for response bias is to compare characteristics of volunteer sub-groups with those of randomly chosen subgroups.

Dropout Bias

Dropout bias is the mirror image of response bias. In prospective studies, a certain proportion of participants for reasons of their own, choose to dropout.

Participant Bias

It is an interesting form of bias that derives from the participant's knowledge of being a member of the experimental or control group and his or her perception of the research objectives.

Memory Bias

It is also known as subjective bias. Memory for recent events is more accurate than for remote events. Hence, persons interviewed concerning past illnesses tend to report a greater prevalence in the recent past than in the distant past.

CONCLUSION

Two fundamental research tools, the health survey and the research protocol, are inseparable parts of the same process: that of aiding scientists, managers, and public officials in their decision making. Health surveys need careful planning; a systematic stepwise procedure is the best means of avoiding error in their use.

⌖⌖⌖⌖⌖

CHAPTER
20

Computers in Medical Field

- *Software*
- *Telemedicine*
- *Internet*
- *PDA*
- *Image Guided Surgery*
- *Pharmacogenomics*

COMPUTER IN MEDICINE

Computers play a key role in almost every sphere of life. They facilitate storage of huge amounts of data, they enable speedy processing of information and they possess an inbuilt intelligence, which if supplemented with human intellect, can work wonders. Owing to their intelligence and speed, computers function on a level close to that of the human brain. Computers can be employed in different fields like engineering, data processing and storage, planning and scheduling, networking, education as well as health and medicine. Computer systems are also used for hospital administration, including hospital bed tracking, admissions scheduling, billing and payroll, facility scheduling and inventory control.

Computers are the excellent means for storage of patient-related data. Hospitals employ computer systems to maintain patient records. It is often necessary to maintain detailed records of the medical history of patients. Physicians often require information about a patient's family history, physical ailments in the family (if any), already diagnosed diseases and prescribed medicines. This information can be stored in a computer database. Computers can keep track of prescriptions and billing information. They can be used to store information about the medicines prescribed to a patient as well as those, which cannot be prescribed to him/her. Computers enable an efficient storage of huge amounts of medical data such as medical journals, research and diagnosis papers, important medical documents and reference books, etc. Innovations such as MEDLINE are a tribute to the way in which computers can be used to help physicians and others to find the information that they need to make good decisions. Personal Digital Assistant (PDA) devices are widely used by physicians and nurses for tasks such as looking up drug information, reading medical journals and textbooks, viewing practice guidelines by using e-mail. Many programs have been developed to address such problems. Since the 1950s, researchers have recognized the relevance of Bayes' rule to the task of diagnosis, with computers being used to manipulate the pertinent conditional probabilities. Many bayesian programs are highly accurate in selecting among competing explanations of a patient's disease state. The results of such analyses are probabilities, and their defense is based on Bayes' formula plus the accuracy of the sensitivity, specificity, and prevalence data used. With the emergence of medical informatics as an academic discipline and the training of individuals who can work effectively at the interface between medicine and computer science, it is likely that physicians and other health professionals will see rapid development of clinically useful tools that are sensitive to the realities of the health care environment. Among such systems will be decision-support programs that are integrated with patient data-management systems. They will serve as knowledge-access and management tools for physicians who will rely on their support much as they rely on paper-based reference tools today.

COMPUTER IN SURGICAL PROCEDURES

Computer software is used for diagnosis of diseases. It can be used for the examination of internal organs of the body. Some of the complex surgeries can be performed with the help of computers. Computer-assisted Surgery (CAS) is a fast-advancing field in medicine, which combines medical expertise with computer intelligence to give faster and more accurate results in surgical procedures. The surgical procedure is simulated on the virtual image of the patient. The sugery can then be performed by a surgical robot, as programmed by a medical professional or the robot may only assist surgeons while they do the actual surgery.

COMPUTER IN DIAGNOSTIC TESTS

The different types of monitoring equipment in hospitals are often based on computer programming. Medical imaging deals with techniques to create images of the human body for medical purposes. Many of the modern methods of scanning and imaging are largely based on computer technology. MRI (Magnetic resonance imaging) employs computer software. Computed tomography makes use of digital geometry processing techniques to obtain 3-D images. Sophisticated computers and infrared cameras are used for obtaining high-resolution images.

COMPUTER IN PHARMACOGENOMICS

Scientists are also working on a way to use computers to prescribe medication. According to doctors, some medications can be harmful if prescribed to a patient who has a certain gene that is not able to properly absorb that medication. A new science called pharmacogenomics is compiling all gene types with corresponding toxic medications. Doctors will soon be able to swipe a DNA sample from the patients blood onto a computer chip that contains gene information. The DNA would stick to the genes that it matched to inform the doctor which medications would be absorbed by the patients genes. For now, researchers are using robots to analyze thousands of drug samples, also called high thoughtput screening. Then, computers are used to process the results to suggest which drugs should be tested with the patients genes.

COMMUNICATION BETWEEN MEDICAL DOCTORS AND PATIENTS

Computers and the Internet have proven to be a boon in all the spheres of life. In the field of medicine, computers allow faster communication between a patient and a doctor. It is possible to obtain experts' opinions within seconds by means of the Internet. Medical professionals sitting on opposite sides of the globe can communicate within minutes with the help of the Internet. They can discuss medical issues in medical forums, they can blog, write articles, contribute to medical journals available online. Updates in the medical field, advancements in medicine, information about new methods of treatment, etc. can reach the common man within minutes. Doctors can seek advice and share knowledge in a convenient manner over the Internet.

INTERNET

The Internet has served medicine in a variety of ways:

- ❖ It has enabled the growth of telemedicine including teleradiology, remote surgery and patient monitoring.
- ❖ PUBMED is an online database of medical journal citations used extensively by physicians and researchers, but also available to the general public.

- A wealth of health information is available on the World Wide Web, enabling consumers to research their own symptoms. Google Health (http://www.google.com/Top/Health/).
- Online comparison-shopping for hospitals and doctors is a growing trend among consumers. The data that feeds such programs comes from medical records provided by doctors and hospitals as well as patient surveys.
- Online solutions like WebMD are available that allow consumers to enter and track their personal medical histories.
- The Internet has also played a role in aiding biomedical research, for example the use of grid computing to help unravel the mysteries of genetic diseases.

MEDICAL SOFTWARE

In computers, **medical software** is a significant branch of software engineering. Many medical devices that monitor or control patients are predominantly controlled by software. Medical devices are frequently regulated and must comply with local and regional laws. The Food and Drug Administration (FDA) is focused on regulatory oversight on medical device software development process and system-level testing. For example, IEC 62304 has become the benchmark standard for the development of medical software.

Types of Medical Software

Monitors

Heart rate, blood pressure, breathing rate, use software to interpret the sensor information and display it in a meaningful way on a monitor.

Medication Pumps

These devices are programmed to pump a certain amount of plasma, blood, saline solution, or other medication into a patient at a certain rate. The software provides the ability to control many aspects of treatment procedures.

Analysis

Many devices, such as X-ray computed tomography scanners (CT or CAT scans), measure raw data that is essentially meaningless to people. Software reinterprets this data to create images that doctors can read and understand.

Expert Systems

A variety of expert systems help clinicians and practitioners in decision making for diagnostic and therapeutic purposes.

Therapy Delivery

The software in implantable pacemakers and defibrillators provides fault-tolerant, real-time, mission-critical monitoring of cardiac rhythms and associated therapy delivery.

Medical and Healthcare Educational Software

Software used as an educational or study tool for health care professionals.

Medical Informatics

Software for the business and informational aspect of medicine; these include electronic medical record (EMR), electronic health record (EHR), practice management, and the analytics software that works with these systems.

Classification of Medical Software

Medical Software could be classified simply into the following groups, depending on its use.

1. **Educational Medical Software** (Educational Medical Software, EMS):
   (a) Built-in Device and
   (b) Not built-in appliances.
2. **Medical Diagnostic Software** (Diagnostic Medical Software, DMS):
   (a) Built-in Device and
   (b) Not built-in appliances.
3. **Therapeutic Medical Software** (Therapeutic Medical Software, TMS):
   (a) Built-in Device and
   (b) Not built-in appliances.
4. **Medical Design Software** (Design Medical Software, DEMS):
   (a) Built-in Device and
   (b) Not built-in appliances.

Computer Aided Medical Diagnosis, CAD

Computer Aided Diagnosis is a procedure in which an appropriate Medical Software can diagnose illness and assist doctors in the interpretation of medical images using patient data processed by the computer.

Medical Software Internationally

The internationally applied Medical Software has settled in the following areas:

1. **Integrated Medical Software:** The first major area is the Integrated Medical Software in Medical Devices of any kind (often unavailable). Of

course there century companies that manufacture and sell medical software for imaging and other medical devices. Such is the SANTESOFT AEBE with many products on the website http://www.santesoft.com/customers.html

2. **Surgery Management Programs:** The second segment is simple and Programs Management Clinic patient records. There is no single way to design these programs, and - unfortunately - when once the user have a problem, looking for the company that designed it, he discovers that no longer exists. (Examples: The project concerns the management ORTHO orthopedic Surgery. The program "CardioData" to administer cardiac Surgery, etc.).

3. **Application Software Specifically:** The third sector is usually On Line web programs, Software Specifically Application. (Examples: There is free On Line web software that explores the interactions between drugs and inform your doctor or pharmacist what medicines do not match the shot). website http://www.medscape.com/druginfo/druginterchecker

   website http://eof1.eof.gr/Syntagologio. The American Society for Medical Software Unbound Medicine offers free via its website http://www.unboundmedicine.com/store/android.

4. **Computer Differential Diagnosis (Computer Aided Diagnosis):** The fourth area is the network On Line Software Differential Diagnosis. Existing diagnostic systems Computer Aided (CAD, Computer Aid Diagnosis) divided into two basic categories, as to how building (development):

   (a) *Probability Systems (Probability Systems):* These models are probabilistic type and not of particular interest.

   (b) *Knowledge Base Systems (Knowlesge Based Systems):* These are applications of AI (Artificial Intelligence) and known as Expert Systems (Expert Systems). One such free software on the internet, is the American Diagnosis Pro website http://en.diagnosispro.com/.

5. **Medical Software Telemedicine:** Telemedicine is the use of combining IT and communication technology. It defines new levels in all areas that constitute the functioning of the Medical Sciences: Education, access to knowledge, research, clinical practice, control of medical instruments, assistance in inaccessible areas, prevention and generally minimizes the limitations of space and time in exercise.

⌖⌖⌖⌖⌖

Glossary

Absolute value: The positive value of a number, regardless of whether the number is positive or negative. The absolute value of a is symbolized as | a |.

Absolute error: Absolute error in statistics is defined as the actual difference between the true value and the estimated (or observed) value.

Acceptance region: This is the region of null hypothesis in normal curve, called (1 – α).

Addition rule (of probability): The probability of occurrence of one of two or more mutually exclusive events is the sum of probabilities of their individual occurrence.

Adjusted rate: A rate adjusted so that it is independent of the distribution of a possible confounding variable, *e.g.*, age-adjusted rates are independent of the age distribution in the population to which they apply.

Age standardization: A procedure of adjustment to remove the effect of differences in age composition of the groups to be compared. This increases comparability. The standardization can be done by direct and indirect methods.

Age-specific death rate: Number of deaths in one year of persons of specified age-group per thousand population of that age-group.

Age-specific fertility rate: Number of live births to the women of particular age-group per thousand women of that age-group.

Algorithm: Logical arrangement of instructions to perform a task.

Alpha (α): The probability of a Type I error.

Alpha value (α-value): The level of alpha (α) selected in a hypothesis test.

Alternative hypothesis: A hypothesis that is accepted by default when the null hypothesis is rejected.

Analysis of variance: A statistical method of breaking variance into its components such as which subjects and between subjects. This method is more commonly used for comparing three or more means. It is also represented by ANOVA.

Antecedent: A characteristic that procedes the outcome. It may or may not be responsible for the outcome.

APACHE score: Acronym for Acute Physiology and Chronic Health Evaluation. A scoring system that helps to assess the prognosis in case of critical condition of a patient. This is based on state of consciousness, reflexes, eye movements, BP, etc.

Apgar score: Sum total of (0 to 2) scores assigned to each of heart rate, respiration, muscle tone, skin colour, and response to stimulation in a newborn. A low score such as less than 4 out of possible 10 is an indication of poor prognosis.

Association: The property of change in one qualitative factor being accompanied by the change in the other. This change can be causal, incidental, or due to an intervening factor. The association can be fall or partial of various degrees and can be negative or positive.

Attack rate: Number of new cases of a disease during a specified time interval (*i.e.,* period of an epidemic) as percentage of the total population at risk in the same time interval.

Attribute: An attribute is a variable that describes a characteristic by classifying it into categories to which a subject either belongs or does not belong. It is a property or quality that a subject either possesses or does not possess.

Bar diagram: A diagram appropritate for disjoint categories to show the number of subjects or mean or rates by bars of corresponding height. It may be horizontal or vertical.

Beta (β): The probability of a type II error.

Bias: A systematic error in measurement or observation or in the result.

Bimodal distribution: A distribution of data points in which two values occur more frequently then the rest of the values in the data set.

Binary variable: A characteristic that is assessed only as present or absent (or yes/no), *e.g.*, gender: Male or femal ; survival : yes or no.

Binomial distribution: A statistical distribution that describes the probabilities of various number of subjects with a characteristic out of total when tha chance of one subject being positive is known.

Bivariate analysis: A statistical analysis of data by considering two variables together, such as age and blood pressure, MI and obesity. One or both variables can be either qualitative or quantitative.

Block design: In analysis of variance, a design in which subjects within each block (or startum) are assigned to a different treatment.

Body Mass Index (BMI): Weight (in kg) divided by square of height (in meters). It is a measure of obesity in adults.

(BMI < 20 kg/m² is interpreted a 'lean', 20.0 – 24.9 kg/m² as 'normal'. 25.0 – 29.9 kg/m² as overweight, and ≤ 30.0 as obese).

Case: A person or unit of interest possessing a specified characteristic, such as a person with the disease or condition of interest.

Case group: The group of subjects that already has the disease or the condition under study.

Case-control study: An observational study that begins with patient cases who have the outcome or disease being investigated and control subjects who do not have the outcome or disease and then looks backward to identify possible risk factors.

Categorical variable: A categorical variable has measurements in which the notion of magnitude is absent or implicit.

Census: A complete count of the population. This done in every 10th year (*i.e.*, the first year of each decade).

Central limit theorem: A theorem that states that the distribution of means is approximately normal if the simple size is large enough ($n \geq 30$), regardless of the underlying distribution of the original measurements.

Central tendency: A tendency of a set of values together around a central value. Mean, median and mode are measures of central tendency (*i.e.*, central values).

Chance: Unknown or too complex to comprehend.

Child mortality rate: Number of deaths below five years of age in one year period per 1000 live births in the same year.

Child-women ratio: Number of children less than five years per woman of reproductive phase (*i.e.*, 15 to 49 years).

Chi-square test: A versatile statistical procedure that is used to test different types of hypothesis on proportions, such as equality, trend and relationship.

Clinical trials: Clinical trials are commonly used by clinicians. The main aim of a clinical trial is to make comparisons between one type of treatment with another.

Closed birth interval: Interval between two successive births.

Close-ended question: A question for which list of possible answers is already provided.

Cluster: A group of subjects (or persons) with common characteristics (*i.e.,* close proximity).

Coefficient of determination (r^2): The square of the correlation coefficient. It is interpreted as the amount of variance in one variable that is accounted for by knowing the second variable.

Coefficient of Variation (CV): The standard deviation divided by the mean (general expressed in percentage). It is used to obtain a measure of relative variation.

Cohort: A well-defined subject or a group of persons with some common features that are followed for a specific period beginning from a defined common baseline.

Complete enumeration: Counting or inclusion of all individuals in the target population.

Conditional probability: The probability of occurrence of an event such as disease when some prior information such as signs-symptoms are known. It is denoted by P(AIB), (*i.e.,* probability of A given B).

Confidence interval: The interval within which a parameter value is expected to lie with a certain confidence levels as could be revealed by repeated samples.

Confidence level: The degree of assurance for an interval to contain the value of a parameter.

Confidence limit: The upper and lower boundaries of a confidence interval.

Confounding variable: A variable more likely to be present in one group of subjects than another that is related to the outcome of interest and thus potentialy confuses (or confounds) the results.

Contingency table: A table containing the frequency of subjects with different characteristics, which should be mutually exclusive.

Continuous variable: A continuous variable is one with potentially an infinite number of possible values in any interval.

Control: A person or unit of interest but not possessing the specified characteristic, such as a person not having the disease of interest.

Correlation: The degree or strength of relationship between two quantitative variables. It is measured by correlation coefficient (r) that ranges from – 1 to + 1.

Covariance: A measure of how the product of two variables-behave used in evaluating correlation.

Critical ratio: The term for the Z-score used in statistical tests.

Critical value: The value that a test statistic must exceed (in absolute value) in order for the null hypothesis to be rejected.

Cross-sectional study: An observation study that examines a characteristic (or set of characteristic) in a set of subjects at one point of time ; a "snap shot" of a characteristic or condition of interest ; also called survey or poll.

Cross-over trial: A trial in which patients act as their own controls by receiving both the treatment being assessed and the control treatment, in random order.

Cross-tabulation: The process of dividing a group of individuals by two characteristics simultaneously such as distribution of Myocardial Infarction (MI) cases by their lipoprotein and homocysteine levels.

Crude rate: A rate for the entire population that is not specific or adjusted for any given subset of the population.

Cumulative frequency (or percentage): In a frequency table, the frequency (or percentage) of observations having a given value plus all lower values.

Data: A set of observations, generally in numerical format but can be in text format also. Data is a plural form of Greek word datum.

Database: A collection of items of data arranged in a predefined format.

Defacto census: The method of counting the actual population present in the census area on census day.

Demographic gap: The difference between birth rate and death rate over a long period of time.

Demographic transition: The process by which, over a number of years, continuous changes in one or more of the fertility, mortality and migratory rates in the population produce alterations in the characteristics and structure of the population.

Demogrophic cycle: Over a long duration, from high birth and death rates, the changing phases of quick decline in death rate, slow decline in bith rate, and finally both rates setting down to a low level.

Demogrphy: The study of population structure.

Dependency ratio: Number of people who need care (*i.e.,* children < 15 years and aged persons of 60 plus) to the people who provide care (*i.e.,* persons of age 15-59 years).

Descriptive statistics: Statistics such as the mean (median, mode, geometric mean, harmonic mean), the standard deviation (or mean deviation), the proportion, and the rates used to describe attributes of a set of data.

Design: The format of collection, compilation and analysis of observations.

Determinant: A factor that is responsible, fully or partially, for an outcome.

Discrete variable: A discrete variable has measurements that occur as integers. It can only have a finite number of values in any given interval.

Dispersion: The spread or variability in a set of data.

Distance measure: A measure of dispersion in terms of the difference between two values in the data set.

Distribution (population): The values of a characteristic or variable along with the frequency of their occurrence. Distributions may be based on empirical observations or may be theoretical probability distributions, *e.g.*, Binomial, Poisson, Normal.

Doctor-population ratio: Number of qualified doctors per 1000 populations (or the average population served by one qualified doctor).

Double-blind trial: A trial in which neither the experimental subject nor the assessor knows that the subject has received the test regimen or the control regimen.

Early expanding phase: The phase of demographic cycle when birth rate is high and death rate starts to decline. The difference between birth and death rate increases, and the population starts to expand.

Effect size: The magnitude of a difference or relationship. It is used for determining sample sizes and for combining results across studies in meta-analysis.

Estimator: A sample statistic used to estimate a population parameter.

Expectation of life at birth: The estimated years of life of a person at the time of birth considering the current death pattern.

Expected frequency: The number of observations to be expected in a class or cell if the null hypothesis is true.

Experiment: A study on effect of intentionally introduced intervention or alteration of a factor under controlled conditions.

Experiment design: The structure of an experiment in terms of inclusion and exclusion criteria for subjects, method of allocation of subjects to intervention, details of assessments, their reliability and validity, etc.

Ex-post facto study: Ex-post facto study, where the event has already occurred and only trace the events and no manipulation of variables are possible.

Extrapolation: The use of the regression line to predict a value of the dependent variable from that of the independent variable outside the range of values actually observed.

Family: People who are related by blood or marriage, and live together sharing a common kitchen.

Fecundity: The capacity to reproduce.

Fertility: The actual reproductive performance in terms of live births taking place.

Field trial: An experiment on human subjects in a community, such as Vit. A supplementation to children less than 3 years for examining the improvement in their nutrition status.

Genral fertility rate: Number of live births per 1000 women of reproductive age-group (15-49) years.

Goal (of a health programme): The ultimate aim of a health programme, *e.g.*, Polio eradication.

Gold standard: In diagnostic testing, a procedure that always identifies the true conditions (*i.e.*, diseased or diseased free) of a patient.

Goodness of fit: How well the actual observations fit into a specified model, *i.e.*, mathematical model. The goodness of fit is generally tested by Chi-square.

Gross reproduction rate: Average number of female live births per woman during her entire reproductive span according to the existing age-specific fertility.

Health Information System (HIS): Health information system is defined as a mechanism for the collection, processing, analysing and transmitting information required for organising and operating health services and also for research and training.

Household: A group of persons living together in a house and sharing common food.

Hypothesis: A statement of belief that is made before the investigation regarding the status of parameters under study including those that measure relationship.

ICD: International Classification of Diseases that assigns a group and a code to each cause of morbidity, injury, mortality, etc. The objective is to promote uniformity and comparability.

Impairment: Any loss or abnormality of psychological, physiological or anatomical structure or function.

Incidence: A rate giving the proportion of people who develop a given disease or condition within a specified period of time.

Index: A composite of two or more indicators, such as BMI for obesity that combines height and weight.

Indicator: A single measurement that indicates the existence or magnitude of a condition signs-symptoms are indicators of a disease; smoking an indicator of MI risk, and IMR is an indicator of mortality.

Inference (statistical): The process of drawing conclusions about a population of observations from a sample of observations.

Interpolation: The use of a regression line to estimate a value of the dependent variable from that of the independent variable within the range of values actually observed.

Interquartile range: The difference between the 25th percentile and the 75th percentile.

Interval estimate: A range of value used to estimate an unknown population paamater.

Intervention study: A study of the impact of an intentionally introduced intervention experiments and trials are intervention studies.

Kappa statistic: A measure of agreement in excess of chance between two or more observers or methods which is used for qualitative data.

Keywords: The set of words that describes the essential features of a study.

Kurtosis: The degree of peakness of a distribution of points.

Late expanding phase: The phase of demographic cycle when birth rate starts to decline and death rate is at a low level. The difference between birth rate and death rate is large and the population continues to expand.

Level of significance: The maximum tolerable probability to type I error that is fixed in advance, such as 0.05 (or 5%) and denoted by α.

Life table: A summary of the death and survival pattern of a group people, generally for the entire population of an area but can also be used for patients particular disease.

Likelihood ratio: In diagnostic testing, the ratio of true positives to false-positives.

Literacy: Ability to read and write with understanding.

Literacy rate: Percentage of literates in population of age 7 years and above.

Logistic regression: The regression technique used when the outcome is a binary or dichotomous variable.

Longitudinal study: A study where the same set of individuals is periodically assessed for one or more defined outcomes.

Lorenz curve: It is a cumulative percentage curve in which the percentage of items (or frequencies) are shown with the corresponding percentage of factors like income, wealth, profits, etc.

Low stationary phase: The phase of demographic cycle when both birth rate and death rate are at low level. The difference between birth rate and death rate is nearly zero, and the population is stationary.

Medical record: A cumulative narrative of the history of a patient, the treatment given, final diagnosis, and continuing medical care after the patient discharged.

Medical uncertainties: Uncertainties arising from various kinds of variations, lack of knowledge, partial compliance, errors, etc. in medical decsion process.

Medically significant: A result that is capable of modifying the management of any aspect of health or disease.

Meta analysis: A procedure of combining evidence in different reports on the same aspect. It different trials in the same regimen report efficacy, they can be combined to come to a unified conclusion which may command substantially more confidence then result of any one of the individual trials.

Migration: Movement of people from on geographical location to another within the same country or across country borders.

Model: A simplified version of a complex process. A model could be mathematical, graphical, structural, etc.

Morbidity: Deviation from normal health.

Multiple correlation: The degree of relationship existing between three or more variables is called multiple correlation.

Multiple regression: A multivariate method for determining a regression or prediction equation to predict an outcome from a set of independent variables.

Mutually exclusive events: The set of events wherein only one can occur at a point of time. Blood group of a patient would either be A, or B or AB or O. These are mutullay exclusive. Signs-sympotms such as pain, vomitting and diarrhoea are not mutually exclusive, they can occur together in a patient.

Natural growth rate: The diference between birth rate and death rate in particular year.

Negative trial: A trial that reports that difference between the test and control regimen is not statistically significant.

Net reproduction rate: Rate of replacement of females in the population per generation, with the current schedules of fertility and mortality.

Nonsense correlation: A correlation between two variables that incidently, occurs because each is related to a third irrlevant variable. Such correlation has no biological plausibility.

Nuclear family: Husband, wife and their children.

Null hypothesis: A hypothesis that says that there is no difference, or that asserts the existing knowledge or claim, and is tested for refutation by the study.

Odds: The probability that an event will occur divided by the probability that the event will not occur, *i.e.*, odds = P/(1 – P), where P is the probability.

Ogive: A cumulative frequency curve.

Open birth interval: Interval between last birth and the date of the study.

Open ended question: A question whose answer is allowed to be recorded in verbatim as given by the respondent.

Parameter: A summary measure or value for any characteristic in the targe population. It pertains to the entire population of interest and not to be sample.

Partial correlation: The degree of relationship between dependent variable and one particular independent variable when all other variables involved are kept constant, *i.e.*, when the effects of all other variables are removed.

Percentiles: Those values in a series of observations, arranged in ascending order of magnitude, which divide the distribution into 100 equal parts.

Performa: A prototype or a format on which the observations are to be recorded.

Person-years: The sum total of years observed for different individuals. For example, if one person is followed up for 3 years, second for 2 years and third for one year, then the person-years of follow up is 3 + 2 + 1 = 6 years. Similarly there could be person- months or person-weeks.

Pie chart: Sectors of a circle, with areas proportional to class frequencies, used to present data in nominal classes.

Pilot study: A small-scale forerunner study to know about the situation and the variables.

Placebo: An inert substance or a procedure that is neither harmful nor beneficial. The objective of placebo is that subject gets the perception that he or she is receiving treatment.

Point estimate: Estimate of a parameter by a single value.

Point prevalence: The frequency of the disease at a designed point in time.

Poisson distribution: A probability distribution used to model the number of times a rare event occurs.

Polygraph: Apparatus for recording severe responses con-currently, such as a lie detector.

Polytomous variable: A characteristic divided into three or more categories, such as severity of disease into mild, moderate and severe. A quantitative measurement such as cholesterol level can be made polytomous when divided into a number of categories such as < 100, 100-179, 180-249, and 250 mg/dl and above.

Population density: It is the number of persons living in one sq. km area.

Population dynamics: The changing scenario of the structure of population as the time passes.

Population pyramid: A typical graphical presentation of the age-sex strructure of a population.

Precision: The ability of an instrument to provide the same or a very similar result with repeated measurements.

Prevalence rate: All current cases (old and new) existing at a given point in time, or over a period of time in a given population.

Prevalence ratio: Ratio of prevalence rate in one group to the other.

Primary data: Data that are directly collected from the respondents.

Probability: If there are 'n' mutually exclusive, exhaustive and equally likely cases and 'm' of them are favourable to a certain event A, then the probability (or chance) of the occurrence of A is defined as the ratio $m \div n$.

Probability of survival: Chance that somebody alive at a particular age will still be alive at a given older age.

Process indicator: A measure of the extent, efficiency or quality of service performance.

Proportion: The number of observations with the characteristic of interest divided by the total number of observations.

Proportional mortality: Deaths due to a cause or in any specific age-group as a fraction of the total deaths.

Protocol: A comprehensive but concise statement regarding steps to be taken *i.e.,* plan of a study.

P-value: The probability of type I error, *i.e.,* the chance that a difference or association is concluded when actually there is none.

Quartiles: The values which divide a series of observations, arranged in ascending order, into four equal parts.

Questionnare: A survey instrument that contains a predetermined series of questions that are supposed to put in verbatim to the respondents, or can be self-administered. It contains space for recording responses also.

Quintiles: The values which divide an arranged series of observations into five equal parts.

Quota sample: A sample which includes subgroups of people or items in the same proportion as they are represented in the population.

Random: Unperdictable, like lottery *i.e.,* when each unit has equal chance of being selected.

Random error (or variation): The variation in a sample that can be expected or occur by chance.

Random variable: A variable in a study in which subjects are randomly selected or randomly assigned to treatments.

Randomization: Allocation of subjects to different groups in a random manner. The objective is that unaccounted factors are almost equally distributed among groups and there is no bias on this count.

Randomized controlled trial: A trial where there is a control group and the allocation of subjects to the control and test groups is done by random method. This is considered to be the ideal methodology to evaluate efficacy of a new regimen particularly when it is double-blind.

Rate: A proportion associated with a multiplier, called the base, (*e.g.,* 1,000, 10,000, 1,00,000) and computed over a specific period of time.

Ratio: A part divided by another part. It is number of observations with the characteristic of interest divided by the number without the characteristic.

Realth birth cohort: A group of births occurring at the same time.

Recall bias: Bias resulting from differential recall of exposure to causal factors among those who have the disease as compared with those who do not have it.

Regression analysis: Given data on a dependent variable 'y' and an independent variable 'x', regression analysis involves finding the best mathematical model (within some restricted form) to describe 'y' as a function of 'x' (or to predict y from x).

Rejection region: This is the region of null hypothesis in normal curve, called α.

Relative error: Relative error in statistics is defined as the ratio of the absolute error to the true value, often expressed as a percentage.

Reliability: Reliability deals with the inherent performance of the procedure. A reliable procedure is one that gives consistent results when it is applied more than once to the same unit under similar conditions.

Reseach protocol: Statement on steps of research, including background information and rationale, objectives and hypothesis, review of literature, methodology, ethics, statistical evaluation, and references.

Residual: The difference between the predicted value and the actual value of the outcome (*i.e.,* dependent) variable in regression.

Risk event: Death, disease, or injury.

Risk factor: A characteristic which, if present and active, clearly increases the probability of a particular disease in a group of persons who have the factor compared with an otherwise similar group of persons who do not. A risk factor is neither a necessary cause nor a sufficient cause of the disease.

Sample registration system: It is in adhoc system to get quick required data for policy making and measures to be taken.

Sampling: The process of selecting a sample from a population.

Sampling error: The difference that occurs by chance between sample values and population values.

Scale of measurement: The degree of precision with which a characteristic is measured. It is generally classified into nominal, ordinal, and numeric (or interval and ratio) scales.

Schedule: A form which contains a set of items on which information is to be obtained. It contains space also to record the responses.

Score: Quantification of a set of qualitative (or ordinal) measurements such as APGAR score. In medicine, scores are used either to grade severity of a condition or as an aid to diagnosis.

Selection bias: Bias resulting when allocation of participants to study, or a particular study group, is influenced by characteristics of the participants that also influence the probability of the outcome.

Sensitivity: Sensitivity of a screening test is a measure of the probability of correctly diagnosing a case. It is the proportion of truly diseased persons in the screened population who are identified as diseased by the screening test.

Sex ratio: Number of females per 1000 males.

Single blind: When the subject alone is not informed that he/she is reveiving test regimen or the control regimen in a trial. The doctor or assessor knows.

Skewness: Any deviation from symmetry is called skewness.

Smoking index: A measure of life long burden of smoking with weightage for age at limitation, quantity of smoking, duration of smoking, type of smoking (filter, nonfilter, bidi or cigar), and duration elapsed since quitting by exsmokers.

Specificity: Specificity is a measure of the probability of correctly identifying a non-diseased person with a screening test. It is the proportion of persons who are not truly diseased, who are so identified by the screening test.

Spurious correlation: An association between two variables that may be false or due to all kinds of non-causal associations resulting from chance or bias.

Stable population: A population with same growth rate over a substantial period, *i.e.,* 5 years or more.

Standard error: Standard deviation of a statistic, e.g., the standard error of mean is the standard deviation divided by the square root of the sample size.

Stationary population: A population with zero growth.

Statistic: A summary measure (or value) for any characteristic in the sample, *e.g.,* mean, median or standard deviation of a sample, or proportion of subjects found affected in a sample.

Statistical inference: The process of drawing conclusions about a population of observations from a sample of observations.

Statistical significance: The concept by which results are judged as due to chance or not.

Still birth ratio: The number of still births per thousand live births in the same period of time.

Strata: The divisions (or groups) obtained after the division of subjects into relevant groups. Strata is the plural of stratum.

Surrogate variable: A make shift substitute variable when the measurements on actually required variable are not available. If the respondents are shy of revealing income, surrogates such as presence of own house, vehicle, television and telephone etc. can be used to assess the level of income. Since they are surrogate so they may or may not reveal the true status.

Survey: An observational study that generally has a cross-sectional design to collect opinions.

Symmetrical: A characteristic of a distribution in which each half is the mirror image of the other half.

Tabulation: Arrangement of data in rows and columns of a table in a manner that makes them intelligible for the analysis.

Target (or reference) population: The larger group of persons or patients of interest to which the sample results would finally apply. Sample is generally chosen from the target population.

t-distribution: A symmetric distribution with mean zero and a standard deviation larger than that for the normal distribution for small sample sizes. As 'n' increases, the t-distribution approaches the normal distribution.

Trials: Experiments on human subjects in which results can not be predicted in advance.

Two-way classification: Simultaneous division of subjects by two characteristics, such as dividing cases of MI by their CPK level and cholesterol level.

Type I error: The error that results if a true null hypothesis is rejected or if a difference is concluded when there is no difference.

Type II error: The error that results if a false null hypthesis is not rejected or if a difference is not detected when there is a difference.

Unbiasedness (of a statistic): A term used to describe a statistic whose mean based on a large number of samples is equal to the population parameter.

Validity: A measurement is valid if it measures what it is supposed to measure.

Vital registration: The formal recording of events of human life, such as births, deaths, marriages and divorces.

Yetes correction for continuity: An adjustment made to the chi-square procedures when the counts in a contingency table are small or when any expected cell count is less than 5.

Z-distribution: The normal distribution with mean zero and standard deviation one. It is also called the standard normal distribution.

Z-ratio : The test statistic used in the Z-test. It is formed by subtracting the hypothesized mean from the observed mean and dividing by the standard error of the mean.

Z-score: The deviation of X value from the mean divided by the standard deviation.

Z-test: A statistical test of hypothesis based on normal distribution, generally used to compare two means or two proportions in large samples ($n > 30$).

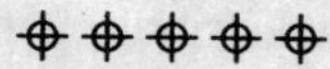

Multiple Choice Questions

1. **Summary value of a population (data) is called as:**
   (a) A variable (b) A parameter
   (c) A statistic (d) An observation.
2. **Which of the following is not a discrete variate?**
   (a) Skin colour (b) Blood pressure
   (c) Weight (d) Boys in the class.
3. **Which of the following is a discrete variable?**
   (a) Mass (b) Length
   (c) Temperature (d) Offspring.
4. **Which of the following is a continuous variable?**
   (a) Parity (b) Siblings
   (c) Angles (d) Beds in a hospital.
5. **All of the following are continuous variables except:**
   (a) Incidence rate (b) Severity of disease
   (c) Width (d) Volume.
6. **Which of the following variables would be considered as continuous?**
   (a) Age (b) Gender
   (c) IQ score (d) Religion.
7. **All of the following are discrete variables except:**
   (a) Pulse rate (b) WBC count

(c) Glands (d) Birth weight.

8. Which of the following is not a continuos variable?

(a) Parity (b) Height

(c) Weight (d) Temperature.

9. All of the following are examples of nominal scale except:

(a) Sex (b) Socio-economic status

(c) Marital status (d) Religion.

10. When variables are not measurable. Which of the following is used to be represented?

(a) Nominal (b) Ordinal (c) Interval (d) Ratio.

11. When variables are not measurable, which of the following is used to be represented?

(a) Nominal (b) Oridinal (c) Interval (d) Ratio.

12. The scale used in measuring pressure or absence of risk factor is:

(a) Nominal (b) Ordinal (c) Interval (d) Ratio.

13. The variable 'length of stay' falls upon which of the following scales of measurement?

(a) Nominal (b) Ordinal (c) Interval (d) Ratio.

14. When frequency of a variable is given in form of mild, moderate and severe, the data scale used is:

(a) Nominal (b) Ordinal (c) Interval (d) Ratio.

15. The scale used in measuring serum creatinine (mg/dl) is :

(a) Nominal (b) Ordinal (c) Interval (d) Ratio.

16. Which of the following is not a nominal scale?

(a) Goals of RCH programme (b) Sex of a body

(c) Grade of malnutrition (d) Outcome of cancer.

17. Which of the following is not an interval scale?

(a) Temperature (b) Serum creatinine

(c) Heart rate (d) IQ level.

18. Which of the following is not a ratio scale?

(a) Height (b) Weight

(c) Time (d) Disease condition.

19. Which of the following is a ratio scale?

(a) Age (b) Rank in class

(c) Temperature in °F (d) Height.

20. In which of the following epidemiological measurements is numerator not a component of denominator?

(a) Rate (b) Ratio
(c) Proportion (d) Percentage.

21. Which of the following type of diagrams can be used to find out the relationship between two variables:

(a) Pictogram (b) Bar diagram
(c) Histogram (d) Scatter diagram.

22. A pictorial diagram of frequency distribution is denoted by:

(a) Line chart (b) Bar chart (c) Histogram (d) Pie chart.

23. Low Birth Weight (LBW) statisitcs of a hospital is best shown by:

(a) Bar chart (b) Histogram
(c) Frequency polygon (d) Pie chart.

24. Line chart shows:

(a) Trend of an event with passage of time
(b) Arithmetic mean
(c) Most commonly occurring value
(d) Difference between the highest and lowest value.

25. The percentage age is depicted by:

(a) Bar diagram (b) Histogram
(c) Line diagram (d) Pie diagram.

26. A graph of a cumulative frequency distribution is called :

(a) Line diagram (b) Histogram
(c) Ogive (d) None of the above.

27. Sex composition is demonstrated in which of the following:

(a) Pie chart (b) Component Bar chart
(c) Age Pyramid (d) Multiple Bar chart.

28. All of the following are graphical representation of grouped data except:

(a) Bar diagram (b) Histogram
(c) Frequency polygon (d) Ogive.

29. If you want to display the average length of stay by gender and service for the month of March. The best choice is a:

(a) Line graph (b) Bar diagram
(c) Scatter diagram (d) Pie chart.

30. To represent the number of deaths by year due to cervical cancer. The best choice is a:

(a) Line graph (b) Bar graph
(c) Pie chart (d) Scatter diagram.

31. If you want to compare average discharged patients and length of stay in a hospital, then the best choice is a:
(a) Scatter diagram (b) Pie chart
(c) Line graph (d) Bar diagram.

32. The age and sex structure of population may be described by:
(a) Bar chart (b) Pie chart
(c) Life table (d) Population pyramid.

33. The width of a class interval is 3, and the mid point is 9, the apparent lower limit of the class is:
(a) 3 (b) 8
(c) 9 (d) 15.

34. The 'real limits' of the class interval (2-4) are:
(a) 2.5 and 4.5 (b) 2 and 4
(c) 1.5 and 4.5 (d) 1.5 and 3.5.

35. 30 babies were born in a hospital. 10 were less than 2.5 kg. and 20 were greater than 2.5 kg., the average is:
(a) Arithmetic mean (b) Median
(c) Geometric mean (d) Mode.

36. Median height can be easily identified from:
(a) Bar diagram (b) Line diagram
(c) Ogive (d) Pie diagram.

37. Which of the following diagrams can not be drawn from quantitative data?
(a) Flow chart (b) Pie chart
(c) Scatter diagram (d) Histogram.

38. Man on the street is referred to:
(a) Bar diagram (b) Histogram
(c) Line diagram (d) Pictogram.

39. The weight (kg) of 7 persons are 62, 58, 52, 60, 95, 55, 120. What is the appropriate measure of average weight of 7 persons?
(a) Mean (b) Median
(c) Geometric mean (d) Mode.

40. In a frequency distribution, the average is 16, if each score is divided by 2, the mean of the new distribution is:

(a) 8 (b) 16
(c) 24 (d) 32.

41. Cumulative frequency is of:
(a) One type (b) Two types
(c) Three types (d) None of the above.

42. Less than cumulative frequency is an arrangement:
(a) In ascending order (b) In descending order
(c) Both (a) and (b) (d) None of the above.

43. More than cumulative frequency is an arrangement in:
(a) Ascending order (b) Descending order
(c) Both (a) and (b) (d) None of the above.

44. Mode is calculated by the formula:
(a) $M_0 = L_{m_0} + \frac{f_1 - f_2}{f_{m_0}}$ (b) $M0 = L_{m_0} + \frac{f_{m_0} - f_1}{2f_{m_0} - f_1 - f_2} \times i_{m_0}$
(c) $M_0 = 3$ Mean – 2 Median (d) $M_0 = 3$ Median ÷ 2 Mean.

45. The geometric mean of the numbers 10, 20, 5 is:
(a) 20 (b) 10
(c) 11.67 (d) 17.5.

46. Mean deviation is calculated by:
(a) $\frac{\Sigma(X - \bar{X})}{N}$ (b) $\frac{\Sigma X - \bar{X}}{N}$
(c) $\frac{\Sigma|X - \bar{X}|}{N}$ (d) $\frac{\Sigma(X - \bar{X})^2}{N}$.

47. Variables are arranged either in ascending or descending order of magnitudes to determine:
(a) Mean (b) Mode (c) Median (d) Range.

48. What is the mode in statistics?
(a) Arithemetic average
(b) Difference between the highest and lowest value
(c) Value of middle observation
(d) Most commonly occurring value.

49. If Mean < Median < Mode, then the distribution is called as:
(a) Negatively skewed (b) Positively skewed
(c) Symmetrical (d) None of the above.

50. Which of the following is not a measure of dispersion?

(a) Mean deviation (b) Median
(c) Range (d) Quartile.

51. Mean deviation of 1, 3, 5, 2, 4 is:
(a) 1 (b) 1.2
(c) 6 (d) Zero.

52. Following measures are known as Quantiles except:
(a) Median (b) Percentile
(c) Quartile (d) Mean.

53. For n = 200 subjects, third quintile is:
(a) 50th value (b) 150th value
(c) 120th value (d) 40th value.

54. For n = 300 subjects, the 3rd quintile is:
(a) 180th value (b) 100th value
(c) 75th value (d) 30th value.

55. For n = 400 observations, the 3rd quartile is:
(a) 100 (b) 200
(c) 300 (d) 400.

56. A percentile rank may take on any of the following values, except:
(a) 10 (b) 22
(c) 57 (d) 102.

57. For the two scores 9 and 13, the $\Sigma(X - \bar{X})^2$ is:
(a) 8 (b) 4
(c) 22 (d) 16.

58. The standard deviation of a frequency distribution is 3. The variance is:
(a) 3 (b) 6
(c) 9 (d) 12.

59. Best method of variability is:
(a) Mean (b) Median
(d) Range (d) Standard Deviation.

60. Which measure is not dependent on the value of each score?
(a) Mean (b) Variance
(c) Range (d) Standard deviation.

61. All are measures of dispersion except:
(a) Range (b) Median
(c) Mean deviation (d) Standard deviation.

62. If each value of a given group of observations is multiplied by 10, the standard deviation of the resulting observations is:

(a) Original std. dev. × 10
(b) Original std. dev. ÷ 10
(c) Original std. dev. – 10
(d) Original std. dev. itself.

63. The weight of each of the 10 babies born in a hospital was 2.5 kg. Considering the distribution was a normal curve. The standard deviation is:

(a) 1 (b) 0 (c) 2.5 (d) 10.

64. Most suitable measure of dispersion in case of open end class distribution is:

(a) Range
(b) Mean deviation
(c) Standard deviation
(d) Quartile deviation.

65. For 20 children height (cm) and weight (kg) are given. To compare variability between heights and weights, all are false, except:

(a) Mean deviation
(b) Quartile deviation
(c) Standard deviation
(d) Coeffficient of variation.

66. Mean and standard deviation can be worked out only if data is on:

(a) Nominal scale
(b) Ordinal scale
(c) Ratio scale
(d) Dichotomus scale.

67. The ratio of 3:1 is achieved by:

(a) Quartile (b) Median (c) 3rd quartile (d) Range.

68. The peakedness of a frequency distribution curve is known as:

(a) Mode
(b) Kurtosis
(c) Skewness
(d) None of the above.

69. The semi-interquartile range is most closely related to :

(a) Mean
(b) Median
(c) Mode
(d) None of the above.

70. If probability of being Rh negative is 1/10, then of being Rh positive will be:

(a) 1/10 (b) 9/10 (c) 1/2 (d) 1.

71. Probability varies between:

(a) 0 and 2 (b) 0 and 100 (c) –1 and +1 (d) 0 and 1.

72. If the probability of new born being female is 0.5, then the probability of new born being male is:

(a) 0.5
(b) 1
(c) 0
(d) None of the above.

73. The probability of a value falling outside 95% confidence limit is:

(a) 1 in 5 (b) 1 in 15 (c) 1 in 20 (d) 1 in 30.

74. The probability of being born with condition A is 0.1 and the probability of being born with condition B is 0.5. If condition A and B are independent. What is the probability of being born with either condition A or condition B, or both?

(a) 0.6 (b) 0.05 (c) 0.55 (d) 0.4.

75. If prevalence of diabetes is 10%, the probability that three persons selected at random from a population will have diabetes is:

(a) 0.1 (b) 0.01 (c) 0.05 (d) 0.001.

76. What is the chance (or probability) that a leap year selected at random will contain 53 Sundays?

(a) 1/7 (b) 2/7 (c) 3/7 (d) 4/7.

77. From the past records of attendance in an office it was found that an employee came late on 73 days in the last year. The probability of his coming late today is:

(a) Zero (b) $\frac{1}{5}$ (c) $\frac{1}{2}$ (d) $\frac{2}{5}$.

78. On a given day a hospital had 100 admissions, 40 females, out of which 10 needed surgery and out of 60 males that were admitted 20 needed surgery. What is the probability of picking up a person requiring surgery?

(a) 3/10 (b) 1/12 (c) 1/3 (d) 1/2.

79. The number of permutations of 'n' things taken 'r' at a time is described as:

(a) npr = n!/(n – r)! (b) $^np_r = n(n - r)$

(c) $^np_r = n(n - 1)(n - 2) \ldots (n - r)$

(d) $^np_r = n \div (n - r)$.

80. The number of combinations of 'n' things taken 'r' at a time is described as:

(a) $^nC_r = n!(n - r)!$ (b) $^np_r = n(n - r)$

(c) $^nC_r = n!/(n - r)!$ (d) $nCr = \frac{n!}{r!(n-r)!}$.

81. Confidence limits can be calculated by using:

(a) Mean and Range (b) Mean and Standard deviation

(c) Median and Range (d) Medain and Standard deviation.

82. For 95% confidence limits, True is:
(a) Reduces 95% of values (b) 1.96 of Standard error or mean
(c) 2.58 of Standard error of mean
(d) 5% of Standard error of mean.

83. True about normal distribution curve is all, Except:
(a) Mean, Median and Mode all coincide
(b) Standard deviation is one (c) Mean of the curve is hundred
(d) Total area of the curve is one.

84. Which is true about normal distribution curve:
(a) Standard deviation-1, Mean-0
(b) Curve skews towards left (c) Curve skews towards right
(d) Mean-1, Standard deviation-0.

85. In a normal curve, true is:
(a) Mean = Standard deviation
(b) Mean = Median (c) Mean = 2 Standard deviation
(d) None of the above.

86. Area between one standard deviation on either side of mean in normal distribution curve is:
(a) 60% (b) 68% (c) 95% (d) 99%.

87. Normal distribution curve depends upon:
(a) Mean and Sample (b) Mean and Median
(c) Mean and Standard deviation
(d) Median and Standard error.

88. If the mean is 220 and the standard error is 10, the 95% confidence limits would be:
(a) 210 to 330 (b) 200 to 240
(c) 215 to 225 (d) 220 to ± 0.2.

89. Normal curve is:
(a) Linear (b) Symmetrical
(c) Curvilinear (d) Parabolic.

90. A non-symmetrical frequency distribution is known as:
(a) Normal distribution (b) Skewed distribution
(c) Cumulative frequency distribution
(d) None of the above.

91. Which of the following is a continuous distribution?
(a) Normal distribution (b) Binomial distribution
(c) Poison distribution (d) None of the above.

92. For normal curve, the coefficient of kurtosis is:

(a) Zero (b) 1

(c) 2 (d) 3.

93. Which of the following conditions is true for normal curve?

(a) Coefficient of skewness is zero

(b) Coefficient of kurtosis is zero

(c) Coefficient of skewness is three

(d) Coefficient of kurtosis is one.

94. Which is true for Mesokurtic:

(a) $\beta_2 = 0$ (b) $\beta2 = 3$

(c) $\beta_2 < 3$ (d) $\beta_2 > 3$.

95. A frequency distribution is called platy-kurtic, when the value of β_2 is:

(a) $\beta_2 = 0$ (b) $\beta_2 = 3$

(c) $\beta2 < 3$ (d) $\beta_2 > 3$.

96. The PEFR of a group of 11 year old girls follow a normal distribution with mean 300 l/min and standard deviation 20 l/min. Which of the following statements is correct?

(a) About 95% of girls have PEFR between 260 and 340 l/min

(b) The girls have healthy lungs

(c) Above 5% of girls have PEFR below 260 l/min

(d) All the PEFR must be less than 340 l/min.

97. 95% C.I. for μ is:

(a) $\bar{X} \pm \sigma$ (b) $\mu \pm 3\sigma$

(c) $\mu \pm$ S.E. (d) $\bar{X} \pm 2$S.E.$(\bar{X})$.

98. In a certain adult population, casual setting systolic B.P. is normally distributed with mean = 120 mm of Hg, variance = 225 mm of Hg. What is the Z-value for a systolic BP of 140 mm of Hg?

(a) 20 (b) 0.75

(c) 1.61 (d) 1.33.

99. Which of the following distribution is symmetric?

(a) Binomial distribution (b) Poisson distribution

(c) Gaussian distribution (d) Chi-square distribution.

100. In which of the following distributions, the mean is equivalent to variance?

(a) Normal distribution (b) Binomial distribution

(c) Poisson distribution (d) Student's t-distribution.

101. For normal curve, the coefficient of kurtosis is:

(a) Zero (b) 1 (c) 2 (d) 3.

102. Which of the following is a continuous distribution?

(a) Normal distribution (b) Binomial distribution
(c) Poisson distribution (d) None of the above.

103. All of the following are the types of kurtosis, except:

(a) Lepto (b) Hecto
(c) Meso (d) Platy.

104. Disperssion of a group of data can be graphically represented by:

(a) Normal curve (b) Lorenz curve
(c) Curvilinear curve (d) Cumulative frequency curve.

105. Which is the best distribution to study the daily admission of head injury patients in a trauma care centre?

(a) Normal distribution (b) Binomial distribution
(c) Poision distribution (d) None of the above.

106. When a null hypthesis is accepted, it is possible that:

(a) A correct decision has been made
(b) A type I error has been made
(c) Both (a) and (b) (d) None of the above.

107. A type I error is committed when a:

(a) False H_0 is accepted (b) True H0 is rejected
(c) True H_A is accepted (d) None of the above.

108. A type II error is committed when a:

(a) False H0 is accepted (b) True H_0 is rejected
(c) False H_A is accepted (d) None of the above.

109. Which is a non-directional alternative hypthesis?

(a) $\mu < 100$ (b) $\mu > 100$
(c) $\mu \neq 100$ (d) None of the above.

110. Another term for a type II error is:

(a) α error (b) β error
(c) γ error (d) None of the above.

111. P-value is the probability of:

(a) Rejecting H0 when it is true
(b) Accepting H_0 when it is true
(c) Rejecting H_0 when it is false
(d) None of the above.

112. The null hypothesis is a statement that is:
(a) Probably true
(b) Considered to be false until proven true
(c) Evaluated statistically as either true or false
(d) All of the above.

113. When α = 0.05, the null hypothesis will be:
(a) Rejected 5% of the time
(b) Accepted 5% of the time
(c) Rejected 5% of the time when it is true
(d) Accepted 5% of the time when it is false.

114. If we change the α-level for a statistically test from 0.05 to 0.01, we are:
(a) Increasing the risk of making a type I error
(b) Decreasing the risk of making a type I error
(c) Decreasing the risk of making a type II error
(d) All of the above.

115. Large sample sizes:
(a) Reduce the risk of type I error
(b) Reduce the risk of a type II error
(c) Make it easier to achieve statistical significance
(d) All of the above.

116. If coefficient of correlation between height and weight is 2.2. What does it mean?
(a) Positive correlation (b) Negative correlation
(c) No association
(d) Calculation of coefficient of correlation is wrong.

117. Correlation coefficient tends to lie between:
(a) Zero to + 1 (b) –1 to Zero (c) –1 to +1 (d) –2 to +2.

118. Not true about correlation is:
(a) Tells about the risk of the diseases
(b) –1 correlation shows linear relationship
(c) Tells association between two variables
(d) Does not tell about causation.

119. The square of the correlation coefficient, r^2 represents :
(a) The risk ratio between two variables
(b) The strength of the association between two variables

(c) The covariance of two variables
(d) None of the above.

120. If $6\Sigma D^2/n\,(n^2-1)$ is zero, then ρ(rho) is:
(a) 1
(b) Zero
(c) – 1
(d) None of the above.

121. The amount of regression toward the mean is least when 'r' is:
(a) Zero (b) Negative (c) Possitive (d) High.

122. Which value of 'r' permits the greatest accuracy of prediction ?
(a) –0.85 (b) –0.25 (c) 0.5 (d) 0.75.

123. To calculate the Pearson's correlation coefficient (r), the two variables should be:
(a) Normally distributed
(b) Linearly related
(c) Random
(d) All of the above.

124. Which of the following values for the Pearson's-r indicates the strongest relationship?
(a) 0.09
(b) 0.58
(c) 0.32
(d) –0.82.

125. Which of the following values for Pearson's-r indicates the weakest relationship?
(a) –0.1
(b) 0.67
(c) 0.01
(d) –0.87.

126. We have calculated a Pearson's-r for length of stay (y) and age (x). Our result is r = –1.12, we, therefore, conclude that:
(a) As age increases, the length of stay decreases
(b) As age increases, the length of stay increases
(c) We cannot predict length of stay from age
(d) We have made error in calculation.

127. If we can not predict y from x, we would conclude that the pearson's-r is:
(a) Zero
(b) Positive
(c) Negative
(d) Not enough information is provided.

128. If D = 0, the Rank correlation coefficient is:
(a) Zero
(b) 1
(c) –1
(d) ±1.

129. About the unit of correlation coefficient between height (cm) and weight (kg), all are false, except:

(a) Centimeter
(b) Kilogram
(c) Cm × kg
(d) No unit.

130. Which is true about the limit of Rank correlation coefficient 'p':

(a) 0 to 1
(b) –1 to 0
(c) –1 to +1
(d) None of the above.

131. Which is true about the correlation between two variables X and Y?

(a) Correlation is AM of two regression coefficients
(b) Correlation is GM of two regression coefficients
(c) Correlation is HM of two regression coefficients
(d) None of the above.

132. All are false about the value of correlation coefficient (r) between two independent variables, except:

(a) r = –1
(b) r = 1
(c) r = 0
(d) None of the above.

133. Mean diastolic B.P. of five individuals is 80 (mm of Hg) with a standard deviation of 10. The coefficient of variation is:

(a) 13%
(b) 12.5%
(c) 12%
(d) 10%.

134. Total cholesterol level = a + b (Caloric intake) + c (Physical activity) + d (BMI) is an example of:

(a) Simple linear regression
(b) Simple curvilinear regression
(c) Multiple linear regression
(d) Multiple curvilinear regression.

135. What will be the standard error (S.E), when n = 100 and σ = 0.5:

(a) 0.05
(b) 0.01
(c) 0.5
(d) 0.02.

136. Mean of 400 variables is 100 and standard deviation is 8. What will be standard error of deviation?

(a) 0.4
(b) 1.0
(c) 2.0
(d) 4.0.

137. Standard error is a measure of:

(a) Conceptual error
(b) Sampling error
(c) Instrumental error
(d) Observer error.

138. $\sqrt{\frac{pq}{n}}$ **indicates:**

(a) Standard error of mean
(b) Difference between proportions
(c) Standard error of proportion
(d) Difference of two probabilities.

139. As sample size increases, standard deviation of sample means:
(a) Decreases (b) Increases
(c) Remains the same (d) Approaches to ∞.

140. The effect sample size depends on:
(a) Power of test (b) Standard deviation
(c) Level of significance (d) All of the above.

141. For quantitative data, the sample size (n) is computed by the formula:
(a) 4 pq/E^2 (b) $2\sigma^2$/E (c) 4σ2/E2 (d) 4σ/E.

142. For qualitative data, the sample size (n) is computed by :
(a) 4pq/L2 (b) $4pq^2$/n (c) pq/L (d) 4pq/L^2.

143. Height for weight of boys in a class room is:
(a) Association (b) Index
(c) Proportion (d) Correlation.

144. In random sampling, chance of being selected is:
(a) Not same and not known (b) Same and known
(c) Same and not known (d) Not same but known.

145. True about Simple Random Sampling is:
(a) Techniques provide least number of possible samples
(b) Every fixed unit is taken for selection
(c) All units have equal chance to be selected
(d) Only selected units have right to be selected.

146. For a survey, a village is divided into 5 lanes the each lane is sampled randomly. It is an example of:
(a) Simple Random Sampling (b) Stratified Random Sampling
(c) Systematic Random Sampling
(d) Multi-phase Random Sampling.

147. Which is true of cluster sampling:
(a) Every nth case is chosen for study
(b) Involves use of random numbers
(c) A natural group is taken as sampling unit
(d) Stratification of population is done.

148. The cluster sampling technique used for evaluating Universal Immunization Programme coverage is:
(a) 30 cluster of 5 children (b) 30 cluster of 10 children
(c) 30 cluster of 7 children (d) 20 cluster of 10 children.

149. Significant 'p' value is:
(a) 0.05 (b) 0.01 (c) 0.1 (d) 0.005.

150. Which of the following is unrelated to the Chi-square test of significance:

(a) Degree of freedom (b) Life table
(c) Significane level (d) Qualitative data.

151. The mean BP of a group of persons was determined and after an intervention trial, the mean BP was estimated again. The test to be applied to determine the significance of intervention is:

(a) Chi-square test (b) Paired t-test
(c) Correlation coefficient (d) Z-test.

152. The Chi-square test for 2 × 2 contingency table is not valid unless:

(a) Both variables are continuous
(b) All the expected frequencies are greater than 5
(c) The sample is very large
(d) Atleast one variable is from a normal distribution.

153. True regarding Chi-square test:

(a) Null hypothesis is equal
(b) Does not test the significance
(c) Tests correlation and regression
(d) Measure the significance of difference between two proportions.

154. The statistical analysis of two unrelated big data (n = 200) is by:

(a) Paired t-test (b) Chi-square test
(c) Z-test (d) Unpaired 't' test.

155. Formula for Chi-square value is:

(a) O – E/E (b) Σ O – E/E^2
(c) $(O - E)^2/N$ (d) Σ (O – E)2/E.

156. For 2 × 2 contingency table, χ^2-test formula is:

(a) $\dfrac{N(ab + cd)}{ab + bc + ac + cd}$ (b) $\dfrac{N(ad - bc)^2}{(a + b)(c + d)(a + c)(b + d)}$

(c) $\dfrac{(ad - bc)}{a + b + c + d}$ (d) $\dfrac{(ad - bc)^2}{N - 1}$.

157. If χ^2 calculated is equal to 28.5 and χ^2 critical is equal to 9.21, then we therefore:

(a) Reject the null hypothesis
(b) Accept the null hypothesis
(c) Conclude that observed frequencies are similar to the expected frequencies
(d) Conclude that not enough information is provided.

158. The chi-square is used to determine difference between:

(a) Mean values (b) Frequencies
(c) Proportions (d) Both (b) and (c).

159. If the difference between two mean values is significant at 1% level, it will significant at:

(a) 0.05 (b) 0.001
(c) 0.003 (d) 0.005.

160. It is easier for a statistical test to achieve statistical significance when we conduct at:

(a) Non directional test (b) One tailed test
(c) Two tailed test (d) All of the above.

161. A condition that is fundamental to statistical inference is:

(a) Random sampling
(b) The population is normally distributed
(c) The mean of the population is known
(d) Both (a) and (b).

162. For paired t-test, the degrees of freedom are equivalent to:

(a) $n - 1$ (b) $n + (n - 1)$
(c) $n_1 + n_2 - 1$ (d) $n_1 + n_2 - 2$.

163. For testing the significance of prevalence rate of a disease to a given proportion, the appropriate test statistic is the:

(a) Z-test (b) t-test
(c) F-test (d) χ^2-test.

164. For testing the significance of gain in weight among 12 rabbits as a result of feeding with a new diet, the appropriate test criterion is:

(a) Paired t-test (b) χ^2-test
(c) Unpaired t-test (d) Z-test.

165. A village with a population of 10,000 has a birth rate of 36 per 1000 population. In one year, there have been five maternal deaths. The maternal mortality rate in this village is:

(a) 0.5 (b) 5.0
(c) 13.8 (d) 14.5.

166. All are true regarding direct standardisation, except:

(a) Vital statistics are required
(b) Age composition of population is required
(c) Age-specific death rate is required for comparison

(d) Without knowledge of the age composition, the two populations can be compared.

167. What does the hospital gross death rate include?

(a) All inpatient deaths and still births
(b) Population at risk
(c) Death of hospital inpatients only
(d) Death of all inpatients and deaths occurring in emergency department.

168. If the annual growth rate of a country is 2%, its population will be double in:

(a) 10 years
(b) 20 years
(c) 35 years
(d) 50 years.

169. In demography, the completed family size is regarded as:

(a) Number of persons in a family
(b) Total number of live births in the family
(c) Total number of live births per women during her child bearing ages
(d) Five members family.

170. The SRS (Sample Registration System) provides adequate information on:

(a) Birth and death rates for the states and country
(b) Causes of death in rural areas
(c) Prevalence of diseases in different segments of the population
(d) Marriages and migration in the country.

171. For calculating adult literacy rate, the age group included is:

(a) ≥ 13 yrs
(b) ≥ 15 yrs
(c) ≥ 17 yrs
(d) ≥ 19 yrs.

172. Best indicator for human reproduction is:

(a) TFR
(b) GRR
(c) CBR
(d) NRR.

173. In which of the following frequency measures is numerator always included in the denominator?

(a) Rate
(b) Ratio
(c) Proportion
(d) Percentage.

174. Survival factor is taken into account in:

(a) TFR
(b) GFR
(c) NRR
(d) GRR.

175. NRR = 1 is equivalent to:

(a) TFR = 1 (b) TFR = 2
(c) TFR = 3 (d) None of the above.

176. Which one of the following is not a socio-economic indicator?

(a) Family size (b) Literacy rate
(c) Per capita income (d) Life expectancy at birth.

177. All of the following are considered as health care delivery indicators except:

(a) Doctor-population ratio (b) Population bed ratio
(c) Doctor-nurse ratio (d) Dependency ratio.

178. In India, on average, the sex ratio at birth is:

(a) 100 : 100 (b) 100 : 105
(c) 100 : 110 (d) 100 : 120.

179. Computation of human poverity index includes, all except:

(a) Percentage of LBWs (b) Adult literacy rate
(c) Percentage of underweight children below 5 years of age
(d) Percentage of people expected to die before age 40 years.

180. Proportion of deaths at age 50 years and above to total deaths is termed as:

(a) Case fatality rate (b) Age specific death rate
(c) Proportional mortality rate (d) Geriatric mortality.

181. The child survival Index is calculated from:

(a) IMR (b) Under five mortality rate
(c) Expectation of life at age one year
(d) (1-4) years mortality rate.

182. There are 5 males in a class of 30 students. What is the best term to describe the comparison?

(a) Percentage (b) Proportion (c) Rate (d) Ratio.

183. There were 20 patients admitted in a hospital two of them were died due to serious condition. What is the best measure to describe the data?

(a) Percentage (b) Rate (c) Proportion (d) Ratio.

184. Percentage of neonatal deaths among total infant deaths is:

(a) 25% (b) 30% (c) 45% (d) 55%.

185. In calculating dependency ratio, the numerator is:

(a) Population under 5 years
(b) Population under 5 years and 60 plus
(c) Population under 15 years and 60 plus
(d) Population of 60 years and above.

186. In dependency ratio, denominator is:
(a) People of age 15-59 years (b) Total population
(c) People of age 10-60 years (d) Poulation under 60 years.

187. If A and B are independent events, then the probability of A and B occurring together, *i.e.*, P(AB) is:
(a) P(A) + P(B) (b) P(A) . P(B)
(c) P(A) ÷ P(B) (d) P(B|A).

188. The distance between the lowest and highest values observed:
(a) Range (b) Dispersion
(c) Standard Error (d) Mean Deviation.

189. Median is almost equivalent to:
(a) 25th percentile (b) 50th percentile
(c) 75th percentile (d) 10th percentile.

190. Which of the following is not a measure of central tendency?
(a) Mean deviation (b) P_{50}
(c) Mode (d) Geometric mean.

191. In Microbiology, the average dilution titers is computed by:
(a) Arithmetic mean (b) Geometric mean
(c) Harmonic mean (d) Median.

192. If mean, median and mode are 10, 16 and 22 respectively, the distribution is:
(a) Symmetric (b) Normal
(c) Positively skewed (d) Negatively skewed.

193. Median is preferred to mean when:
(a) Population is large enough (b) Low variance is seen
(c) Skewed distribution is seen (d) None of the above.

194. Census in India is done:
(a) Every year (b) Every 10 year
(c) Six monthly (d) As and when noted.

195. Sample registration system is done in once in:
(a) 6 months (b) 1 year (c) 2 years (d) 5 years.

196. Population count is taken on:

(a) 1st January (b) 1st April
(c) 1st July (d) 1st August.

197. Randomization is useful to eliminate:
(a) Observer bias (b) Patient bias
(c) Confounding factors (d) Sampling bias.

198. Denominator of maternal mortality rate is:
(a) Per 1000 deaths (b) Per 1000 mother deaths
(c) Per 1000 live births
(d) Per 1000 deaths of children.

199. What is the denominator in General Fertality Rate?
(a) Married women
(b) Women in reporductive age group (15-49) years
(c) Ever married women in the age of 15-49 years
(d) All women.

200. Annual growth rate is:
(a) Crude birth rate – Crude death rate
(b) Crude birth rate + Crude death rate
(c) Crude birth rate + Crude death rate × 100
(d) None of the above.

201. Which of the following is best indicator of health status of a community:
(a) Birth rate (b) Infant mortality rate
(c) Crude death rate (d) None of the above.

202. Sample registration system (SRS) is to acquire information on which of the following:
(a) Morbidity rates of various diseases
(b) Migration statistics
(c) Death rates from rural areas
(d) Birth and death rates for the states and the country

203. Incidence rate is defined as:
(a) Number of new cases occurring during a specified period in a given population
(b) Number of cases existing in a period
(c) Number of old cases present during a specified period in a given population.
(d) Number of new and old cases found during a specified period.

204. Mortality experience is taken into consideration when defining:
(a) General fertility rate (b) Total fertility rate
(c) Net reproduction rate (d) Gross reporduction rate

205. Demographic gap means:

(a) Difference in sex ratio
(b) Differrence between age specific birth and death rates
(c) Difference between birth and death rates
(d) Difference in child and women ratio.

206. Denominator of perinatal mortality is:

(a) Number of live births
(b) Number of deliveries (live and still birth)
(c) Live births – still births
(d) Number of still births.

207. Numerator for neonatal mortality is:

(a) Number of deaths upto 28 days of life
(b) Number of deaths between 28 days to one year
(c) Number of deaths less than or equal to 7 days of life
(d) All infants under one year.

208. Total Fertility Rate (T.F.R.) refers to:

(a) Number of births per one thousand women
(b) Number of women between 15-49 years
(c) Number of female children per women
(d) Approximate completed family size.

209. The denominator to calculate literacy rate is:

(a) Population above 14 years (b) Total population
(c) Population above 7 years of age
(d) Population above 10 years of age.

210. Fertility rate can be reduced by:

(a) Female literacy (b) Compulsory sterilization
(c) Early marriages (d) Spacing of pregnancies.

211. Infantile deaths is taken only below:

(a) 1 month (b) 7 days (c) 1 year (d) 9 months.

212. If TFR in a population is 5 per women, the GRR is:

(a) 2.5 (b) 5
(c) 10 (d) None of the above.

213. Prevalence is a:

(a) Ratio (b) Rate
(c) Proportion (d) Mode of disease.

214. Net Reproduction Rate (NRR = 1) implies a Couple Protection Rate (CPR) of:

(a) 50 (b) 60 (c) 70 (d) 80.

215. Population summary value is known as:

(a) A parameter (b) A statistic

(c) An element (d) Numeric value.

216. The sample mean, $\bar{X}$ is

(a) Always equal to the population mean

(b) Never equal to the population mean

(c) A statistic (d) A parameter.

217. For N = 300 subjects, the 3rd quintile is:

(a) 180th value (b) 100th value

(c) 75th value (d) 30th value.

218. Following measures are known as quantiles, except:

(a) Median (b) Quartile (c) Percentile (d) Mean.

219. For N = 400 observations, the 3rd quartile is:

(a) 100 (b) 200 (c) 300 (d) 400.

220. Which is true for Mesokurtic:

(a) $\beta_2 = 0$ (b) $\beta 2 = 3$ (c) $\beta_2 < 3$ (d) $\beta_2 > 3$.

221. If mean < Median < Mode, then the distribution is called as:

(a) Negatively skewed (b) Positively skewed

(c) Symmetrical (d) None of the above.

222. A percentile rank may take on any of the following values, except:

(a) 10 (b) 22 (c) 57 (d) 102.

223. What is the chance (or probability) that a leap year selected at random will contain 53 sundays?

(a) 1/7 (b) 2/7 (c) 3/7 (d) 4/7.

224. From the past records of attendance in an office it was found that an employee came late on 73 days in the last year. The probability of his coming late today is:

(a) Zero (b) $\frac{1}{5}$ (c) $\frac{1}{2}$ (d) $\frac{2}{5}$.

225. On a given day a hospital had 100 admissions; 40 females, out of which 10 needed surgery and out of 60 males that were admitted 20 needed surgery. What is the probability of picking up a person requiring surgery?

(a) 3/10 (b) 1/12 (c) 1/3 (d) 1/2.

226. If we can not predict y from x, we would conclude that the Pearson's – r is:
(a) Zero
(b) Positive
(c) Negative
(d) No enough information.

227. All are false about the value of correlation coefficient(r) between two independent variables, except:
(a) r = –1
(b) r = 1
(c) r = 0
(d) None of the above.

228. χ^2-test is used to test difference between:
(a) Proportions
(b) Means
(c) Variances
(d) None of the above.

229. Survival factor is taken into account in:
(a) TFR
(b) GFR
(c) NRR
(d) GRR.

230. If the annual growth rate of a country is 2%, its population will be double in:
(a) 10 years
(b) 20 years
(c) 35 years
(d) 50 years.

231. Which of the following is not a socio-economic indicator?
(a) Family size
(b) Literacy rate
(c) Per capita income
(d) Life expectancy at birth.

232. In dependency ratio, Denominator is:
(a) People of age 15-59 years
(b) Total population
(c) People of age 10-60 years
(d) Population under 60 years.

233. Meta analysis is:
(a) A study of materials
(b) A study of multiple studies
(c) A study of chemical reactions
(d) A study of risk factors.

234. Life table is used for:
(a) Incidence
(b) Prevalence
(c) Survival
(d) Migration.

235. Best indicator of health in a community is:
(a) IMR
(b) NMR
(c) MMR
(d) Life expectancy.

ANSWERS OF MULTIPLE CHOICE QUESTIONS

1. (b)	2. (c)	3. (d)	4. (c)	5. (d)	6. (a)	7. (d)	8. (a)
9. (b)	10. (a)	11. (a)	12. (a)	13. (d)	14. (b)	15. (c)	16. (c)

17. (d)	18. (a)	19. (d)	20. (b)	21. (d)	22. (c)	23. (b)	24. (a)
25. (d)	26. (c)	27. (c)	28. (a)	29. (b)	30. (a)	31. (a)	32. (d)
33. (b)	34. (c)	35. (a)	36. (c)	37. (a)	38. (d)	39. (b)	40. (a)
41. (b)	42. (a)	43. (b)	44. (b)	45. (b)	46. (c)	47. (c)	48. (a)
49. (b)	50. (b)	51. (b)	52. (c)	53. (c)	54. (a)	55. (c)	56. (d)
57. (a)	58. (c)	59. (d)	60. (c)	61. (b)	62. (a)	63. (a)	64. (d)
65. (d)	66. (c)	67. (c)	68. (b)	69. (b)	70. (b)	71. (d)	72. (a)
73. (c)	74. (c)	75. (d)	76. (b)	77. (b)	78. (b)	79. (a)	80. (d)
81. (b)	82. (b)	83. (c)	84. (a)	85. (b)	86. (b)	87. (c)	88. (b)
89. (b)	90. (b)	91. (a)	92. (d)	93. (a)	94. (b)	95. (c)	96. (a)
97. (d)	98. (d)	99. (c)	100. (c)	101. (d)	102. (a)	103. (b)	104. (b)
105. (c)	106. (a)	107. (b)	108. (a)	109. (c)	110. (b)	111. (a)	112. (c)
113. (c)	114. (b)	115. (d)	116. (d)	117. (c)	118. (b)	119. (b)	120. (a)
121. (d)	122. (a)	123. (d)	124. (d)	125. (c)	126. (d)	127. (a)	128. (b)
129. (b)	130. (c)	131. (b)	132. (c)	133. (b)	134. (c)	135. (a)	136. (a)
137. (b)	138. (c)	139. (a)	140. (b)	141. (c)	142. (a)	143. (d)	144. (b)
145. (c)	146. (b)	147. (c)	148. (c)	149. (a)	150. (b)	151. (b)	152. (b)
153. (d)	154. (c)	155. (d)	156. (b)	157. (a)	158. (d)	159. (c)	160. (b)
161. (d)	162. (a)	163. (a)	164. (a)	165. (c)	166. (d)	167. (c)	168. (c)
169. (c)	170. (a)	171. (b)	172. (b)	173. (c)	174. (c)	175. (b)	176. (d)
177. (d)	178. (b)	179. (a)	180. (c)	181. (b)	182. (d)	183. (c)	184. (d)
185. (c)	186. (a)	187. (b)	188. (a)	189. (b)	190. (a)	191. (b)	192. (d)
193. (a)	194. (b)	195. (a)	196. (c)	197. (c)	198. (c)	199. (b)	200. (a)
201. (b)	202. (d)	203. (a)	204. (c)	205. (b)	206. (c)	207. (a)	208. (d)
209. (c)	210. (b)	211. (c)	212. (a)	213. (a)	214. (b)	215. (a)	216. (c)
217. (a)	218. (d)	219. (c)	220. (b)	221. (a)	222. (d)	223. (b)	224. (b)
225. (b)	226. (a)	227. (c)	228. (a)	229. (c)	230. (c)	231. (d)	232. (a)
233. (b)	234. (c)	235. (a)					

⊕⊕⊕⊕⊕

APPENDIX

Table I

Areas under the Normal Curve

Z	.00	.01	.02	.03	.04	.05	.06	.07	.08	.09
0.0	.0000	.0040	.0080	0.120	0.160	.0199	.0239	.0279	.0319	.0359
0.1	.0398	.0438	.0478	.0517	.0557	.0596	.0636	.0675	.0714	.0753
0.2	.0793	.0832	.0871	.0910	.0948	.2517	.1026	.1064	.1103	.1141
0.3	.1179	.1217	.1255	.1293	.1331	.1368	.1406	.1443	.1480	.1517
0.4	.1554	.1519	.1628	.1664	.1700	.1736	.1772	.1808	.1844	.1879
0.5	.1915	.1950	.1985	.2019	.2054	.2088	.2123	.2157	.2190	.2224
0.6	.2257	.2291	.2324	.2357	.2389	.2422	.2454	.2486	.2517	.2549
0.7	.2580	.2611	.2642	.2673	.2704	.2734	.2764	.2794	.2823	.2852
0.8	.2881	.2910	.2939	.2967	.2995	.3023	.3051	.3078	.3106	.3133
0.9	.3159	.3186	.3212	.3238	.3264	.3289	.3315	.3340	.3365	.3389
1.0	.3413	.3438	.3461	.3485	.3508	.3531	.3554	.3577	.3599	.3621
1.1	.3643	.3665	.3686	.3708	.3729	.3749	.3770	.3790	.3810	.3830
1.2	.3849	.3869	.3888	.3907	.3925	.3944	.3962	.3980	.3997	.4015
1.3	.4032	.4049	.4066	.4082	.4099	.4115	.4131	.4147	.4162	.4177
1.4	.4192	.4207	.4222	.4236	.4251	.4265	.4279	.4292	.4306	.4319
1.5	.4332	.4345	.4350	.4370	.4382	.4394	.4406	.4418	.4429	.4441
1.6	.4452	.4463	.4474	.4484	.4495	.4505	.4515	.4525	.4535	.4545
1.7	.4554	.4564	.4573	.4582	.4591	.4599	.4608	.4616	.4625	.4633
1.8	.4641	.4649	.4656	4664	.4671	.4678	.4686	.4693	.4699	.4706
1.9	.4713	.4719	.4726	.4732	.4738	.4744	.4570	.4756	.4761	.4767
2.0	.4772	.4778	.4783	.4788	.4793	.4798	.4803	.4808	.4812	.4817
2.1	.4821	.4826	.4830	.4834	.4838	.4842	.4846	.4850	.4854	.4857
2.2	.4861	.4864	.4868	.4871	.4875	.4878	.4881	.4884	.4887	.4890
2.3	.4893	.4896	.4898	.4901	.4904	.4906	.4909	.4911	.4913	.4916
2.4	.4918	.4920	.4922	.4925	.4927	.4929	.4931	.4932	.4934	.4936
2.5	.4938	.4920	.4941	.4943	.4945	.4946	.4948	.4949	.4951	.4952
2.6	.4953	.4955	.4956	.4957	.4959	.4960	.4961	.4962	.4963	.4964
2.7	.4965	.4966	.4967	.4968	..4969	.4970	.4971	.4972	.4973	.4974
2.8	.4974	.4975	.4976	.4977	.4977	.4978	.4979	.4979	.4980	.4981
2.9	.4981	.4982	.4982	.4983	.4994	.4984	.4985	.4985	.4686	.4686
3.0	.4987	.4987	.4987	.4988	.4988	.4989	.4989	.4989	.4990	.4990

APPENDIX
Table II
Random Mumber Tables

Row number										
00000	10097	32533	76520	13586	34673	54876	80959	09177	39292	74945
00001	37542	04805	64894	74296	24805	24037	20636	14037	0822	91665
00002	08422	68953	19645	09303	23209	02560	15953	34764	35080	33606
00003	99019	02529	09376	70715	38311	31165	88676	74397	04436	27659
00004	12807	99970	80157	36147	64032	36653	98951	16877	12171	76833
00005	66065	74717	34072	76850	36697	36170	65813	39885	11199	29170
00006	31060	10805	45571	82406	35303	42614	86799	07439	23403	09732
00007	85269	77602	02051	65692	68665	74818	73053	85237	18623	88579
00008	63573	32135	05325	47048	90553	57548	28468	28709	83491	25624
00009	73796	45753	03529	64778	35808	34282	60935	20344	35273	88435
00010	98520	17767	14905	68607	22109	40558	60970	93433	50500	73998
00011	11805	05431	39808	27732	50725	68248	29405	24201	52775	67851
00012	83452	99634	06288	98033	13746	70078	19475	40610	68711	77817
00013	88685	40200	86507	58401	36766	67951	90364	76493	29609	11062
00014	99594	67348	87517	64669	91826	08928	93785	61368	23478	34113
00015	65481	17674	17468	50950	58047	76974	73039	57186	40218	16544
00016	80124	35635	17727	08015	45318	22374	21115	78253	14385	53763

Table II (continued)...

00017	74350	99817	77402	77214	43236	00210	45521	64237	96286	02655
00018	69916	26803	66252	29148	36936	87203	76621	13990	94400	56418
00019	09893	20505	14225	68514	46427	56788	96297	78822	54382	14598
00020	91499	14523	68479	27686	46162	83554	94750	89923	37089	20048
00021	80336	94598	26940	36858	70297	34135	53140	33340	42050	82341
00022	44104	81949	85157	47954	32979	26575	57600	40881	22222	06413
00023	12550	73742	11100	02040	12860	74697	96644	89439	28707	25815
00024	63606	49329	16505	34484	40219	52563	43651	77082	07207	31790
00025	61196	90446	26457	47774	51924	33729	65394	59593	42582	60527
00026	15474	45266	95270	79953	59367	83848	82396	10118	33211	59466
00027	94557	28573	67897	54387	54622	44431	91190	42592	92927	45973
00028	42481	16213	97344	08721	16868	48767	03071	12059	25701	46670
00029	23523	78317	73208	89837	68935	91416	26252	29663	05522	82562
00030	04493	52494	75246	33824	45862	51025	61962	79335	65337	12472
00031	00549	97654	64051	88159	96119	63896	54692	82391	23287	29529
00032	35963	15307	26898	09354	33351	35462	77974	50024	90103	39333
00033	59808	08391	45427	26842	83609	49700	13021	24892	78565	20106
00034	46058	85236	01390	92286	77281	44077	93910	83647	70617	42941
00035	32179	00597	87379	25241	05567	07007	86743	17157	85394	11838
00036	69234	61406	20117	45204	15956	60000	18743	92423	97118	96338
00037	19565	41430	01758	75379	40419	21585	66674	36806	84962	85207
00038	45155	14938	19476	07246	43667	94543	59047	90033	20826	69541
00039	94864	31994	36168	10851	34888	81553	01540	35456	05014	51176

APPENDIX

Table III

Significant values of t-distribution

Prob (P). d.f. (υ)	.10	.05	.025	.01	.005
1.	3.078	6.314	12.706	31.821	63.567
2.	1.886	2.920	4.303	6.965	9.925
3.	1.638	2.353	3.182	4.541	5.841
4.	1.533	2.132	2.776	3.747	4.604
5.	1.476	2.015	2.571	3.365	4.032
6.	1.440	1.943	2.447	3.143	3.707
7.	1.415	1.895	2.365	2.998	3.499
8.	1.397	1.860	2.306	2.896	3.355
9.	1.383	1.833	2.262	2.821	3.250
10.	1.372	1.812	2.228	2.764	3.169
11.	1.363	1.796	2.201	2.718	3.106
12.	1.356	1.782	2.179	2.681	3.055
13.	1.350	1.771	2.160	2.650	3.012
14.	1.345	1.761	2.145	2.624	2.977
15.	1.341	1.753	2.131	2.602	2.947
16.	1.337	1.746	2.120	2.583	2.921
17.	1.333	1.740	2.110	2.567	2.898
18.	1.330	1.734	2.101	2.552	2.878
19.	1.328	1.729	2.093	2.539	2.861
20.	1.325	1.725	2.086	2.528	2.845
21.	1.323	1.721	2.080	2.518	2.831
22.	1.321	1.717	2.074	2.508	2.819
23.	1.319	1.714	2.069	2.500	2.807
24.	1.318	1.711	2.064	2.492	2.797
25.	1.316	1.708	2.060	2.485	2.787
26.	1.315	1.706	2.056	2.479	2.779
27.	1.314	1.703	2.052	2.473	2.771
28.	1.313	1.701	2.048	2.467	2.763
29.	1.311	1.699	2.045	2.462	2.756
30.	1.310	1.697	2.042	2.457	2.750
40.	1.303	1.684	2.021	2.423	2.704
60.	1.296	1.671	2.000	2.390	2.660
120.	1.289	1.658	1.980	2.385	2.617
∞	1.282	1.645	1.960	2.326	2.576

APPENDIX

Table IV

Significant Values of χ^2

Prob. (P) d.f.	0.990	0.950	.9000	0.500	0.1000	0.050	0.025	0.010	0.005
				Probability (Proportion of area)					
1	0.00016	0.00393	0.0158	0.455	2.71	3.84	5.02	6.63	7.88
2	0.0201	0.103	0.211	1.386	4.61	5.99	7.38	9.21	10.60
3	0.115	0.352	0.584	2.366	6.25	7.81	9.35	11.34	12.84
4	0.297	0.711	1.064	3.357	7.78	9.49	11.14	13.28	14.86
5	0.554	1.145	1.61	4.251	9.24	11.07	12.83	15.09	16.75
6	0.872	1.64	2.20	5.35	10.64	12.59	14.45	16.81	18.55
7	1.24	2.17	2.83	6.35	12.02	14.07	16.01	18.48	20.28
8	1.65	2.73	3.49	7.34	13.36	15.51	17.53	20.09	21.96
9	2.09	3.33	4.17	8.34	14.68	16.92	19.02	21.67	23.59
10	2.56	3.94	4.87	9.34	15.99	18.31	20.48	23.21	25.19
11	3.05	4.57	5.58	10.34	17.28	19.68	21.92	24.73	26.76
12	3.57	5.23	6.30	11.14	18.55	21.03	23.34	26.22	28.30
13	4.11	5.89	7.04	12.34	19.81	22.36	24.74	27.69	29.82
14	4.66	6.57	7.79	13.31	21.06	23.68	26.12	29.14	31.32
15	5.23	7.26	8.55	14.34	22.31	25.00	27.40	30.58	32.80
16	5.81	7.96	9.31	15.34	23.54	26.30	28.85	32.00	34.27

Table IV (continued)...

17	6.41	8.67	10.09	16.34	24.77	27.59	30.19	33.41	35.72
18	7.01	9.39	10.86	17.34	25.99	28.87	31.53	34.81	37.16
19	7.63	10.12	11.65	18.34	27.20	30.14	32.85	36.19	38.58
20	8.26	10.85	12.44	19.34	28.41	31.41	34.17	37.57	40.00
21	8.90	11.59	13.24	20.34	29.62	32.67	35.49	33.93	41.40
22	9.54	12.34	14.04	21.34	30.81	33.92	36.78	40.29	42.80
23	10.20	13.09	14.85	22.34	32.01	35.17	38.03	41.64	44.18
24	10.86	13.85	15.66	23.34	33.20	36.42	39.36	42.98	45.56
25	11.52	14.61	16.47	24.34	34.38	37.65	40.65	44.31	46.93
26	12.20	15.38	17.29	25.34	35.56	38.89	41.92	45.64	48.29
27	12.83	16.15	18.11	26.34	36.74	40.11	43.19	46.96	49.64
28	13.56	16.93	18.94	27.34	37.92	41.34	44.46	48.28	50.99
29	14.26	17.71	19.77	28.34	39.09	42.56	45.72	49.59	52.34
30	14.95	18.49	20.60	29.34	40.26	43.77	46.98	50.89	53.67
40	22.16	26.51	29.05	39.31	51.81	55.76	59.34	63.69	66.77
50	29.71	34.76	37.69	49.33	63.17	67.50	71.42	76.15	79.49
60	37.43	43.19	46.46	59.33	74.40	79.09	83.30	88.33	91.95
70	45.44	51.74	55.33	69.33	85.53	90.53	95.02	100.4	104.2
80	53.54	60.39	64.28	79.33	98.58	101.9	106.6	112.3	116.3
90	61.75	69.13	73.29	89.33	107.6	113.1	118.1	124.1	128.3
100	70.06	77.93	82.36	99.33	118.5	124.3	129.6	135.8	140.2

APPENDIX

Table V(a)

5% Points of Fisher's F-Distribution

υ_2 \ υ_1	1	2	3	4	5	6	7	8	9	10	12	15	20	30	60	∞
1	161.45	199.50	215.71	224.58	230.16	233.99	236.77	238.88	240.54	241.88	243.95	245.95	248.01	250.09	252.20	254.32
2	18.513	19.000	19.164	19.247	19.296	19.330	19.353	19.371	19.385	19.396	19.413	19.429	19.466	19.462	19.479	19.496
3	10.128	9.5521	9.2766	9.1172	9.0135	8.9406	8.8868	8.8452	8.8123	8.7855	8.7446	8.7029	8.6602	8.6166	8.5720	8.5265
4	7.7086	6.9443	6.5914	6.3883	6.2560	6.1631	6.0942	6.0410	5.9988	5.9644	5.9117	5.8578	5.8052	5.7459	5.6878	5.6281
5	6.6079	5.7861	5.4095	5.1922	5.0503	4.9503	4.8759	4.8183	4.7725	4.7351	4.6777	4.6188	4.5581	4.4957	4.4314	4.3650
6	5.9874	5.1433	4.7571	4.5337	4.3874	4.2839	4.2066	4.1468	4.0990	4.0600	3.9999	3.9381	3.8742	3.8082	3.7398	3.6688
7	5.5914	4.7374	4.3468	4.1203	3.9715	3.8660	3.7880	3.7257	3.6767	3.6365	3.5747	3.5108	3.4445	3.3758	3.3043	3.2298
8	5.3177	4.4590	4.0662	3.8378	3.6875	3.5806	3.5005	3.4381	3.3881	3.3472	3.2840	3.2184	3.1503	3.0794	3.0053	2.9276
9	5.1174	4.2565	3.8626	3.6331	3.4817	3.3738	3.2927	3.2296	3.1789	3.1373	3.0729	3.0061	2.9365	2.8637	2.7872	2.7067
10	4.9646	4.1028	3.7083	3.4780	3.3258	3.2172	3.1355	3.0717	3.0204	2.9782	2.9130	2.8450	2.7740	2.6996	2.6211	2.5379
11	4.8443	3.9823	3.5874	3.3567	3.2039	3.0946	3.0123	2.9480	2.8962	2.8536	2.7876	2.7186	2.6464	2.5705	2.4901	2.4045
12	4.7472	3.8853	3.4903	3.2592	3.1059	2.9961	2.9134	2.8486	2.7964	2.7534	2.6866	2.6169	2.5436	2.4663	2.3842	2.2962
13	4.6672	3.8056	3.4105	3.1791	3.0254	2.9153	2.8321	2.7669	2.7144	2.6710	2.6037	2.5331	2.4589	2.3803	2.2966	2.2064
14	4.6001	3.7389	3.3439	3.1122	2.9582	2.8477	2.7642	2.6987	2.6458	2.6021	2.5342	2.4630	2.3879	2.3082	2.2230	2.1807

Table V(a) (continued)...

15	4.5431	3.6823	3.2874	3.0556	2.9013	2.7905	2.7066	2.6408	2.5876	2.5437	2.4753	2.4035	2.3254	2.2468	2.1601	2.0658
16	4.4940	3.6337	3.2389	3.0069	2.8524	2.7413	2.6572	2.5911	2.5377	2.4935	2.4247	2.3522	2.2756	2.1938	2.1058	2.0096
17	4.4513	3.5915	3.1968	2.9647	2.8100	2.6987	2.6143	2.5480	2.4943	2.4499	2.3870	2.3077	2.2304	2.1477	2.0584	1.9604
18	4.4139	3.5546	3.1599	2.9277	2.7729	2.6613	2.5767	2.5102	2.4563	2.4117	2.3421	2.2686	2.1906	2.1071	2.0166	1.9168
19	4.3808	3.5219	3.1274	2.8951	2.7401	2.6283	2.5435	2.4768	2.4227	2.3779	2.3080	2.2341	2.1555	2.0712	1.9796	1.8780
20	4.3513	3.4928	3.0984	2.8661	2.7109	2.5990	2.5140	2.4471	2.3928	2.3479	2.2776	2.2033	2.1242	2.0391	1.9464	1.8432
21	4.3248	3.4668	3.0725	2.8401	2.6848	2.4727	2.4876	2.4205	2.3661	2.3210	2.2504	2.1757	2.0960	2.0102	1.9165	1.8117
22	4.3009	3.4434	3.0491	2.8167	2.6613	2.5491	2.4638	2.3965	2.3419	2.2967	2.2258	2.1508	2.0707	1.9842	1.8895	1.7831
23	4.2793	3.4221	3.0280	2.7955	2.6400	2.5277	2.4422	2.3748	2.3201	2.4747	2.2036	2.1282	2.0476	1.9605	1.8649	1.7570
24	4.2597	3.4028	3.0088	2.7763	2.6207	2.5082	2.4226	2.3551	2.3002	2.2547	2.1834	2.1077	2.0267	1.9390	1.8424	1.7331
25	4.2417	3.3852	2.9912	2.7587	2.6030	2.4904	2.4047	2.3371	2.2821	2.2365	2.1649	2.0889	2.0075	109192	1.8217	1.7110
26	4.2252	3.3690	2.9751	2.7426	2.5868	2.4741	2.3883	2.3205	2.2655	2.2197	2.1479	2.0716	1.9898	1.9010	1.8027	1.6906
27	4.2100	3.3541	2.9604	2.7278	2.5719	2.4591	2.3732	2.3053	2.2501	2.2043	2.1323	2.0558	1.9736	1.8842	1.7851	1.6717
28	4.1960	3.3404	2.9467	2.7141	2.5581	2.4453	2.3593	2.2913	2.2360	2.1900	2.1179	2.0411	1.9586	1.8687	1.7689	1.6541
29	4.1830	3.3277	2.9340	2.7014	2.5454	2.4324	2.3463	2.2782	2.2229	2.1768	2.1045	2.0275	1.9446	1.8543	1.7537	1.6377
30	4.1709	3.3158	2.9223	2.6896	2.5336	2.4205	2.3343	2.2662	2.2107	2.1626	2.0921	2.0148	1.9317	1.8409	1.7396	1.6223
60	4.0012	3.1504	2.7581	2.5252	2.3683	2.2540	2.1665	2.0970	2.0404	1.9926	1.9174	1.8364	1.7480	1.6491	1.5343	1.5089
120	3.9201	3.0718	2.6802	2.4472	2.2900	2.1750	2.0867	2.0164	1.9588	1.9105	1.8337	1.7505	1.6587	1.5543	1.4290	1.2539
∞	3.8415	2.9957	2.6049	2.3719	2.2141	2.0986	2.0096	1.9384	1.8799	1.8307	1.7522	1.6664	1.5705	1.4591	1.3180	1.0000

APPENDIX

Table V(b)

1% Points of Fisher's F-Distribution

v_1 / v_2	1	2	3	4	5	6	7	8	9	10	12	15	20	24	30	60	120	∞
1	4052	4999.5	5403	5625	5764	5859	5928	5982	6022	6056	6106	6157	6209	6235	6261	6313	6339	6336
2	98.50	99.00	99.17	99.25	99.30	99.33	99.36	99.37	99.39	99.40	99.42	99.43	99.45	99.46	99.47	99.48	99.49	99.50
3	34.12	30.82	29.46	28.71	28.24	27.91	27.67	27.49	27.35	27.23	27.05	26.87	26.69	26.60	26.50	26.32	26.22	26.13
4	21.20	18.00	46.69	15.98	15.52	15.21	14.98	14.80	14.66	14.55	14.37	14.20	14.02	13.93	13.84	13.65	13.56	13.46
5	16.26	13.27	12.06	11.39	10.97	10.67	10.46	10.29	10.16	10.05	9.89	9.72	9.55	9.47	9.38	9.20	9.11	9.02
6	13.75	10.92	9.78	9.15	8.75	8.47	8.26	8.10	7.98	7.87	7.72	7.56	7.40	7.31	7.23	7.06	6.97	6.88
7	12.25	9.55	8.45	7.85	7.46	7.19	6.99	6.84	6.72	6.62	6.47	6.31	6.16	6.07	5.99	5.82	5.74	5.65
8	11.26	8.65	7.59	7.01	6.63	6.37	6.18	6.03	5.91	5.81	5.67	5.52	5.36	5.28	5.20	5.03	4.95	4.86
9	10.56	8.02	6.99	6.42	6.06	5.80	5.61	5.47	5.35	5.26	5.11	4.96	4.81	4.73	4.65	4.48	4.40	4.31
10	10.04	7.56	6.55	5.99	5.64	5.39	5.20	5.06	4.94	4.85	4.71	4.56	4.41	4.33	4.25	4.08	4.00	3.91
11	9.65	7.21	6.22	5.67	5.32	5.07	4.89	4.74	4.63	4.54	4.40	4.25	4.10	4.02	3.94	3.78	3.69	3.60
12	9.33	6.93	5.95	5.41	5.06	4.82	4.64	4.50	4.39	4.30	4.16	4.01	3.86	3.78	3.70	3.54	3.45	3.36
13	9.07	6.70	5.74	5.21	7.86	4.62	4.44	4.30	4.19	4.10	3.96	3.82	3.66	3.59	3.51	3.34	3.25	3.17
14	8.86	6.51	5.56	5.04	4.69	4.46	4.28	4.14	4.03	3.94	3.80	3.66	3.51	3.43	3.35	3.18	3.09	3.00

Table V(b) (continued)...

v_1 / v_2	1	2	3	4	5	6	7	8	9	10	12	15	20	24	30	60	120	∞
15	8.68	6.36	5.42	4.89	4.56	4.32	4.14	4.00	3.89	3.80	3.67	3.52	3.37	3.29	3.21	3.05	2.96	2.87
16	8.53	6.23	5.29	4.77	4.44	4.20	4.03	3.89	3.78	3.69	3.55	3.41	3.26	3.18	3.10	2.93	2.84	2.75
17	8.40	6.11	5.18	4.67	4.34	4.10	3.93	3.79	3.68	3.59	3.46	3.31	3.16	3.08	3.00	2.83	2.75	2.65
18	8.29	6.01	2.09	4.58	4.25	1.01	3.84	3.71	3.60	3.51	3.37	3.23	3.08	3.00	2.92	2.75	2.66	2.57
19	8.18	5.93	2.01	4.50	4.17	3.94	3.77	3.63	3.52	3.43	3.30	3.15	3.00	2.92	2.84	2.67	2.58	2.49
20	8.10	5.85	4.94	4.43	4.10	3.87	3.70	3.56	3.46	3.37	3.23	3.09	2.94	2.86	2.78	2.61	2.52	2.42
22	7.95	5.72	4.82	4.31	3.99	6.76	3.59	3.45	3.35	3.26	3.12	2.98	2.83	2.75	2.67	2.50	2.40	2.31
24	7.82	5.61	4.72	4.22	3.90	3.67	3.50	3.36	3.26	3.17	3.03	2.89	2.74	2.66	2.58	2.40	2.31	2.21
26	7.72	5.53	4.64	4.14	3.82	3.59	3.42	3.29	3.18	309	2.96	2.81	2.66	2.58	2.50	2.33	2.23	2.13
28	7.64	5.45	4.57	4.07	3.75	3.53	3.36	3.23	3.12	3.03	2.90	2.75	2.60	2.52	2.44	2.26	2.17	2.06
30	7.56	5.39	4.51	4.02	3.70	3.47	3.30	3.17	3.07	2.98	2.84	2.70	2.55	2.47	2.39	2.21	2.11	2.01
40	7.31	5.18	4.31	3.83	3.51	3.29	3.12	2.99	2.89	2.80	2.66	2.52	2.37	2.29	2.20	2.02	1.92	1.80
60	7.08	4.98	4.13	3.65	3.34	3.12	2.95	2.82	2.72	2.63	2.50	2.35	2.20	2.12	2.03	1.84	1.73	1.60
120	6.85	4.79	3.95	3.48	3.17	2.96	2.79	2.66	2.56	2.47	2.34	2.19	2.03	1.95	1.86	1.66	1.53	1.38
∞	6.63	4.61	3.78	3.32	3.02	2.80	2.64	2.51	2.41	2.32	2.18	2.04	1.88	1.79	1.70	1.47	1.32	1.00

APPENDIX
Table VI
Critical Values of n_+ for the Sign Test

n	α (two-sided) / α (one-sided)	0.10 / 0.05	0.05 / 0.025	0.02 / 0.01	0.01 / 0.005
1					
2					
3					
4					
5		0, 5			
6		0, 6	0, 6		
7		0, 7	0, 7	0, 7	
8		1, 7	1, 8	0, 8	0, 8
9		1, 8	1, 8	0, 9	0, 9
10		1, 9	1, 9	0, 10	0, 10
11		2, 9	1, 10	1, 10	0, 11
12		2, 10	2, 10	1, 11	1, 11
13		3, 10	2, 11	1, 12	1, 12
14		3, 11	2, 12	2, 12	1, 13
15		3, 12	3, 12	2, 13	2, 13
16		4, 12	3, 13	2, 14	2, 14
17		4, 12	4, 13	3, 14	2, 15
18		5, 13	4, 14	3, 15	3, 15
19		5, 14	4, 15	4, 15	3, 16
20		5, 15	5, 15	4, 16	3, 17
21		6, 15	5, 16	4, 17	4, 17
22		6, 16	5, 17	5, 17	4, 18
23		7, 16	6, 17	5, 18	4, 19
24		7, 17	6, 18	5, 19	5, 19
25		7, 18	7, 18	6, 19	5, 20
26		8, 18	7, 19	6, 20	6, 20
27		8, 19	7, 20	7, 20	6, 21
28		9, 19	8, 20	7, 21	6, 22
29		9, 20	8, 21	7, 22	7, 22
30		10, 20	9, 21	8, 22	7, 23

(Cont...)

n	α (two-sided) α (one-sided)	0.10 0.05	0.05 0.025	0.02 0.01	0.01 0.005
31		10, 21	9, 22	8, 23	7, 24
32		10, 22	9, 23	8, 24	8, 24
33		11, 22	10, 23	9, 24	8, 25
34		11, 23	10, 24	9, 25	9, 25
35		12, 23	11, 24	10, 25	9, 26
36		12, 24	11, 25	10, 26	9, 27
37		13, 24	12, 25	10, 27	10, 27
38		13, 25	12, 26	11, 27	10, 28
39		13, 26	12, 57	11, 28	11, 28
40		14, 26	13, 27	12, 28	11, 29
41		14, 27	13, 28	12, 29	11, 30
42		15, 27	14, 28	13, 29	12, 30
43		15, 28	14, 29	13, 30	12, 31
44		16, 28	15, 29	13, 31	13, 31
45		16, 29	15, 30	14, 31	13, 32
46		16, 30	15, 31	14, 32	13, 33
47		17, 30	16, 31	15, 32	14, 33
48		17, 31	16, 32	15, 33	14, 34
49		18, 31	17, 32	15, 34	15, 34
50		18, 32	17, 33	16, 34	15, 35
51		19, 32	18, 33	16, 35	15, 36
52		19, 33	18, 34	17, 35	16, 36
53		20, 33	18, 35	17, 36	16, 37
54		20, 34	19, 35	18, 36	17, 37
55		20, 35	19, 36	18, 37	17, 38
56		21, 35	20, 36	18, 38	17, 39
57		21, 36	20, 37	19, 38	18, 39
58		22, 36	21, 37	19, 39	18, 40
59		22, 37	21, 38	20, 39	19, 40
60		23, 37	21, 39	20, 40	19, 41
61		23, 38	22, 39	20, 41	20, 41
62		24, 38	22, 40	21, 41	20, 42
63		24, 39	23, 40	21, 42	20, 43
64		24, 40	23, 41	22, 42	21, 43
65		25, 40	24, 41	22, 43	21, 44

(Cont...)

n	α (two-sided) 0.10 α (one-sided) 0.05	0.05 0.025	0.02 0.01	0.01 0.005
66	25, 41	24, 42	23, 43	22, 44
67	26, 41	25, 42	23, 44	22, 45
68	26, 42	25, 43	23, 45	22, 46
69	27, 42	25, 44	24, 45	23, 46
70	27, 43	26, 44	24, 46	23, 47
71	28, 43	26, 45	25, 46	24, 47
72	28, 44	27, 45	25, 47	24, 48
73	28, 45	27, 46	26, 47	25, 48
74	29, 45	28, 46	26, 48	25, 49
75	29, 46	28, 47	26, 49	25, 50
76	30, 46	28, 48	27, 49	26, 50
77	30, 47	29, 48	27, 50	26, 51
78	31, 47	29, 49	28, 50	27, 51
79	31, 48	30, 49	28, 51	27, 52
80	32, 48	30, 50	29, 51	28, 52
81	32, 49	31, 50	29, 52	28, 53
82	33, 49	31, 51	30, 52	28, 54
83	33, 50	32, 51	30, 53	29, 54
84	33, 51	32, 52	30, 54	29, 55
85	34, 51	32, 53	31, 54	30, 55
86	34, 52	33, 53	31, 55	30, 56
87	35, 52	33, 54	32, 55	31, 56
88	35, 53	34, 54	32, 56	31, 57
89	36, 53	34, 55	33, 56	31, 58
90	36, 54	35, 55	33, 57	32, 58
91	37, 54	35, 56	33, 58	32, 59
92	37, 55	36, 56	34, 58	33, 59
93	38, 55	36, 57	34, 59	33, 60
94	38, 56	37, 57	35, 59	33, 60
95	38, 57	37, 58	35, 60	34, 61
96	39, 57	37, 59	36, 60	34, 62
97	39, 58	38, 59	36, 61	35, 62
98	40, 58	38, 60	37, 61	35, 63
99	40, 59	39, 60	37, 62	36, 63
100	41, 59	39, 61	37, 63	36, 64

APPENDIX
Table VI(a)
Critical Values of T for the Sign Test

Level of significance α					Level of significance α				
Two-sided	**0.10**	**0.05**	**0.02**	**0.01**	**Two-sided**	**0.10**	**0.05**	**0.02**	**0.01**
One-sided	**0.05**	**0.025**	**0.01**	**0.005**	**One-sided**	**0.05**	**0.025**	**0.01**	**0.005**
n					**n**				
1	–	–	–	–	31	11	13	15	17
2	–	–	–	–	32	12	14	16	16
3	–	–	–	–	33	11	13	15	17
4	–	–	–	–	34	12	14	16	16
5	5	–	–	–	35	11	13	15	17
6	6	6	–	–	36	12	14	16	18
7	7	7	7	–	37	11	13	17	17
8	6	8	8	8	38	12	14	16	18
9	7	7	9	9	39	13	15	17	17
10	8	8	10	10	40	12	14	16	18
11	7	9	9	11	45	13	15	17	19
12	8	8	10	10	46	14	16	18	20
13	7	9	11	11	49	13	15	19	19
14	8	10	10	12	50	14	16	18	20
15	9	9	11	11	55	15	17	19	21
16	8	10	12	12	56	14	16	18	20
17	9	9	11	13	59	15	17	19	21
18	8	10	12	12	56	14	18	20	22
19	9	11	11	13	65	15	17	21	23
20	10	10	12	14	66	16	18	20	22
21	9	11	13	13	69	15	19	23	25
22	10	12	12	14	66	16	18	22	24
23	9	11	13	15	75	17	19	23	25
24	10	12	14	14	70	16	18	22	24
25	11	11	13	15	79	17	19	23	25
26	10	12	14	14	76	16	20	22	24
27	11	13	13	15	89	17	21	23	27
28	10	12	14	16	90	18	20	24	26
29	11	13	15	15	99	19	21	25	27
30	10	12	14	16	100	18	22	26	28

APPENDIX

Table VI(b)

Critical Values of T for the Signed Rank Test for paired differences

(n is the number of pairs of observations)

	Level of significance α						Level of significance α				
n	Two-sided			One-sided		n	Two-sided			One-sided	
	0.05	0.01	0.001	0.05	0.01		0.05	0.01	0.001	0.05	0.01
6	0			2		36	208	171	130	227	185
7	2			3	0	37	221	182	140	241	198
8	3	0		5	1	38	235	194	150	256	211
9	5	1		8	3	39	249	207	161	271	224
10	8	3		10	5	40	264	220	172	286	238
11	10	5	0	13	7	41	279	233	183	302	252
12	13	7	1	17	9	42	294	247	195	319	266
13	17	9	2	21	12	43	310	261	207	336	281
14	21	12	4	25	15	44	327	276	220	353	296
15	25	15	6	30	19	45	343	291	233	371	312
16	29	19	8	35	23	46	361	307	246	389	328
17	34	23	11	41	27	47	378	322	260	407	345
18	40	27	14	47	32	48	396	339	274	426	362
19	46	32	18	53	37	49	415	355	289	446	379
20	52	37	21	60	43	50	434	373	304	466	397
21	58	42	25	67	49	51	453	390	319	486	416
22	65	48	30	75	55	52	473	408	335	507	434
23	73	54	35	83	62	53	494	427	351	429	454
24	81	61	40	91	69	54	514	445	368	550	473
25	89	68	45	100	76	55	536	465	385	573	493
26	98	75	51	110	84	56	557	484	402	595	514
27	107	83	57	119	92	57	579	504	420	618	535
28	116	91	64	130	101	58	602	525	438	642	556
29	126	100	71	140	110	59	625	546	457	666	578
30	137	109	78	151	120	60	648	567	476	690	600
31	147	118	86	163	130	61	672	589	495	715	623
32	159	128	94	175	140	62	697	611	515	741	646
33	170	138	102	187	151	63	721	634	535	767	669
34	182	148	111	200	162	64	747	657	556	793	693
35	195	159	120	213	173	65	772	681	577	820	718

APPENDIX
Table VII
Wilcoxon Signed Rank Test
(n – number of pairs)

	Critical Values			
n	**$\alpha \leqq 0.10$**	**$\alpha \leqq 0.05$**	**$\alpha \leqq 0.02$**	**$\alpha \leqq 0.01$**
1				
2				
3				
4				
5	0, 15			
6	2, 19	0, 21		
7	3, 25	2, 26	0, 28	
8	5, 31	3, 33	1, 35	0, 36
9	8, 37	5, 40	3, 42	1, 44
10	10, 45	8, 47	5, 50	3, 52
11	13, 53	10, 56	7, 59	5, 61
12	17, 61	13, 65	9, 69	7, 71
13	21, 70	17, 74	12, 79	9, 82
14	25, 80	21, 84	15, 90	12, 93
15	30, 90	25, 95	19, 101	15, 105
16	35, 101	29, 107	23, 113	19, 117
17	41, 112	34, 119	28, 125	23, 130
18	47, 124	40, 131	32, 139	27, 144
19	53, 137	46, 144	37, 153	33, 156
20	60, 150	52, 158	43, 167	37, 173
21	67, 164	58, 173	49, 182	42, 189
22	75, 178	66, 187	55, 198	48, 205
23	83, 193	73, 203	62, 214	54, 222
24	91, 209	81, 210	69, 231	68 239
25	100, 225	89, 236	76, 249	68, 257

APPENDIX
Table VIII
Critical values of the smallest rank sum for the Wilcoxon-Mann-Whitney test

n_1 = number of elements in the largest sample;
n_2 = number of elements in the smallest sample.

		Level of significance α			
Two-sided		0.20	0.10	0.05	0.01
One-sided		0.10	0.05	0.25	0.005
n_1	n_2				
3	2	3	–	–	–
3	3	7	6	–	–
4	2	3	–	–	–
4	3	7	6	–	–
4	4	13	11	10	–
5	2	4	3	–	–
5	3	8	7	6	–
5	4	14	12	11	–
5	5	20	19	17	15
6	2	4	3	–	–
6	3	9	8	7	–
6	4	15	13	12	10
6	5	22	20	18	16
6	5	30	28	26	13
7	2	4	3	–	–
7	3	10	8	7	–
7	4	16	14	13	10
7	5	23	21	20	16
7	6	32	29	27	24
7	7	41	39	36	32
8	2	5	4	3	–
8	3	11	9	8	–
8	4	17	15	14	11

8	5	25	23	21	17
8	6	34	31	29	25
8	7	44	41	38	34
8	8	55	51	49	43
9	1	1	–	–	–
9	2	5	4	3	–
9	3	11	9	8	6
9	4	19	16	14	11
9	5	27	24	22	18
9	6	36	33	31	26
9	7	46	43	40	35
9	8	58	54	51	45
10	1	1	–	–	–
10	2	6	4	3	–
10	3	12	10	9	6
10	4	20	17	15	12
10	5	28	26	23	19
10	6	38	35	32	27
10	7	49	45	42	37
10	8	60	56	53	47
10	9	73	69	65	58
10	10	87	82	78	71
11	1	1	–	–	–
11	2	6	4	3	–
11	3	13	11	9	6
11	4	21	18	16	12
11	5	30	27	24	20
11	6	40	37	34	28
11	7	51	47	44	38
11	8	63	59	55	49
11	9	76	72	68	61
11	10	91	86	81	73
11	11	106	100	96	87
12	1	1	–	–	–
12	2	7	5	4	–
12	3	14	11	10	7
12	4	22	19	17	13
12	5	32	28	26	21
12	6	42	38	35	30
12	7	54	49	46	40

(Cont...)

12	8	66	62	58	51
12	9	80	75	71	63
12	10	94	89	84	76
12	11	110	104	99	90
12	12	127	120	115	105
13	1	–	–	–	–
13	2	7	5	4	–
13	3	15	12	10	7
13	4	23	20	18	14
13	5	33	30	27	22
13	6	44	40	37	31
13	7	56	52	48	44
13	8	69	64	60	53
13	9	83	78	73	65
13	11	114	108	103	93
13	12	131	125	119	109
13	13	149	142	136	125
14	1	1	–	–	–
14	2	7	5	4	–
14	3	16	13	11	7
14	4	25	21	19	14
14	5	35	31	28	22
14	6	46	42	38	32
14	8	72	67	62	54
14	9	86	81	76	67
14	10	102	96	91	81
14	11	118	112	106	96
14	12	136	129	123	112
14	13	154	147	141	129
14	14	174	166	160	147
15	1	1	–	–	–
15	2	8	6	4	–
15	3	16	13	11	8
15	4	26	22	20	15
15	5	37	33	29	23
15	6	48	44	40	33
15	7	61	56	52	44
15	8	75	69	65	56
15	9	90	84	79	69
15	10	106	99	94	84
15	11	123	116	110	99

(Cont...)

15	12	141	133	127	115
15	13	159	152	145	133
15	14	179	171	164	151
15	15	200	192	184	171
16	1	1	–	–	–
16	2	8	6	4	–
16	3	17	14	12	8
16	4	27	24	21	15
16	5	38	34	30	24
16	6	50	46	42	34
16	7	64	58	54	46
16	8	78	72	67	58
16	9	93	87	82	72
16	10	109	103	97	86
16	13	165	156	150	130
16	14	185	176	169	155
16	15	206	197	190	175
16	16	229	219	211	196
17	1	1	–	–	–
17	2	9	6	5	–
17	3	18	15	12	8
17	4	28	25	21	16
17	5	40	35	32	25
17	6	52	47	43	36
17	7	66	61	56	47
17	8	81	75	70	60
17	9	97	90	84	74
17	11	131	123	117	105
17	12	150	142	135	122
17	13	170	161	154	140
17	14	190	182	174	159
17	15	212	203	195	180
17	16	235	225	217	201
17	17	259	249	240	223
18	1	1	–		–
18	2	9	7	5	–
18	3	19	15	13	8
18	4	30	26	22	16
18	5	42	37	33	26
18	6	55	49	45	37
18	7	69	63	58	49
18	8	84	77	72	62

(Cont...)

18	9	100	93	87	76
18	10	117	110	103	92
18	11	135	127	121	108
18	12	155	146	139	125
18	13	175	166	158	144
18	14	196	187	179	163
18	15	218	208	200	184
18	16	242	231	222	206
18	17	266	255	246	228
18	18	291	280	270	252
19	1	2	1	–	–
19	2	10	7	5	3
19	3	20	16	13	9
19	4	31	27	23	17
19	5	43	38	34	27
19	6	57	51	46	38
19	7	71	65	60	50
19	10	121	113	107	94
19	11	139	131	124	111
19	12	159	150	143	129
19	13	180	171	163	147
19	14	202	192	182	168
19	15	224	214	205	189
19	16	248	237	228	210

APPENDIX
Table IX
Runs above and below the Median

	Critical Values			
n′	α = 0.10	α = 0.05	α = 0.02	α = 0.01
1				
2				
3				
4	2, 8			
5	3, 9	2, 10	2, 10	
6	3, 11	3, 11	2, 12	2, 12
7	4, 12	3, 13	3, 13	3, 13
8	5, 13	4, 14	4, 14	3, 15
9	6, 14	5, 15	4, 16	4, 16
10	6, 16	6, 16	5, 17	5, 17
11	7, 17	7, 17	6, 18	5, 19
12	8, 18	7, 19	7, 19	6, 20
13	9, 19	8, 20	7, 21	7, 21
14	10, 20	9, 21	8, 22	7, 23
15	11, 21	10, 22	9, 23	8, 24
16	11, 25	11, 22	10, 24	9, 25
17	12, 24	11, 25	10, 26	10, 26
18	13, 25	12, 26	11, 27	11, 27
19	14, 26	13, 27	12, 28	11, 29
20	15, 27	14, 28	13, 29	12, 30
21	16, 28	15, 29	14, 30	13, 31
22	17, 29	16, 30	14, 32	14, 32
23	17, 31	16, 32	15, 33	14, 34
24	18, 32	17, 33	16, 34	15, 35
25	19, 33	18, 34	17, 35	16, 36
26	20, 24	19, 35	18, 36	17, 37
27	21, 35	20, 36	19, 37	18, 38
28	22, 36	21, 37	19, 39	18, 40
29	23, 37	22, 38	20, 40	19, 41
30	24, 38	22, 40	21, 21	20, 42

31	25, 39	23, 41	22, 42	21, 43
32	25, 41	24, 42	23, 43	22, 44
33	26, 42	25, 43	24, 44	23, 45
34	27, 43	26, 44	24, 46	23, 47
35	28, 44	27, 45	25, 47	24, 48
36	29, 45	28, 46	26, 48	25, 49
37	30, 46	29, 47	27, 49	26, 50
38	31, 47	30, 48	28, 50	27, 51
39	32, 48	30, 50	29, 51	28, 52
40	33, 49	31, 51	30, 52	29, 53
41	34, 50	32, 52	31, 53	29, 55
42	35, 51	33, 53	31, 54	30, 56
43	35, 53	34, 54	32, 56	31, 57
44	36, 54	35, 55	33, 57	32, 58
45	37, 55	36, 56	34, 58	33, 59
46	38, 56	37, 57	35, 59	34, 60
47	39, 57	38, 58	36, 60	35, 61
48	40, 58	38, 60	37, 61	36, 63
49	41, 59	39, 61	38, 62	36, 64
50	42, 60	40, 62	38, 64	37, 65
51	43, 61	41, 63	39, 65	38, 66
52	44, 62	42, 64	40, 66	39, 67
53	45, 63	43, 65	41, 67	40, 68
54	45, 65	44, 66	42, 68	41, 69
55	46, 66	45, 67	43, 69	42, 70
56	47, 67	46, 68	44, 70	42, 72
57	48, 68	47, 69	45, 71	43, 73
58	49, 69	47, 71	46, 72	44, 74
59	50, 70	48, 72	46, 74	45, 75
60	51, 71	49, 73	47, 75	46, 76
61	52, 72	50, 74	48, 76	47, 77
62	53, 73	51, 75	49, 77	48, 78
63	54, 74	52, 76	50, 78	49, 79
64	55, 75	53, 77	51, 79	49, 81
65	56, 76	54, 78	52, 80	50, 82
66	57, 77	55, 79	53, 81	51, 83
67	58, 78	56, 80	54, 82	52, 84
68	58, 80	57, 81	54, 84	53, 85
69	59, 81	58, 82	55, 85	54, 86

70	60, 82	58, 84	56, 86	55, 87
71	61, 83	59, 85	57, 87	56, 88
72	62, 84	60, 86	58, 88	57, 89
73	63, 85	61, 87	59, 89	57, 91
74	64, 86	62, 88	60, 90	58, 92
75	65, 87	63, 89	61, 91	59, 93
76	66, 88	64, 90	62, 92	60, 94
77	67, 89	65, 91	63, 93	61, 95
78	68, 90	66, 92	64, 94	62, 96
79	69, 91	67, 93	64, 96	63, 97
80	70, 92	68, 94	65, 97	64, 98
81	71, 93	69, 95	66, 98	65, 99
82	71, 95	69, 97	67, 99	66, 100
83	72, 96	70, 98	68, 100	66, 102
84	73, 97	71, 99	69, 101	67, 103
85	74, 98	72, 100	70, 102	68, 104
86	75, 99	73, 101	71, 103	69, 105
87	76, 100	74, 102	72, 104	70, 106
88	77, 101	75, 103	73, 105	71, 107
89	78, 102	76, 104	74, 106	72, 108
90	79, 103	77, 105	74, 108	73, 109
91	80, 104	78, 106	75, 109	74, 110
92	81, 105	79, 107	76, 110	75, 111
93	82, 106	80, 108	77, 111	75, 113
94	83, 107	81, 109	78, 112	76, 114
95	84, 108	82, 110	79, 113	77, 115
96	85, 109	82, 112	80, 114	78, 116
97	86, 110	83, 113	81, 115	79, 117
98	87, 111	84, 114	82, 116	80, 118
99	87, 113	85, 115	83, 117	81, 119
100	88, 114	86, 116	84, 118	82, 120

⌖⌖⌖⌖⌖

Index

D

E

F

G

H

I

Q

R

S

T

U

V

W

Z

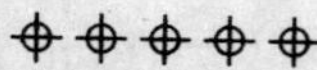

NOTES

NOTES